CALIFORNIA GOVERNMENT TODAY
Politics of reform

The Dorsey Series in Political Science
Consulting Editor   **Samuel C. Patterson**   The University of Iowa

CALIFORNIA GOVERNMENT TODAY
Politics of reform

CHARLES G. BELL
Department of Political Science
California State University, Fullerton

CHARLES M. PRICE
Department of Political Science
California State University, Chico

1980

 THE DORSEY PRESS   Homewood, Illinois   60430
Irwin-Dorsey Limited   Georgetown, Ontario   L7G 4B3

ISBN 0-256-02185-6
Library of Congress Catalog Card No. 79–55222

Printed in the United States of America

1 2 3 4 5 6 7 8 9 0 ML 7 6 5 4 3 2 1 0

Dedicated to Gary L. Wilhelm and Frank Mesple.
Their untimely deaths prevented us from thanking them
for their contribution to this book—and to California.

Preface

This new text on California government and politics appears at a time of significant social change in the golden state. But that could have been said at almost any time in California's dynamic history. For in fact, the hallmark of California is change and reform and that is the central theme of this text.

In the past few years students and faculty alike have rediscovered state and local government. This is understandable since so many day-to-day governmental services are delivered by state and local government. And, of course, each of us in one way or another pays a substantial amount in taxes to these same governments. Thus, it is reasonable that each of us should be concerned about what happens at the state capitol, county court house, city hall, school district, and other special districts. Equally important, we will show, it is quite possible for each of us to have a direct and substantial effect on these governments.

California is not only the most populous state in the nation but is most frequently a model for innovation and reform in other states. What happens here, at the edge of the Pacific Ocean, is often predictive of the future in other states and in the nation as a whole. Thus, it is fair to assert that the study of California government and politics assumes added significance.

This book combines both the fruits of academic research and personal political participation. Each of us brings to this text over 20 years of experience as both teachers of, and participants in, the government and politics of California. We have tried to present what we believe to be the basic patterns and themes underlying politics in the golden state and the major consequences of governmental actions—or inaction.

We want to thank our students and colleagues who have challenged and stimulated our thoughts; and our wives who not only suffered through the process but who also read, criticized, and helped edit this work. We also want to thank the many, many writers and researchers not only of academic stature but those whose efforts appeared in the *California Journal, Los Angeles Times,* and *Sacramento Bee.* The fruits of their efforts have made a substantial contribution to this text. As usual, and in all fairness, we must assume responsibility for any errors and omissions.

February 1980   Charles G. Bell
                                                                                Charles M. Price

Contents

1

California—Critical state, reform model

For better or for worse, and hopefully, with a minimum of chauvinistic chest pounding, we argue in this chapter and throughout the volume that California is without question one of the most important, if not *the* most important, state in the United States. Its significance is based on a number of factors including: size, location, resources, people, climate, and economy. California, the proverbial "Land of Plenty," represents what America believes is (or will be) the "good life," i.e., sprawling ranch-style homes, color TVs, swimming pools, shopping centers, inexpensive franchise food chain restaurants, backyard patios, outdoor living, and above all—affluence. Paradoxically, California is also the harbinger of the technological society run amok—smog, water pollution, threatened redwoods, bulldozed orchards, prime soil and farmlands lost to new shopping centers and apartment complexes, chain restaurants and assembly-line food, unemployment, and urban crime. This duality of promise and peril helps create the mystique surrounding California.

Yet, notwithstanding the paradox, Mervin Field (1977) in a recent California Poll noted that most Californians continue to rate California as "one of the best" places to live (75 percent), and only a few (3 percent) thought it a "rather poor" place to live. A recent article in *California Journal* eloquently summarized this point:

> As Joseph Kraft pointed out from Sacramento a year ago, "Most Californians come here to get away from a harsher life in the East. Whatever the difficulties here, they like the lifestyle, the relatively good job opportunities, and the sun and the surf." Given a choice, most of us who live in San Diego, Los Angeles, San Francisco, and Sacramento would not trade places with our fellow Americans in New York, Washington, Philadelphia, and Chicago,

1

and that's probably the best test of the quality of life in California today (Salzman, May 1977, 15).

For the time being, notwithstanding its problems, California still seems to be a relatively good place to live.

In considering California's importance, four central areas will be examined in this chapter: (1) California's political significance—much of which depends upon its spectacular population spiral, (2) its economic significance, (3) its social significance, and (4) its reform significance.

POLITICAL SIGNIFICANCE

No state exerts more political clout on the national scene than California. At present, California has more than 23 million citizens residing within its borders. Additionally, approximately 1 million permanent resident aliens reside in the state, and another 1 to 2 million illegal aliens live here as well. This means that California is by far the most populous of the 50 states. (New York, the second most populous state has only 18 million people.) Of the 23 million California citizens, approximately 8 million are under 18 years of age and not eligible to vote. However, California has more than 15 million people 18 and over in its potential voting pool. While voting turnout percentages are higher in some of the other states (California is close to the national average in this respect), no other state has as many participating voters or as many potential voters as California.[1]

While there has been a steady growth in California's population ever since it became a state, there has been a partial slowing of the growth rate since 1964. In the early 1960s, California was gaining nearly 350,000 per year in net migration alone. This new population, along with a baby boom, meant the state was adding several hundred thousand elementary students and many thousands of high school and college students each year. Hundreds of schools had to be built and staffed. In the 1960s, policymakers confronted the problem of spectacular population growth with its inevitable demands for new schools, highways, welfare, and water.

Over the past several years, migration into California has tapered off somewhat. Indeed, in 1970–71, net gain from migration plummeted to 25,000 per year. However, by the early 1970s, net gain from migration was averaging about 100,000 per year, and projections for the 1980s suggest

---

[1] If permanent resident aliens were allowed to vote in California as they were historically in some western states, hundreds of thousands of potential voters would be added to the registration totals; and if President Carter's amnesty for long-term illegal residents plan were accepted, there would be hundreds of thousands of additional new voters.

ILLUSTRATION 1–1

In search of the golden dream By covered wagon or Dust Bowl auto, California has historically offered another chance to those who needed it.

Photo courtesy California State Library

United Press International

that this figure may inch even higher. Further complicating the population trends are the many undocumented workers (illegal aliens) moving north of the border from Mexico. Also, the birth rate has declined since the 1960s and has now stabilized at a 0.9 fertility rate.

California politicians in the decade of the 1970s had to adjust to the population growth slowdown, and this trend may continue into the 1980s. Hence, contemporary California politicians confront problems of "steady-state" rather than spectacular growth. In particular, public schools are faced with declining enrollments and an overabundance of teachers.

Yet, even a substantially reduced growth rate (one approximating the national average) means that California will add 300,000 per year at a minimum—200,000 through natural increase and another 100,000 in migration, and this, of course, does not include illegal aliens. A population gain of 300,000 per year, it should be emphasized, is about equal to Alaska's entire population. Furthermore, if the unemployment situation in the state were to brighten, or if Mexico's unemployment worsens, or if the other problems of the state could be solved—smog, pollution, crime, or overcrowding—the short-range leveling of the population growth cycle could reverse itself in prodigious new population increases.

Presidential politics

Undoubtedly, California is the key state in American presidential politics. California is equally important in both the nominating process and the general election.

NOMINATION PROCESS

Throughout the 19th century, delegates selected to go to national nominating conventions were handpicked by party leaders. The state party leaders controlled not only who was selected but how they voted at the convention. Early in this century, in California, Oregon, and a few other western states, the reform-oriented Progressives became the ascendant political force. They adopted the presidential primary system that allowed voters to elect their state's delegates. Throughout this century, presidential candidates attracted by the rich delegate potential of California have campaigned extensively in the state.

Additionally, the California primary held on the first Tuesday in June every four years has been historically, and is currently, the last major election hurdle for presidential candidates prior to the party conventions. The New Hampshire primary, traditionally the first in the nation, and the California primary are the two most critical primaries presidential candidates face. As William J. Crotty (1977:214) notes:

> The Golden State's primary was easily the most significant and decisive of all . . . a primary victory in this state awarded the winner about one-fifth of the total votes needed for nomination. Historically, candidates who lost California seldom won their party's nomination.

Further enhancing the importance of the California presidential primary is the fact that until 1972 California operated under a "winner take all" rule. The candidate receiving the most votes in the Democratic or Republican primary elected his or her entire state of delegates to the party convention. For example, in 1972 Senator George McGovern captured all 271 California delegates to the Democratic National Convention while receiving only 43 percent of the Democratic primary vote; Hubert Humphrey, who gained 38 percent of the Democratic vote, received no delegates.[2] In 1976, California Democrats reformed their primary by eliminating the "winner take all" approach and adopting a proportional representation system. California Republicans, however, continue to operate under the "winner take all" system. At the 1976 Democratic and Republican conventions, the California delegations were the largest from any single state.

GENERAL ELECTIONS

California is not only a key state in the nomination phase of presidential politics, it is also the most critical state in presidential elections. California's 45 electoral votes (which will probably be increased by at least one after the 1980 census) comprise the largest single state bloc in the electoral college. In terms of electoral impact, California is more important to presidential candidates than the 12 smallest electoral states combined: Alaska, Delaware, Hawaii, Idaho, Maine, Montana, Nevada, New Hampshire, New Mexico, North Dakota, Vermont, and Wyoming. Further enhancing California's importance is the pivotal quality of the state's electorate in national elections. Over the last several decades, Republican and Democratic presidential candidates have alternated in capturing the "Golden State."

The California electoral cornucopia helps encourage the national parties to nominate Californians for the presidential or vice-presidential spots (the hope being that these local products will help carry the state for the party ticket). Earl Warren, Republican vice-presidential candidate in 1948 and former perennial Republican candidate, Richard M. Nixon, vice-presidential candidate in 1952 and 1956 and the presiden-

---

[2] A coalition of the Democratic presidential candidates challenged the results of the 1972 California primary and appealed to the convention's credentials committee which upheld them—but this decision was later overturned on a floor vote of the entire convention.

tial candidate in 1960, 1968, and 1972 are two examples. While there has been some trend away from major party candidates *having* to come from major electoral states—Barry Goldwater, Arizona; George Mc-Govern, South Dakota; or Jimmy Carter, Georgia—it is interesting to note that in 1976 Gerald Ford's prime opponent for the Republican nomination was former California Governor, Ronald Reagan, while Jimmy Carter's most formidable opponent was Governor Jerry Brown of California. These two Californians were again major contenders for their respective party's nominations in 1980.

Congressional politics

It has become a cliché to state that power in Congress rests with its committees and committee chairpersons. The sheer volume of federal legislation along with its complexity and diversity have helped foster the development of the powerful congressional committee system. Traditionally, seniority in Congress has been the main criterion for determining who is appointed to which committees as well as who becomes chair of a committee. The member of the majority party with the longest continuous service on a standing committee has automatically become chair of the committee.

In years past, Southern Democrats, who represented safe, one-party districts, were often able to win easy reelection. They were able to build up sufficient seniority to chair key congressional committees. California members of Congress, on the other hand, have traditionally had difficulty accumulating sufficient seniority to attain leadership positions. This has probably been due, in part, to the relative closeness of the Republican-Democratic balance in the state, and, in part, due to the somewhat older age of the new California congressional representatives (many had already spent years in the California legislature). Some California Republican legislators may also have decided to retire early because of the distinct improbability that there would ever be a Republican Congressional majority in the foreseeable future—and hence, no chairpositions. Indeed, the only really powerful California legislators have tended to be those elected to *party* leadership positions (former U.S. Senators Thomas Kuchel, William Knowland, or present incumbent, Alan Cranston). These party leadership positions were not tied to seniority.

More recently, the California House delegation has been rent by strong political feuds further dissipating its influence in the House. The California congressional delegation tends to be extremely diverse—ranging from the radical leftist politics of Ron Dellums to the radical right-wing views of John Rousellot. Differences are further compounded by sporadic north-south and rural-urban cleavages in the delegation. Thus, though the California House delegation is the largest in Congress, it has usually been unable to match the power of many of the unified, seniority-laden southern state delegations.

Currently, California's traditional weakness in Congress appears to be changing—to an extent at least. In the Senate, Alan Cranston has become a major force in the Democratic Party majority caucus. In the House, California representatives have begun to acquire the necessary seniority to qualify for committee and subcommittee chairs.

In the early 1970s, congressional reform forces led by Phillip Burton, augmented by a host of newly elected "Watergate" Democratic freshmen; emboldened by committee chair scandals; and encouraged by the powerful new "public interest" lobbies such as Common Cause and Ralph Nader's Congress Watch were able to apply sufficient pressure to force the House to reform its seniority system. Today, committee chairs must win periodic approval from the majority party caucus in order to retain their positions. In 1974, three different committee chairs lost their positions on votes of the majority party caucus, and another would have (Wilbur Mills), if he had not resigned his Ways and Means chair just prior to the caucus deliberations. Clearly, power in the House of Representatives has begun to shift away from the once fiercely independent seniority-laden committee chairs to the majority party caucus, and this, in turn, should help increase the power of California Democrats in the House. Additionally, more and more California members of Congress have begun to build up the necessary years of service to qualify for chair positions. On the Democratic side, in particular, members from the major cities (Los Angeles, San Francisco, Oakland, or Sacramento) and several from the rural Central Valley have become virtually unbeatable incumbents, almost as safe as their southern or midwestern counterparts used to be. Moreover, a number of California legislators serve as subcommittee chairs, chosen today under the new reform rules by majority party members of the committees. These subcommittee chairpersons often rival standing committee chairpersons in terms of power and autonomy.

Thus, several factors coming together should increase the overall impact of the California congressional delegation in the years ahead: (1) the growing ability of California legislators to build up seniority; (2) the new reform rules lessening the importance of seniority and increasing the role of the majority party caucus; and (3) the candidacy of Congressman Phillip Burton of San Francisco for speaker once Thomas "Tip" O'Neil retires.

Supreme Court politics

It is more difficult to assess the impact California has on U.S. Supreme Court politics than it is to discuss California's role in presidential or congressional politics. By design, the Court is less overtly political than the other two branches. Nonetheless, California has had a substantial influence on the deliberations of the U.S. Supreme Court.

During the tumultuous 1950s–60s decades, former California Governor Earl Warren served as Chief Justice of the Supreme Court. In these decades, the Warren Court issued a number of landmark decisions on a variety of topics such as school desegregation, voting rights, reapportionment, and rights of defendants that have strongly influenced the future direction of American constitutional law.

A number of California legal controversies have been appealed on to the U.S. Supreme Court for adjudication. The Court's decisions on some of the cases generated in California have had major national significance. Perhaps the best and most recent example is the *Bakke* Case. Alan Bakke had been denied admission to the University of California at Davis Medical School. In this critical case, the Supreme Court had to weigh affirmative action principles designed to assist minorities against potential reverse discrimination.

The *Bakke* dispute was probably the most important racial case to be settled by the U.S. Supreme Court since the Warren Court's landmark decision of 1954, *Brown* v. *Board of Education of Topeka* requiring public schools to desegregate. In 1978, the Court ruled that Bakke had been wrongfully denied admission to the Davis Medical School under an unconstitutional quota system. The Court also went on to say, however, that race could be used as a criterion for admission to assist minority applicants.

Probably the most significant way California has executed an influence on the U.S. Supreme Court has been the leadership role played by the California State Supreme Court. Over the last several decades, the state court has developed a national reputation for innovation. For example, California granted many due-process rights to children long before the U.S. Supreme Court provided for them. Indeed, in a number of critical legal areas, the U.S. Supreme Court has tended to follow the lead of the California court. As one writer put it:

> In 1961, when the U.S. Supreme Court held that all states were forbidden to use illegally seized evidence in a criminal trial, it cited a 1955 California decision. In 1965, the U.S. Supreme Court struck down Arizona and New York Supreme Court decisions when it announced the *Miranda* rule against confessions from a suspect not informed of his rights. A companion California case was upheld because the state's court already had reversed this conviction. California has led, too, in civil rights cases. In 1948, California was the first to strike down a statute prohibiting interracial marriage. Nineteen years later the U.S. Supreme Court followed the California example. And when California voters repealed fair housing legislation in 1964, the State Supreme Court set aside the voters' decision in reasoning followed by a later U.S. Supreme Court ruling. (*Sacramento Bee,* October 6, 1974, section P, p. 1.)

However, ideological divisions, internal dissension, an increasing number of socially and politically sensitive cases, leaks to the press, and alleged politically motivated delays in announcing court decisions all culminated in a public investigation of the state supreme court in the summer of 1979. While the investigation was, in itself, inconclusive, the court's reputation was damaged, and several justices lost considerable dignity (see Chapter 12).

ECONOMIC SIGNIFICANCE

California grows more crops, produces more food, raises more cotton, builds more airplanes, and manufactures more space-military hardware than any other state in the nation. Perhaps the most unique feature of the California economy is its diversity. Unlike many of the major industrial states of the eastern seaboard, California has an exceedingly important and varied agricultural sector. Distinct from the major industrial states of the Midwest which do have important agricultural bases, the California economy includes other diverse fields such as mining, communications, finance, lumber, and petroleum.

Overall, when we consider the major economic factors shaping the state—rapid population growth, climate, type of industrial activity (emphasis on space-defense), percentage of work force in defense-related jobs, and sizable retirement population, California probably most resembles some of the southern or southwestern states such as Florida, Texas, or Arizona.

Again though, it should be emphasized that the diversity of California agriculture; the continued importance of manufacturing; the significance of the motion picture, record, and television industries headquartered in the state; and trade/exporting help make the state unique economically. California politicians have long noted with pride that the Golden State itself surpasses nearly all countries of the world in GNP (gross national product). Only the rest of the United States, West Germany, the United Kingdom, France, and Japan currently produce more.

Last, as is the case with many of the other western states, a large percentage of California land is federally owned (45.2 percent). When state and county land is added to the federal total, we can note that over half of California is government-owned (50.2 percent). Table 1–1 has been compiled to show how California land is productively apportioned.

Table 1–1 shows that in addition to a large percentage of California land being government-owned, a handful of major corporations control vast tracts of California's privately owned land. Interestingly, the great majority of Californians live on only 2½ percent of the land. However, there has been a recent alarming trend in California for prime agricultural land to be gobbled up by new shopping units, housing developments, and freeways, though some farm spokespeople claim there is no problem,

TABLE 1–1
California land use and ownership

Class of land	Number of acres	Percent of state's area
Total	100,185,000	100.0
Forest land	42,416,000	42.3
Agricultural	35,722,000	35.7
Urban and suburban land	2,200,000	2.2
Other land	19,847,000	19.8

Government-owned	Number of Acres	Percent of area
Total	50,335,946	50.2
Federal	45,251,036	45.2
State	2,437,809	2.4
Cities	865,895	.86
Counties	691,827	.69
Special districts	461,868	.46
Indian land	540,471	.54
School districts	80,025	.08
Junior college districts	7,012	.01

Privately owned	Number of acres	Percent of area
Total	49,847,735	49.8
Southern Pacific	2,411,000	2.4
Newhall Land Co.	1,590,000	1.6
Shasta Forest Co.	479,196	.4
Tenneco Inc.	362,843	.4
Tejon Ranch Co.	348,000	.3
Standard Oil of California	306,000	.3
Boise Cascade	303,000	.3
Georgia Pacific	278,000	.3
Pacific Gas and Electric Co.	250,000	.2
Occidental Petroleum	200,000	.2
Sunkist Corporation	192,000	.2
Other, "smaller holdings"	43,127,714	43.0

Source: California Land Use Task Force, Department of Finance, *California Statistical Abstract,* and Ralph Nader's *Who Owns California?*

since there are hundreds of thousands of acres of potential farm land that could be converted into agricultural use if needed.

Governor Jerry Brown (Office of Planning and Research, 1978) recently proposed a new "urban strategy" policy for California designed to cope with this problem:

> to lend legitimacy to the idea that people can live well in densely populated areas . . . Californians can no longer avoid city problems by moving farther and farther from the central cities. Crime rates generally are increasing at the urban fringe. Smog has spread past the suburbs into the deserts and mountains. The loss of jobs caused by movement of industry from the central cities has caused increasing unemployment in the cities, with a growing need for unemployment and financial assistance. These costs are borne by all residents of the state.

The result is waste: waste of land, particularly valuable agricultural land; waste of older cities and suburbs; waste of air, water and other natural resources; waste of energy; waste of time spent in commuting; and, in the long run, a waste of money.

California is the most urbanized state in the nation with 94 percent of its population living in cities and suburbs. Paradoxically, it is also the nation's leading farm state with Iowa ranking second based on overall value of agricultural crops and livestock.

Agriculture

Agriculture, or perhaps more accurately, agribusiness, remains the state's most important industry. Key features of California farming include: large acreages, highly mechanized, scientific, extensive use of pesticides, a rapidly growing percentage of prime agricultural land owned by foreign conglomerates, increasing unionization and organization in the United Farm Workers Union of poorly paid farm workers; and extensive use of illegal aliens, "Braceros," by many farmers.

Nationally, the average farm size is 384 acres and has an average total value of $115,000. But in California, the average farm size is 573 acres and has an average total value of $315,000. Recent efforts at the national level by the Department of the Interior to limit federal water deliveries in the Westlands area of California to farms of 160 acres has run into considerable opposition from a wide spectrum of California politicians and now appears hopelessly doomed.

With just two percent of the nation's farms and ranches, California produces 9 percent of the agricultural output. California ranked first among the states in 47 different crop and livestock commodities in 1974.[3] Overall, California produces some 200 different crop and livestock commodities, and more are being added to the list each year. For example, kiwi fruit is just beginning to be grown in California (seedlings were imported several years ago from New Zealand); in time, this fruit is likely to become yet another major cash crop for California farmers. Addi-

---

[3] *California Agriculture* (State of California, Department of Food and Agriculture, 1975) reports the following crops in this category:

Alfalfa seeds	Celery	Lima beans	Persimmons
Almonds	Cotton	Melons	Plums
Apricots	Cut flowers	Nectarines	Pomegranates
Artichokes	Dates	Nursery stock	Potted plants
Asparagus	Eggs	Olives	Prunes
Avocados	Figs	Onions	Rabbits
Blackeye beans	Flower seeds	Oriental	Strawberries
Broccoli	Garlic	vegetables	Spinach
Brussel sprouts	Grapes	Peaches	Safflower
Cantaloupes	Ladino clover	Pears	Sugarbeets
Carrots	Lemons	Peppers, bell	Tomatoes
Cauliflower	Lettuce	Peppers, chili	Walnuts

Photo courtesy Sacramento Bee

tionally, three California counties (Fresno, Kern, and Tulare) rank among the top ten in the entire country in terms of the total value of their agricultural production. The impact of agriculture on the California economy including farm receipts, processing, transportation, distribution, and sales runs into the billions of dollars each year.

Looking ahead, as worldwide food shortages inevitably plague many countries of the world, California's importance to the nation and the world community of nations as a food producer is likely to continue to grow. At the same time, development pressures pose mounting concern to California environmentalists concerned with preserving the state's prime agricultural land.

Other facets of the California economy

In addition to its agricultural base, California is also a leading industrial state. Table 1–2 enumerates the number of workers in various job categories in the state and emphasizes the diversity of the state employment picture.

The fastest growing employment sectors in California recently have been government employment, transportation, and trade. However, the new fiscal constraints on state and local government imposed by the Jarvis-Gann Proposition 13 property tax reform of June 1978 may drastically slow the growth of government employees. Particularly interesting when considering California employment patterns is the proportion of the

TABLE 1–2
California employment and population, 1975

Employment	Number of workers (000)
Contract Construction	321
Mining	32
Manufacturing	1,579
Aerospace	472
Durable except aerospace	574
Nondurable	533
Transportation, communication, and utilities	471
Trade	1,779
Finance, insurance, and real estate	452
Government	1,609
Federal	311
State and local	1,298
Agricultural	296
Unemployed	913
Total	7,452

Source: *UCLA Business Forecast for the Nation and California in 1975 (Proceedings of the 23d Business Forecasting Conference* held at UCLA, December 5, 1974).

labor force in services (78 percent) rather than manufacturing and in white-collar rather than blue-collar jobs. California has a higher proportion of engineers than any other state in the nation. Moreover, 1 out of every 4 defense-industry jobs in this country is in California, and 1 out of every 7 manufacturing jobs in the state is in weapons production. One expert, Ted Bradshaw, (1976:1–61) contends that California is the *world's* most advanced industrial society because of its high technology industry, heavy concentration of workers in service-sector industries, considerable interdependence, rapid change, and innovation. In this same vein, Todd La Porte and C. J. Abrams (1976:101) argue that California is one of the world's best examples of a postindustrial society. These authors note that the state's innovations in petrochemicals, agriculture, transport, aerospace, electronics, nuclear energy, medicine, education, and biology are examples of the sophisticated nature of the California economy.

California in the decade of the '70s led all other states in total personal income. Additionally, California has ranked in the top ten of the states in terms of per capita income for a number of years. Projections for the mid-1980s show the average wage earner in California earning about $15,000 a year, while workers in the rest of the nation will average about $14,000.

Four prime problem areas for the California economy in the 1980s are housing, aerospace/military, unemployment, and the business climate.

HOUSING

As the state's population continues to grow and as the cost of land, lumber, labor, and loans skyrocket, the number of new homes constructed declined in California and in the rest of the nation as well. By the late 1970s, the average cost of a single family home in California was almost $60,000 and rising steadily! Crosscutting pressures from environmentalists to preserve agricultural land versus the demands of developers, builders, and realtors for new housing further contributed to the controversy. To house the expected 1982 California population, it is estimated that at a minimum some 250,000 new housing units must be constructed. Clearly, the long cherished dream of so many Californians— to have a new home in a quiet suburban setting—is becoming an increasingly remote possibility for many middle- and lower-income Californians. The shift in the California housing market is towards mobile homes, apartments, town houses, and condominiums.

AEROSPACE/DEFENSE

California's aerospace/defense industry has always been heavily dependent upon the federal government for health and vitality. Approximately one fourth of the federal defense dollar goes to California. Leo Rennert of the *Sacramento Bee* reported that the Pentagon spent more than $16.2 billion in California in 1977—a sum larger than the entire state budget for that year.

The end of the Viet Nam War, cutbacks in space research and new economies in military spending have combined to curtail the flow of federal defense dollars into California. Obviously, jobs and the California economic picture are heavily dependent upon the steady infusion of federal defense dollars. Governor Brown and U.S. Senators Alan Cranston and S. I. Hayakawa have fought zealously to maintain this federal flow of dollars into California. Without federal augmentation, the California economy would be in trouble.

UNEMPLOYMENT

The unemployment rate in California traditionally has been higher than for the rest of the nation. Future projections indicate that unemployment will continue to be a problem in California. In the 1970s, unemployment in California was running at nearly 10 percent of the work force, some 3 percent higher than the national average. Over the last year or two California's unemployment percentage has only been a little higher than the national average. To keep up with population growth, some 200,000 new jobs must be created annually!

BUSINESS CLIMATE

There is little question that many state business leaders are convinced, rightly or wrongly, that contemporary California government is not very sympathetic to business community needs. Increasingly effective environmental and consumer groups have won some governmental victories over business/labor opposition. The recent decision by Dow Chemical Company not to construct a major petrochemical facility in the state because of alleged governmental and environmental red tape symbolized this governmental indifference to the business community. Further adding to the sentiment, Fauntus, a private business consulting firm, rated California 47th out of the 48 contiguous states as a good place to build a plant a few years ago. But, according to a current *Fortune* (1979:46) article, passage of Prop. 13 in 1978 has provided a healthy stimulus to California's economy. For example, personal income and spending for consumer goods rose to record highs in 1978–79.

SOCIAL SIGNIFICANCE

Two prominent features of California life have been extensively discussed by journalists describing social patterns in this state: (1) it has been the haven and at times the birthplace for a variety of exotic religious cults, offbeat political movements, and extremist groups, and (2) it has been a major contributor to American "pop" culture and social patterns. It may well be that the endless discussions of the zany California social milieu have been overdone by writers—after all, a large, diverse, populous state is sure to have a certain number of eccentric types. However, there is little denying that much of this nation's political exotica either started in California or found particularly fertile growing soil in the state. Extremist groups such as the Black Panthers and the Symbionese Liberation Army got their start in California and then later became part of the national picture. The John Birch Society and the American Nazi Party, while not starting in California, certainly attracted sizable numbers of recruits in the state.

As an example of the unique California political makeup, we might note the growing political assertiveness of the state's homosexuals. While homosexuals are organizing politically throughout the nation, it is in California where they have their largest local following. According to *Newsweek,* no city has a larger proportional homosexual population than San Francisco (a reported 120,000 out of a total 680,000), and no city has taken a more tolerant view of homosexuals (*Newsweek,* June 6, 1977:16–26). In San Francisco, there are gay Democratic clubs, gay office seekers and holders, and even gay police officers. Candidates running for office in many wards of San Francisco must receive support from the gay community to have a chance to win. Gay politics, which may appear to be a bizarre facet of California life to citizens in other states, has become increasingly mainstream in California. California voters in 1978 rejected an initiative that would have allowed school districts to fire homosexual teachers. In time, gay political activism will probably be accepted in other areas of the country as well.

California has also served as a sanctuary for a wide variety of unusual religious cults and sects. From Aimee Semple McPherson and the Foursquare Gospel Church in the 1930s to the People's Temple, Hare Krishna, Scientology, or the "Moonies" of the 1970s, the state has long served as a beacon to unorthodox religious movements or bizarre cults. Most recently, the People's Temple and the mass suicide at Jonestown of members of this cult have put California in the international spotlight.

California, inevitably, seems to be in the center of the American political-social swirl: the Watts race riots, the 1960s' student protest movement, the anti-Viet Nam War crusade, the Watergate political scandal, the environmental movement, the anti-environment movement, or the Jarvis-Gann property tax revolt are some examples. Bradshaw (1976:1–6) notes, ". . . new issues often seem to demand attention in California long before they emerge in other places." Kenneth Lamott (1971:4) writes, "California *is* our distant warning system for the rest of

ILLUSTRATION 1–3

Robert Englehart and the Copley News Service

the United States. California *is* our window into the future. California *is* the center of the whirlpool, where all currents come to a focus."

Clearly, a great many features of contemporary American social life are Californian-inspired—fashions, new sport crazes, music, food fads, movies and television programs, liberalized divorce laws, and hardcore pornography.

California always seems to be the springboard for national foils and new trends. Hang gliding, scuba diving, cross-country skiing, hot air ballooning, off-road vehicles, hot-tubbing, or the current craze, skateboarding, are some examples of this phenomenon. The drive-in revolution from movies to restaurants to banks and even churches is a California innovation.

California also seems to be the home for some of this country's major newsmakers: Jerry Brown, Ronald Reagan, Richard Nixon, John Wayne, Farrah Fawcett, Jane Fonda, Charles Manson, Charles Schultz, Cesar Chavez, Patty Hearst, Henry Winkler, Werner Erhard, Jonas Salk, or

Johnny Carson. They do have one feature in common—they are Californians.

California is a trendsetter in so many features of contemporary American social life for several reasons. Part of the explanation hinges around the communications industry (TV, movies, radio, and records) headquartered here; the media have certainly trumpeted what is going on in the state. Another factor is the large, restless, mobile citizenry comprising California. Californians seem more willing to try something new or different. In any case, California, has undoubtedly, been a major influence on American "pop" culture.

REFORM SIGNIFICANCE

California has long been in the vanguard of states, primarily western, promoting political reform and experimentation. As noted previously, a continuing theme running throughout the state's political history has been the attempt to grapple with entrenched special interests and root out corrupt political power. A reformist tradition in California and suspicion of traditional politicians can be traced from the Workingman's Party and Populist Movement of the latter part of the 19th century through the Progressive Movement early in this century; to the EPIC (End Poverty in California Movement) of Upton Sinclair in the 1930s; clear through to present-day reform groups such as Common Cause, People's Lobby, and perhaps, Paul Gann's People's Advocate.

Obviously, reform sentiment has arisen in different parts of the nation at different historical periods. However, the "clean government" crusade and the populist "direct democracy" revolution (let the voters have the ultimate voice) have clearly had their greatest successes and most profound impact in the western states. Entrenched political power and hide-bound political traditions had not yet been established in the West when the Populist and Progressive reform movements swept the nation. For example, William J. Crotty (1977:214) notes in his discussion of the extension of the franchise in this country:

> The weight of public opinion in the western states was overwhelmingly against any property limitations on the vote and by 1851, 12 states had proceeded to the point of eliminating any taxpaying provision as a prerequisite to the vote. The contrast between the western states and those in the East was pronounced. The latter were older, more comfortable with the established ways, and more conservative and elitist.

Or, in discussing alien voting, Crotty (1977:213) comments:

> The hostility the immigrants found in the East contrasted sharply with the warmness of the reception accorded Germans, Poles, Swedes, and even the Irish and Italians in the Midwest, the Great Lakes states, and the Plains states. A number of far western states did exclude aliens explicitly, espe-

cially Orientals, from the franchise, but for the most part newcomers were welcomed to the sparsely populated frontier regions.

Not surprisingly, voting rights for women were granted in the western states first—Wyoming, Utah, Washington, Colorado, Idaho, California, Arizona, Kansas, and Oregon.

California, the most populous and politically powerful of the western states came to play a central leadership role in this reform movement. Most authorities would agree that compared to many eastern states, California government is reasonably honest, substantially open and above-board, and *relatively* free of corruption. Indeed, in a major new text on political corruption (Berg et al., 1976:176) in America, the authors subtitle one section of their book, "Political Reform in California: An Alternative National Model."

Progressive era

Without question, the Progressive era at the beginning of this century was the period of the most profound political reform experimentation ever in the western states. Overall, Progressives sought to secure passage of reform legislation aimed at weakening political parties, reducing the power of special interests, rooting out corruption, and expanding the citizen's role in the political process. (In Chapter 4 we discuss the Progressive era in California.)

Some of the Progressive reform proposals were never extended beyond a particular state's borders. Thus, the Nebraska unicameral state legislature instituted in 1934 is still the only single-house legislature in the country, but periodic efforts continue in other states by reformist forces to institute the Nebraska unicameral system. A few reforms such as California's cross-filing ("vote for the person, not the party") have long since been abandoned. However, much of the Progressive reform package remains in place in California and other western states.

Indeed, many of these earlier western Progressive reforms are now being promoted in the eastern half of the nation. For example, from just a handful of states that adopted the presidential preference primary early in the 20th century, today over 30 states offer various types of presidential preference primaries. Or another example, a great many eastern states have begun to consider adopting the initiative, particularly in the wake of the popular Jarvis-Gann property tax initiative.

Legislative reform

The movement to upgrade, reform, and professionalize American state legislatures got its primary impetus in California during the speakership years of Jess Unruh. Today, the California state legislature is one of the best-paid, best-staffed, best-equipped, most professionalized state legislatures in the nation and has become a model for other state legislatures.

Political reform

In 1974, prompted by the revelations of Watergate, California voters adopted the most stringent political reforms ever imposed in any state (Proposition 9). This measure established new standards for campaign contribution reporting, set spending limits for statewide campaigns, established a tough new conflict of interest code, and established new lobby regulations. (In Chapter 7 we discuss in detail the ramifications of Proposition 9 of 1974.) California's pioneering Political Reform Act provisions are likely to be pursued in other states and, possibly, even at the federal level. Indeed, a new Iowa lobby reform measure, in the California vein, prohibits an Iowa lobbyist from providing *any* gift or service to an Iowa legislator—even a cup of coffee!

Policy leadership

Last, the leadership California has exerted in reform has also been manifested in important substantive policy areas as well. Two separate studies by political scientists using differing methodologies came to one similar conclusion: California is one of the most innovative states in the nation (Walker, 1969:880–89 and Gray, 1973:1174–85).

Perhaps the best current example of California policy leadership has been the Proposition 13 phenomenon. The overwhelming vote for this citizen-sponsored initiative has sparked a tax revolt that has spread across the nation. Moreover, Governor Jerry Brown has positioned himself as the leading politician favoring a constitutional convention to balance the federal budget. Whether one agrees with the Brown constitutional convention approach or not, there is no denying the fact that Proposition 13 of California started the tax revolt momentum and that Governor Brown has become the leading spokesperson for the national tax protest movement. Governor Brown's comments in his support of a new urban strategy ". . . this (policy) could have repercussions beyond the borders of California because California, the nation's most populous state, has a history of grappling with problems ahead of the country," could have been said about tax reform or air quality standards or many other issues. California is, clearly, a trend-setting state.

SUMMARY

Politically, economically, and socially California is one of the most important states in the nation. It is unique because it is the most advanced state technologically. By understanding something about the issues and political crosscurrents confronting California today, one can also discern something of the shape of national issues in the near future. Additionally, California and other western states have played important roles in promoting political reform and change in government and in innovating new public policy.

2

California—Past and present

California, here they come;
Doctor, lawyer, merchant, bum;
They come by car and train and plane,
Straight from Kansas, Georgia, Maine,
Massachusetts, Minnesota,
Iowa and North Dakota,
Rich folk, poor folk, young folk, codgers
Moving westward like the Dodgers.

RICHARD ARMOUR[1]

In this chapter we will look at some of the major features underlying California's politics and government. The state's people, geography, natural resources, and climate are basic features. The clash of people over ideas, policy, and allocation of resources—which we call politics—flows from these basic features. This chapter provides a foundation for a better understanding of the state's political history which we look at in the following chapters.

THE LAST FRONTIER

For years, California was the last frontier in America, physically and psychologically. Many without hope came to the Golden State, and many others who came brought only hope. Between 1850 and 1980, the state's population grew 138 times—from 165,000 to 23 million. In the same period, the United States grew nine times (see Illustration 2–1). Had the nation grown at the pace set by California, there would be today almost 3 billion Americans rather than the present 223 million.

---

[1] Richard Armour, "I Loved You, California," *Look*, September 25, 1962, p. 54.

ILLUSTRATION 2–1
California's population by decades

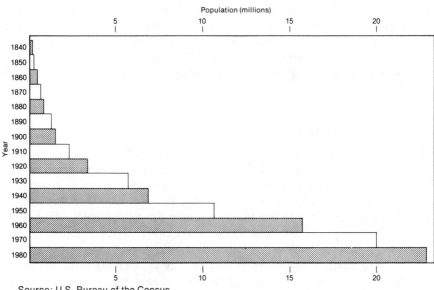

Source: U.S. Bureau of the Census.

One feature that makes California's growth so startling is its continuously high rate. Only two other states have had similar growth rates—Florida since 1850 and Arizona since 1900. Many other states have had short periods of rapid growth, but they then settled down to slow growth. In every case, the rapid growth phase was due to migration—a part of the westward expansion of the United States. What distinguishes California growth is that it continued over such a long period of time—119 years (1848–1968). Millions came to California, lured by the gold rush, land speculation, completion of the transcontinental railroad, oil booms, climate, and rapidly growing economy.

For many, California was more than a "last frontier"—it was a *last chance.* Long after the Old West was gone, California remained a place where the young, the poor, and the disadvantaged had a chance to make it. It was also a place to retire—if you'd made it someplace else. Migrants have always outnumbered the natives since the Gold Rush of 1849. After all, even the original Indians were migrants.

The California Indians

The first people to live in what we now know as California were Indians. These were probably descendants of nomadic tribes that crossed the Bering Strait some 25,000 years ago. When Spain made its first serious effort to colonize California in the 1760s, the total Indian population was probably about 140,000. According to archeologists, California Indians led a simple life in a primitive culture. The ocean, mountains, and deserts, which proved formidable barriers to the Spanish, Americans, and other explorers trying to get into California, also helped keep other Indians out, thus reducing competition. In addition, California's mild climate and the availability of natural foods provided little challenge for the native inhabitants.

The earliest explorers

The Chinese were probably the first to explore the west coast of North America. Ancient Chinese implements, including a bronze fan and a bronze coin 3,000 years old have been unearthed in British Columbia. In fact, at times, it was impossible for early Oriental sailors not to come to the west coast! Winds and currents would drive them helplessly across the Pacific. In the 18th and 19 centuries alone, about 60 Oriental craft were unwillingly "delivered" to the west coast.

The Japanese had an even better chance to settle the area. Unlike the Chinese, they had a unified nation and actively considered a policy of trade with the Indians in the area we now know as Mexico. However, due to fear of foreign influence, they retreated into isolation, effectively shutting out all foreigners and forbidding Japanese citizens from leaving their island kingdom. This policy continued until the mid-1800s, eliminating Japan as a contender for territory in the New World.

THE SPANISH–MEXICAN ERA

Early European explorers

The Spaniards came to the New World looking for riches that had been described in *Las Sergas de Esplandian* by Garci Ordonez de Montalvo, published about 1498. In a fanciful tale of adventure, he described the beautiful island of California:

> . . . at the right hand of the Indies there is an island named California, [which] . . . abounds with gold and precious stones . . . .

Of course, no one had ever seen California—it was a myth.

Eighty-two years before the first English colony was established in Virginia, the Spanish landed in Mexico looking for the cities of gold and the worldly paradise described by Christopher Columbus. None existed, but the Spaniards believed these tales and kept looking for over 250 years.

In 1542, Juan Rodriquez Cabrillo (a Portuguese) sailed along the

California coast, passing San Diego, Catalina Island, Ventura, and finally going as far north as the present-day Fort Ross area. The next year, Bartolome Ferrelo sailed up the coast and got as far as the northern border of contemporary California. These two were the first *discoverers of California.*

Another early explorer, Sir Francis Drake, landed north of San Francisco Bay in 1579, named the land Nova Albion ("New England"), and claimed it for England: (Drake's "New England" was discovered 41 years before the Pilgrims landed at Plymouth.) Essentially, though, California was ignored by the Spanish and other European nations for almost 250 years, until 1765.

The mission period

The mission had been used extensively during the 1600s and 1700s as a colonizing device in several of Spain's New World colonies including Mexico, southern Chile, Paraguay, Central America, Florida, Texas, and even Virginia (these last failed). Not surprisingly, they also used missions in colonizing California. Under the command of Gaspar de Portola, soldiers, Franciscan priests (including Father Junipero Serra), and Baja California Indians reached San Diego in 1769 and established the first California mission.

Thus began the mission era in California history. Under the direction of Father Serra, the missions combined religious conversion of the Indians with practical instruction in the day-to-day activities of agriculture and building. A few missions were quite large and had carpentry shops, blacksmithing, weaving, pottery, and candle making. They were supposed to be, and usually were, self-supporting. The last mission was established at Sonoma in 1823 and marks the end of the Spanish and mission periods.

California was a marginal colony in the Spanish empire. Ruled from Mexico City by a Royal viceroy, little attention was actually given to, or control exercised over, this vast territory. At most, the Spanish had about 3,000 citizens, soldiers, and missionaries in California. Their control was limited to a narrow coastal strip from San Diego to the Sonoma, Petaluma, and Santa Rosa area north of San Francisco. (Ironically, this strip of land today contains most of the state's population.)

The Mexican period

California was not involved in the Spanish-Colonial Wars of Independence (1808–1820s). In early 1822, when the Mexican Revolution became successful, Californians easily accepted the new regime. The Spanish Governor simply swore allegiance to the new government. The new Mexican government was largely concerned with staying in power in

Mexico and devoted little attention to California—even less than had the Spanish.

Under Spanish rule, the missions were important in California. Under Mexican rule, they were dismantled and to some degree replaced by the rancheros. Mission properties were sold by the government or given in grants to favored individuals. Most of the famous "Spanish Land Grants" were actually made by the Mexican government.

During the Mexican period, foreign influence, long feared by the Spanish, began to develop. A thin trickle of outsiders came to the state including whalers, fur traders, and "mountain men." Most visited California and returned home, but a few stayed. Richard H. Dana wrote his famous *Two Years Before the Mast* after sailing to California on a hide and tallow ship in 1834. And, in 1841, the Bidwell party arrived by land from the Middle West, thus opening a new route for the thousands of Americans who were to arrive in the next few years.

BEAR FLAG REVOLT

A number of Americans encouraged by the weakness of the Mexican government, anticipating war between Mexico and the United States, and concerned about British interests in California, staged a brief revolt in June 1846. Led by the adventurer, John C. Frémont, they seized a herd of horses, captured two Mexican generals and raised a flag displaying a grizzly bear. Their revolution was cut short by the war between Mexico and the United States, and today all that remains of the revolt is the California state flag.

THE MEXICAN-AMERICAN WAR

Most people believe that the Mexican-American War was over Texas. President James K. Polk could probably have secured Texas without war. But Polk wanted much more. Specifically, he wanted California, and that meant war. Ironically the major object of the war was hardly touched by battle, since the real fighting took place in Mexico. With American occupation of Mexico City, the war was over. In February 1848, Mexico signed the Treaty of Guadalupe Hidalgo giving California (and other lands) to the United States. This ended the short period of time (1822–48) when Mexico had title to California.

THE AMERICAN ERA

The American era began with the Gold Rush of 1849 which had an incredible impact on California. In 1840, the total state population was about 116,000, of which most (110–112,000) were Indians. By 1860, the

ILLUSTRATION 2-2
Ishi: The last known full-blooded California Indian   Ishi
died a natural death in this century, but most California
Indians were killed or died of starvation or disease
by the late 1880s.

Photo courtesy California State Library

state's population had reached 380,000. By 1870 it had reached a half-million, but the Indian population had been reduced to about 30,000. The Spanish and Mexicans had unintentionally reduced the Indian population through disease and ignorance, but the Americans killed them outright.[2] One of Frémont's expeditions reported:

> We killed plenty of game and an occasional Indian. We made it a rule to spare none of the bucks.

Tragically, by 1870 there were probably more Chinese (brought into work on the railroad) in California than Indians.

Almost all of the Indian, Spanish, and Mexican cultures were swept aside by the onrushing American civilization. The most obvious remnants are the names of some of our major cities—San Francisco, San Jose, Monterey, Santa Barbara, Los Angeles, San Bernardino, and San Diego. Several restored missions, Old Town in San Diego and Olvera Street in Los Angeles, and parts of old Monterey have become tourist attractions. Some of the large land holdings—the Spanish grants—were confirmed, but many others gave rise to lawsuits, some lasting well into this century. The state's community property laws are based on the Spanish legal system, and some of our architecture and furniture reflect a lingering Spanish influence. But, while the Constitution of 1849 stipulated that all laws be published in Spanish as well as English, that requirement was dropped in the Constitution of 1879. Essentially, California quickly became as American as Massachusetts, Missouri, or Illinois. In fact, much of the Constitution of 1849 was borrowed from Iowa and New York, copies of which were available to the convention delegates (see Chapter 3).

The Land

GEOGRAPHY

California is the third largest state in the nation—its 160,000 square miles stretch 650 miles from the Mexican border to the Oregon state line. The traveler going from San Diego near Mexico to Crescent City near the Oregon line faces an 876-mile drive, a distance longer than the trip between New York and Chicago.

The Sierra Nevada Mountains, stretching for some 400 miles along the eastern border of the state with over 50 peaks higher than 13,000 feet, presented a formidable barrier to explorers and early settlers attempting to enter California. Those mountains, combined with the Cascade and Klamath ranges in the north, the Coastal Range on the west,

---

[2] In 1963, representatives of the remaining California Indians and the U.S. Justice Department agreed on a $30 million settlement for the 64 million acres of land taken from them (47 cents per acre).

and the Tehachapis in the south, enclose one of the world's most fertile agricultural regions—the Central Valley. In most years, the mountains that rim the state in the north and central region trap much of the snow and rain that comes in from the northwest Pacific area. Thus, northern California has ample water, sometimes floods, while southern California has had to import water. Use of the state's water, its allocation for agriculture, and transport to the southern parts of California are vital issues. The water and the fertile valley make California the leading agricultural producer in the nation.

CLIMATE

For many Californians, the state's climate is its most important quality. While the state has widely ranging climatic extremes—the harsh cold and deep snows of the High Sierras and the blistering arid heat of Death Valley—it is the mild weather of the coastal regions that has lured millions to California. Dry, moderate warmth in the summer contrasts markedly with the muggy heat of the South, the central states, and much of the Atlantic seaboard. And, the warm, sunny days of winter, with no snow or ice contrast dramatically with the cold of the eastern and central states. During the great blizzard of 1976–77, residents of the snowbound East, shivering in their homes, could watch the televised Rose Bowl game played under warm, sunny skies.

The land, its mineral wealth, its agricultural potential, and climate, provided the lures that have brought wave after wave of immigrants to the Golden State.

The economy

THE GOLD RUSH

Discovery of gold in January 1848 at Sutter's Mill on the American River began what we know as the "gold rush." News of the find spread, and by late May 1848, San Francisco, Monterey, and San Jose were largely deserted for the gold fields on the American River. By 1849, the news had spread around the world, and the gold rush was on. In the mid-50s, perhaps as many as 100,000 people were at the diggings—over a third of the state's population! The value of gold mined in 1852 alone was $80 million. Most of the miners came to make their fortune and then leave. Many did leave but few made a fortune. Rather, more fortunes were made by those who served the mining camps.

The gold rush not only swept aside the pastoral Spanish-Mexican lifestyle, but it also established roads and stores, mills and small manufacturing plants, built cities from the towns of San Francisco, Sacramento,

ILLUSTRATION 2–3
Gold: Where it all began at Coloma in 1849

Photo courtesy California State Library

and Stockton, and began a rush to the golden dream. Looking back, we can now see that the miners of '49 found much more than gold, though few realized it at the time. They came to a state whose potential wealth in agriculture, manufacture, trade, and services was soon to far exceed the riches of the mother lode.

THE RAILROAD-LAND BOOM

When the Central Pacific Railroad joined the Union Pacific at Promontory Point, Utah, in May 1869, California was finally linked to the rest of the nation, Prior to that, those who came to California traveled by sailing ship, stage coach, wagon, horse, or on foot. Most trade was carried by

ILLUSTRATION 2–4
Building the railroad   Chinese labor built much of the railroad that linked
California to the rest of the nation. Chinese coolies riding a wood-burning train
in the Bloomer cut, Placer County, California.

Photo courtesy California State Library

sail around the horn or across the Panama Isthmus after completion of
the Panama Railroad. But, the ocean route was slow and dangerous. At
best, in the mid-1860s it took 21 days to get to California by ship (using
the Panama Railroad). Several ships were lost and hundreds drowned.

The overland stage from Tipton, Missouri to San Francisco took 25
days—subject to delay due to Indian attacks or floods. With no stops
except to change horses, no pretense at providing sleeping accommo-
dations, and little preparation for meals, traveling the Butterfield Stage
was hard work.

Upon completion of the railroad one century after Portola and Serra
had arrived in San Diego in 1769, California was opened to massive
migration and economic development (it also gave the railroad a stranglehold on the state's economy). Many were drawn to southern California by
promise of the health-giving climate. One writer of the time described
it thus:

> The purity of the air of Los Angeles is remarkable . . . The air . . . gives to the individual a stimulus and vital force which only an atmosphere so pure can ever communicate.

Many came in search of inexpensive land. The railroad has received over 10 million acres of land from the federal government as a construction reward—most of it in southern California. Wanting to "cash out," to sell the land, the Southern Pacific began flooding the United States with sales propaganda. Special trains were prepared for land seekers, and as a final inducement, the price of the ticket was applicable to the cost of the land. If an immigrant bought railroad land in California, the trip was free. By the 1880s, 350,000 people had come to the state—half to southern California.

Real estate speculators were not far behind buying land and reselling it. Developers laid out cities from the Pacific Ocean to the Mojave Desert. Some cities had a sound base and a good future; others were simple frauds. Ballona was swamp land; Chicago Park was nothing more than a dry rocky river bed; Border City had nothing to recommend it except a fine view of the Mojave Desert. In their promotion, the "boomers" used outrageous tactics to lure buyers. Slogans such as these were printed in newspapers:

> Buy land in Los Angeles and wear Diamonds.

> San Diego has a population of 150,000 people, only they are not all here yet.

Barbecues, free lunch excursions, and brass bands were also used. The two railroads serving southern California engaged in a rate war that finally drove down the price of a Kansas City-Los Angeles ticket to one dollar in March 1887.

From 1887 to mid-1889, 60 towns were mapped out, but little cash changed hands; most sales were by contract. Land prices soared higher and higher, and most people bought with the expectation of selling again at a profit—often within a day or two.

Suddenly, the whole tower of paper fell. In the spring of 1888, the land boom became a bust. Inflated prices, speculation, and the beginnings of a national depression ended southern California's first real estate binge. Commenting on the crash, a fictional character in a contemporary novel, *Millionaires of a Day* said:

> I had a half million dollars wiped out in the crash and what's worse, $500 of it was cash.

The land boom of the 1880s was significant to the development of southern California. Until then, most migration had been to the northern part of the state—first for gold, then to the San Francisco Bay and Sacramento areas for jobs and land. Few people had come to southern California. Los Angeles was considered to be the last frontier, a tough cow town where in the mid-1850s the murder rate reached one a day, an ominous figure, since the county had a total population of only 5,000! But, the small boom of the 1870s and the big boom of the '80s brought thousands of people to the southern part of the state. By the end of the 1880s, southern California was growing at a rate much greater than northern California and continued to do so until the 1970s.[3]

BLACK GOLD

The earliest oil wells were simply pits dug in oil seeps in Kern and Santa Clara County. The first well *drilled* in California was in Humboldt County in 1861. Fifteen years later the first commercially successful well, Pico 4, came into operation, producing 30 barrels a day in 1876 near Newhall. But, it was not until the internal combustion engine and the advent of the automobile at the turn of the century that California oil began its boom.

The early 1900s were a period of massive oil discoveries, gushers, and wild oil land speculations. Petroleum production increased dramatically between 1900 and 1910, took another leap upward between 1920 and 1930, and again during the war decade of 1940–50. In the late 1920s, offshore drilling and production began in California at Summerland near Santa Barbara.

Until recently, California's oil production has been greater than state needs, and millions of barrels were exported each year, mostly to other states. Since 1968, however, production has declined while demand has increased. As a result, California now imports oil.

THE MILITARY-DEFENSE INDUSTRY BOOM

World War II had a great impact on California's population and economic growth. Before the war, the military establishment was not a significant part of the population (less than 1 percent). But, at the height of the war, 11 percent (1 out of 9 in the state) were in uniform. Of greater importance, California became a major center for war production and shipping.

Almost 2 million people came to California during the war: some were drawn by work opportunities in the war plants to replace the half-million who enlisted or were drafted; others came to take new jobs created by a booming economy; and, finally, many came as members of the armed forces brought here for training. In 1940, before the war, unemployment had been over 12 percent, but by 1943–44 it was less than 1 percent.

---

[3] The northern 51 counties grew by 11 percent in 1970–78, compared to the southern 7 counties' growth of 8 percent.

Following the war (1945–47), almost 700,000 servicemen were discharged in California. Remembering the cold, rain, and snow of their Middle West and eastern homes, 300,000 stayed in the Golden State. Thousands who went home soon returned.

Later, the Korean War increased the state's military population to nearly a half-million in 1952. Since then, the military population has fluctuated around 300,000.

The steel mills, airframe plants, shipyards, and ports built or expanded to meet the needs of World War II were converted after 1945 to the needs of a peacetime economy. In the 16 years between 1929 and 1945 (the Depression and war periods), home construction had stagnated, and new schools, hospitals, highways, automobiles, and a host of other consumer goods had fallen into short supply. The pent-up consumer demand multiplied by the increased population created yet another boom period in California. Moreover, federal spending in the state continues to be an important dimension of California's economy—adding several billion dollars per year to the net income.

The people

Throughout the history of California, the poor and the foreign-born have come seeking their fortune, sometimes recruited, sometimes escaping grinding poverty, or fleeing discrimination. The Chinese, Japanese, Mexicans, blacks, and Dust Bowl migrants are prime examples.

THE CHINESE

During the gold rush, some 25,000 Chinese came to California. After the rush, many returned to China, but some stayed. Another 20–25,000 were brought to California in the 1860s to work on railroad construction gangs. By 1870, perhaps as many as 150,000 Chinese had arrived under labor contracts that came close to being a debt-bondage system. The large number of Chinese (about 18 percent of the state's population) caused much concern to unemployed whites.

Due to brutal harassment and lack of opportunity, many Chinese returned to their native land. The Chinese Exclusion Act of 1881 stopped further immigration. By 1920, there were only 29,000 Chinese in the state. Since then, their numbers have slowly increased, and by 1970 there were 170,000.

THE JAPANESE

Between 1900 and 1910 the number of Japanese increased from 10,000 to 41,000 and by 1920 had reached 72,000. But, even these relatively few reminded Californians of the earlier "Yellow Peril," and pressures for their exclusion soon began. What particularly irritated many white Californians was the success of the Japanese in agriculture. While constituting only 2 percent of the population, they controlled more than 11 percent of the state's agricultural land in 1920. In 1924 Congress excluded further Japanese immigration.

ILLUSTRATION 2–5
Japanese-American children waiting to be sent to an Owens Valley relocation center

Library of Congress; photograph by Russell Lee

After the bombing of Pearl Harbor in 1941, many Californians were more than willing to believe that all Japanese were potential traitors. In 1942, in one of the state's most shameful episodes, all Japanese (citizens and aliens) were rounded up and forced into relocation centers. They were, to all intents and purposes, concentration camps. Released at the end of the war, the Japanese rebuilt their shattered lives and today number about 250,000.

THE MEXICANS

No one knows for sure how many people of Mexican origin live in California. In 1970 the U.S. Bureau of the Census counted 3.1 million people with Spanish surnames but later revised the figure upward to 3.7 million. Of these, at least 200,000 are not of Mexican origin (Indians, Filipinos, and a few from other Latin American states). But, the vast majority are of Mexican origin. And, looming large is the issue of the illegal alien. No one knows, of course, but there are probably well over a million illegal Mexican aliens in California.

Mexican-Americans constitute the single largest minority in California, about 18 percent of the state's population. They outnumber blacks 5 to 2. The first wave of Mexican immigrants came to California (and other southwestern states) as a result of the Mexican Revolution in 1910. Exclusion of Japanese and Chinese migrants created a demand for cheap farm labor which was filled by the Mexicans in the 1920s. By 1930 there were probably about 170–200,000 Mexicans in California, a large number of them immigrants. During the Depression, many returned to Mexico, and many were deported. Many also disappeared into barrios.

World War II created a tremendous need for farm labor again, and the Mexicans came back to California—many of them illegally. These workers were subject to great abuse, leading to an agreement between the Mexican and U.S. governments to provide some protection and controls between 1951 and 1964.

Under this agreement, hundreds of thousands of braceros worked in the fields of California. Under pressures from organized labor, the agreement was terminated in 1964. But, thousands of Mexicans continued to cross the border looking for work, and, in increasing numbers, they also went to the urban areas looking for jobs.

It would be a mistake today to think of the Mexican-American or Chicano as essentially a farm laborer, since over 90 percent live in urban areas. The typical Chicano has less formal schooling and less income than his Anglo counterpart. While many Chicanos are better off economically than blacks, those who are illegal immigrants are subject to immediate deportation. In time of economic hardship, they are the most vulnerable of the disadvantaged.

ILLUSTRATION 2–6
Illegal aliens camping out in orange grove, and the packing crates in which they
live while picking fruit

Photos courtesy United Press International

THE DUST BOWL

Oklahoma, Arkansas, and other Plains states were swept by drought in the 1930s. At a time when migration to California had dropped to an all-time low as a result of the Depression, the "Okies" and "Arkies" came looking for jobs that didn't exist and helped swell the migration numbers again. Many of them went to the Central Valley looking for farm work. While California grew by only 22 percent in the 1930s, Kern County grew by 64 percent, Kings and Tuolumne Counties by 39 percent each, and Madera County by 36 percent. Other Central Valley farm counties also grew more than the rest of the state.

BLACKS

World War II's booming economy in northern industrial centers and in California lured millions of blacks away from their southern homes. About 300,000 came to California during the war and in the late 1940s—for a whopping increase of 272 percent. In the 1950s the black population increased another 91 percent and in the 1960s by 58 percent.

Today blacks are the second largest minority in California, approximately 7 percent of the state's population. Two out of three live in the central cities—many of them in ghettos—Watts and Hunter's Point, for example. On the average, a typical black's income is 70 percent of a white person's. A few blacks have been able to continue to college. About 1 out of 7 have had 1 to 3 years of college, but, social, political, and economic equality have not yet been achieved. When California's economy stagnates, blacks and Chicanos suffer most.

NEW TRENDS

In the aftermath of Vietnam, the newest wave of immigrants seeking "the good life" are Vietnamese refugees. Thus far, more of these refugees have settled in California than in any other state.

Today

WHERE WE LIVE

California is an urban state. In fact, with 91 percent of the population living in metropolitan areas, it is one of the most urbanized states in the nation. But, the urban pattern is substantially different from most other urbanized states. Due to relatively low land costs, the desire for room, the extensive freeway system, and the willingness to commute long distances to work (and earlier fears of earthquakes), we have spread out across the land. Thus, California is also a suburban state. One national columnist once referred to Los Angeles as "seven suburbs in search of a soul." (Today, it's more than *107* suburbs in search of a soul.) More than half of all Californians live in suburbs.

In the 1950s and 1960s, California's suburban growth was massive in scale—whole counties seemed to mushroom overnight. Orange County, south of Los Angeles, grew by 99 percent in the '60s, while Santa Clara, south of San Francisco, grew by 63 percent. Indeed, Orange and Santa Clara Counties accounted for over two thirds of the state's total growth between 1960 and 1970.

On the other hand, because of the suburban trend, many older metropolitan areas have lost population. San Francisco County began losing population in the 1950s, and in 1972 Los Angeles County began losing people too.

Another area—the state's so-called inland empire, the Central Valley, experienced a net out-migration in the 1960s. More people moved out of Kern, Fresno, Madera, Merced, and other Central Valley counties than moved in. The only in-migration in this area was in the suburbs of Sacramento and in Butte County.

But, in the early 1970s, this population trend appears to have been reversed. Between 1970 and 1979, the Central Valley's population grew by 17 percent (more than southern or northern California). This growth was largely centered in the rural counties at the edge of some of the valley's larger cities. El Dorado, Lake, Mariposa and Nevada Counties grew by more than 60 percent. Some of the smaller counties also began to grow in the 1970s. Alpine and Mono Counties more than doubled in population.

Growth in the '70s was not as massive as in the '60s, but here and there, pleasant, quiet semirural towns suddenly attracted substantial numbers of people fleeing the suburban "rat race." Santa Rosa and Napa in northern California are good examples.

In southern California, people moved farther out from the Los Angeles complex, buying homes in Riverside or Ventura Counties. And, San Diego continued to grow, luring thousands to its sunny smog-free atmosphere.

But, wherever we live, many of us—most of us—will move again soon. One third of all Californians have moved from one home to another in the same county within the last five years. Another 12 percent have moved from one county to another within the state in that period. Finally, 10 percent moved into the state. Less than half of us have not moved in the last five years.

This propensity to move—and to move to suburbs—has produced a 500-mile-long strip city along the coast from the Mexican border to Santa Rosa north of San Francisco. About 75 percent of the state's population lives in this coastal strip. Hills, mountains, and deserts cover about two thirds of the state and few people live there. Relatively few people live in the inland agriculture areas. Not only do most of us live in this "strip city," but there is every reason to believe that we will continue to do so.

Cosmopolitan California

Many kinds of people live in California. San Francisco's city-county 1975 ballot was printed in seven separate languages. Thirty-nine other counties, including Los Angeles, Orange, San Diego, Alameda, Contra Costa, Santa Clara, and Sacramento print ballots in Spanish as well as English. The Department of Motor Vehicles published instructions in three languages other than English for its 1975 license renewal notices, and as of 1979, driver's instruction booklets were published in seven languages. Scattered throughout the state are at least 33 newspapers printed in 16 different languages. In the larger urban areas, several radio and television theaters broadcast in different languages, and some movie theaters feature foreign language films.

Making a living

California was originally an agricultural area that experienced its first growing pains in the Gold Rush of 1849. Today, ironically, less than 4 out of 100 are employed in farming or mining.

In fact, California's economy is now well into the postindustrial stage. More people are employed in trade (20 percent) than in any other activity. They work in stores of all kinds—grocery, clothing, or music, for example. Manufacturing ranks second with government, and service employment is a close third and fourth in importance. Moreover, if present trends continue, manufacturing will drop to fourth place in a few years.

Today over 2 million Californians belong to a labor union, which is about 25 percent of the labor force. But, union membership was 30 percent 20 years ago; so union membership has dropped. Northern California is more unionized than southern California. Thirty-two percent of the workers in the San Francisco Bay area belong to a union. In Los Angeles County, the percentage is 24 percent, and in Orange County it is 20 percent.

Until the gasoline shortages of 1973–74 and 1979, many thought nothing of driving long distances to work as a part of their suburban living style. In Los Angeles County, the average worker has a daily round trip of about 35 miles. One out of four Orange County workers commute daily to Los Angeles County. Forty to 60 percent of those living in some of the San Francisco Bay suburbs commute to work from communities such as Walnut Creek, Menlo Park, Mill Valley, and Daily City.

ILLUSTRATION 2–7
Passengers waiting for a BART (Bay Area Rapid Transit) train at the Embarcadero station BART serves the San Francisco Bay Area and is California's only mass public rapid transit system.

Photo courtesy of BART

California's two cultures

According to many observers of the state scene, California is really two states—southern California, that area south of the Tehachapi mountains, and northern California, north of the mountains. This split is delineated in the state's division of gas tax funds, organization of political parties, professional organizations, and the administration of many state government agencies. The north-south split makes sense geographically, in patterns of communication and travel, and in basic cultural differences.

At one time, when transportation was difficult and communications slow, there wasn't much exchange between north and south in California. Today, with Los Angeles and San Francisco only one hour away by jet plane, with instant telephone and televised news, and with the freeways making it easy to travel, the state is not as divided as it once was. However, now and then, when issues such as water distribution or allocation of tax funds become important, the north versus south division reappears.

The final fling—1950–1970

Accelerated by both the population and economic growth of the 1940s —California enjoyed what may have been its last tango in the sun. Between 1950 and 1960, population grew from 10.5 million to almost 16 million, and by 1970 it had grown to almost 20 million. Real personal income increased by half over the 20-year period. Additionally, the labor force grew by about half between 1950 and 1960 and then almost doubled between 1960 and 1970.

Growth meant more jobs, jobs for young people just out of school, jobs for women entering the labor market in mid-life, jobs for the semi-skilled, and jobs for the migrants. Young or middle-aged, black, brown or Oriental, poor whites or prosperous businesspeople; all could come to California expecting to do better. Growth also meant increased tax revenues for government.

Growth also meant air and water pollution, jammed freeways, crowded schools, hospitals, and jails, increasingly expensive housing, and a water shortage. So, government needed all the money it could get.

But, there have been substantial signs of a slowdown. Starting in 1964, population growth dropped from 3.6 percent a year to 1 percent by 1970. In the decade of the '70s, this very slow growth rate appears to have been stabilized. Thus, 1970–80 may see the lowest growth rate in the state's history (about 14 percent). Employment growth will be about 30 percent for the decade. And, as in the rest of the United States, energy is now in short supply. The state's oil production has dropped, and imports now are about one quarter of consumption.

THE FUTURE

The supply of energy and its costs are major uncertainties in California's future. High energy costs mean fewer jobs and an increase in the cost of living. At the same time, more Californians will be looking for jobs. Ours is a young state, and even though population growth has slowed, many young people will soon be entering the labor market. Between 1975 and 1985, about 2.25 million young people will be looking for jobs in California, but less than a million workers will reach age 65 and retire. Thus there will be a need for more than 1.25 million *new jobs.* In a period of slow economic growth, where will the young, the blacks, Chicanos, or women find the jobs they seek? Will unemployment become a chronic major problem? In a period of recession, who will be fired first?

Will the rising costs of gasoline increase the demand for public transportation? Or, will people move closer to work? But, on the other hand, the high cost of housing is forcing people to move farther away from the central cities and many suburbs.

Will environmental protection be eliminated in order to meet the demand for jobs, energy, and construction?

If the economy stagnates, what will happen to the present welfare program? If many middle-class and blue-collar workers join the ranks of the unemployed, will they have a different view of welfare?

Will our political institutions respond effectively to the new problems? What kinds of political reforms are needed? Should the solutions be left to the present economic system? As we suggested in Chapter 1, California's problems are usually the same as the nation's. How we solve them may show the way for the rest of the United States.

3

California's constitution

Each of the 50 states, as well as the national government, has a written constitution. And each is rooted in its own particular history and circumstances. The constitution may be long or short, specific in detail or broad in generalizations, and easy or difficult to amend. But, every constitution has a unique set of characteristics that *makes it a constitution.* These characteristics include:

1. Establishing the agencies of government.
2. Granting some powers to those agencies.
3. Denying some powers to these agencies.
4. Providing for change.

Of these four characteristics, the single most important is the limit on governmental power. The California Constitution, like those of the other 49 states, limits the authority of government and protects the rights of the people. The essence of constitutional government is that it is *a limited government* (Friedrich, 1950).

In general, state constitutions differ from the national constitution in that the U.S. Constitution is one of *delegated powers.* Theoretically, the national government may not exercise any power that cannot be found in the U.S. Constitution. All powers not delegated to the national government are, in theory, reserved to the states and the people. (The 10th Amendment to the U.S. Constitution is an explicit statement of that division of powers.) State governments, on the other hand, are assumed to have power unless it is explicitly denied by the state's own constitution or the U.S. Constitution. It is important to note that Article XIV of the U.S. Constitution also places a limit on the powers of state governments.

Agencies of government/grants of power

California's constitution establishes the major agencies of government —legislative, executive, and judicial. Provisions for local government— counties, cities, schools, and special districts—may also be found. In addition, the powers and authority of government are derived from the constitution. Authority to tax and borrow money, to enact and administer laws, and to adjudicate conflicts are all found in the constitution. These agencies and their powers are discussed later in the text.

Limit on powers

Most important in a democratic political system are the statements of the constitution limiting the powers of government. Article I of the California Constitution spells out its citizens' rights and freedoms and the limits on governmental powers.

The 14th Amendment to the U.S. Constitution has also become a major restraint on state powers. The U.S. Supreme Court has ruled that the 14th Amendment's "due process of law" clause includes some of the rights guaranteed by the Federal Bill of Rights. Thus, for example, states may not violate an individual's rights of free speech and press which are protected by the U.S. First Amendment (*Gitlow* v. *New York,* 1925). More recently, the U.S. Supreme Court held that states could not segregate public schools on the basis of race (*Brown* v. *Board of Education,* 1954). Such segregation, the court ruled, violated the "equal protection" clause of the 14th Amendment.

Change

The fourth component of any workable constitution is its capacity and provisions for change. The California Constitution has been changed by each of the following three methods: (1) convention (1879), (2) amendments proposed by the legislature, and (3) amendments proposed by initiative. Regardless of the method by which constitutional amendments are proposed, each must be approved by a majority of the voters in a statewide election.

The most frequently used method has been by legislative action. Over 260 separate constitutional amendments have been referred to the people by the legislature since World War II (1945). The second most frequently used method is the initiative. Almost 50 constitutional amendments have been placed on the ballot by initiative since 1945.

Amendments proposed by the legislature are much more likely to be approved than are amendments by initiative. Many of the legislature's amendments are technical modifications and engender little or no opposition. And many potentially controversial amendments are modified and altered in the legislative process so that they have less opposition on the ballot. Two thirds of the amendments proposed by the legislature have been approved by the voters, whereas less than a third of the initiative amendments have been approved (see Chapter 6).

California leads all other states in the number of constitutional amendments proposed and approved (Strum, 1976:161–80). On the other hand, the Golden State has not used the constitutional convention device as frequently as have other states. Since most amendments to the constitution are piecemeal—by ballot measure—it is not surprising that California has a very long constitution. Indeed, only ten states have longer constitutions.

But this frequent constitutional change is not because it is easy. Two thirds of both legislative houses must approve a proposed constitutional amendment which must then be approved by a majority of voters. In 10 states the requirements are more difficult, but in 15 states it is easier to amend the constitution. The other 24 states are similar to California. California, like other initiative states, does tend to have a longer than average constitution, but the low success rate of initiative constitutional amendments suggests that they have not had much to do with the overall length of the constitution or its many amendments. (Only 13 out of 185 approved amendments since 1945 were by initiative.)

Of all methods, the constitutional convention has been used least. The original constitution (1849) was, of course, drafted in convention and ratified by the voters. The second constitutional convention was held 30 years later (1879). Since then, there have been no more conventions, though several attempts have been made to call such a convention in the last 40 years.

CONSTITUTIONAL HISTORY

California's constitutional history may be divided into six periods of time:

1. Spanish, 1769–1821.
2. Mexican, 1821–49.
3. Early American, 1849–79.
4. Early industrial, 1879–1910.
5. Progressive, 1910–62.
6. Contemporary reform, 1962–

While the first two periods were colorful and exciting, nothing of contemporary constitutional significance remains of those early times (Mason, 1973).

Early American

California's first constitution (1849) was adopted before California became part of the United States. Shaping the now dry words of debate and the document were the westward expansion of American settlers, slavery, the emerging gold boom, and a desperate need for effective government.

Called into convention at Monterey on September 1, 1849, 48 delegates drafted the first constitution in six weeks. Hastily written, and largely borrowed from the Iowa and New York state constitutions, this document served the people of California for 30 years. After overwhelming ratification, the election of a legislature, a governor, and two United States Senators, California had to wait until September 1850 before it was admitted to the Union.

But the first constitution, a hurry-up patchwork effort, was soon found to have several weaknesses. There was too little in it about taxes and government finance. There were no specific provisions in regard to legislative districts—some counties had no representatives at the state capitol. And, there were complaints about the extent of the governor's powers. Most important, mounting economic problems and public unrest made it clear that the original constitution could not do the job. In 1879, a second constitutional convention was called.

Emerging industrial

By the meeting of the 1879 constitutional convention, California had become a part of the rapidly industrializing United States. An isolated agricultural and mining state in the 1850s, it became linked to the nation by the railroad in 1869. It was economically linked too. California was suffering from the massive national depression of the time: high unemployment, low farm produce prices, unregulated railroad rates, and a large number of Chinese workers competing for scarce jobs.

Of the 152 delegates sent to the 1879 constitutional convention, 85 were "nonpartisan," and 50 were "Kearneyites" or members of the Workingman's Party (see Chapter 4). Only 17 were elected on a regular party basis (9 Republicans and 8 Democrats).

Major features of the 1879 Constitution were an expanded and strengthened Bill of Rights (Article I) and severe limits placed on the legislature (Article IV). The state judiciary was reorganized, but the executive was not changed. Specific attention was aimed at limiting the rights of Orientals.

One of the lasting features of this constitution was its length and detail. The delegates put a large number of specific provisions into the second constitution hoping, thereby, to protect and to promote their own interests and values. They also hoped to reduce control of the legislature by special interests. But errors in the specifics and changing needs led to repeated constitutional amendments in the next few decades. Nor were special interests effectively controlled. By 1911, the Progressives had to make several major constitutional changes.

The Progressive movement was a major feature in California's political history (see Chapter 4). Among significant constitutional changes implemented by Progressives were the initiative, referendum and recall (see Chapter 6), the direct primary, women's suffrage, nonpartisan election of local government officials, a presidential primary, and a strengthened public utility commission.

Twentieth century

As California moved into the 20th century of industrialization and urban living, demands for constitutional revision increased. On four separate occasions—1898, 1914, 1920, and 1930—voters rejected a proposal to call a third constitutional convention. In 1933, in the depths of the Depression, the voters approved such a convention, but the state legislature failed to act on it. Conventions were proposed at every session of the state legislature between 1935 and 1947. Increasingly, as more amendments were added and as needs changed, the constitution became more cumbersome and out of date.

In 1947, the legislature appointed a citizen's advisory committee to study constitutional revisions. The committee's recommendations were submitted to the voters in a special election in 1949. Six amendments were approved, which eliminated about 14,500 unnecessary words from the state constitution. Again, in 1960, voters approved removal of more obsolete constitutional wordage (Proposition 12).

But at the same time, legislators and voters were busy adding to the constitution. Some of these additions and changes were the work of special interest groups using the initiative methods of constitutional amendment (see Chapter 6). Some of these initiatives dealt with young fig trees, marine insurance, parking facilities, minor government offices, or increasing the size of the Chiropractors Examining Board. An obvious example of using the constitution to protect a special interest was the requirement that the legislature had to have a two-thirds vote to increase business or corporate taxes. In contrast, income tax or sales tax change could be made with a simple majority. (The two-thirds requirement was abolished in 1976).

Between 1946 and 1962, 148 constitutional amendments were submitted to the voters who approved 89 (60 percent). While some were trivial, others were important: establishing regional forms of local government, reorganizing the state's inferior courts, and reapportioning the state senate (rejected by voters). Most significantly, voters approved in 1962 the establishment of a constitutional revision commission (Proposition 7).

Contemporary reform

Under authority of Proposition 7, the California legislature appointed a Citizens' Advisory Commission on Constitutional Revision. The commission's task was to examine the Constitution of 1879 and its numerous amendments and to submit recommended changes and a "clean-up" in the form of proposed new amendments to the legislature.

Meeting almost monthly for two years, the commission presented to the legislature a package of major revisions and deletions to the state's constitution. After some modification, the legislature submitted these proposals to the voters in 1966 in the form of a massive constitutional amendment—Proposition 1A.

Proposition 1A dealt with about one third of the state's constitution and deleted about 16,000 words. It eliminated several procedural restrictions on the state legislature (see Chapter 9), modified the initiative process (see Chapter 6), and streamlined the executive branch (see Chapter 10).

Supported by both the Democratic and Republican candidates for governor, State Chamber of Commerce, AFL-CIO, League of Women Voters, League of Cities, and the County Supervisors Association, as well as many major newspapers (including the *Los Angeles Times* and McClatchy *Bee* chain), Proposition 1A was approved by California's voters 3 to 1.

Continuing to meet on a monthly basis, the commission presented another set of proposed constitutional amendments to the legislature in 1968. Submitted to the voters as Proposition 1 on the November 1968 ballot, the amendment would have made substantial changes in seven articles including education, state civil service, and local government. However, there was little support for this proposition, and the *Los Angeles Times* opposed it. The electorate rejected it by 856,000 votes.

The commission continued to meet and offered a third set of proposed constitutional changes to the legislature. Four propositions were placed on the November 1970 ballot. Proposition 14 revised the state's civil service, reducing the number of exempt employees (see Chapter 11). Proposition 15 slimmed down one of the more cumbersome constitutional articles (XX) eliminating such out-of-date provisions as a prohibition on dueling. Proposition 16 amended Article XVIII, eliminating the awkward convention provisions and replaced them with a simple requirement for calling a convention after a majority vote by the California electorate. Finally, Proposition 17 eliminated a useless article (XXVIII) from the constitution. All four amendments were approved by the voters. Thus, much that had been rejected by the voters in 1968 was accepted as revised in 1970.

Subsequently, in the elections of 1972 and 1974, other commission recommendations were approved by the voters. Of the 14 commission-legislature constitutional amendments submitted to the voters, 13 were approved.

At the same time, the legislature was proposing its own amendments at the rate of 13 per election year (79 amendments between 1964–74). The legislature's amendments were approved by the voters 70 percent of the time.

From 1946–74, there was a steady flow of constitutional amendments offered to the voters. Of the approximately 16 per election year, voters approved two thirds. Interestingly, the use of the initiative process to place amendments in the constitution increased during this period of time. The success rate of initiative amendments increased too.

Obviously, in spite of the good efforts of the Constitutional Revision Commission and the legislature, the people of California have felt compelled to use the initiative amendment process more frequently in recent years. Moreover, those initiative measures have become more frequently successful.

It may be that a greater number of interest groups and reform organizations have turned to the initiative process. Sometimes the proponents of an initiative measure will threaten to "go to the people" if the legislature fails to act as it wants. Sometimes the legislature will respond—for example Proposition 8 in 1978. But sometimes the legislature is unable to respond (or unwilling). An examination of one of the most recent and dramatic initiative constitutional amendments illustrates some of these factors.

Proposition 13—A case study

Perhaps no other subject is so complex as tax reform. California's tax structure is the result of decades of tax legislation. Parallel to the tax

TABLE 3–1
Constitutional amendment activity 1946–1978

Time period	Legislative proposals			Initiative proposals		
	Passed	Failed	Total	Passed	Failed	Total
1946–62	89	59	148	3	16	19
1964–78	90	35	125	11	15	26
Total:	179	94	273	14	31	45

Source: California Secretary of State, *Statement of Vote*, 1946–78.

structure is the state and local budget structure. It is equally complex (see Chapter 11). Numerous attempts have been made to change the tax-budget structure in California. One largely successful attempt, resulting from the state supreme court's decision in *Serrano* v. *Priest* (1971), substantially altered the state-local funding of public education. And a recent change in the state's income tax was instituted by Governor Ronald Reagan and the legislature.

Several attempts had also been made to reform the property tax. In 1968 an initiative ballot measure authored by Los Angeles County Tax Assessor Philip Watson forced the legislature into some minor relief. But the Watson initiative failed at the polls. Watson's next measure (1970) failed to get enough signatures to be placed on the ballot. His 1972 measure (Proposition 14) qualified but lost too. In general, the Watson measures (and others like it) were too complex and generated confusion.

However, by the mid-70s, property taxes increasingly became a subject of debate. Homeowners in most urban areas throughout the state found that inflation and demand rapidly increased the value of their residences—doubling and tripling their market value in the early and mid-1970s in some areas. Along with the rapid increase in market values came an equally rapid increase in property taxes. But few homeowners' incomes increased as rapidly as their taxes, and those who retired found their incomes actually cut. Perhaps more than anything else, it was the method of collecting the tax that hurt the most.

Unlike the personal income tax that is withheld from the paycheck, property taxes are collected twice a year (December and April). Paying several hundred or a thousand dollars in property taxes at the start of the holiday season hurt! But April was the cruelest month of all. While preparing federal and state income tax forms (due April 15th), the beleaguered taxpayer had to pay the second half of the property tax! These taxes have the highest political visibility of any in California.

In the fall of 1977, Howard Jarvis and Paul Gann started an initiative campaign for what was to become the major political issue in California in the 1978 elections—Proposition 13. Essentially, they simply proposed that the property tax should not be more than 1 percent of the assessed market value of the property. That meant an average cut in the tax of about 57 percent. Proposition 13 easily qualified for the ballot with over 1.2 million signatures. Public opinion rapidly firmed-up in support of the initiative, and it was approved in the June 1978 primary election by 65 percent of the voters.

Local government revenues were immediately cut by 27 percent. Governor Brown, attempting to assist local government, trimmed the state's budget by $1½ billion (about 10 percent). While the arguments continue to rage about the merits and effects of Proposition 13, it is obvious that the voters forced state and local governments to cut their budgets. Whether or not government spending will continue at a reduced level is unclear (see Chapter 11), but, it is clear that property taxes were cut by an initiative constitutional amendment.

SUMMARY

As we examine the political institutions and process of California government, it will become increasingly clear that the state's constitution—the way government is organized, its powers, and its limits—are very important. And, we will also see that these institutions and processes can be changed.

In the following chapters, a more detailed discussion of constitutional provisions will be found as they relate to the topic at hand. For example, the constitutional provisions dealing with the governor (Article V) will be considered in Chapter 10, which examines the governor's powers. Similarly, the chapters dealing with other California political institutions will also consider relevant constitutional sections.

4

The kaleidoscope of
California politics

To appreciate and comprehend contemporary California politics fully, and to understand the future better, one first needs to examine the major features of the state's political past and the many changes that have occurred. Although this chapter will describe major historical features, it will focus only on those events or individuals that either had a lasting impact on California politics or are good examples of basic political patterns in the state. In particular, emphasis will be given to California's substantial political reform tradition.

California political history can be divided, roughly, into six time segments:

1. Democratic dominance .... 1850–61.
2. Civil War politics .... 1862–67.
3. Two-party competition .... 1868–98.
4. Republican dominance .... 1899–1958.
5. Two-party competition .... 1959–74.
6. Emerging Democratic dominance ...... 1975–?.

Obviously, the state's politics are not fixed; over time one party and then the other appears to dominate. And, many burning issues of the past are no longer important. If one thing is clear, it is that California politics change.

The first two historical periods have had little lasting impact on contemporary California politics. Subsequent events have obliterated their major features. In the third period, there were three events that have had lasting impact. They are: (1) the railroad era of the late 1800s; (2) the

Workingman's Party of the 1870s, and; (3) the Populist movement of the 1890s. The three are significant because they illustrate the long struggle for reform and the basic relationship between the state's political system, its people, and the economy.

19th-CENTURY FEATURES

The railroad era

California's railroad magnates, Leland Stanford, Mark Hopkins, Collis Huntington, and Charles Crocker—the "Big Four," as they were known—dominated California's economy and politics from the 1880s into the 20th century. Controlling transportation into and out of the state, as well as much of it within the state, the owners of the Southern Pacific Railroad used that economic power to gain political control of California. Their greed and corrupt politics gave rise to several protest movements—the Workingman's Party and the Progressive movement as well as fueling California's version of Populism.

Each of the Big Four became major economic powers in the state. Today their names are institutionalized in a major university, bank chain, and hotels. Moreover, the Southern Pacific is still one of the largest private landholders in California.

Workingman's Party

Led by Denis Kearney, the Workingman's Party was a response to major social and economic forces in California: first, high unemployment brought about by the economic recession of the late 1870s; and, second, rapid growth of cheap Chinese labor in the state. White animosity toward the "Yellow Peril" grew steadily in California as thousands of Chinese were brought in to work on the railroad. After completion of the railroad (1869), Chinese immigrants were forced to look for other kinds of work, and unemployed white workers resented the new job competition. The Workingman's Party strongly opposed the import and use of Chinese labor.

Kearneyism (as it was also known) came to stand for establishing state regulation of railroads, utilities, and banks; a fair tax system; an eight-hour day; compulsory education, and the direct election of United States Senators. (Some of these proposals were later adopted at the California Constitutional Convention of 1878–79.)

But, California's economy improved, and as various portions of the Workingman's program came to be adopted by both Democrats and Republicans, the Workingman's Party soon disappeared.

Populists

This minor party that emerged toward the end of the 19th century was a mixture of agrarian reformers, nonpartisans, and socialists. While never achieving significant political power, the Populists helped alert the public to many needed reforms. In several instances, they provided the balance of power between Democrats and Republicans. Populists were staunch early advocates of such reforms as: women's suffrage, railroad regulation, monetary reform ("free silver"), municipal ownership of utilities, the secret ballot, the initiative, referendum and recall, direct primaries, income tax and unemployment relief—all of which are accepted policy today.

Kearneyism and Populism were both clear manifestations of citizen discontent with the existing economic and political system. While neither movement gained sufficient strength to implement its programs fully, each did help pave the way for later successful reform.

REPUBLICAN DOMINANCE: 1899–1958

In 1898, California Republicans won control of both houses of the California legislature and the governor's office. For the next 60 years, Republicans effectively controlled California government. Early in this period, the Progressives, led by Hiram Johnson (a liberal Republican), briefly captured control of the party and instituted far-reaching fundamental reforms. In the 1930s and '40s, California voters flirted with the Democratic Party, and, at the same time, the state acquired a national reputation for being a hotbed of radical, crazy political movements.

Finally, toward the end of the period, came the Warren era of moderate Republicanism and "nonpartisan" politics. This long period of Republican control finally came to an end with (1) fundamental changes in the California primary election laws, (2) a bitter internal fight in the Republican Party, and, (3) an increase in the loyal Democratic vote.

The Progressives

As California government increasingly came under control of the Republican Party in the late 1800s, so, too, did the Republican and Democratic parties come under control of the Southern Pacific Railroad and its corporate allies. According to Fremont Older, a leading newspaper reporter of the time, by 1896 the entire state was controlled by the Southern Pacific (Older, 1926).

> In those days there was only one kind of politics and that was corrupt politics. It didn't matter whether a man was a Republican or a Democrat. The Southern Pacific Railroad controlled both parties, and he either had to stay out of the game altogether or play it with the railroad.

Older's statement should be taken seriously, since his newspaper was one of those on the railroad's payroll!

In addition to Southern Pacific machinations, another corrosive political force emerged in the state during this period—big city bosses and party machines. The most notorious California political "boss," Abe Ruef of San Francisco, was eventually convicted of bribery. But his partners in corruption—labor leaders and corporate executives of Pacific Gas & Electric, Pacific States Telephone & Telegraph, and other major California companies—were indicted but never convicted. In fact, their indictments cooled much of the city's elite reform fervor. Several of the state's major newspapers, including the *Los Angeles Times, San Francisco Chronicle,* and William R. Hearst's *Examiner* chain staunchly defended the indicted business leaders.

The Ruef bribery trial received maximum publicity when the prosecuting attorney was brazenly shot by a witness *in the court room.* More publicity developed when the witness was later found dead under mysterious circumstances in his own jail cell. Hiram Johnson, an obscure attorney at that time, accepted the job as prosecutor and helped secure Ruef's conviction.

Appalled by the railroad's activity, corruption in state and local politics, and the need for social and economic betterment, a small group of liberal Republicans began a statewide campaign to eliminate Southern Pacific control and implement reforms. Some of the state's newspapers were either directly involved in, or actively supported the Progressives, but there were notable major exceptions, such as the *Los Angeles Times, Oakland Tribune,* and *San Francisco Chronicle* which bitterly fought them.

Most Progressives expected a long uphill fight against the entrenched regular Republicans and their railroad allies. But the railroad made a tactical error in the spring of 1910. Instead of making an early selection of *their Republican candidate* for governor, Southern Pacific hesitated, and four "regular" Republicans entered the primary. Progressives supported a fifth candidate—Hiram Johnson. Building on his Ruef trial publicity, Johnson, a fire-breathing "give-'em-hell" candidate, toured the state with his battle cry, "Kick the Southern Pacific machine out of California politics." Nor did he ignore the regular Republican press. Describing Harrison Gray Otis, owner of the *Los Angeles Times,* Johnson said (Delmatier, 1970:168):

> . . . he sits in senile dementia, with gangrened heart and rotting brain, grimacing at every reform and chattering in impotent rage against decency and morality, while he is going down to his grave in snarling infamy . . . .

The four regular Republicans split 113,000 votes between themselves, while Johnson won with 102,000. A few months later he defeated the

ILLUSTRATION 4–1
Hiram Johnson on the campaign trail   No TV or radio in 1910. The candidate appeared in person.

Photo courtesy California State Library

Democratic candidate in the general election. Equally important, Progressive candidates won control of both the state assembly and state senate. This gave them the power to enact the most comprehensive and far-reaching political reforms in California history. It should be emphasized that Progressive success was partially built on the earlier "failures" of the Workingman's Party and the Populists.

Though Progressives dominated the state for only a few years, their legacy has been enormous. Among their social reforms were:

1. Prohibiting child labor.
2. Establishing workmen's compensation.
3. Expanding and strengthening of the state railroad commission.
4. Providing free school texts.
5. Extending the eight-hour work day.
6. Expanding conservation programs.

These social-economic programs clearly distinguished Progressive Republicans from old-line "regular" Republicans.

More important were the Progressive political reforms, since they involved significant changes in the processes of government. These included:

1. Direct democracy legislation—the initiative and referendum.
2. Recall.
3. Direct primary system and a presidential preference primary.
4. Nonpartisan local elections.
5. Restructured political party organizations.
6. Extended civil service.
7. Cross-filing.

Of these reforms, only cross-filing has been subsequently eliminated. The other reforms continue to exert a substantial influence on California politics.

Several reforms—cross-filing, nonpartisan local elections, civil service expansion, and restructured party organizations—greatly weakened political parties in California. Progressives sought to eliminate corrupt politics by reducing the role of political parties (see Chapter 8). Indeed, in 1915, they nearly succeeded in establishing nonpartisan elections to the state legislature.

For a short time, the Progressive reforms sharply reduced corruption and special interest power in the state. However, by the late 1920s special interests were as active as ever, and by the 1930s and '40s they had probably reached new heights of power (see Chapter 7). On the other hand, California, for the most part, has continued in the Progressive tradition of honest government. Certainly, in contrast to many eastern states, it is a model of pristine purity.

In 1916, Hiram Johnson was elected to the United States Senate. His departure from California for Washington, D.C. left the Progressives without a leader. By 1921, conservative Republicans were back in power.

Depression politics

The Depression era in California is more significant *for what did not happen* than for what did. Nationally, the Depression hit with stunning force in the early 1930s, putting millions out of work and sweeping Republicans out of office everywhere. In 1930, for example, California sent only one Democrat to Congress. But two years later, the state sent *ten* Democrats to Congress. Democratic presidential candidate Franklin D. Roosevelt captured California's electoral votes with 60 percent of the popular vote.

This marks the beginning of 14 years of Democratic successes in federal elections in California. Democratic presidential candidates captured the state from 1932 through 1948, while the congressional delegation had a Democratic majority from 1932 to 1946. In addition, Democratic Party registration leaped upward, from a low of 22 percent in 1930, to over 60 percent in 1936, where it remained until 1952.

While Democrats made impressive gains in national elections, they were unable to wrest control of the state away from Republicans. Democrats failed to gain control of California government for several reasons: (1) the party was weak, even by California standards; (2) their candidates were sometimes personally unattractive and sometimes politically offensive; (3) the registration majority was an illusion (see Chapter 5); and (4) the state's press was almost solidly Republican.

The Democratic Party was so weak in 1932 that it failed to field Democratic candidates in 17 of the 80 assembly districts. And, in eight other districts, a Republican won the Democratic nomination. As a result, there were no Democratic candidates running in approximately one third of the assembly districts. Cross-filing and incumbency protected most Republican legislators from defeat.

In 1934, the Democratic Party gubernatorial nomination was captured by party newcomer, Upton Sinclair. Sinclair, a prolific left-wing writer, had previously run for governor as a Socialist. Seeing a good chance to gain power, Sinclair switched to the Democratic Party and ran for its gubernatorial nomination on a platform of *End Poverty in California* (EPIC).

EPIC proposed state operation of idle factories—"for production, not for profit"—state distribution of farm and industrial produce; shifting the tax burden to the utilities and "wealthy"; and a pension of $50 a month for the elderly and disabled. Sinclair received approximately half of the primary vote, defeating eight other Democrats for the gubernatorial nomination.

The general election was hard-fought. Sinclair, a fiery speaker in the Hiram Johnson mold, campaigned throughout the state, but his campaign staff lacked both money and experience. Republican candidate, Frank Merriam, a bland personality at best, had the overwhelming support of an experienced party organization, much of the state's press, the badly frightened business community, and many conservative Democrats. Finally, William R. Hearst, a powerful Democrat and owner of the influential *Examiner* newspaper chain, threw his support to a third candidate—Raymond L. Haight.

Merriam won the election with less than half of the votes cast. His margin of victory over Sinclair was 260,000 votes—40,000 less than the 300,000 votes received by Haight. Though Sinclair lost, 29 EPIC candidates were elected to the assembly. But, Democrats (EPIC or otherwise) were still in the minority in the state legislature.

It was not until 1938, six years after Roosevelt's landslide presidential victory, that Democrats were able to elect a governor in California.

Culbert Olson, an EPIC state senator from Los Angeles, defeated incumbent Merriam, 1,391,000 votes to 1,171,000. Merriam got almost the same number of votes as he had in 1934; Haight, running again but without Hearst support, received only 64,000 votes! Thus, Olson became the first Democratic governor in 40 years. As the *Sacramento Bee* described it then: the situation ". . . presents the elements of novelty, surprise and speculation."

A number of offbeat political reform groups sprang up in southern California during this period. Among them were the Townsend Plan, "Thirty Every Thursday" (better known as "Ham and Eggs"), the Utopian Society, and Technocracy.

The Townsend Plan and Ham and Eggs were essentially the same. Government would be required to pay a substantial pension to the old and disabled. The pensioners, in turn, would be required to spend all they received every month. The pensions would be financed by a transaction tax—a tax on the sale of goods or services—essentially a sales tax. The basic idea was to stimulate production and create new jobs by required expenditures of the pensions. None of these plans was implemented, and most of the sponsoring organizations quickly disappeared.

Governor Olson approached his 1942 reelection campaign with a faulty understanding of California politics and a badly divided party. Many of his appointees were inept. They lacked experience, and they were often selected for political/patronage purposes. His administration was plagued by errors that the state's Republican press played up. In addition, his personal relations with the legislature were poor. Olson's dogmatic partisanship badly damaged his programs in a legislature dominated by Republicans. On 5 separate occasions unsuccessful attempts were made to recall Olson—an all time high.

Olson apparently did not understand the real nature of California party registration. While registered Democrats outnumbered Republicans by almost 2 to 1, many Democrats were not strong in their professed party allegiance—about 1 out of 5 had been Republicans in 1930. Olson had also been involved in a bitter presidential primary fight in 1940. And, finally, most of the state's press opposed him.

Olson campaigned confidently, deliberately taking strong partisan stands. The Republican candidate, Earl Warren, better understood the nature of California politics. Warren filed for both the Republican and Democratic gubernatorial nominations (i.e., cross-filed), receiving 404,000 votes in the Democratic primary (4 out of 10 votes cast).

The Warren era

Earl Warren had developed a solid reputation of nonpartisan efficiency and integrity as California State Attorney General and earlier as Alameda

County District Attorney. His record contrasted sharply with Governor Olson's largely ineffective and highly partisan record. Warren, in fact, was a partisan Republican. He had been co-founder of the then-powerful California Republican Assembly and had served as Chair of the Republican State Central Committee. He later ran for vice president with Tom Dewey on the GOP ticket in 1948. And, Warren was considered a prime Republican presidential possibility in 1952.

However, Warren ran for attorney general and then governor at a time when the nonpartisan emphasis was most useful. Thus, he did not run as a Republican but rather as a nonpartisan—stressing his record for honest, effective administration and a moderate policy position. This stance is best illustrated by his 1942 statement of candidacy in the *San Francisco Chronicle:*

> I believe in the party system and have been identified with the Republican Party in matters of party concern, but I have never found that the broad questions of national party policy have application to the problems of state and local government in California.

Warren's strategy was successful. He won by a large margin in 1942.

Four years later, Warren successfully cross-filed and had no Democratic opponent in the general election. In 1950, when he ran for an unprecedented third term, he received 4 out of 10 votes in the Democratic primary against James Roosevelt, son of the late president. Warren went on to win the general election by an incredible two-thirds vote—getting some 700,000 Democratic votes.

Warren's tenure in office brought stability to the state Republican Party. He so completely dominated the party that there was very little internal conflict. In 1953, when he resigned the governorship to accept appointment as Chief Justice of the U.S. Supreme Court, he left an apparently strong and united party in firm control of the state.

The end of Republican dominance

Warren's appointment to the U.S. Supreme Court moved Lieutenant Governor Goodwin "Goodie" Knight up to the governorship. When Knight became governor, he quickly assumed the Warren middle-of-the-road, nonpartisan stance. And, significantly, he worked closely with the state's labor union leaders.

But California's three leading Republicans, Vice President Richard Nixon, U.S. Senator William Knowland, and Knight soon began to fight over control of the state Republican Party. Knowland wanted to be elected governor in 1958, because he thought it would help his campaign for president in 1960. Only after a bruising intraparty fight could Knowland build up enough support to force Knight out of the race for governor. Knight grudgingly announced he would run for the vacant U.S. Senate seat instead. Thus, Republicans entered the 1958 election badly divided.

Further, Knowland abandoned the Warren victory formula. Instead of offering voters a moderate nonpartisan candidacy, he ran as an arch-conservative partisan.

Knowland's campaign was also hurt by a split in the usually solid Republican press. The *San Francisco Chronicle,* which had supported him in the primary, withdrew its support; three of the four Hearst *Examiner* newspapers endorsed Democrat Pat Brown, as did the three Central Valley *Bee's.* Even the very conservative *Long Beach Press Telegram* attacked Knowland for his willful shattering of the Republican Party.

The Democratic candidate, Pat Brown, taking advantage of Knowland's partisan conservative stance, easily occupied the political middle of the road. Brown, once a Republican who had reregistered as a Democrat in the Depression, fit the political patterns of Warren and Knight, while Knowland did not.

Knowland took his party down to crashing defeat. Not only did he lose badly (getting 4 out of 10 votes), but Democrats won four statewide offices, took Knowland's vacated U.S. Senate seat, won a majority of the state's congressional delegation, and even won a majority in both houses of the state legislature. Adding insult to injury, Knowland's antilabor or right-to-work initiative (Proposition 18) was soundly defeated.

The Democratic vote had been increasing slowly since 1948, and Democrats had been steadily increasing their numbers in the legislatures since 1952. (See Illustration 4–2). A substantial change in voter feeling had clearly been taking place—California Democrats were more frequently voting for Democratic candidates. Probably the single most important initial factor in the strengthening of the Democratic vote was the virtual elimination of cross-filing in 1954.

Further, after Adlai Stevenson's defeat in 1952, his supporters built an effective statewide volunteer political organization—the California Democratic Council. The party also recruited more attractive candidates. Given their basic majority, Democrats were almost bound to win if the trend continued. But the bitter intraparty Republican fight hastened the GOP defeat, making it more certain and overwhelming.

The 1958 elections terminated 60 years of Republican rule in California. It also ushered in a series of bitter internal GOP party battles between moderates and conservatives which further weakened the party until 1970. Most significantly, it was the start of a period of two-party competitive politics in the Golden State which, by the late 1970s seemed to be slowly shifting into a period of Democratic dominance.

ILLUSTRATION 4–2
Changes in party strength, 1930–1979

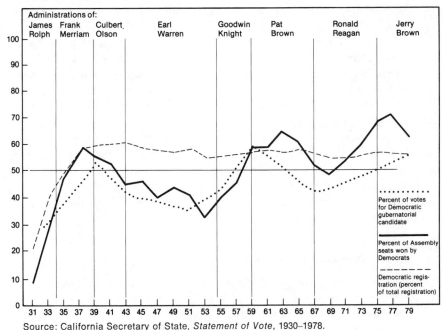

Source: California Secretary of State, *Statement of Vote,* 1930–1978.

TWO-PARTY COMPETITION: 1959–1974

This period of California's political history featured a dramatic change in the Republican Party's traditional ideological moorings, while clearly establishing the Democrats as the state's majority party. The Republican Party's share of registered voters began to decline in this period, too, slowly dropping to an all-time low by the mid-1970s (see Chapter 5). While Republicans continued to win state and national offices occasionally, they lost so many legislative elections that they became, essentially, a permanent minority in the state assembly, state senate, and congressional delegations.

The 1962 elections: Conservatives emerge

In March 1961, after losing the 1960 presidential race to John Kennedy, Richard Nixon announced that he would not be a candidate for governor in 1962. In September he changed his mind, but by this time, Joe Shell, a conservative Republican and party leader in the state assembly, had already announced his candidacy. Denouncing Nixon's switch as a blatant attempt to use the governor's office as a stepping stone to the presidency, Shell refused to drop out of the Republican primary. Nixon won the Republican primary, but Shell's hard-hitting conservative campaign cost Nixon 1 out of 3 Republican votes.

Pat Brown ran for reelection on his record and stressed party loyalty (since Democrats had 57 percent of the state's registered voters). Nixon combined an appeal for conservative Democratic votes with an attack on Brown for being "soft" on Communists. Brown won, along with several other Democrats, but incumbent Republican U.S. Senator Thomas Kuchel was easily reelected too.

On November 7, 1962, a tired, bitter Richard Nixon, stung by defeat, "retired" from politics, and in a morning-after blast at the press, accused them of "shafting" him. He concluded with his now famous parting shot, "You won't have Dick Nixon to kick around any more." Nixon moved to New York and entered private law practice. Everyone agreed—his political career was finished.

A new Republican Party—Moderation denied

Conservatives, who had lost in 1958 with Knowland, had been suspicious of Nixon since the mid-1950s. Tired of what they viewed as "me too" moderate Republican candidates, GOP conservatives mounted a concerted effort to capture the California Republican Party organizations in 1963–64.

"Operation take-over" was phenomenally successful. In two years, 1963 and 1964, conservatives gained control of the Young Republicans and the California Republican Assembly and also established a new conservative volunteer worker organization—United Republicans of California (UROC).

The 1964 elections

The Young Republicans, UROC, and John Birch Society attacked several moderate Republicans in the 1964 Republican primary elections. Four Birch Society members won Republican nominations. And, finally, U.S. Senator Barry Goldwater's narrow presidential primary victory over New York Governor Nelson Rockefeller put Republican conservatives in firm control of the state party.

Interestingly, as the Republican Party was becoming more conservative, so it appeared was the California electorate as a whole. For example, in a classic conflict between human rights and property rights, the governor, legislators, and citizens all focused on ballot Proposition 14 —the 1964 fair housing initiative.

At Governor Pat Brown's urging, the California legislature passed a fair housing bill (Rumford Act) in 1963. The bill banned racial discrimination in the sale or rental of all publicly assisted housing as well as most of the privately financed apartments in the state. Bitterly opposed to the new law, the 40,000-member California Real Estate Association placed an initiative measure on the 1964 ballot to repeal the Rumford Act. The initiative was also designed to prohibit any such legislation in the future.

Proposition 14, the repealer, tapped deeply held feelings about race, personal and general property rights, and government power. Sentiment was so strong on the issue that more people cast a vote on it than on any other measure on the ballot. Sixty-five percent of the vote was against fair housing. The vote was statewide. According to the California poll, Democrats split 6 to 4 for repeal, while Republicans favored it by 4 to 1. (Later, the California State Supreme Court struck down the vote as a violation of basic federal constitutional rights. But public opinion was clear).

ENTER RONALD REAGAN—STAGE RIGHT

Ronald Reagan got his first taste of big-time politics in the 1964 Goldwater campaign. As state co-chair of Citizens for Goldwater-Miller, Reagan made a favorable impression on both the party's leadership and financial backers as well as the general public during the campaign. A prominent actor and nationally popular as the host of two television shows ("General Electric Theater" and "Death Valley Days") his name was indeed a household word.

Toward the end of the 1964 Goldwater campaign, when even the most ardent of the Senator's supporters had all but conceded defeat, Reagan made a successful last-minute televised fund-raising appeal that raised over one-half million dollars. His speech, "A Time for Choosing," repeated the themes he had followed in earlier years speaking to General Electric employees across the nation. He attacked a wide range of government programs and big government itself.

> . . . government has laid its hand on health, housing, farming, industry, commerce, education, and to an ever increasing degree interferes with the people's right to know.

The speech so impressed the Goldwater campaign directors that they had it retelecast a dozen times in the last days of the election. Reagan's sincerity, his convincing knowledge of the issues, and his ability to project an image of reasonable indignation were impressive to voters.

It also impressed a powerful group of conservative state Republican party leaders looking for a winning gubernatorial candidate for 1966. A small group of wealthy Republicans (Henry Salvatori, Holmes

Tuttle, and A. C. Rubel) organized the "Friends of Ronald Reagan." They raised a relatively small campaign fund and acquired the professional campaign services of Spencer-Roberts, a high-powered Republican campaign management firm. On June 26, 1965, the Friends sent a letter to 7,500 leading Republicans exploring the possibility of a 1966 Reagan candidacy. Reagan also traveled around the state speaking to select audiences—building support.

The 1966 elections

Between mid-1965 and the spring of 1966, Spencer-Roberts, the Friends, and the candidate developed a superbly orchestrated campaign. Rejecting the pure Goldwater conservative stance, Reagan moved to a more moderate position. The key phrase of his campaign became "The Creative Society," concentrating on three themes:

1. Morality.
2. Government spending and taxes.
3. Professional politicians.

Not surprisingly, Reagan was for morality, against government spending and taxation, and offered himself as a "citizen politician."

Reagan sailed through the Republican primary, convincingly defeating his only major opponent, moderate Mayor George Christopher of San Francisco. His win was statewide, taking 53 of the state's 58 counties, swamping Christopher in southern California 4 to 1, and almost beating him in the Bay Area.

Liberal influence in the GOP was clearly shrinking. Some liberal Republicans had perhaps become more conservative and perhaps a few had left the party. More important, southern California, the bastion of conservative Republicans, had grown more rapidly in population than the liberal Republican Bay Area. Between 1946 and 1966 Republican registration in southern California grew by 125 percent. But in the Bay Area it grew by only 65 percent. In 1966, southern California conservative Republicans outnumbered northern liberal Republicans almost 3 to 1. In eight years, the Republican Party had changed from a moderate to a conservative philosophy.

Unlike Reagan, Governor Brown's campaign was not well organized, staffed, or financed. Sam Yorty, the conservative Democratic mayor of Los Angeles, entered the race repeating the old charge that Brown was supported by Communists. (Yorty, a maverick Democrat supported Richard Nixon for president against John F. Kennedy in 1960.) Even though Yorty did not wage a vigorous campaign, he got 38 percent of the Democratic primary vote (four other candidates got 9 percent), leaving the incumbent Brown with a slim majority of 53 percent. Yorty gave voice to the frustrations and fears of conservative Democrats concerned with race riots, welfare costs, and rising taxes.

On the other hand, many liberal Democrats were also unhappy with Brown. The liberal California Democratic Council (CDC) had supported Brown in 1958 more out of need than desire—he was the only strong candidate available. But, his moderate philosophy and history of "non-partisanship" as attorney general were not popular with more liberal partisan club members. In 1962 they again supported him because they had no choice. But in 1966, the CDC and Brown quarreled over the Viet Nam War. Club Democrats opposed the war and attacked the national Democratic administration on the issue.

After a bitter floor fight, the CDC reluctantly endorsed Brown for a third term in 1966. The vote was 874 to 280, but most of those 280 delegates walked out after the endorsement.

The general election was never in doubt. Brown's image contrasted starkly with Reagan's. Brown could (and sometimes would) walk un-recognized down a street even after eight years as governor. He often appeared (and was) indecisive, and he agonized over alternatives until he had a reputation in Sacramento as a "tower of jelly." Brown was badly hurt by both the Watts and Hunter's Point riots as well as the ideological splits within his party. Finally, the Brown campaign grossly underesti-mated Reagan. They dismissed Reagan as an amateur politician and—even worse—an actor.

Reagan won by almost 1 million votes (58 percent) out of 6½ million cast. His sweep helped elect three other Republicans to statewide of-fice. Also important to the Republicans, they won seven more assembly seats, five more state senate seats, and three more congressional seats.

The 1968 elections

Though faced with a growing budget, welfare reform, higher education needs, and a host of other major problems, much of Reagan's energies in his first two years as governor were devoted to his presidential aspira-tions and the 1968 Republican Presidential Convention in Miami. Reagan was the first California governor to openly and vigorously pursue the presidency. His California backers, believing that Reagan had an out-side chance, spent almost $400,000 in promoting him. But, in one of the most dramatic political comebacks in American history, Richard Nixon received the Republican nomination and then captured the presidency in November 1968.

In California, the Republican Party's normally efficient campaign or-ganization was badly hurt by a bitter primary fight between archconservative Max Rafferty and moderate incumbent U.S. Senator Thomas Kuchel. Conservative Republicans had tried unsuccessfully to defeat Kuchel in 1962.

Rafferty narrowly defeated Kuchel after a bitter ideological fight, with southern conservatives supporting Rafferty and northern moderates voting for Kuchel. However, Rafferty's slashing attacks on his fellow Republican so alienated Kuchel's moderate followers that they did little in the general election for Rafferty, and a Democrat (Alan Cranston) won.

The 1968 elections were an even sadder and more bitter experience for the Democrats. Badly split by the Viet Nam War and the presidential candidacies of Senators Hubert Humphrey, Eugene McCarthy, and Robert Kennedy; stunned by the murder of Senator Kennedy on primary election night in California; and bitter over their experience at the National Democratic Convention in Chicago; state Democrats were unable to work together to defeat Richard Nixon. Senator Humphrey, the party's Presidential candidate, was not warmly supported by California Democrats and lost the state to Nixon by 223,000 votes.

The 1970 elections

Republicans went into the 1970 elections in a strong position. Reagan's tightened controls on higher education had substantial public support while budget, tax, and welfare issues hurt him very little. The *California Poll* of February 1970 showed that two thirds of the state's voters thought he was doing a "good" or "fair" job as governor. Republicans also had real hopes of gaining control of both legislative houses and being able to reapportion the state's legislature in 1971—thereby improving their political power in the state through the 1970s. Banking on Reagan's popularity, the Republicans ran a straight party campaign with the slogan of "Team '70."

But, in mid-March it was revealed that incumbent Republican Senator George Murphy had received $125,000 over the previous six years from Technicolor, Inc. The *Los Angeles Times* immediately declared that Murphy had forfeited the privilege of representing California in the U.S. Senate. Several Republicans were pressured to run against Murphy and at the last minute, Norton Simon, a liberal Republican millionaire, entered the race. The Murphy-Simon primary was fought on both moral and ideological grounds, with a majority of Republican moderates and liberals voting for Simon, and the rest of the party supporting Murphy. Simon lost, 670,00 votes to 1.3 million for Murphy.

Jess Unruh, no longer assembly speaker, gave up his safe assembly seat in a long-shot bid for the governor's office. His slim chance of

ILLUSTRATION 4–3

ONE AND ONE-HALF
MILLION
PRIMARY VOTES
FOR KENNEDY

Source: *Los Angeles Times,* June 7, 1968. Copyright, 1968, *Los Angeles Times.* Reprinted
with permission.

defeating the very popular Reagan was further damaged by his past fights
with other Democrats. One of those Democrats, Mayor Sam Yorty, ran
for the party's nomination again and got 660,000 votes—mostly from the
southern conservative part of the state. Unruh won the primary but entered the general election with little real hope of winning.

The general election was hard-fought. Murphy, badly hurt by both the

Technicolor scandal and his bitter primary fight, narrowly lost to Congressman John Tunney, who had substantial support from the Kennedy family. On the other hand, Reagan defeated Unruh by 500,000 votes in a race that was never in doubt.

Most significantly, the Democratic campaign destroyed Team '70. The Republican slate campaign, led by Reagan's popularity, did not work. Three statewide Republican candidates *did better* than Reagan, while one statewide office, secretary of state, was lost to a Democratic Party newcomer, Edmund (Jerry) G. Brown, Jr., son of the earlier Democratic governor. Most painful of all to Reagan was the loss of both legislative houses to the Democrats. As Unruh said: "We cut off his (Reagan's) coat tails clear up to the lapels." Not only would Reagan be facing a hostile legislature again, but the Democrats would have a powerful voice in reapportionment.

California's voters also elected a black to statewide office for the first time—Wilson Riles as California State Superintendent of Public Instruction. Riles, in defeating the incumbent Max Rafferty, received considerable quiet help from liberal Republicans seeking revenge for Kuchel's defeat in 1968.

The 1972 elections

Presidential politics and several controversial ballot measures dominated California politics in 1972. Richard Nixon, the incumbent President, faced no serious opposition in the California Republican primary and won an easy victory. Democrats, on the other hand, were still badly divided with nine candidates on the ballot.

U.S. Senator George McGovern, representing the more liberal left-wing Democrats, succeeded in defeating most moderate Democrats in the spring series of presidential primaries. California's 271 delegates (about one sixth of the votes needed for the nomination) were the big prize. Only U.S. Senator Hubert Humphrey remained to contest actively for them. After a bruising primary battle, McGovern won with less than half of the vote. (Though Humphrey captured almost as many votes as McGovern, he received none of the delegates in the winner-take-all primary.)

Victory in California assured McGovern of the Democratic presidential nomination. But having abandoned the middle ground in his quest and inclined to take quick, simplistic positions on complex issues, he rapidly alienated the middle-of-the-road Democrats he needed to defeat Nixon. In some ways, McGovern's 1972 ideological campaign resembled Senator Barry Goldwater's 1964 campaign. Like Goldwater, McGovern abandoned the middle ground to his opponent and lost badly. With 1 out of 3

Democrats voting for Nixon, McGovern lost the state by over a million votes.

Nixon's election was a personal victory over a weak opponent. There was no Republican team effort as in previous campaigns. The Nixon campaign, looking like a sure winner, drew most available financial support from Republican sources. Local Republicans, ignored by the President's campaign, focused on state legislative races. And, Democrats, having quietly given up on McGovern, did so too.

In California Republicans fared poorly. While Nixon captured over 4½ million votes, the combined Republican assembly vote total was nearly 1 million less. Democrats, having voted in large numbers for Nixon, returned to the party fold in the lesser elections. Democrats won eight new assembly seats. They also picked up five new congressional seats. For California Republicans, the state elections were a disaster.

California's November 1972 ballot was also loaded with controversial items: legalizing use (but not sale) of marijuana, local censorship of "obscene materials," restoring the death penalty, restricting organizing farm workers, prohibiting busing to achieve school integration, and regulating coastal lands. The state's voters appeared to take a conservative stand on some issues—voting for the death penalty and against school busing and marijuana, but they also took what looked like a liberal position by voting against obscenity censorship, against restrictions on farm labor organizing, and for regulation of coastal development.

A new Democratic Party?

In 1974, voters gave Democrats clear control of California government: with heavy majorities in both the assembly and state senate, the governor's office, and, 4 out of 5 statewide partisan offices. A black, Mervyn Dymally, was elected Lieutenant Governor, and an Oriental woman, March Fong Eu, captured the secretary of state's office.

Most of the political drama came from the nation's capital with Watergate, impeachment hearings and finally—the key event—President Richard Nixon's resignation. Aside from a close governor's race, the general elections were not very exciting. Public opinion polls confirmed what most people believed—Republican candidates were in trouble. Apathetic and/or disgusted voters stayed away from election booths in record numbers. Even the press was bored.

Watergate crushed Republican hopes in California. Several potentially strong candidates decided not to run for office—perhaps sensing defeat. Houston I. Flournoy won the Republican gubernatorial nomination by default but was not popular with Republican voters.

Republican candidates for other statewide offices were unknown and had little voter appeal. For example, one of the two obscure Republicans running for the U.S. Senate candidly admitted there was no chance to win.

In contrast, several prominent Democrats ran for each of the major statewide offices. The most hotly contested primary race was for governor. Of the 18 candidates running, at least half a dozen were initially serious contenders. Jerry Brown, son of former governor Pat Brown, benefited both from superior name recognition and his vigorous reform record as secretary of state. San Francisco Mayor Joseph Alioto was also a known political figure. A third candidate, Speaker Bob Moretti, though not as well known, had a substantial power and money base as leader of the assembly.

In addition to his well-known name, Brown had a firm grip on the central issue of 1974. For four years, as secretary of state, he had been enforcing the state's minimally effective clean election laws and promoting stronger ones. He was a major factor in the Proposition 9 political reform measure (see below.) Moretti never found an issue to attract voters. Alioto was constantly plagued by personal and city problems while running for governor.

Brown stayed in the lead during the entire primary and won the Democratic Party gubernatorial nomination with a third of the vote. Alioto and Moretti trailed far behind—each with about one fifth of the vote. Alioto, essentially a regional candidate, won in five of the Bay Area counties, *but* Brown took the other 53 counties.

Equally interesting and important was the June 1974 election battle over Proposition 9, the political reform initiative. This measure had four major provisions:

1. Regulate lobbying.
2. Require strict campaign finance reporting.
3. Limit campaign spending.
4. Prohibit conflict of interest.

Developed by the People's Lobby, Common Cause, and staff from Secretary of State Jerry Brown's offce, the measure won early support from many voters. Indeed, in the post-Watergate era, few would publicly oppose it. It passed by a margin of 3 to 1 (see Chapter 5).

The general election was anticlimatic. The only question was whether Jerry Brown could hold onto his early lead over Houston Flournoy. Brown waged a low-key campaign—doing as little as possible. Flournoy just narrowly missed catching Brown (3.1 million votes to 3.0 million.) Except for incumbent Attorney General Evelle Younger, Republicans lost all other statewide offices. Alan Cranston was easily reelected to the U.S. Senate, and the Democrats won almost two thirds of the seats in the state's legislature.

ILLUSTRATION 4–4

Source: Campaign Committee for Proposition 9.

EMERGING DEMOCRATIC DOMINANCE: 1975–?

The 1974 and 1976 elections may have signaled the end of Republican hopes to be the majority party in California for the foreseeable future. Statewide, Democrats outnumbered Republicans 2 to 1. But more significantly, Democratic voters were not crossing party lines as much as in the past. In particular, party loyalty had become a prime feature of legislative races—elections for the state assembly, state senate, or U.S. House of Representatives. Here and there a Republican would win against heavy odds, but it was a *personal win,* not a party victory.

The 1976 elections

The presidential elections included two California favorite sons, Democrat Jerry Brown and Republican Ronald Reagan. Each won his party's primary in California, and each lost his party's presidential nomination at the convention. Reagan's challenge to incumbent Republican President Gerald Ford was expected. He had run for the Republican nomination in 1968 only two years after being elected governor. After losing to Richard Nixon, Reagan shifted his target date to 1976. Even after Ford became president, Reagan continued to pursue the office.

Brown's run at the presidency was not as well planned. He converted his "favorite son" campaign to serious contention when the Gallup Poll showed him ranked fourth across the nation among Democratic hopefuls. Like Reagan's first presidential bid (1968), Brown's 1976 effort was belated. But, he gained national attention and laid the groundwork for his 1980 attempt.

The U.S. Senate race featured a primary fight in both parties. Antiwar activist Tom Hayden, in a well-organized and well-financed campaign, cut into incumbent Democrat John Tunney's strength by capturing nearly one third of the Democratic primary vote. Tunney's Republican opponent, S. I. Hayakawa, defeated two well-known Republicans in his primary race. Hayakawa, a folk hero who had earlier suppressed demonstrators during the San Francisco State College student strike, campaigned as an amateur anti-establishment candidate.

Senator Tunney had failed to build a popular support base. He had not caught on with the voters who viewed him as distant and a part of the Washington establishment. Tunney, an incumbent about whom voters had a negative image, lost narrowly to Hayakawa about whom little was known.

The 1978 elections

In spite of having lost California to Gerald Ford and S. I. Hayakawa in 1976, California's Democrats entered the 1978 elections in an apparently strong position. Heading the ticket was the popular governor, Jerry Brown. Democrats held lopsided majorities in both houses of the state legislature and enjoyed a substantial majority in voter registration.

Republicans, who had been steadily losing support among voters, had four political unknowns and one bland but familiar candidate in their party's gubernatorial primary. Early campaign opinion among political observers was that Brown was unbeatable. Brown, when asked whom he'd like to run against, answered that he'd take on whoever "stumbled across the [primary] finish line."

But, as voters began thinking about alternatives, Brown's apparently insurmountable popularity began to disappear. And Attorney General Evelle Younger's large lead among Republicans also disappeared as dark-horse Fresno legislator Ken Maddy and retired Los Angeles police chief Ed Davis began their campaigns.

As Brown's popularity appeared less secure and as the Proposition 13 taxpayer revolt emerged as *the major political issue,* Republican hopefuls bombarded voters with TV spots, personal appearances, and special appeals to political groups. Maddy's early TV blitz moved him into a strong third position by late April. But State Senator John Briggs' support never grew in spite of his campaigning for three highly controversial issues—property tax reform, death penalty, and a ban on homosexual teachers. And, San Diego Mayor Pete Wilson campaigned vigorously throughout the state but was never able to expand on his original support base.

Ed Davis, with his clear-cut law-and-order image immediately established a strong voter base among southern California conservative Republicans. He was unable, however, to attract enough new support and remained in second place throughout the race.

Attorney General Evelle Younger, who had held a series of elective offices in California for years, had a substantial head start over the other candidates in *name recognition*. Both the Davis and Maddy campaigns cut into the Younger lead, but on election day, many undecided Republicans supported Younger and he won with 40 percent of the vote cast.

Governor Jerry Brown, with no meaningful opposition in the primary, lost 1 out of 5 Democratic votes to a half-dozen unknowns. One out of 10 Democrats who went to the polls did not vote in the governor's race. Sensing difficulty, Brown spent almost $1 million in the primary on radio and TV spots to strengthen his image.

But clearly, the most significant election decision was the massive voter support for the Jarvis-Gann property tax relief measure (Proposition 13). Voting in record numbers, the California electorate rose up in what must be described as a massive attack on government and voted 2 to 1 for Proposition 13.

On balance, the "establishment" opposed Proposition 13. Included in that opposition were Governor Brown, most Democratic legislators, most city mayors, school boards, and other local government officials, many business leaders, and union officials. But the voters had had enough. In part, it was a revolt against rapidly rising property taxes, but it was also a revolt against rising government spending, inflation, and other taxes. The Proposition 13 vote, in general, has to be described as antigovernment.

Brown, who had been clearly identified with the "No on 13" campaign and whose support in both the election and in public opinion polls had markedly declined, began his general election campaign two weeks after the primary. Appearing on statewide TV and radio he announced a program of emergency state funding to local government (see Chapters 11 and 13), support for a limit on government spending, and his determination to implement the voter's intent in passing Proposition 13.

GENERAL ELECTION 1978

Jerry Brown's switch on Proposition 13—from bitter opposition to enthusiastic implementation—destroyed any chance that Republican

Evelle Younger might have had. Younger, earlier described by Ed Davis as "exciting as a mashed potato sandwich," never generated much enthusiasm among Republicans, much less the electorate. He lost in November to Jerry Brown by 1.3 million votes.

However, aside from Governor Brown's landslide victory, Democrats suffered several substantial defeats. Lieutenant Governor Mervyn Dymally was defeated by political unknown, Mike Curb. Curb, a self-made millionaire, capitalized on Dymally's uncertain reputation, some implied past wrongdoings, and a supposed FBI investigation.

Further damaging to the Democrats, Republican George Deukmejian defeated Yvonne Brathwaite Burke for attorney general. Burke, a member of Congress for six years, was unknown statewide. Deukmejian, a member of the state legislature, was better known.

In addition, as a woman, Burke may have lost votes for attorney general, because many voters see that office as being mostly concerned with law enforcement. The "super-cop" image of the attorney general's office is incorrect, but many voters believe it (see Chapter 12). Deukmejian, a law-and-order, conservative male legislator was more attractive than a black woman liberal.

Perhaps equally significant, both Burke and Dymally were black. In an era of increased voter concern about school integration and general conservatism, race may have been a silent issue in these two campaigns. On the other hand, it is important to note that black incumbent Superintendent of Public Instruction, Wilson Riles was reelected in the June primary.

The Dymally and Burke defeats damaged not only the Democratic party but hurt Governor Brown, too. The governor, who had never liked Dymally, kept his distance from both Dymally and Burke until the last few weeks of the campaign. Then, spurred by mounting criticism from Democratic Party loyalists and black community leaders, Brown scheduled a few joint appearances with both Dymally and Burke. He also provided both with badly needed campaign funds. But it was too little too late, and Brown's efforts failed.

Equally damaging to Brown's image as a candidate able to lead his party to victory was the loss of seven assembly seats and one in the state senate. As we saw in Illustration 4–2, the 1978 elections restored Republican strength in the legislature to about the same proportion as its basic voter support in the state.

One of the most hotly contested elections in 1978 centered on an unprecedented attempt to defeat three incumbent state supreme court justices. As a rule in California, judges are seldom challenged for reelection. And, in fact, most have no opposition and are automatically reelected under California's election code (see Chapter 12). But since 1970, judges have come increasingly under attack in the Golden State.

The campaign against incumbent judges reached new heights when Chief Justice Rose Bird, Justice Wiley Manuel, and Justice Frank Newman were all subjected to attack by a law-and-order organization directed by State Senator H. L. Richardson. Another organization, made up largely of wealthy Central Valley farmers and allies, also attacked the Chief Justice, who had been instrumental in establishing the state's agricultural labor relations machinery while secretary of California's Department of Agriculture.

The attack on Bird came close to defeating her; she won with a margin of only 210,000 votes out of over 6 million cast (3.4 percent). The votes against the other justices (including a conservative Frank Richardson) were much higher than usual and may signal increased public concern about the courts and their rulings.

Another feature of the 1978 elections was an attempt to restrict public smoking. The tobacco industry broke all campaign finance records in defeating Proposition 5—spending more than $6 million. Proposition 6, an antigay teacher initiative sponsored by State Senator John Briggs, appeared to be a sure winner following victories of similar measures in other states and cities in the United States. But concern about increased government power, protection of personal freedoms, and Proposition 6's thinly veiled hate campaign finally led ex-Governor Ronald Reagan and most major political and community leaders to oppose the measure. It lost by 1.2 million votes, with Los Angeles and San Francisco counties voting very heavily against it.

Finally, in another attempt to establish a strong death penalty law in California, Senator Briggs also qualified Proposition 7 to extend the death penalty to additional violent crimes. Proposition 7 passed by almost 3 to 1, with only one county, San Francisco, voting against it.

SPECIAL ELECTION 1979

Two highly controversial but popular ballot measures were submitted to California voters at a special election in November 1979. One measure, Proposition 1, was designed to stop busing of children to achieve racial integration in public schools. The other measure, Proposition 4, was designed to place a ceiling on government budgets in California.

Proposition 1, sponsored by State Senator Alan Robbins (D. Van Nuys) was approved 3 to 1 by California's voters. Basically, it amended the state's constitution to conform to federal standards for school integration. California courts have required school districts to integrate, whatever the cause of segregation. Federal courts, on the other hand, have required integration only when segregation was the result of some deliberate governmental policy.

Opponents of Proposition 1 called it racist, and immediately chal-

ILLUSTRATION 4–5
Gay parade   A gay and his mother join a march down Hollywood Boulevard.

United Press International

lenged it in the courts. Supporters of Proposition 1 denied any racist motives, asserting they were simply more concerned with the quality of public education than they were with any policy of racial integration.

Proposition 4, a constitutional amendment limiting government budgets was approved by California voters 2 to 1. Essentially, the measure froze all state and local budgets at their 1978–79 levels. The only adjustments allowed were for population growth and inflation.

Proposition 4 was supported by a group called the Spirit of 13—essentially the same people and organizations that were behind Proposition 13 in 1978. Big business and real estate interests were large financial contributors. Governor Jerry Brown endorsed the measure, having been hurt by his opposition to Proposition 13 in 1978. The *Los Angeles Times* and *Oakland Tribune* as well as the AFL-CIO opposed the measure. Howard Jarvis, who had led the Proposition 13 fight in 1978 came out against Proposition 4 because, he said, its effects were uncertain (see Chapter 13).

The 1979 special elections were the last of the decade. At the end of the 1970s, California politics were significantly different from what they had been at the start of the decade and even more different from what they had been at the start of Pat Brown's administration 20 years earlier. Jerry Brown's fiscal conservatism cast the Democrats in a new light. And, the state's Republicans were clearly in the minority with their central issue of fiscal conservatism taken from them.

SUMMARY

There is no simple explanation of California politics. Various events and patterns merge or conflict in different ways in each election. But it is useful to sort out two kinds of factors: (1) basic long-term patterns and (2) short-term events or personalities.

Basic patterns

During the period of time from 1899 to 1958, politics and government in California were Republican. Struggles over power, policy, and reform were between the various segments of the Republican Party. Toward the end of this period, in the 1950s, Democratic Party strength grew to the point that they wrested control of the state from Republicans in the 1958 elections.

The second period (1959–74) can be characterized as one in which Democrats solidified their position while Republican power declined. Ronald Reagan's personal popularity won the governor's office for the GOP two times, but aside from their narrow majority in the assembly for two years (1969–70), Republicans were clearly the minority party. The ability of Republicans to gain support outside of their own party declined substantially in this period of time. Equally significant, GOP registration began a slow decline in this period. Democrats increasingly voted Democratic, and the ephemeral majority of Democratic voters solidified into a base of reliable support for the party.

By 1975, a pattern of Democratic dominance emerged. Republicans, who had been outnumbered about 2 to 1 in party registration for almost 40 years, found themselves outnumbered about 2 to 1 in the legislature for the first time in the century. The myth of registration had become a reality. The GOP was occasionally able to mount an effective campaign for statewide office, if the Democratic candidate was particularly inept or unattractive to voters. Perhaps the elections of S. I. Hayakawa to the U.S. Senate and Mike Curb as Lieutenant Governor illustrate the point.

In sum, Republicans now appear able to win statewide elections only when the Democratic candidate is weak or makes a mistake. In legislative terms, since so few districts have Republican majorities, the same rule holds true, too. Overall, Republicans stand little chance of gaining control of either the assembly or state senate.

Two themes run consistently through the three periods under consideration: (1) reform and (2) weak political party organization. From the Workingman's Party and Populists of the late 1800s, through the Progressive Republicans of the early 1900s, through the watergate era of the early 1970s, and within the Jerry Brown administration, reform has been a constant theme in California politics. Second, the weakness of the major political parties compared to those in other populous urban states has been a root cause of much of the unique politics of California (which we will further discuss in Chapters 5–8). This weak party tradition is a direct heritage from the Progressive Republican reforms of the early 1900s.

A new theme?

A new theme may also have emerged in the 1970s. California politics appear to change from the "go-go," hyperactivity of growth and boom psychology to an attitude of caution and conservation. The suburban car culture may be substantially altered by the price of gasoline and housing. The ability of government to solve problems is questioned. And the capacity of government to solve problems has been restricted by Proposition 13 and Governor Jerry Brown's fiscal conservatism. Approval of Proposition 4 in November 1979 appears to have put a ceiling on government spending.

Concomitant with the basic change in governmental fiscal policy is the changing attitude about government's role in solving social and economic problems. Civil rights concerns now appear to have been replaced by antibusing legislation and constitutional amendments. Traditional programs in welfare, public education, and community services are also under attack.

As we enter the 1980s, California politics promise to be exciting and challenging.

5

Campaigning in California

Elections are a central feature of any "popular" or democratic government. If the election process enables citizens to express their choice of meaningful alternatives, government is legitimate. People will believe in its fairness and will support it.

The election process is not neutral. How elections are organized, who can run, who can vote, and the many factors that influence the results are important. Every practice, technique, or law helps some and places a burden on others. Generally speaking, the process tends to support the status quo—the way things are.

However, in the past, substantial changes have been made in California's election laws and processes that have profoundly affected the system. And, there is every reason to believe that other significant changes will be made in the future.

WHO MAY VOTE

Eligibility

To be *eligible* to vote in California, one must be at least 18 years old by the time of the election, a citizen, and a resident of the district at least 30 days prior to the election. In this state, as well as the rest of the nation, there has been a steady expansion of those eligible to vote. Women, racial minorities, 18–20-year-olds, ex-felons, and, as of 1976, even some "mentally incompetents" are now eligible to vote in California.

Registration

Anyone who is eligible and who wants to vote must be registered (except new residents in presidential elections). Each county has a registrar of voters (smaller counties use the county clerk) who maintains a county list of registered voters. It is easy to register in California. Before the state primary and general elections, the registrar of voters will assign deputies to supermarkets, shopping centers, churches, university and college campuses, sports events, and other places where large numbers of people may gather. Most political parties and many civic groups also conduct registration drives. One can even register by postcard. In 1978, the state's 430 McDonald's restaurants provided patrons with postcards at their fast-food counters.

Even though it is easy to register, only one known substantial registration fraud has occurred in contemporary California history. In the 1975 San Francisco municipal elections, there were over 11,000 registered voters who actually did not live in San Francisco. Typically, these illegal voters were city employees who had registered to vote in San Francisco in order to participate in city elections on matters that concerned them —pay, retirement, and public officials.

It is important to note that in California, registration is semipermanent. Once people have registered, they are on the list of registered voters until they move, die, or fail to vote in the general (November) elections.

WHO MAY RUN

Eligibility

To be eligible to run for state public office in California one must:

1. Be a citizen of the United States and of California.
2. Be a registered voter of the party whose nomination one seeks. For nonpartisan office (superintendent of public instruction or judge), party affiliation is not required—one can be an Independent or Decline to State.
3. Have been a resident of the state for at least three years. Candidates for executive or judicial office must have lived in California for five years. Candidates for assembly, state senate, the Board of Equalization must have lived *in their district* for at least one year.

Qualifying

A potential candidate qualifies for the ballot by first filing a *Declaration of Intent* with the county clerk—saying, in effect, "I intend to run for the office of _____."

Second, the potential candidate must file a petition with a small number of signatures of registered voters who assert they support the candidacy. Candidates' petitions for statewide office must have at least 65 valid signatures, while assembly and state senate candidates need 40 valid signatures. The signatures must be from registered voters of the candidate's own political party if the office is a partisan one.

Third, the potential candidate must pay a filing fee or substitute an additional petition with more signatures. The filing fee is 2 percent of the annual salary for statewide office; 1 percent for other offices.

It's easy to get on the ballot in California. Getting elected is not easy. In 1976, 314 candidates ran for 80 assembly seats; 143 (43 percent) did not make it past the June primary. Another 91 lost in the general election. Of the 314 starters, only 80 (25 percent) won a seat. In 1978, 290 candidates started before the primary but only 80 (28 percent) could win in the general. (The factors that contribute to winning and losing will be discussed in the next section of this chapter.)

PRESIDENTIAL BALLOT

Under California law, the secretary of state is required to compile a list of *all potential presidential candidates.* The list must be compiled by January 31 of each presidential election year. The criteria for listing a candidate are vague. Anyone who is actively seeking the nomination or anyone who is "generally advocated for" is put on the list. This law makes it hard for serious candidates to skip the California presidential primary elections. It also makes it difficult for favorite son candidates to dominate the election. In addition, anyone who wants may get on the ballot by petition.

In late 1975, Secretary of State March Fong Eu had 18 Democrats on her list of potential presidential candidates. While Secretary Eu generally included all candidates who qualified for matching dollars under the new Federal Elections Law, she also added to her list potential candidate Senator Ted Kennedy of Massachusetts. During the spring, several candidates dropped out of the race, and several said they were not candidates. At the time of election, there were nine candidates: two Republicans, five American Independents, and two Peace and Freedom candidates on the ballot.

BALLOT FORMS

California uses the *office block ballot*—presenting the competing candidates *by office sought* (see Illustration 5–1). This contrasts to some states where the party column ballot is used. In these states, competing candidates are listed *by party membership.* A single vote at the top of the list is a vote for each of the party's candidates. But in California, it is hard to vote a party ticket. The office block ballot tends to reduce partisanship and accents the candidate as a person.

ILLUSTRATION 5–1
Office block ballot

GOVERNOR	ELIZABETH KEATHLEY	Peace and	1 → ○
	Feminist Writer	Freedom	
Vote for One	EDMUND G. BROWN JR.	Democratic	2 → ○
	Secretary of State		
	HOUSTON I. FLOURNOY	Republican	3 → ○
	California State Controller		
	EDMON V. KAISER	American	4 → ○
	Doctor of Chiropractic	Independent	
LIEUTENANT GOVERNOR	MARILYN SEALS	Peace and	6 → ○
	Secretary, Nursing Student	Freedom	
Vote for One	MERVYN M. DYMALLY	Democratic	7 → ○
	California State Senator		
	JOHN L. HARMER	Republican	8 → ○
	State Senator		
	ALBERTA M. PROCELL	American	9 → ○
		Independent	

Source: Los Angeles County Registrar of Voters, sample ballot, November 1974.

Ballot position

Until 1974, incumbents were always listed first in their office block. This helped incumbents gain reelection, since some citizens merely vote for the first name on the ballot. However, Proposition 9 (1974) eliminated this incumbent's advantage. Subsequent court cases and legislation have led to the present system of a random listing of candidates.

ELECTIONS

Primaries

The major purpose of the partisan primary is to select a party's nominee for the general election. (Nonpartisan primaries are discussed in Chapter 13.) California's direct primary was one of the major reforms enacted in the Progressive era and was designed to give more power to the people in selecting their parties' candidates.

Primary elections are important not only because they determine the party's nominee, but because they often determine the final outcome of the general election. Only a third of California's legislative districts are competitive. One party or the other has a substantial majority in two thirds of the congressional, assembly, and state senate districts. These are "safe seats." Winning the majority party primary is the same as winning the seat. The general election is a formality.

When an incumbent decides not to seek reelection, there is usually substantial competition for the dominant party's nomination (see Table 5–1). In some districts, as many as a dozen candidates will campaign for the dominant party nomination. Whoever gets the most votes wins in the primary. An absolute majority is not required.

TABLE 5–1
Safe seats and competition in the 1978 primary

	Average number of candidates seeking their party's nomination	
	Democrats	Republicans
Safe and open Republican districts	3.00	4.76
Safe and open Democrats districts	5.86	2.00

Source: Data, California Secretary of State, *Statement of Vote,* June 1978.

Thus, another important aspect of the primary election is that a candidate will often win it with less than a majority of the vote—*a plurality victory*. This happens quite often in safe districts where there is no incumbent seeking reelection (an open seat). As we saw above, in such cases several candidates run. In recent primary elections (1974, '76, and '78), 22 out of the 28 open primaries in safe districts were won with a plurality. That means that in 79 percent of those elections, the real decision was made in the primary by a minority of the voters.

The same situation can happen in statewide elections, too. All but one of the Democratic candidates for statewide office in 1974 won their party's primary with less than a majority of the votes. Yet, each of the plurality victors went on to win in the general election.

TABLE 5–2
1974 Democratic primary winners statewide races

Office	Candidate	Percent of vote received in primary election	Won general election
Governor ....Brown		37.8%	Yes
Lieutenant Governor ....Dymally		29.9	Yes
Secretary of state ....Fong		28.7	Yes
Controller ....Cory		44.5	Yes
Treasurer ....Unruh		45.5	Yes
Attorney general ....Norris		57.7	No

Source: California Secretary of State, *Statement of Vote,* June 1974.

PRESIDENTIAL PRIMARIES

Presidential primary elections determine which candidates will get California's delegate votes in their party's national presidential convention. Unlike other primaries, this election does not directly select the partys' nominee. Though the Democratic and Republican Parties allocate convention delegates in different ways, the Golden State's delegations usually account for about one-tenth of the total vote at both major party's national conventions. In recent years, California's presidential primary has been a "make or break" election for several presidential hopefuls.

Before 1976, whoever received the most votes in the primary won all the state's presidential delegates. But under a recent change in California election law (and Democratic National Convention rules), California Democrats converted their primary from a winner-take-all to a proportional distribution of delegates. Roughly speaking, each candidate receives a share of delegates equal to his or her share of the total vote cast.

Democratic candidates select their potential convention delegates in a rather cumbersome way. People wishing to be considered as possible delegates attend their candidate's congressional district caucus. If elected at the caucus, their names are submitted in rank order to a state delegate selection committee. While the candidate's delegation selection committee is not required to appoint caucus nominees, clearly there is considerable pressure to appoint a reasonable number from the top of the list along with party leaders and campaign contributors. Each Democratic presidential candidate's slate gets a share of the state's convention delegates proportionate to their primary vote.

Republicans continue to select their presidential convention delegates on a winner-take-all basis. The candidate's committee prepares a slate of party and community leaders and major campaign contributors. The slate that gets the most votes in the primary gets all of California's delegates to the Republican Presidential Convention.

General elections

Usually, political excitement is greater in the general election than in the primary elections. It is the pay-off of a long hard campaign. The issues are more clear-cut, and the opposition is *between party candidates* rather than *within parties* as in the primary. General elections are the finals in each election race.

In about two thirds of the legislative races, the real decision is made in the primary. However, for statewide elections and for about one third of the legislative races, the general elections are crucial.

Statewide campaigns for governor, lieutenant governor, other minor executive offices, and U.S. Senate are hard-fought, the outcome is often in doubt, and the victory is frequently narrow. In 1976, S. I. Hayakawa won his U.S. Senate election with barely half the votes cast. And President Ford captured all the state's presidential electoral votes with 49.7 percent of the vote compared to Jimmy Carter's 48 percent. In 1974, Jerry Brown won the governorship with only 50.2 percent of the votes cast, while two other Democrats won their offices with less than half the votes cast.

In the last ten years, out of 20 statewide elections, 12 were won with less than 53 percent of the vote, and 3 were won with less than a majority. General elections are clearly not to be taken for granted.

THE ELECTORATE

Partisanship

As discussed in Chapter 4, from 1935 to 1958, California's Democrats had a substantial majority of the voter registration but were unable to transform it into victory at the ballot box. That difference between party registration and political control is at the heart of the state's reputation for having a fickle electorate. But today most voters tend to support their party's candidates—particularly for legislative office and usually for minor statewide office.

There are three ways to measure party strength in California. First, how do voters register? Second, what do people say when asked about their party preference? And, third, how do they vote?

REGISTRATION

Democratic Party registration has averaged about 56.5 percent since 1960. Republican registration averaged 38.5 percent in the same period, declining to a low of less than 35 percent in the late 1970s.

California has many minor parties. The Peace and Freedom and the American Independent Party attracted modest followings in the 1960s but declined by the mid-1970s. More recently, the Libertarian Party has attracted some following. But Californians, like voters in most states, do not give much support to minor parties.

California law permits voters to register as Decline to State if they have no party choice, though some voters prefer Independent. These nonparty registrants have increased substantially in the last 20 years. In particular, it appears that many young, first-time voters are uncertain about their basic party affiliation.

Three significant facts are apparent in California party registration figures. First, Democrats are in the clear majority. Second, most voters are members of one of the two traditional parties. And, third, a growing number of people do not affiliate with either of the two major parties.

PARTY PREFERENCE

Statewide opinion polls conducted in 1970, 1974, and 1978 show that a consistent majority of those asked considered themselves Democrats. Table 5–3 shows the results of those three surveys and compares them with the party registration for the same time. Two patterns clearly emerge: first, voter registration tends to slightly overstate Democratic party strength compared to Republican party strength; second, however measured, Republican party strength declined in the 1970s.

TABLE 5–3
Party registration and party preference, 1970–1978

	1970	1974	1978
Democrats as defined by:			
Voter registration	54.9	56.2	57.1
Public opinion poll	50.8	54.6	53.1
Republicans as defined by:			
Voter registration	39.8	36.8	34.7
Public opinion poll	43.7	41.4	37.7

Source: California Secretary of State, *Statement of Vote,* 1970, 1974, and 1978, and *California Poll,* 1970, 1974, and 1978.

VOTING BEHAVIOR

Party strength, as measured by statewide votes, changes markedly from election to election. Between 1966 and 1970, Republicans were stronger than Democrats, winning 10 of the 13 statewide races. But, from 1974–78 Democrats were stronger, winning 10 out of 14 elections. Such substantial changes over a short period of time suggests that statewide election results are strongly influenced by incumbency, candidate appeal, and impact of issues.

On the other hand, if we use election results from the state assembly races, we can reasonably assume that the effects of incumbency, personality, and issues are significantly reduced. Over time, these figures seem to be reasonably good measures of basic party strength. The results of these races are provided in Table 5–4. Measured this way, basic Democratic party strength appears to be about 54 percent, while basic Republican party strength appears to be about 44 percent.

Party strength measured three different ways gives us three slightly different answers. But the pattern is consistent. Democrats are clearly the majority party, and Republicans are in the minority.

This does not mean that Republicans cannot win office. Election history tells us otherwise. Ronald Reagan's candidacy in 1966 and 1970, and S. I. Hayakawa's win over John Tunney in 1976 amply illustrate that Republicans can win if they offer attractive candidates. But, making

TABLE 5–4
**Total vote cast for Democratic and Republican candidates
for State Assembly 1972–1978 general elections***

Vote for	1972	1974	1976	1978
Democrats	52.3%	55.5%	55.0%	53.6%
Republicans	46.4	42.4	43.4	44.7

* Excluding districts with no contests.
Source: Data, California Secretary of State, *Statement of Vote,*
1972–78.

candidates "attractive" depends on media coverage—particularly TV.
Such coverage, as we will discuss later in this chapter, is usually available for statewide races but seldom for local or legislative elections.
Thus, Republicans are more likely to overcome their basic party weakness in statewide races where image and personality are more apparent
than in local legislative races.

Ideology

Illustration 5–2 shows the ideological structure of the California electorate. Clearly, most Republican voters are conservative—2 out of 3
describe themselves as "strongly conservative" or "conservative." Thus,
it is not surprising that most Republican candidates are conservative.

Democrats are almost evenly divided ideologically with about 40 percent each in both the conservative wing and liberal wing of the party.

ILLUSTRATION 5–2
Ideology of California's voters—Democrats, Republicans, and all voters

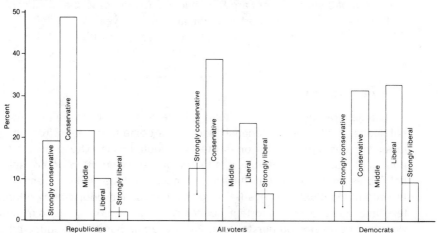

Source: *California Poll,* several different surveys in the 1970s.

Thus, the middle-of-the-road Democrats (about 20 percent) hold the balance of power. As one might expect, Democratic candidates tend to span the ideological spectrum—some are liberals, some are conservatives, and some vacillate between the two philosophies.

Overall, California voters tend to be considerably more conservative than liberal. Half are conservatives, while only a third are liberal. Hence, middle-of-the-road voters hold a key position. This suggests that California may swing back and forth from moderate to conservative candidates depending on other factors.

Social and economic characteristics

Two clear-cut patterns are apparent when we look at the social and economic characteristics of California voters in Table 5–5. First, in virtually every category, there are more Democrats than Republicans. And, second, those differences are substantial. A clear understanding of this information will go a long way in explaining much of California election politics.

The Democratic Party is favored by the state's racial and religious minorities—Roman Catholics, Jews, and other nonprotestant groups; blacks, Chicanos, and Orientals. Lower- and middle-income groups and union households also clearly favor the Democratic Party. In a sense, the typical Republican is wealthy, Protestant, white, older, and does not belong to a labor union. All others are likely to be Democrats. Thus, one of the greatest difficulties for the Republican Party in California is its lack of any substantial support base among a large part of the population.

The age patterns may be the most crucial, however. Clearly, relatively few young voters (ages 18–30) are attracted to the Republican Party. Less than 1 out of 3 young voters are Republicans. On the other hand, almost half of the state's registered Republicans are 50 years or older. The GOP is an "old" party and needs to attract younger citizens if it is to survive.

Voter participation

As a general rule, Democrats tend to be less politically active than Republicans. Partly, this is because Democrats come more often from the lower socioeconomic categories than do Republicans. Those who are poor, lack education, hold unskilled jobs, or are young often do not see politics as important. Often, they do not have the time, skills, or energy to become politically involved. Blacks, Chicanos, and poor whites often feel that they are not important politically; they are alienated from the system and do not bother to vote. On the other hand, well-educated, wealthy, professional people usually see politics as important to them.

TABLE 5–5
Partisan characteristics of various socio-economic groups

Group:	Democrats	Republicans
Race		
White	54%	46%
Chicano/Hispanic	80	20
Black	94	6
Asian	75	25
Other	59	41
Religion		
Protestant	49%	51%
Roman Catholic	71	29
Jewish	91	9
Other	55	45
No preference	71	29
Income		
Less than $7,000 per year	69%	31%
$7,000 to $9,999	64	36
$10,000 to $14,999	69	31
$15,000 to $19,999	61	39
$20,000 to $29,999	59	41
$30,000 or more	43	57
Home ownership		
Owns home	54%	46%
Rents	70	30
Union membership		
Someone in family is		
union member	72%	28%
No one in family is		
union member	56	44
Age		
18–24	67%	33%
25–29	71	29
30–39	61	39
40–49	55	45
50–59	57	43
60 or older	54	46

Source: *California Poll,* four surveys conducted between May and September 1978.

They know they can have an impact on the system, and they vote.

In recent general elections, for example, Republican turnout has been greater than Democratic turnout by an average of about 4 percentage points. Less than 77 out of every 100 registered Democrats went to the polls. But 81 out of every 100 registered Republicans voted.

This higher level of voting by Republican voters helps offset the GOP registration deficit. Republicans also tend to be more active in other forms of political effort—campaign work, financial contributions, and club membership.

Even though a large proportion of elections are decided in the primary, fewer voters go to the polls in the primary than in general elections. In the last six election years (1968–78) general election turnout has averaged 10 percentage points higher than in the primary. About a million voters, on the average, who do not vote in the primary will vote in the general election.

And, of course, millions of potential voters do not even bother to register to vote. One recent report by the secretary of state showed that of 14.2 million eligible citizens, 9.9 million had registered, and only 6.3 million voted in the general election. Over 7.8 million did not vote!

RUNNING FOR OFFICE

Money

"Money is the mother's milk of politics," declared Jess Unruh, past assembly speaker, and one of the most knowledgeable and able politicians in California history. Any campaign for public office will cost money. Even candidates for minor office need literature that must be printed. And, for bigger campaigns, candidates must spend money for postage, headquarters rent, telephones, bumper strips, advertisements in community newspapers, lawn signs, and staff. Candidates for statewide office also need substantial amounts for TV, radio, and travel. Campaign budgets for ballot measures are almost totally devoted to media costs.

In the 1960s and 1970s campaign costs skyrocketed. This was due, in part, to the increased use of expensive TV (more than $3,000 for a 30-second spot). Two other factors contributed to increased spending: population growth (up 33 percent between 1960 and 1970) and increased competition. California became a competitive two-party state in the 1960s. Both sides (Republicans and Democrats) had to spend more money just to stay "even." Like the international arms race, as each candidate, party, or ballot measure committee spent more money, the opposition felt obliged to spend more too.

WHY PEOPLE GIVE

Why do people give money to political candidates?

Joe Cerrell, a leading California campaign manager, suggests the following reasons:

1. They like the candidate personally.
2. Giving is an ego trip—having the candidate (governor, U.S. Senator, or president) ask for money feels good.
3. Insurance—the contributor does business with or is regulated by the government and may need help someday.

4. Investment—the contributor is doing business with or is regulated by government and needs help now.

One insight into motive is the fact that interest groups are by far the largest source of campaign money. According to the Fair Political Practices Commission, about 85 percent of all funds contributed to candidates were from interest groups. Clearly, insurance and investment loom large in motivating campaign contributions.

Motives for contributions to campaigns "for" or "against" a ballot measure are less complex. Basically, these are issue campaigns. In 1972 *Playboy* magazine gave $125,000 to defeat Proposition 18 which would have given local governments power to control obscene materials. In 1976 the California Farm Bureau contributed over $200,000 to defeat a farm labor initiative (Proposition 14). And, in 1978 tobacco companies contributed over $6 million to defeat a ballot measure that would have regulated smoking (Proposition 5).

RAISING CAMPAIGN MONEY

Asking people to give is probably the most hated part of campaigning. Former Assembly Speaker Bob Moretti once described it as "embarrassing and degrading." Every campaign of any size has a finance chair who is supposed to raise money. But, large contributions ($10,000—$20,000—$50,000) often require a personal meeting between the donor and the candidate.

While large individual campaign contributions probably amount to no more than 5 percent of the total raised statewide, they can sometimes be very important to a specific candidate. Dr. Louis Cella gave $287,000 to Ken Cory's 1974 controller campaign, obviously providing a substantial part of the total spent ($730,000). But, the all-time record for individual donations belongs to Jane Fonda who gave her husband (Tom Hayden) $400,000 toward his 1976 U.S. Senate campaign.

Obviously, too, the candidate who is wealthy has an advantage. Multimillionaires like Norton Simon or William Matson Roth can use their own money. However, ironically, wealthy candidates often have difficulty in getting campaign contributions. Potential contributors think that wealthy candidates should use their own money.

Another useful source of campaign funding is the early loan. Max Palevsky, a liberal Los Angeles Democrat, likes to give campaigns a fast early start with an early massive loan. This gives his candidate a headstart on the opposition and a better chance to win.

Large amounts are also raised at cocktail parties, campaign dinners. and lunches. A contribution to the candidate at a cocktail party may be $100 or $150. Campaign dinners may also cost $100 or $150 a plate, but there are many more people who come to a dinner—so more money is raised. Governor Jerry Brown, as the star attraction at a 1977 dinner, helped assembly Democrats raise over $100,000 for their 1978 campaigns. A year later, the Governor raised almost $250,000 for his own reelection effort with a posh gourmet dinner—stuffed avocado, caviar, and chateaubriand. Tickets for the event were $250 per person. These dinners are an easy way for interest groups to give money. Buying a table for 12 usually means a contribution of between $1,200 and $3,000.

An important state like California will also attract outside campaign money. Republican gubernatorial candidate Evelle Younger flew to San Antonio, Texas, after the 1978 primary to meet the Eagles. Not the rock concert group; these Eagles are a group of substantial GOP campaign contributors.

A recent development in campaign fund raising is the computerized fund-raising "personal" letter. The Orange County campaign management firm of Butcher-Forde has raised hundreds of thousands of dollars for initiative campaigns this way.

In 1976 over 700 special fund-raising groups reported contributions of almost $9 million in California. Half of this money was raised by business groups. Another 17 percent from unions, and 13 percent was from agricultural groups. Thirty-nine groups gave over $50,000 each.

In 1978, even more money was raised—over $58 million. Among large donors, who gave more than $200,000 each, were the California Real Estate Association, United for California (a business group), the Law and Order Committee (an antigun group); and the California Teachers Association.

AMOUNTS SPENT

Campaign expenditures in 1978 of over $58 million compare markedly with the some $28 million spent in 1976. The substantial increase was due to several factors. First, the governor's races (both primary and general) and other statewide executive campaigns were not held in 1976. And second, huge amounts were spent on some ballot measures in 1978.

On the other hand, the amounts spent on legislative candidates remained about the same. The average assembly candidate spent about $130,000; the average senate candidate about $250,000.

Governor Jerry Brown spent $3.4 million to defeat Evelle Younger, who spent $2.3 million and lost. The many candidates for other statewide offices spent as much as $1 million in their campaigns.

Expenses for ballot measures were also very large. Four tobacco companies spent a total of $6.1 million to defeat Proposition 5.

Campaigns in a large city are also expensive. Tom Bradley spent $1.3 million in 1973 defeating Mayor Sam Yorty, who spent almost $1 million. Campaigns for county supervisor in large counties (Los Angeles, Orange,

San Diego, and Alameda, for example) can cost between $200,000 and $500,000.

HOW IT IS SPENT

How campaign funds are spent depends on several factors. How much money is available? What and where is the constituency? What other resources are available? Is the candidate an incumbent or not?

For most statewide campaigns—governor, attorney general, etc., large sums are spent on media—TV, radio, and newspapers. For example, in 1974 both Jerry Brown and Houston Flournoy spent over half their money on media. In 1978, Brown spent almost *all his* money on media. Other major costs of campaigning included: literature, campaign management firms and professional personnel (accountants and attorneys), travel, office rent, and supplies. In-kind contributions are often a major help. Brown's 1974 campaign received over $100,000 worth of free office space. Ken Maddy's 1978 campaign received over $12,000 worth of travel in private airplanes.

Local campaigns face different problems. Often the local TV and radio stations cover much more than the candidate's particular district. Thus, they can be both inefficient and expensive. Local candidates will often rely on direct mailing and use little or no TV and radio. The ability of the candidate to attract volunteer precinct workers is an important factor too.

Media

California is a *media state.* It is the center for much of the nation's radio, TV, and movie industry. Over 100 daily newspapers, 49 commercial television, and 11 educational TV stations serve the state. Television reaches a wider audience than do newspapers. Almost all homes have at least one set. Total newspaper circulation in the state is about 5,500,000, reaching 8 out of 10 households. Most homes receive both newspaper and TV news coverage. With little competition from political parties, media exercises a powerful political influence in the state.

Historically, the press has been a power in government and politics and continues to play a substantial role today. The most important newspapers in the state were (and are) the *Los Angeles Times, San Francisco Chronicle,* and *Oakland Tribune.* In the past, they dominated the state Republican Party and much of state and local government. These three papers trumpeted the GOP position in news columns and editorials.

The Republican bias of the state's newspapers was reduced by three factors. First, emergence of TV, second, a new generation of owners and management, and third, William Knowland's disastrous gubernatorial candidacy in 1958.

Television provides substantial competition to newspapers in essentially every area of the state. Since the early 1950s, newspapers no longer have a monopoly on the news. And, as a result, newspaper reporting has become less biased.

Also, in the last 20 years, the *Times, Tribune,* and *Chronicle* and several other major urban newspapers have come under new management or ownership. The new management has established higher levels of professional journalistic ethics that give high priority to objective comprehensive news coverage. Many newspapers no longer make endorsements in major partisan campaigns. Some purposely present conflicting opinion on the editorial pages. The *Los Angeles Times* has developed into one of the nation's best newspapers, while the *Sacramento Bee* has long enjoyed a solid reputation for its coverage of state politics.

Finally, the gubernatorial campaign of William Knowland in 1958 broke the cozy relationship between the *Times, Chronicle,* and *Tribune.* Knowland, who owned the *Tribune,* ran a campaign that bitterly divided the Republican Party and led it to defeat in the general election (see Chapter 4). The *Times* supported Knowland but was forced to reevaluate its traditional role within the Republican Party. The *Chronicle* withdrew its support of Knowland. Today, the major urban newspapers continue to play significant roles in state politics, but it is more as responsible critics rather than as partisan advocates.

Because of California's size, each newspaper and TV station can cover only a small fraction of the state. Essentially, there are eight news regions in the state, each of which is isolated from the others by distance or mountains.

Only three newspapers have a substantial share of the state's total circulation. The *Los Angeles Times* is read in 1 out of 5 California homes, while both the *Chronicle* and *Los Angeles Examiner* are read in about 1 out of 10 homes. No other newspaper gets more than 5 percent of the state's total readership. And, only three newspapers are read in a majority of their own county's homes. The *Chronicle* is read in about 3 out of 4 San Francisco homes. The *Union* has half the readers in San Diego, and the *Bee* chain has about half the readers in three Central Valley home counties. But most newspapers get only a small fraction of their hometown circulation. Even the mighty *Times* gets only one third of the circulation in L.A. County.

This multiplicity of newspapers and TV stations which serves each region is significant. Over 19 million (90 percent) of the state's residents have some choice of news source. And in the Los Angeles and San Francisco areas, the number and kind of alternatives are staggering. It is important to note that while most of us read only one newspaper, we have several TV stations from which to choose.

The precise impact of TV, newspaper, radio endorsements, and news coverage is hard to assess. However, based on the few studies conducted in California, it appears that the press has more impact on local and nonpartisan races than on national or partisan elections. Newspaper readers will sometimes follow their paper's endorsements in a school board election, for example, but not in the presidential race. There is some research that also supports the conclusion that the media have an impact on voting for or against ballot measures.

In the long run, media endorsements are probably less significant than day-to-day news coverage and content. Incumbents often get publicity; challengers usually do not. How an issue is presented (offshore oil spills, the state's annual budget, an increase or decrease in the welfare load) will have an impact on the voters' basic perceptions of the issues.

All major candidates budget immense amounts of money for their media campaigns. Ken Maddy, in an all-out effort to win the Republican gubernatorial nomination in 1978, spent hundreds of thousands of dollars on TV. Governor Jerry Brown, realizing he was in trouble before the June primary, launched a major radio and TV blitz. Both Brown and Evelle Younger (eventual winner of the Republican nomination) spent about $800,000 on their primary election media efforts.

Media, money, and professional campaign management are closely tied together. As a whole, they have become a central component of California election techniques.

Public opinion polls

Public opinion polls have become a key part of most major campaigns for public office—partisan and nonpartisan. However, public opinion polls are expensive. A well-designed poll will cost as much as $30,000 to $40,000. Serious candidates for major public office will try to have at least one public opinion survey taken early in the campaign. Known as internal polls, they are never made public. Such polls usually are the base for a candidate's strategy.

Candidates use public opinion survey information to:

1. Identify major issues.
2. Assess their own strengths and weaknesses.
3. Assess the strengths and weaknesses of their opponents.
4. Help raise campaign funds and other support.

For example, polls taken in early 1978 revealed that Governor Jerry Brown's public support had deteriorated badly. As a result, Brown strategists ran a massive media blitz before the primary elections, even though the governor had no substantial opposition in the June primary.

Polls are also used to identify potential winners and losers. Many Republicans appear to have voted for Evelle Younger in the 1978 primary, simply because polls revealed that Younger would have the best chance to defeat Brown. Ken Maddy's primary campaign received substantial new help when early 1978 polls showed him gaining strength. On the other hand, State Senator John Briggs dropped out of the gubernatorial race when polls showed him getting only 2 percent or 3 percent of the vote. And San Diego Mayor Pete Wilson's financial support dwindled when polls revealed him in a distant fourth place.

INCUMBENCY

If there is anything like a "sure bet" in politics, it is the incumbent. Legislative incumbents, in particular, are almost always reelected. In California's last five legislative elections (1970–78) 379 out of 414 (92 percent) incumbents seeking reelection were successful. Incumbent governors, attorney generals, and U.S. Senators also do very well. Since World War II, 14 out of 19 of these statewide incumbents have been reelected (74 percent). Several reasons account for the high success rate of incumbents: name recognition, advantages of office, and better access to campaign dollars.

Name recognition

Governors, attorney generals, and U.S. senators are often prominent in the news. What they do *makes news.* In a very real sense, their names become household words. Challengers running against a statewide incumbent have to overcome at least four years' publicity given to the incumbent.

However, once in a while incumbents are defeated. For example, Republican U.S. Senator Tom Kuchel was defeated in his own party primary by conservative Max Rafferty in 1968. Sometimes a bitter primary battle can contribute to defeat in the general election. Governor Pat Brown (1966) and U.S. Senator John Tunney (1976) are examples of this. Sometimes too much publicity can be a disadvantage. For example, a well-publicized financial scandal led to the defeat of U.S. Senator George Murphy in 1970.

A massive national disaster or political scandal will also badly damage incumbents. In office, they are considered to be at fault or to blame for what happened. The Depression of the 1930s and Watergate scandals of the early 1970s clearly hurt incumbents who were in no way involved in either of the problems.

Office advantages

Most legislative incumbents do not get the publicity given to statewide officeholders. The advantages they enjoy are substantial, however. All state legislators have district offices and staff who are busy year-round. This staff varies in size according to the legislator's interests, seniority, and powers. But, there will be at least an office director, secretary, and an assistant. Many incumbent legislators will also have some unpaid interns. (For more detail, see Chapter 9).

District staff spend most of their time doing casework and assisting constituents who need help. Problems may range from lost social security checks to revoked drivers' licenses. The staff also sets up speaking engagements for the legislator on weekends.

Lawmakers try to be in their districts on weekends when the legislature is in session and fulltime during recess. Their days and nights are packed with breakfast, lunch, and dinner meetings; coffees and teas; Rotary, Kiwanis, Chamber of Commerce, and union meetings; schools and churches; PTAs and Boy Scouts; League of Women Voters; American Association of University Women; and dozens of other community groups concerned with government policy. The incumbent "reports" on the Sacramento scene and soon builds an image of a hard-working, effective lawmaker.

Incumbents also send out newsletters, press releases, questionnaires, and letters of congratulations to constituents for honors and achievements. In 1977, legislative newsletters cost taxpayers $3.4 million. Another $95,000 was spent on press releases. Press releases and newsletters combined, each lawmaker gets about $15,000 worth of publicity per year at taxpayer expense.

Money

Incumbent candidates get about three times as much money as do their challengers. A recent detailed examination of campaign contributions by Common Cause revealed that interest groups gave mostly to incumbents while challengers had to look elsewhere. Michael Walsh, head of Common Cause in California, has observed that ". . . there's a sweetheart relationship between incumbent legislators and the special interests . . . ." In short, interest groups want access to government, and incumbents need campaign money. The "smart" contributions go to the incumbents, since they almost always win.

PUBLIC FIGURES

Some candidates who are not incumbents but who are public figures also enjoy the advantage of *name recognition*. Actors, TV personalities, and sports figures can often build a successful political career on their name recognition.

Ronald Reagan is an obvious example. A well-known Hollywood actor, Reagan was able to use his movie and TV fame as a springboard to political success. Another actor, George Murphy (U.S. Senate), is a similar example.

TV newscaster Stan Statham, a Republican, was able to overcome a 59 percent Democratic Party registration to win a seat in the state assembly in northern California. Baxter Ward, a muckraking TV newscaster, won a seat on the Los Angeles County Board of Supervisors, and another broadcast personality, Robert K. Dornan, won a west Los Angeles congressional seat.

Offspring of famous people also have an advantage. Governor Jerry Brown's campaign for secretary of state in 1970 and his campaign for governor in 1974 were substantially helped by the fact that his father (Pat Brown) had been governor from 1959–66. Name recognition and quiet assistance from father's friends helped a lot. John Tunney's U.S. Senate victory in 1970 was due, in part, to his father's fame as a boxing champion.

S. I. Hayakawa, who achieved national fame in battling student demonstrators, was later elected to the U.S. Senate (1976). Tom Hayden, a leading student activist in the 1960s, capitalized on his fame in attacking John Tunney in the Democratic primary, winning a third of the votes in June 1976.

But fame cannot be instantly purchased—even in a media-campaign-firm public relations state like California. Several unknowns have tried to buy name recognition during a campaign and have failed. Assembly member Ken Maddy tried and failed in 1978. Millionaire Norton Simon spent over $2 million in 1970 running against incumbent George Murphy and got a third of the vote. (It cost him $3 per vote to lose.) Another millionaire, Democrat William Matson Roth spent $1.3 million to get 300,000 votes in the 1974 gubernatorial primary ($4.33 per vote).

It takes time to acquire name recognition (or fame) in a nonpolitical field of activity. But once acquired, it can be an effective campaign asset.

REGIONALISM

As in many other states, California exhibits *regional* patterns in some of its voting behavior. In the Golden State, regionalism is typically north versus south—the south usually being the seven counties south of the Tehachapi Mountains and the rest of the state making up the north.

Historically, apportionment of the state senate (see Chapter 9), water, and gas tax allocations have been major regional issues dividing California. Additionally, in party primary elections, if one candidate is from the south and another from the north, votes will sometimes divide for the candidates along regional lines (partially due to name familiarity). Both major political parties maintain state central committee offices in each of the two regions. And, many state agencies and professional groups maintain northern and southern state offices.

Regionalism as a political factor emerges when other factors are absent or weak—usually in a party primary or nonpartisan race and sometimes in the vote for a ballot measure.

Several candidates have won or lost an election because of a regional vote. In 1974, March Fong Eu, a candidate for the office of secretary of state and a northern resident, won 45 of the northern counties but lost all 7 of the southern counties. Her two strongest opponents were both from southern California, and they split the southern vote. Ms. Eu won the primary with 29 percent of the vote.

Perhaps one of the most dramatic regional votes occurred in 1964, when U.S. Senator Barry Goldwater narrowly defeated New York Governor Nelson Rockefeller in California's Republican presidential primary. Goldwater took all of the southern counties which gave him enough votes to narrowly defeat Rockefeller. Goldwater's California win gave him the 1964 Republican Presidential nomination.

Regionalism will sometimes become *localism* with a particular candidate winning hometown votes but doing badly in the rest of the state. In 1966, Ronald Reagan defeated San Francisco Mayor George Christopher in 53 counties. Christopher won only four San Francisco Bay area counties. In 1978, San Diego Mayor Pete Wilson, Fresno Assembly member Ken Maddy, and Los Angeles police chief Ed Davis found that they were unable to build strong statewide campaigns. They were each essentially hometown or semiregional candidates. They lost the Republican gubernatorial nomination to Evelle Younger who had a statewide base as attorney general.

Because a majority of the voters live in Southern California, most candidates for state-wide office are residents of the southern region.

REFORMS

Some argue that reforms never work; others argue that they are not needed. It is our position that some reforms do not produce the changes desired by reformers; some have little effect; and some do what reformers wanted. Frequently, a reform will also produce an unanticipated effect. In sum, reforms often do produce substantial change, but that change may not be what was desired or anticipated.

Proposition 9

"Clean politics," "campaign reform," "lobby regulation," and "conflict of interest" are terms familiar to all politically aware citizens. And more than any single event, the political scandal known as "Watergate" helped set the stage for political reform in the 1970s.

In California, that reform was Proposition 9, an initiative jointly sponsored by Common Cause, People's Lobby, and Secretary of State Jerry Brown. Supported by a wide range of civic and community groups and by many politicians as well, it was overwhelmingly passed by the voters in the June 1974 primary elections.

PROVISIONS OF ACT

The Political Reform Act (PRA as it became known) had four major goals: limiting campaign expenditures, requiring disclosure of campaign expenditures and sources, limiting lobbying expenditures (see Chapter 7), and prohibiting conflict of interests. In addition, the PRA set up a Fair Political Practices Commission to administer the act. In this chapter we will discuss only campaign finance regulations.

After the PRA was adopted, it was attacked in the courts by those who opposed limits on campaign spending. The California Supreme Court struck down expenditure limits on initiative measures in 1977. Since then all such limits have been removed. The remainder of the act is still in effect. In 1979 the Court also struck down the restrictions on lobbyists making, or arranging for the making of, campaign contributions. The FPPC immediately appealed to the U.S. Supreme Court where it lost.

CAMPAIGN DISCLOSURES

All campaign contributions and expenditures of $50 or more must be reported by all candidates for state and local elective office. The contributor's name, address, occupation, and employer's name must be given. This information must be filed both 40 and 12 days before and 65 days after election day. Thus, voters may know before the election who is supporting various candidates if local newspapers report the information—and most do. The same provisions apply to ballot measures and campaign committees.

FAIR POLITICAL PRACTICES COMMISSION

The commission established by the PRA has five members: the chair and one other are appointed by the governor, and one member each is appointed by the attorney general, secretary of state, and controller. Members serve four-year terms.

The Fair Political Practices Commission is empowered to establish rules needed to implement the PRA, hear complaints hold hearings, and investigate where needed. A major task of the commission is the receipt and filing of reports from lobbyists and campaigns. Given the number of lobbyists, candidates, ballot measure campaigns, etc., the commission can reasonably expect over 20,000 filings in an election year.

IMPACT OF THE PRA

For the first time, California's citizens have a fairly clear idea of what campaigns cost, who gives, and who receives. On the other hand, it is clear from our discussion earlier that big contributors and interest groups continue to dominate campaign finance in California. It is not surprising, then, that the incumbent's advantage in raising funds has not been diminished either.

In a 1977 study of the PRA, 1 out of 5 candidates reported that the act hindered their campaign in some ways. But *1 out of 3 challengers* reported that the PRA hindered their campaign against the incumbent, Inexperienced candidates were much more likely to report that the PRA hindered them. Experienced candidates had less difficulty with the act (See Table 5–6).

The PRA also had substantial impact on some specific campaign activities. Most notable was the increased use of paid legal and accounting personnel, increased use of paid campaign managers and other staff, and increased use of professional advertising. The PRA also decreased the number of large contributors and increased the number of small contributors (See Table 5–7). In addition, other data strongly suggest that the PRA has increased the use of radio, TV, and newspaper advertisement and the use of direct mail.

TABLE 5–6
Impact of the disclosure provisions on political campaigns

	Increased	No effect	Decreased
Advantage of incumbents	59%	34%	7%
Role of special interests	36	46	19
Citizen awareness of the role of money in politics	50	47	3
Honesty in campaigning	30	64	6
Level of political information among voters	27	65	8

Source: Putt & Springer (1977).

TABLE 5–7
Impact of PRA on specific campaign activities

	Increased	No effect	Decreased
Use of paid legal/ accounting staff	65%	33%	2%
Use of paid campaign manager	46	53	1
Use of other paid staff	42	58	1
Use of professional advertising	34	61	5
Number of large contributors	6	45	49
Number of small contributors	23	63	14

Source: Putt & Springer (1977).

On balance, the PRA has been a limited success. It has not reduced campaign spending. It may have helped increase the role of interest groups in campaign financing, and it appears to have strengthened the ability of incumbents to win reelection. It may also have had a part in the increased use of media—particularly for statewide campaigns.

On the other hand, it has provided detailed information about campaign finance and expenditures that was unavailable before. This may well provide the information needed to enact laws effectively restricting campaign spending and giving. Jess Unruh has observed that "there is a tendency of reformers to skim off the easy reforms and skip over the others . . . [Proposition 9 is] more cosmetic surgery than it is a cure for our system's basic ills." According to Unruh (and others), the greatest need is to restrict the contributions that any one individual or group may make.

Public financing of campaigns

At present, the public finances political campaigns in two ways. Under federal law, presidential candidates receive matching funds from the U.S. Treasury in the primary and outright grants in the general election. And, as discussed earlier in this chapter, incumbents in California have the direct advantage of newsletters, district offices, and district staff. These are paid for out of the state's general funds.

Several proposals have been made for the public financing of campaigns in California, but none have been approved. Supporters of public financing make the argument that public financing with limits on contributions and expenditures is the only way to keep campaign costs within reason and minimize the influence of special interests. Skyrocketing campaign costs, it has been argued, keep many potential candidates from seeking public office.

Opposition to public financing comes from those who fear it will destroy direct public involvement in politics and those who see public financing as encouraging all kinds of kooks, idiots, and ideologues to run. There is concern that limiting a person's right to give a large campaign contribution is, in effect, limiting his or her freedom of expression. There is also fear that public financing will strengthen the two major parties, whose candidates would easily qualify, but weaken or destroy the minor parties, whose candidates would probably not qualify.

Generally, most Republicans have opposed public financing of campaigns, while Democrats tend to support it. However, recent money problems Republican candidates have had may change their position.

Even if all of the political and legal problems were solved, several difficult administrative problems remain. First, would public campaign funding be provided in primary elections? What is a "reasonable" amount to spend on a campaign? Should incumbents get as much as challengers?

Primary campaigns are important as we have seen. They often are the real election. Thus, if used, public finance should be made available in primary elections. But, the requirements for running for assembly or state senate are so minimal at present that almost any registered voter can get on the ballot. Clearly, the requirements demonstrating public support for a candidate would have to be made higher if public funds were made available to primary candidates. Such requirements could include a specific amount and number of private contributions and/or a special petition demonstrating that the candidate has the support of a large number of people.

After a candidate qualifies for public financing, how much should be spent on the campaign? The answer depends on several factors, the most significant being the number of voters in the constituency. But, as we also know, statewide and regional campaigns can make very effective use of TV and radio, while local campaigns usually have to use direct mail. So, a campaign may actually cost more per voter in an urban assembly district than it does in a statewide race.

If incumbents get the same amount to spend as their challengers, the incumbent has a very real advantage. Having been able to send newsletters to the voters in the previous two or four years, having a district office to help constituents, and having had the advantage of press coverage for two or four years, the incumbent has a big head-start on challengers. Should challengers be permitted to spend more than incumbents? How much more?

Ballot change

"NONE OF THE ABOVE"

Often, critics say, the average voter doesn't like any of the candidates running. This may be particularly true in the general election. At present, if the voter is unhappy with the alternatives, the only action that he or she may take is *not to vote.*

One suggested reform would be to place a line on the ballot for each office reading "None of the Above." Voters could mark their ballot for that alternative. Nevada has used this to a limited extent. But, what would happen if "None of the Above" got more votes than any of the candidates?

SHORT BALLOT

California's long ballot has been the object of considerable criticism in the past. Voters, it is argued, are confused by such a long ballot and often do not know whom or what they are voting for. However, changing the ballot would require a constitutional amendment. It is unlikely that California voters will vote to deny themselves the vote!

ABSENTEE BALLOT

Until 1979, only those voters who were ill or who would be traveling on election day could qualify for an absentee ballot. However, a new law enacted in 1978 permits anyone who wants to use an absentee ballot to do so. In two 1979 special elections (Long Beach and Fresno), vigorous attempts were made to get people to vote in the convenience of their homes. In both cases there was an unusually high number of absentee ballots cast. What might this latest election reform do to the political process? (Eacker, 1979)

Fair campaigning

Last-minute smear attacks, false and/or misleading statements, and bogus photographs have been used all too frequently in California campaigns. But attempts to regulate or legislate on the subject have largely failed. Even so, almost 20 states have laws of some kind designed to curb so-called unfair campaign tactics.

Essentially, the problem of campaign regulation centers on the First Amendment guarantees of free speech. According to several decisions by the U.S. Supreme Court, if state laws restrict political advertising, mailings, or other forms of communication, those restrictions must be narrowly and specifically aimed at false statements. Further, the Supreme Court has ruled that candidates for public office or elected public officials place themselves in the public spotlight. They may be attacked, criticized, or subject to comment that would be illegal if they were not public figures.

Nor does there appear to be a way to legislate against false and/or misleading, flattering statements a candidate may make about him- or herself. The normal concept of "consumer protection" does not apply, again, because of the prime importance in a democracy of the free and unrestricted flow of campaign materials. At present, the most effective regulation of campaign practices and materials appears to be community standards rather than law.

Multilingual voting materials

Under a 1975 amendment to the Civil Rights Act, 37 of California's 58 counties are required to print ballots, voter pamphlets, voting instructions, and other similar materials in at least two languages—English and Spanish.

Large numbers of citizens in California (and several other states) do not speak or write English with any degree of competence. The congressional action of 1975 was designed to provide basic election materials in those languages used by these citizens.

In California with almost 1 out of 5 residents of recent Mexican origin, Spanish is the obvious second language. But in San Francisco and a few other areas, Chinese and Tagalog (a Filipino language) are also used.

Initial use of the multilanguage election materials in 1975–78 does not appear to have produced any substantially larger election participation among the language minorities. On the other hand, it may take some years for the "language minorities" to become politically active.

SUMMARY

As we have shown, the ways in which election laws work are not neutral. And, while almost anyone can run for public office in California—that is, qualify for the ballot—few can command or attract the resources required for victory.

And, as shown, primary elections are most often the crucial election. Whoever wins the dominant party's primary in about two thirds of the legislative districts will go on to win the general election.

While California politics have traditionally been viewed as nonpartisan or independent, today there is good reason to believe that the state's voters have become more partisan in their voting behavior. At the same time, they have become more consistently Democratic in their voting behavior.

Ronald Reagan and Jerry Brown appear to signal the end of the traditional depression-liberals versus economic-conservatives politics. So, while voters may be looking more for party identification on the ballot, the party label may mean less than it once did.

6

Direct democracy—
Power to the people?

At the turn of this century, the United States was swept by the Progressive political reform movement (described previously in Chapter 4). Though the movement was national in scope, affecting to varying degrees cities and towns in nearly every state, there is little question that the Progressive impact was felt most keenly in a few midwestern states, such as Wisconsin and Minnesota, and in the western portions of the United States in what had formerly been strongholds of 19th-century political reform—Populism.

Progressives wanted to clean up politics, control politicians, and curb excessive special interest power. In California, the chief special interest target of this state's Progressives was the Southern Pacific Railroad. According to former newspaper editor, Fremont Older (1926:14), in 1896 Southern Pacific dominated the legislature, courts, municipal governments, county governments, and the newspapers of California. Southern Pacific, in turn, was the recipient of state and federal largesse—cash subsidies, no rate regulations, a sympathetic railroad commission, massive land grants, and favorable loans.

To combat this political and economic power, one of the main stratagems of California Progressives focused on providing citizens a greater voice in governmental decision making. Clearly, no reform elements in the Progressive program were more important than their holy trinity— the initiative, referendum, and recall. Underlying these three reform proposals was the implicit assumption that *ordinary* citizens using the petition process and voting booth, ought to have the ultimate decision-making power.

ILLUSTRATION 6-1

Proposition 4, placed on the November 6, 1979 ballot by initiative   The first three measures were placed on the ballot by the state legislature.

SAMPLE BALLOT

MARK ROUND DOT (●) ON BALLOT ONLY WITH VOTING STAMP, NEVER WITH PEN OR PENCIL.

(ABSENTEE BALLOTS MUST BE MARKED WITH BLUE STICKERS PROVIDED.)

(Fold ballot to this line, leaving top margin exposed)

OFFICIAL BALLOT

INSTRUCTIONS TO VOTERS:
To vote for the candidate of your selection, stamp a round dot (●) in the voting square to the right of the candidate's name. Where two or more candidates for the same office are to be elected, stamp a round dot (●) after the names of all candidates for that office for whom you desire to vote, not to exceed, however, the number of candidates to be elected.

To vote for a qualified write-in candidate, write the person's name in the blank space provided for that purpose after the names of the other candidates for the same office and stamp a round dot (●) in the voting square to the right of the name.

written in. The vote will not be counted unless the round dot (●) is stamped in the voting square to the right of the name written in.

To vote on any measure, stamp a round dot (●) in the voting square after the word "Yes" or after the word "No." All distinguishing marks or erasures are forbidden and make the ballot void.

If you wrongly stamp, tear, or deface this ballot, return it to a precinct board member and obtain another.

On absent voter ballots use ONLY the round dot (●) stickers provided for marking ballot.

RANCHO SANTIAGO COMMUNITY COLLEGE DISTRICT
DISTRITO DE COLEGIOS DE LA COMUNIDAD DE RANCHO SANTIAGO

TRUSTEE AREA 1
REGENTE AREA 1

For Member of the Governing Board
Para Miembro del Consejo Gubernativo
Vote for no more than Three
Vote por Tres nada mas

HECTOR G. GODINEZ
Incumbent

MICHAEL "TELL" ORTELL
Incumbent
Professor of Mathematics

RICHARD C. HERNANDEZ
Incumbent

RUDY MONTEJANO
Trustee, Rancho Santiago Community College District
Regente, Distrito Consejo de Comunidad Rancho Santiago

WATSON J. W. WARREN
Pintor de Pintura Recinda

GRACIE A. KEYS
Incumbent
Asistente de Terapia Fisica

TRUSTEE AREA 3
REGENTE AREA 3

For Member of the Governing Board
Para Miembro del Consejo Gubernativo
Vote for One
Vote por Uno

ORANGE UNIFIED SCHOOL DISTRICT
DISTRITO ESCOLAR UNIFICADO DE ORANGE

TRUSTEE AREA 2 (FULL TERM)
REGENTE AREA 2 (TERMINO COMPLETO)

For Member of the Governing Board
Para Miembro del Consejo Gubernativo
Vote for One
Vote por Uno

ELEANORE CATHERINE PLEINES
Incumbent
Teacher

LAWRENCE (LARRY) R. LABRADO
Incumbent
Administrador Universitario—Ejecutivo

TRUSTEE AREA 3 (FULL TERM)
REGENTE AREA 3 (TERMINO COMPLETO)

For Member of the Governing Board
Para Miembro del Consejo Gubernativo
Vote for One
Vote por Uno

KARL BAKER, JR.
Businessman/Electronics Manufacturing
Negociante, Manufactura de Electronica

JOYCE S. TRAINOR
Incumbent
Mantin/Tutora Privada

F BERT SKILES
Incumbent

TRUSTEE AREA 4 (FULL TERM)
REGENTE AREA 4 (TERMINO COMPLETO)

For Member of the Governing Board
Para Miembro del Consejo Gubernativo
Vote for One
Vote por Uno

SANTIAGO COUNTY WATER DISTRICT
DISTRITO DE AGUAS DEL CONDADO DE SANTIAGO

For Director
Para Director
Vote for no more than Three
Vote por Tres nada mas

WARREN K. VanINGEN
Accountant/Business Consultant
Contador/Consultor de Negocios

RUSSELL C. MANNING
Incumbent
Businessman

LESLIE WIELAND
Teacher
Maestra

JOHN MICHAEL COVAS
Incumbent

JOE CHERRY
Incumbent

SILVERADO-MODJESKA PARK AND RECREATION DISTRICT
DISTRITO DE PARQUES Y RECREACION DE SILVERADO-MODJESKA

FULL TERM
TERMINO COMPLETO
For Director
Para Director
Vote for no more than Two
Vote por Dos nada mas

MONA ENGEL
Realtor Associate/Owner, Bakers

CHARLES L. CRON
Incumbent

MICHAEL A. LIMA
Appointed Incumbent

BALOTA DE MUESTRA

MARQUE CON PUNTO REDONDO (●) LA BALOTA UNICAMENTE CON SELLO VOTANTE, NUNCA CON PLUMA O LAPIZ.

(LAS BALOTAS DE VOTANTE AUSENTE SERAN MARCADAS CON ETIQUETA ENGOMADA AZUL PROPORCIONADA.)

(Doble la balota a esta linea, dejando margen de arriba descubierto)

BALOTA OFICIAL

Orange County
November 6, 1979

INSTRUCCIONES A LOS VOTANTES:
Para votar por el candidato de su selección, estampe un punto redondo (●) en el cuadro de votante a la derecha del nombre del candidato. Cuando mas de dos candidatos deberan ser elegidos para el mismo oficio estampe un punto redondo (●) despues de los nombres de las candidatos para ese oficio por quien Ud. desee votar, siempre que no exceda el total de candidatos para ser elegidos.

Para votar por algun candidato calificado para ser escrito, escriba el nombre de esa persona en el espacio en blanco proporcionado para ese fin abajo de los nombres de los candidatos elegibles para el mismo este oficio y estampe un punto redondo (●) en el cuadro de votante a la derecha del nombre escrito.

que el punto redondo (●) sea estampado en el cuadro de votante a la derecha del nombre escrito.

Para votar por cualquier medida, estampe un punto redondo (●) en el cuadro del votante seguido de la palabra "Si," o en seguida de la palabra "No."

Cualquier borradura o marca que se distingo por ser diferente esta prohibido y nulifica la balota.

Si por error estampa mal, rota o estropea esta balota, regrese el miembro del distrito electoral y obtenga otra.

En balotas de votante ausente use unicamente la etiqueta engomada de punto redondo (●) proporcionada para marcar la balota.

MEASURES SUBMITTED TO VOTE OF VOTERS
MEDIDAS SOMETIDAS A VOTACION

1 — SCHOOL ASSIGNMENT AND TRANSPORTATION OF PUPILS. Provides that U. S. Constitution will govern pupil school assignment or pupil transportation in California. Financial impact: Potential savings if school districts elect to reduce or eliminate pupil transportation or assignment programs as a result of this measure.

ASIGNACION DE ESCUELAS Y TRANSPORTACION DE PUPILOS. Proporciona que la Constitucion de los Estados Unidos gobernara la asignacion de escuelas y la transportacion en California. Impacto economico: Ahorro economico Indeterminable. Economia potencial si los distritos electos reducen o eliminan los programas de transportacion de pupilos o programas de asignacion a resultad de esta medida.

YES Si — NO

2 — LOAN INTEREST RATES. On loans other than for personal, family or household purposes, permits interest rates higher than 10 percent if Legislature approves. Financial impact: No direct fiscal effect on state or local government.

TIPO DE INTERES DE PRESTAMOS. Sobre prestamos aparte de esos para proposito personal, de familia o domesticos, permite tipos de interes mas altos del 10 por ciento si la Legislatura aprueba. Impacto economico: Ningun efecto economico sobre el gobierno del estado o local.

YES Si — NO

3 — PROPERTY TAXATION—VETERANS' EXEMPTION. Requires the Legislature to adjust the valuation of veterans' assessable property if assessment ratio is changed. Financial impact: No effect on the amount of property taxes levied. No effect on tax liability of taxpayers claiming the veterans' exemption. Minor initial costs to local government.

IMPUESTOS DE PROPIEDAD—EXENCION DE VETERANOS. Requiere que la Legislatura ajuste la valuacion de propiedad acensible de veteranos si la proporcion de tasacion es cambiada. Impacto economico: Ningun efecto sobre la cantidad de impuestos de propiedad impuesto. Ningun efecto en la obligacion de impuestos de los contribuyentes reclamando la exencion de veteranos. Costas iniciales minimas al gobierno local.

YES Si — NO

4 — LIMITATION OF GOVERNMENT APPROPRIATIONS. Establishes annual appropriation limit for state and local governments. Financial impact: Indeterminable. Financial impact of this measure will depend upon future actions of state and local governments with regard to appropriations that are not subject to the limitations of this measure.

LIMITACION DE APROPIACIONES DEL GOBIERNO. Establece limites de apropiacion anuales para gobiernos del estado y locales. Impacto economico: Indeterminable. El impacto economico de esta medida dependera sobre acciones futuras de los gobiernos del estado y locales referente al apropiacion en regardo al apropiaciones que no estan sujetas a las limitaciones de esta medida.

YES Si — NO

PROCEDURES

Initiative procedures

The initiative provides citizens with an opportunity to propose and to formulate laws. Basically, there are two types of initiatives—statute and constitutional. California and most of the other western states provide for both initiative options, while a few states provide for only one or the other initiative device. The statute initiative allows citizens to make changes in the laws, and the constitutional initiative allows citizens to amend the Constitution.

The basic steps in the California initiative process are as follows: (1) interested citizens draft a proposed measure; (2) the measure is submitted to the Office of Attorney General for titling and summary; (3) proponents pay a $200 fee; (4) petitions are circulated among voters with backers having 150 days to qualify their petition; (5) the secretary of state's office determines whether the proper number of valid signatures has been collected within the time frame—a statute initiative requires 346,119 valid signatures (5 percent of the total vote cast for governor at the last election) and a constitutional initiative requires 553,790 valid signatures (8 percent);[1] and (6) voters at the next election either approve or disapprove the proposed initiative. If the initiative has more "Aye" than "Nay" votes, it becomes the law. Additionally, if provisions of two or more propositions approved at the same election conflict, the measure receiving the highest affirmative vote prevails.

In order to further protect this citizen weapon from the "politicians," Progressives also made it difficult for the legislature to amend an approved initiative. Constitutional initiatives may be changed only through passage of another initiative. Statutory initiatives can be amended by a majority vote of the legislature and then submitted to the electorate, unless the initiative specifically permits amendment without voter approval. Proposition 9, the Political Reform Act of June 1974, established particularly tough amendment provisions. A two-thirds vote of each house is required to amend.

Finally, initiatives are subject to review by the courts. For example, the antischool-busing Proposition 21 of 1972 was ruled unconstitutional by the California Supreme Court, and, the Senator Robbins' antischool busing Proposition 1 of November 1979, approved by a more than 2–1 voter margin, is likely to be challenged in the courts. Proposition 9, the Political Reform Act of 1974, has undergone a series of challenges in the courts with some portions having been declared unconstitutional. Proposition 13, the property tax relief measure of June 1978, was immediately chal-

---

[1] Based on 6,922,380 votes cast in the 1978 gubernatorial election.

lenged but was quickly upheld by the California Supreme Court. Initiatives at variance with the U.S. Federal Constitution may also be declared unconstitutional in the courts. Proposition 14 of 1964, which effectively rescinded the Rumford Fair Housing Law, was ruled unconstitutional by the U.S. Supreme Court.

According to the California Constitution, initiatives may cover only one topic, but this is sometimes hard to define. Thus, Proposition 9, the Political Reform Act of 1974, was appealed to the state supreme court on the contention that it encompassed more than one subject—spending limits, conflict of interest, reporting requirements, and the like. Proposition 9 backers have argued that these topics are all subsumed under the general heading—political reform—and that the measure is constitutional. The state supreme court has upheld the constitutionality of this reform measure.

Referendum procedures

The *referendum* provides citizens with an opportunity to "veto" bills recently passed by the legislature and signed by the governor. Briefly, the process works as follows: (1) the legislature passes and the governor signs a controversial bill; (2) certain citizens strongly oppose the new law and decide to attempt to qualify a referendum for the ballot before the law goes into effect 61 days after the legislative session; (3) citizens attempting to qualify a referendum have only 90 days after the governor has signed the bill to collect the necessary number of valid signatures—5 percent of the total vote cast for governor in the preceding election. Last, certain type of bills are excluded from the referendum process: calls for special elections, tax levies, urgency measures, and appropriations bills.

Recall procedures

The *recall* provides citizens with an opportunity to remove incumbents from office using the same petition/election procedure. For a statewide recall, valid signatures of qualified voters equalling 12 percent of the total vote cast in the last general election for that particular office must be gathered (between 1979 and 1982, 830,686 signatures would have to be collected within 180 days to place a recall of Governor Jerry Brown on the ballot.)[2] At the local level, signatures equalling as much as 25 percent of the votes cast in the last previous election are required.

---

[2] At the state level, the petition effort to recall an officeholder theoretically could begin on the first day of the officeholder's term. If the correct number of valid signatures is collected, a special election would then have to be called. The ballot for a statewide recall would be divided into two parts. On the top half of the ballot the list of charges brought

Before proceeding to our analyses of the three direct democracy devices in California, let us briefly consider the background of the initiative, referendum, and recall in a regional context.

DIRECT DEMOCRACY: A WESTERN PHENOMENON

In all, some 23 states currently provide for the initiative, and in many of these same states the referendum and recall are also allowed. Moreover, some of the other 27 states that offer no statewide direct democracy options do allow for the initiative, referendum, or recall at the local level.

Unlike some of the Progressive reforms—such as the secret ballot, the direct primary, or the presidential preferential primary that have been voted in by ever-increasing numbers of states—the initiative, referendum, and recall, after an initial adoption surge in the early part of this century, have been adopted by only a very few new states in the last several decades. However, renewed interest in the nondirect democracy states has been generated in the initiative process with the successful adoption of Proposition 9 of June 1974, the Political Reform Act, and Proposition 13, the property tax relief measure of June 1978.

Clearly, direct democracy devices have been adopted primarily in the western states. Only 4 states (15 percent) out of the 26 east of the Mississippi River currently provide for the initiative, compared to 16 (66 percent) out of the 24 west of the Mississippi River. Indeed, the further west one travels in the continental United States, the more likely it will be that a particular state provides for the direct democracy option. Interestingly, the state most often identified as the cradle of Progressivism, Wisconsin, allows for neither the initiative nor the referendum but does provide for the recall.

The Progressives' middle-class reformism, their antipathy toward the two major establishment parties, their suspicions of officeholders, and their reliance on ordinary citizens to exercise ultimate political power clearly have their modern-day parallels. The reform momentum following the Watergate political scandals of the early 1970s is not unlike the reform surge at the turn of the century. Recent public opinion polls suggest

---

against the incumbent would be set forth, as well as the incumbent's defense of his or her position. Then the question would be posed: *Shall _____ be recalled from the office of _____?* On the bottom half of the ballot, the various nominees for the office (to be placed on the ballot as a candidate one would need to secure the signatures of 1 percent of the vote cast for that particular office in the last election) would be listed. Not surprisingly, the challenged incumbent may not qualify as one of the candidates on the bottom portion of the ballot. If there are more "No" votes than "Yes" votes, the incumbent remains in office, and votes on the bottom half of the ballot are not counted. Additionally, the state must reimburse the incumbent for the expenses of the campaign. If there are more "Yes" than "No" votes, the officeholder is removed from office, and the candidate with the most votes on the bottom portion of the ballot is elected and serves out the remainder of the recalled officeholder's term.

that few voters today consider themselves as strong Democrats or strong Republicans, and a growing percentage of Americans, particularly young people, consider themselves Independent or Decline to State. Pollster Louis Harris (*Sacramento Bee*, March 5, 1979) recently reported that only 18 percent of the American public had confidence in Congress, and only 15 percent had confidence in the president.

In the decade of the '70s, a number of new public interest citizen groups such as Common Cause, Ralph Nader's Public Citizen, and in California, People's Lobby emerged on the political horizon. Unlike the futile efforts of public-interest lobbies of earlier years, these new groups have been able to exert a significant impact at the state and national level. The philosophy of these new public-interest lobbies parallels the political goals of the Progressives decades ago—cleansing and reforming the political system.

Using the initiative process, careful research, grass-roots organizing, and governmental lobbying, these new groups have promoted many Progressive-type reform issues, such as public financing of campaigns, rigid monitoring of campaign spending, officeholder's income disclosure, and lobby regulation. Competing against powerful entrenched special interests and "big money," they have scored some remarkable achievements.

ILLUSTRATION 6–2
Usage patterns of states providing for the constitutional initiative and/or the statute initiative

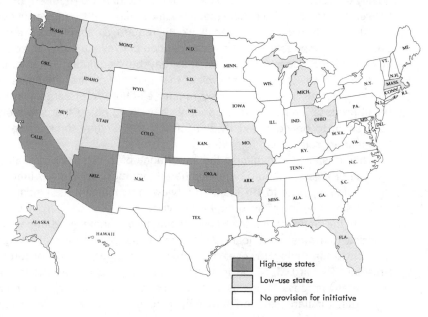

High-use states
Low-use states
No provision for initiative

Also in the progressive tradition are contemporary tax crusaders Howard Jarvis and Paul Gann. In 1978 they successfully qualified Proposition 13, property tax relief for the ballot with an unprecedented 1.2 million signatures. Their successful election campaign was built around the theme, "Teach the politicians a lesson." This same theme carries through in Gann's "Spirit of 13" Prop. 4 of November 1979 dealing with limiting government spending and Jarvis' current initiative proposal to reduce state income taxes.

In the next section of the chapter we shall consider these three direct democracy devices—the initiative, referendum, and recall—and the role they play in California politics. It is apparent when considering these three techniques that over the years the initiative has been far more significant in California than the recall or referendum. Hence, we shall discuss only briefly the recall and referendum and then concentrate our attention on an analysis of initiative usage in California.

RECALL USE

No recall effort directed against a statewide officeholder has ever successfully qualified for the California ballot. The few abortive statewide recall attempts (directed primarily against governors) have always fallen far short of securing the necessary signatures.

Several factors probably contribute to this notable lack of recall use at the state level. First, massive numbers of signatures are required to qualify the recall petition for the ballot, far more than are required for initiatives or referenda. To collect the awesome number of signatures necessary to qualify a statewide recall would require a monumental effort. Second, like impeachment, the recall petition conveys to some citizens a kind of radical, desperate action that may be disquieting to potential petition signers. These people might feel that the normal channels for throwing out the rascals (the next regular election) is preferable to the recall process. Third, recall proponents have long noted that some citizens seem to be confused by the term "recall"—they think it means "remember" rather than removal.

While it is easy to minimize the importance of the statewide recall as a viable process, it should be remembered that most scholars writing on the presidency prior to 1973 tended to view impeachment as a meaningless scarecrow, too. The thought of removing a president from office through the impeachment process seemed so remote in 20th-century America that most American government texts gave only cursory discussion to the topic. However, the forced resignation in 1974 of former President Richard M. Nixon to head off the ongoing congressional impeachment process suggests that impeachment is now no longer unthinkable. Similarly, though recalling a governor, for example, seems remote, the machinery is there, and the potential for its use in an extreme situation should not be totally ignored.

Though the recall has seldom even been attempted at the state level, it has been successfully used at the local level against county supervisors, mayors, sheriffs, city council members, and school board members. Obviously, one critical difference between local and statewide use is the ability of citizens in small election districts to organize successfully to secure the requisite number of signatures. Perhaps, too, anger and bitterness are more easily directed at visible local incumbents rather than at distant figures like the governor or attorney general. One author (Georges, 1976:105–106) has noted that local recalls generally revolve around three types of issues: lack of responsiveness, ineffective administration, and misbehavior in office. In a recent two-year period, there were 20 local recall elections; in half of these elections the incumbent was successfully ousted. In the latter half of the 1970s there has been a substantial upsurge in local recall politics in California.

Critics of the recall process can cite any number of problems inherent in the device, including: intimidation of officeholders by disgruntled minorities, heightened acrimony, and partisan hanky-panky. For example, part of the motivation to recall Ronald Reagan as governor in 1968 was an attempt to discredit his presidential ambitions. In 1979, Democratic Assembly representative Carmen Perino was the subject of a recall effort launched just a day or two after his successful, narrow reelection. Recall-Perino backers (mainly associates of the defeated Republican candidate Doug Carter) contend that Perino mailed out an unfair and unethical campaign flyer.

At the local level where the recall has been used successfully, the targets have generally been *nonpartisan* elective officeholders such as: mayors, supervisors, city council members, or school board members. In the last analysis, whether the recall process has been used or abused frequently depends on "whose ox is being gored." All too often, if one dislikes the incumbent, a recall effort against this officeholder is "necessary and justifiable"; if one supports the incumbent, the recall effort is "unwarranted, partisan, and interferes with the democratic process."

One final point should be considered: should the requirements to qualify a statewide recall be reduced to give disgruntled citizens a more realistic opportunity to recall an incumbent? Clearly, the Progressives in promoting the recall option did not want citizens to pursue this course casually; hence, the substantial number of signatures required and the relatively short time frame allowed to collect signatures. But, with a California population of 23 million citizens, the sheer number of signatures necessary to qualify is overwhelming. Since no statewide recall has ever qualified, it does seem arguable, at least, that the percentage necessary to qualify should be reduced to 10 percent or eight percent to make it a remotely possible option, but the legislature is unlikely to move rapidly in this direction.

REFERENDUM USE

Nearly all of the states providing for the statute and/or constitutional initiative also provide for its alter ego, the referendum. However, the pattern in these states is similar; very few referenda have qualified for the ballot over the last several decades. Indeed, New Mexico has *never* had a referendum successfully qualify for its ballot.

Before proceeding further, it should be noted that the *compulsory referendum* is widely used in nearly all of the states; however, this device should not be confused with the *petition referendum.* The petition referendum is a direct democracy technique using the petition/election format. The compulsory referendum, on the other hand, goes on the ballot automatically after passing the legislature and being signed by the governor (for example, a bond issue or constitutional amendment). Compulsory referenda sometimes deal with relatively innocuous matters eliciting little attention from the media. For example, voters have been asked to cast votes on such technical and mundane issues as: Should postsecondary education personnel be under civil service? Should local government employees be required to live in the city where they work? Should a board of chiropractic examiners be authorized to adopt rules and regulations governing chiropractors? Or, should the legislature be allowed to amend or reverse the boxing and wrestling contests initiative act of November 1924? In the period between 1960 and 1979 in California, *no petition referendum* qualified for the ballot, *32 initiatives* qualified, and *190 compulsory referenda* were placed on the ballot by the legislature.

Indeed, only one petition referendum has successfully qualified for the California ballot since 1942, and this proposal was later defeated by the voters. While there have been sporadic attempts to qualify referenda for the ballot over the last decade or two, none has amassed sufficient signatures to qualify. In 1964, the California Real Estate Association attempted to qualify a referendum for the ballot that would have prevented the enactment of the Rumford Fair Housing Law, but the effort failed. After failing to qualify their referendum, realtors proceeded to qualify an initiative (Proposition 14, 1964) for the ballot. In 1975, a coalition of conservative church leaders attempted to prevent enactment of the consenting adult sex bill which had been passed by the legislature and signed by the governor, but once again, not enough signatures were collected in the requisite time.

Exactly why the petition referendum has nearly disappeared from the political scene, while its counterpart, the initiative, continues to play a significant role is not altogether clear. Clearly, one key reason is the time constraints imposed on referendum backers. Referendum proponents have only 90 days to qualify their measure, and the stopwatch starts running as soon as the governor signs the bill. To have any realistic hopes of qualifying a referendum, a group would probably have to begin anticipating a referendum campaign while a measure was progressing through the legislature. Initiatives are frequently generated by legislative inaction. Powerful special interests are unable to work out satisfactory compromises, but inaction or watered-down legislation do not spur a referendum effort. A referendum effort is likeliest to occur on a controversial, emotional issue such as race relations, abortions, sexual practices, gun control, or the like, where the legislature and governor take a principled stand realizing, at the same time, that a majority of the public may believe otherwise. This is not a very frequent occurrence.

Finally, is the referendum worth keeping? The answer to this question, as with any of the other direct democratic devices, is not simple. Obviously, many politicians do not care for the procedure, since it can potentially undermine what they have done. In any case, in defense of the referendum: first, it has not been used that extensively—though this is admittedly a weak defense; and, second, its potential for overturning an unpopular law justifies keeping it.

Last, proponents of the referendum probably would argue for one important change in the present process, i.e., lengthening the time a referendum can be circulated to give angry voters at least a reasonable chance to qualify a measure for a vote.

INITIATIVE

The statewide initiative (statutory and/or constitutional), while provided in some 23 different state constitutions, is used frequently in only a few states—California, Washington, Colorado, Oregon, North Dakota, Oklahoma, and Arizona. In considering these seven states, one feature stands out: they are all western states—either Plains, Rocky Mountain, or Pacific Coast. In the other 16 initiative state, this technique is used either infrequently or almost never.

While part of the difference in initiative use in the various states may hinge around formal requirements, such as the number of signatures required, the fee for circulating petitions, the length of time allowed for circulation, or the question of whether signers must be precincted, the differences between the various states on these procedural requirements are not really very great. The reason that initiatives are used extensively in some states and not in others seems less a question of legal requirements and more one relating to the political-social makeup of a state.

It is interesting to note that while there was a steady drop-off in the number of initiatives qualifying for the ballot in the 1940s, 1950s, 1960s, there has been a remarkable upsurge in the number of initiatives qualifying in the 1970s. In Table 6–1, the number and percent of initiatives circulating, qualifying, approved, and rejected are listed by decade.

What types of issues, generally, are brought to voters via the initiative? Clearly, they run the gamut, but often they comprise some of the most controversial issues of the day—the death penalty, political reform, property taxes, property rights and racial exclusion, marijuana penalties, pay TV, school busing, farm labor rights, dam construction, nuclear energy safety, and homosexual teachers. Additionally, a wide range of other issues have at least begun to be discussed by a portion of the public in initiative campaigns that failed to qualify for the ballot or are in the process of circulation. Some of these potential issues are: allowing for 18-year-old drinking, establishing a unicameral legislature, off-track betting, prohibiting the sales tax, legalizing casino-style gambling, abolishing compression chambers for killing unclaimed dogs and cats, limiting attorney fees in malpractice cases, and taxing oil companies profits.

The initiative process, which allows voters an opportunity to express their opinions on a host of controversial issues as a sort of "court of last resort," is, not surprisingly, the subject itself of considerable controversy. From the very first years immediately after the adoption of the initiative to the present, there have been persistent criticisms of the process. Many legislators dislike the process because it takes power away from them and dilutes representative government. Knowledgeable observers worry about the public's capacity to vote on initiatives. Even the initiative process' most vehement supporters recognize problems with the device.

TABLE 6–1
Number and percent of initiatives submitted to voters

Decade	Number titled by attorney general as eligible for circulation	Number and (percent) qualifying	Voters' action Adopted	Rejected
1912–19	45	30 (67%)	8 (27%)	22 (73%)
1920–29	51	35 (69)	10 (29)	25 (71)
1930–39	66	35 (53)	9 (26)	26 (74)
1940–49	42	19 (45)	6 (32)	13 (68)
1950–59	17	10 (59)	2 (20)	8 (80)
1960–69	44	9 (20)	3 (33)	6 (67)
1970–78	140	21 (15)	6 (28)	15 (72)
Grand total	405	159 (39%)	44 (28%)	115 (72%)

Source: This table, though modified and updated, is adopted from Eugene Lee, *Referendums: A Comparative Study of Practice and Theory.* Eds. Daniel Butler and Austin Ranney (Washington D.C.: American Enterprise Institute, 1979), p. 91.

Let us examine some of the criticisms of the initiative and then consider some of the counterarguments to these criticisms.

Drafting phase

CRITICISMS

One of the major complaints direct democracy critics level against initiatives is that they tend to be poorly or hastily drafted. Most legislative bills move slowly through the legislative labyrinth. In the legislature, bills are repeatedly scrutinized, polished, and amended by various legislative committees.

The initiative comes to the voter full-blown. There is no screening nor any give-and-take. Moreover, literally anyone, including cranks and crackpots, can submit an initiative idea to the attorney general and then begin circulating the petition forms. In 1974, two private citizens alone proposed 30 separate California initiatives! Finally, given this situation, initiatives can be unclear, weird, lengthy, complicated, and, potentially, unconstitutional. Over the years, a number of initiatives which had been approved by the voters were declared unconstitutional by the courts.

REBUTTAL

While there is some truth to these charges, there is another side. Initiatives are at least put into proper legal form in the titling and summary written by the Office of Attorney General. If an initiative is patently hare-brained, it is unlikely to win acceptance from the voters in the signature-gathering campaign. Obviously, one can note (see Table 6–1) that over the last several decades, while many initiative proposals circulated, few qualified for the ballot and fewer passed. For example, from 1970 to 1978, 140 initiatives were officially titled, 21 qualified for the ballot, and only 6 were approved by the voters.

It may be true that some initiatives are not well thought out or are poorly drafted, but, in fairness, for years the legislature has been guilty of passing legislation hastily without careful scrutiny, especially during the last week or two of a session when there is inevitably a tremendous backlog of bills. Furthermore, given the fact that legislators are expected to vote on thousands of bills and resolutions each year, few can give more than cursory attention to these many votes. Voters, on the other hand, have only a few initiatives that they have to vote upon.

Finally, while some initiatives have been declared unconstitutional by the courts, so too have measures passed by Congress or the state legislatures. Obviously, the final word on constitutionality must come from the courts, and one is never really sure until a measure is tested in court.

Qualifying phase

CRITICISMS

Critics of the initiative process frequently contend that in order to amass the requisite number of signatures necessary to qualify a statute or constitutional initiative in the time allotted,[3] it is necessary to have either enormous financial resources or a large mass organization. Hence, it is argued that the initiative, rather than being an important citizen weapon, is in reality a tool of narrow, special interests—the petroleum industry, automobile manufacturers and dealers, land developers building interests, and the like.

Under the original provisions of the Political Reform Act initiative of 1974, groups would have been limited in how much they could spend to qualify a measure for the ballot (25 cents times the number of signatures necessary to qualify). These limits were struck down by the state court as being unconstitutional, since they violated the free speech provisions of the First Amendment to the U.S. Constitution. They noted the U.S. Supreme Court's action striking down campaign expenditure limits in *Buckley* v. *Valeo.*

ILLUSTRATION 6–3
Getting signatures on a petition

---

[3] The court has ruled the 150-day period to gather signatures is a reasonable limit.

Large mass-member organizations such as the California Teachers Association or the California State Employees Association can mail out petition forms to their many members, but smaller groups cannot hope to qualify an initiative relying only on their own membership. Wealthy groups can hire expensive public relations firms to collect their signatures for them. The most legendary of the professional petition pushers was the Joe Robinson firm of San Francisco. Through his statewide network of experienced professionals plus a volunteer army of paid amateurs (25 cents per signature), the Robinson firm could virtually guarantee qualifying a proposed initiative. Instead of commitment to a cause, these mercenary signature gatherers were earning a fee. Motivations for signing also became suspect; Robinson volunteers would go first to family, friends, and neighbors. These people would sign petitions in order to help the signature collector earn some extra income, not because they had any commitment to the issue.

Critics of the initiative process also argue that opportunities for deception and skulduggery in gathering signatures are legion. In some initiative campaigns, "dodger cards" reportedly have been used to cover up the attorney general's summary of the measure. Petition signers can then be misled on the details of the initiative. Some groups such as People's Lobby emphasize only the signing aspect and feel it is impractical to spend much time explaining the substance of an initiative to potential signers. People's Lobby founder, the late Edwin Koupal (Duscha: 1975) stated:

> Generally, people who are getting out signatures are too goddamned interested in their ideology to get the required number in the required time. We use the hoopla process.
>
> First, you set up a table with six petitions taped to it, and a sign in front that says, SIGN HERE. One person sits at the table. Another person stands in front. That's all you need—two people.
>
> While one person sits at the table, the other walks up to people and asks two questions. We operate on the old selling maxim that two yeses make a sale. First, we ask them if they are a registered voter. If they say yes, we ask them if they are registered in that county. If they say yes to that, we immediately push them up to the table where the person sitting points to a petition and says, "Sign this." By this time, the person feels, "Oh goodie, I get to play," and signs it. If a table doesn't get 80 signatures an hour using this method, it's moved the next day . . . people don't ask to read the petition and we certainly don't offer. Why try to educate the world when you're trying to get signatures?

Last, all signatures are supposed to be witnessed and the signature collector must so affirm when he or she signs the petition, however, this requirement is sometimes violated. On many college campuses, one will find various initiative petitions left in departmental offices or at unmanned card tables to be signed by interested passers-by, and no witness is present.

REBUTTAL

While money and/or large organizations can help in qualifying initiatives, they are not, as it has been argued, indispensable. Clearly, over the last several elections, small nonaffluent groups have scored some impressive victories in signature-gathering campaigns. For example, People's Lobby successfully qualified the environment initiative of June 1972, the Political Reform Act of November 1974, and the Nuclear Safety Act of June 1976. A coalition of environmental groups spearheaded signature gathering for the coastline initiative. The 1972 marijuana initiative was successfully qualified through the work of a few dedicated volunteers. The "People's Advocate," a small taxpayers' group, secured the signatures for Proposition 13, property tax relief measure of June 1978.

The point is: small, less affluent groups have been able to qualify initiatives for the ballot without enormous financial resources or large-scale mass organization. Grass-roots appeal and ingenuity can be critical factors.

Paul Gann, "People's Advocate" founder, after successfully masterminding Proposition 13, the property tax relief measure, to victory in June 1978, launched a new government-spending-limit initiative on election day, November 7, 1978. Under his ingenious scheme, Gann placed volunteer signature gatherers at polling places across the state (carefully positioned more than 100 feet away from the polls). The California Real Estate Association also helped supply some of these volunteers. As people finished voting, they would walk a few paces over to the colorfully marked card table of the Gann volunteer and sign the new initiative. It was estimated that more than 300,000 signatures were gathered on this day alone! Gann hoped that if sufficient signatures were collected, the governor might exercise his executive option and call a special election for the initiative. Or, another example, the new Jarvis income tax reduction initiative secured *all* of its signatures and campaign money through a unique mass mailing campaign.

Campaign phase

CRITICISMS

Clearly, the most frequently heard criticism of the initiative process is the role of big money in direct democracy campaigns. Undoubtedly, enormous sums have been spent by proponents and opponents in initiative campaigns. In 1976, nearly $4 million was spent on the nuclear power initiative and over $3 million on the farm labor initiative. An historic high point (or all-time low?) was recorded in the general election of 1978, when several cigarette companies raised and spent more than $6 million to defeat the antismoking initiative, Proposition 5.

A more serious objection is the considerable advantage wealthy groups have when pitted against less affluent groups in an initiative campaign. Obviously, the side with the most money can buy more billboards, newspaper ads, TV spots, and the like to help influence the electorate. In some initiative campaigns, the spending disparity between proponents and opponents has reached outlandish proportions. For example, in 1972 opponents of Proposition 20 (the coastline initiative) spent five times as much as the proponents—$1.1 million versus $210,000; public employee groups spent nearly $2 million in their campaign on the state employee salaries initiative, while opponents spent a paltry $37,000. In 1978, cigarette companies spent more than ten times as much as anti-cigarette forces in the Proposition 5 campaign.

Critics of the initiative also emphasize that these direct democracy campaigns are frequently managed by professional public relations firms. The firms have little interest in informing or educating voters; their goal is to win elections. Public relations firms using techniques pioneered originally from advertising campaigns for commercial products (toothpastes, mouthwashes, and underarm deodorants) have transferred them to the political campaign area. Distortions, gimmicks, deceptive slogans, half-truths, and outright lies have characterized many initiative campaigns. Though public relations firms also manage some statewide candidates' campaigns, their impact is greater in initiative campaigns, because voters do not have the usual candidate or partisan cues to guide them in this type of election.

Examples of confusing claims and counterclaims are extensive in the history of California initiative campaigns. For example, Artie Samish (1971:37–38), the most notorious lobbyist in California history, blitzed the billboards of the state in a now legendary campaign with a picture of a large, ugly pig and the caption, "Drive the Hog from the Road! Vote yes on Proposition Number 2." Samish knew voters would despise road hogs—and vote "Yes" on Number 2. However, road hogs had nothing to do with the Proposition 2 campaign of that year. The measure was designed to give tax breaks to bus and truck companies. It was simply a Samish "joke" on the voters.

In 1972 advocates of Proposition 14 argued that a vote "Yes" would reduce taxes, and opponents of Proposition 14 countered with a vote "No" would reduce taxes. In November 1973, former Governor Ronald Reagan argued that a "Yes" vote on Proposition 1 would help reduce taxes; opponents said a "Yes" vote would actually contribute to raising taxes. State employee ads in 1972 proclaimed, "It's your money, keep state pay in line, vote Yes on 15." In reality, a vote "Yes" would have made it easier for state employees to receive salary increases. Advocates of the measure argued that "keeping state pay in line" referred to having state employees paid at a level commensurate with what they would earn in the private sector! Opponents of Proposition 20 of 1972 argued that a "Yes" vote would lock up the coast from the people; proponents argued that they were trying to save the coast for the people. Proposition 22 of 1972 had proponents contending that a "Yes" vote was to support farmworkers' rights, but opponents made the same claim!

In the Jarvis-Gann property tax relief measure, (Proposition 13), voters were innundated with bewildering sets of figures on the number of state, county, and city employees who might be laid off or the amount of money citizens would receive if Proposition 13 were to pass. Pro and antismoking forces waged a bitter campaign in 1978 over Proposition 5 and how much it would really cost to be implemented. In short, potential opportunities for razzle-dazzle, hocus-pocus politics seem unparalleled in initiative campaigns.

REBUTTAL

Campaign spending on initiatives has risen steadily, it is true, but so has spending on candidate races. While the side with the most money obviously has a distinct advantage, it is not insurmountable. Indeed, in several recent initiative campaigns the side spending the most money lost. Professor Gene Lee (1978:113) notes that from 1972–76, in the 16 initiative campaigns of that period, the side spending the most money in the campaign won 8 times and lost 8 times. The eight initiatives where the better financed side lost were: property tax limits, state employee salaries, highway patrol salaries, death penalty, marijuana, coastline, agricultural labor, and expenditure and tax limits. On several of the above, spending was incredibly lopsided (highway patrol, 100 percent–0 percent; state employee salaries, 98 percent–2 percent), and yet they lost. What this suggests, of course, is that an expensive, professional campaign is helpful, but it will fail if it runs counter to substantial public sentiment.

A serious attempt to limit the impact of money in initiative campaigns came with the passage of the Political Reform Act of 1974, Proposition 9. Under Proposition 9 provisions, spending on ballot propositions was to be limited to 8 cents times the voting age population.

Unfortunately for advocates of spending limits, the U.S. Supreme Court in 1976, in *Buckley* v. *Valeo,* ruled that expenditure ceilings set for candidates running for federal office were unconstitutional. The Court did rule that expenditure limits for candidates receiving federal funds (presidential candidates only) were permissible. FPPC Chair, Dan Lowenstein, announced a few weeks after the Supreme Court decision that the limits on ballot spending in California would not be enforced, since they had been effectively nullified by the Court's decision, and the state supreme court has since struck down the campaign spending limits of Proposition 9. Hence, spending on the 1976 nuclear initiative campaign and all initiative campaigns since has been unlimited.

Last, while one can be concerned with devious, misleading initiative campaigns oftentimes skillfully orchestrated by expensive public relations firms, it does appear that regular candidate election campaigns have similar features. Thus, initiative campaigns are not really all that different from other statewide campaigns. What can be noted is that over the last several elections, California voters seemingly have been able to pierce through some of the fog of misleading claims and hyperbole and cast their votes in what they perceive to be their own best self-interest, e.g., for a coastline commission, for the death penalty, against pay TV, against school busing, or for property tax relief.

Voting

CRITICISMS

Critics of the initiative process have emphasized that most voters are woefully uninformed about the host of incredibly complex, lengthy propositions confronting them. The Political Reform Act of 1974 contained more than 22,000 words; it is unlikely that many voters read all (or any) of its various provisions. Other initiatives, such as Governor Reagan's 1973 property tax proposal or the 1978 Jarvis-Gann property tax limit, were highly technical and complicated and, hence, impossible for the average voter to grasp fully.

It is argued that voters have a difficult enough time knowing something about the races at the top of the ticket; expecting them to have informed views on a host of propositions including initiatives at the bottom of the ticket is not realistic. Further reinforcing this view, pollsters have repeatedly noted that there is enormous ignorance and confusion among voters during campaigns dealing with highly publicized and controversial initiatives. For example, as of October 1, 1972, in the midst of the fall election campaign, a Mervin Field Poll (The California Poll, October 26, 1972) noted voter attitudes on the controversial initiatives of that election (see Table 6–2 on page 126). Other surveys of public awareness about initiatives since 1972 have arrived at similar conclusions. One recent study of Washington State voters concluded that 95 percent of voters there were unable to give at least one pro and one con argument on a few key ballot propositions (Bone 1974).

Last, some critics believe some citizens vote for propositions on the basis of their lucky ballot positions such as 7 or 11, or they may vote

126

TABLE 6–2
Initiatives of 1972—Voter attitude

Proposition	Voters with opinions		Voters who were unaware/undecided*
	Yes	No	
Proposition 20 (coastline)	8	4	88
Proposition 14 (tax amendment)	4	3	93
Proposition 18 (obscenity)	5	4	91
Proposition 21 (school busing)	6	4	90
Proposition 22 (farm labor)	5	8	87

* It is interesting to contrast these exceedingly high unawareness/undecided percentages with the national Gallup Poll of September 25 dealing with attitudes toward the presidential candidates. At time, respondents in the Gallup Poll showed the following support figures: Nixon, 61 percent; McGovern, 33 percent; Other, 1 percent; *Undecided, 5 percent.* *San Francisco Chronicle,* October 2, 1972, p. 1.
Source: Mervin Field, *Release,* October 26, 1972.

against 13. Do they tend to favor measures at the top of the proposition list or oppose those at the bottom? Concerns have been voiced by initiative critics that given the absence of party cues, voters will more likely follow the lead of newspaper endorsements.

REBUTTAL

Few supporters of the initiative process would deny that *some* initiatives are long and complex, and voters are faced with a host of difficult voting decisions. Yet, most voters expressing a preference at the top of the ballot do take the time and, evidently, feel competent enough to vote on initiatives at the bottom of the ballot. The more controversial and widely discussed the proposition, the greater the vote cast. In 1972, approximately 8.3 million Californians voted in the presidential election, but nearly 8.1 million also voted that year on the marijuana initiative, and nearly 8 million voted on the death penalty initiative and on the coastline initiative. In 1974, approximately 6.25 million Californians voted in the gubernatorial election, but 5.5 million voted aye or nay on the complicated Stanislaus River initiative. Thus, while there is usually some drop-off in initiative voting, clearly most citizens who vote seem willing (or anxious?) to vote on the various ballot propositions. In June 1978, 6,607,000 votes were cast on Proposition 13—750,000 more than were cast in the gubernatorial primary.

Field polls do indicate there is *usually* a substantial lack of voter awareness about ballot propositions during the campaign. Interestingly, however, most of the public knew about Proposition 13 of 1978, the property tax relief measure, long before the election. Field reported the voter mood on Proposition 13 at several different points in the campaign (see Table 6–3).

One factor helping account for low voter awareness of initiatives

TABLE 6–3
Proposition 13—Voter attitude

Will vote	Feb. 11–23 (percent)	Mar. 27–Apr. 3 (percent)	May 1–8 (percent)	May 29–31 (percent)
Yes	20	27	42	57
No	10	25	39	34
Undecided/ unaware	70	48	19	9

Source: Mervin Field, *Release 975*, June 2, 1978.

during the campaign derives from the typical strategy of an initiative campaign: "Save your campaign money until the last week or two and then spend it all in a last-minute blitz." Additionally, the public receives its *California Voters Pamphlet* just a few weeks prior to the election. It is likely that some voters learn about the initiatives when reading through portions of the pamphlet.

Hence, the Field Poll surveys, while accurately capturing voter unawareness a month or so prior to the election, may be somewhat misleading, since so many voters receive their information on these measures toward the end of the campaign. Finally, does it really matter whether a voter decides two months prior to or the day before the election? The important point is that voters cast an informed ballot.

In further rebutting critics of the initiative, a recent study of ballot proposition voting by Professor John Mueller (1969:1197–1212) found (1) little or no evidence that there was a large bloc of "No" voters who voted against everything; (2) little evidence to support the contention that many voters blindly followed the endorsements of newspapers; and (3) only a slight effect on a proposition's chances depending on its ranking among the various propositions. The overwhelming "Yes" vote on Proposition 13 of June 1978 suggests few voters were deterred by unlucky number 13. Finally, Professor James Gregg (1965:532–38) has found that newspaper endorsements are far more important at the local level than in statewide campaigns.

Legislative failure

Before concluding our discussion of the pros and cons of the initiative, one final summary criticism should be noted. It is asserted that when various groups or individuals are forced to resort to the initiative, the legislature has, in effect, failed. Further pursuing this point, supposedly a prime legislative mission is to resolve group conflict. If a legislature is unable to reconcile group differences and groups must resort to initiatives, the legislature, it is argued, has obviously failed. The inability of the legislature and governor to pass satisfactory property tax relief culminating in the passage of Proposition 13 of 1978, the property tax relief initiative, is a good example. However, in fairness to the legislature, this view of legislative failure seems overly simplistic.

Initiatives develop when a group or groups fail to receive satisfactory legislative action. Issues, such as malpractice—pitting doctors versus lawyers versus insurance companies—or coastline planning—pitting developers, builders, and labor unions against environmentalists—are difficult for the legislature and governor to resolve successfully. Inability to pass satisfactory compromise legislation should not necessarily be construed as failure but may merely reflect the relatively even balance of power of the various contending groups in the legislature. Indeed, no action by the legislature on a particular issue is, in effect, a legislative response. It should also be emphasized that many initiatives are promoted and sponsored by legislators. It is interesting to note that Oregon, Washington, California, Colorado—all states where the initiative is frequently used—have legislatures that rank, according to the Citizens Conference on State Legislatures (Burns 1971), among the very best in the nation. Instead of encouraging irresponsibility and failure to innovate, these surveys suggest that the states where initiatives are used frequently have some of the most innovative and responsive legislatures in the nation.

PROPOSED REFORMS

Not surprisingly, a device as controversial as the initiative that provides citizens (informed or uninformed) with the final say on various vital issues has been the focus of a host of proposed reforms. Some of the proposed reforms have aimed at reducing or eliminating the role of public relations firms in initiative campaigns. For example, former state Senator John Dunlap of Napa proposed that initiative proponents be required to secure signatures in public places as defined by law. Another reform proposal would have required an absolute majority of the total vote cast on the election rather than adoption by a majority of those voting on a specific initiative.

One of the more interesting and, we feel, useful initiative reform proposals is the inspiration of Los Angeles attorney, Nick Brestoff. His proposal would both strengthen the initiative process and provide for fuller public discussion of the measure. The Brestoff (1975) proposal would reform the direct initiative process in several important respects:

1. A group or individual would apply to the attorney general for titling and summary of a measure to be circulated.
2. Signatures would be gathered, and as soon as signatures of one percent of the vote for governor at the last gubernatorial election were collected the names would be submitted to the secretary of state for verification.

3. After verification of the names by the secretary of state, the speaker of the Assembly would give the measure to the appropriate policy committee of the legislature and hearings would be scheduled in six different locations in the state (Los Angeles, Santa Ana, San Diego, San Francisco, Sacramento, and Fresno) and proponents and opponents would be allowed to testify on the measure.

4. Upon completion of these hearings, proponents would have the opportunity to alter or amend their proposal.

5. Initiative backers would then have the attorney general put the proposal into final draft form and the process of securing the remaining number of names necessary to qualify the measure, i.e., 4 percent more for a statute initiative and 7 percent more for constitutional initiative, would commence.

6. Upon securing the required number of names and having them verified, the legislature would conduct hearings strictly limited to 30 days in each house on the initiative.

7. If the legislature chooses, it could adopt the initiative and hence shortcircuit the costly campaign period; or if it rejects the measure, the proposal *would automatically* be presented to the voters for their approval at the next election.

The Brestoff reform proposal would improve the initiative process by allowing for more public discussion of various measures, increasing public understanding of various initiatives, providing for legislative input, and offering initiative backers the chance to have their measure scrutinized by experts. Assigned to committee in 1976, the bill was later dropped by the bill's author, Art Torres, prior to public hearings. People's Lobby opposed the measure, fearing it would involve the legislature more directly in the initiative process.

In addition to the improvements in the initiative process encompassed in the Brestoff proposal, one other reform area should be addressed. Hopefully, a new effort will be made to find the proper formula so the courts will allow spending limits on initiative signature gathering and election campaigns. Perhaps some form of public financing of initiative campaigns could be devised which would, in turn, permit limits on spending.

Before the Court had struck down the campaign spending limits of Proposition 9, the FPPC had established extensive rules and regulations governing spending in initiative campaigns. Time periods were established, and proponents and opponents were limited to fixed amounts during the course of the campaign (to minimize the traditional last-minute blitz). One side could not spend more than $500,000 more than the other side. A format such as the FPPC constructed limiting initiative campaign spending excesses would have been of positive value to improving the tone of an initiative campaign.

SUMMARY

Because of the power of various special interests, the legislature at times has had difficulty reaching satisfactory compromises on highly controversial issues. Without the initiative, California voters would not have realized lobby or campaign reform, would have no coastline commission, nor property tax relief. Moreover, the significance of initiatives cannot be measured solely by the number qualifying and winning approval of the voters.

A threatened initiative, such as People's Lobby's hint that they would circulate an initiative changing the way banks and insurance companies were taxed, led to the legislature's submitting a constitutional amendment on this subject to the voters in 1974. Successful qualifying of the nuclear initiative, the farm worker initiative, and the property tax limitation initiative provided the necessary stimulus to the legislature to pass legislation on these topics to head off the initiative.

Some issues, such as medical malpractice, handgun control, no-fault auto insurance, or abortion, perhaps, cannot be resolved legislatively and hence, may have to be resolved eventually through the initiative process. Also, issues that directly effect the legislature, such as reapportionment or the unicameral proposal, may have to be decided by the initiative.

In summary, the initiative provides a last resort to the public to bypass a stymied or recalcitrant legislature and/or governor. Initiatives do allow for decisive decisions on particularly sensitive, hard-to-resolve issues. Reforms can and should be made in the initiative process to make it work more fairly (for example, the Brestoff proposal and spending limitations). However, we argue the initiative should be retained. It is a deeply engrained feature of the California political scene. While there are trade-offs, the pros outweigh the cons in our minds as to initiative use. In fact, today there is a modest movement underway to establish a national initiative, and this idea, hopefully, will be extensively explored.

Finally, adoption by the voters of Proposition 9—the Political Reform Act of 1974, and Proposition 13—property tax relief, highlight the most important advantage of the initiative: it allows the voters to defy the establishment and to collectively thumb their noses at the powers that be. With both propositions, the major figures of the political establishment came away with "egg on their face." This, we feel, in the last analysis, is a healthy feature. What came to be the motto of the proponents of Proposition 13—"show the politicians who's boss"—certainly is in the spirit of the Progressive surge at the beginning of this century and is a healthy feature of California democracy today.

7

Lobbying: In the "good ole days" and the contemporary setting

From the very first day of the California state legislature's beginning session held in December 1849 in their San Jose temporary quarters to the elegant refurbished capitol of contemporary Sacramento, interest groups and "legislative advocates" (a legal euphemism for lobbyists) have always been an integral part of the California political scene. In fact, according to former President Pro Tem of the Senate Hugh Burns, they existed before the legislature:

> Don't forget that the lobbyists were here [in the State Capital] even before we got here. The history shows us that at one of the first [legislative] sessions [in the state's history] in San Jose, the lobbyists had come to town before the legislative members and had taken up all the rooms in the hotels, and there was no room for the members to stay.
>
> That probably gave rise to the first expression about getting in bed with lobbyists—there was no other place to sleep. (*Sacramento Bee,* July 14, 1969:5)

Indeed, it has been argued with some justification that, for much of California's political history, lobbyists have tended to control the legislature and the rest of the state government as well. While it is true that interest groups and their lobbyist representatives have been active and are influential in all the state capitals and Washington, D.C., there seems little question that California has been and remains a particularly strong lobby state (Zeigler, 1971:127).

Given the sorts of decisions that are made by the legislature, governor, commissions, and state bureaucracy, it is not surprising that businesses, trade associations, labor unions, government employees, and literally hundreds of other groups find it useful to station their agents in the state capital.

Overall, lobbyists perform several critical functions. First, they serve as the eyes and ears for groups of citizens at the state capitol—the watchdog function. Since few in the public can really follow what's going on at the different levels of American national, state, and local government (further complicated by the separation of powers format), lobbyists are employed to help keep track of what is happening and report these activities back to their respective groups. Second, they champion "their" group's interests at the capitol. They attempt to get measures favorable to their group passed and unfavorable measures killed. In doing this, they use a variety of techniques to influence decision makers. Third, they provide information to legislators on pending legislation, or perhaps, suggest to the legislator what the group members' views are. It is important to remember that the right to lobby is, in effect, guaranteed by the First Amendment in the Bill of Rights—the right of citizens to petition their government.

LOBBYING IN HISTORICAL PERSPECTIVE

Southern Pacific era and the Progressive reaction

During the latter part of the 19th century and the first years of the 20th century, Southern Pacific Railroad dominated California government. But sweeping across the country in the early 1900s came the Progressive reform movement which sought to eliminate corruption in government (see Chapter 4). California Progressives fought zealously to eliminate the corrupt power of Southern Pacific from California's state government.

Ironically, special interests have flourished ever since in the political power vacuum created by the Progressive reforms—banks, savings and loans, insurance companies, utilities, title and trust companies, oil interests, agribusiness, mortuaries, liquor, and horsetracks are examples of some of the powerful economic interests of this century.

Artie Samish era

During the 1930s and '40s in California, Artie Samish, a former legislative staff employee, became the dominant lobbyist in California. Physically, Samish was a newspaper cartoonist's dream: the perfect stereotype of how a lobbyist should look—straw hat, large cigar, enormous paunch, and loud tie.

Samish became the most infamous state government lobbyist of his time. With only a modest formal educational background and a short stint as a clerk in the state senate Samish soon went into lobbying. Samish quickly became the king of Sacramento lobbyists and, as his lobbyist reputation grew, other businesses and special interests sought him out to represent them, and this further enhanced Samish's political power. At the height of his power, Samish represented more than a dozen major California interests. Samish's power was so immense that the governor of California, Earl Warren, at one point stated, "On matters that affect his clients, Artie unquestionably has more power than the Governor" (Velie, August 13, 1949:13). Samish could raise enormous sums from his grateful clients to bankroll campaigns (in what he called his "select and elect" system) and to "wine and dine" and provide other amenities to public officials. Samish understood the legislative process, had many influential friends, represented many wealthy interests, and had a network of paid tipsters. No wonder he was such a formidable power.

Post-Samish period

Lobby reform characterizes the post-Samish era from 1951 to the present. The lurid, corrupt overtones and flamboyance of the Samish era are today largely gone. Contemporary lobbying is more honest and today's lobbyists more businesslike. No contemporary lobbyist has the dominant power Samish had in the 1940s. Nevertheless, those who follow Sacramento politics would undoubtedly agree that a skilled, professional lobbyist such as Dugald Gillies, representing the California Real Estate Association and others have considerable influence today in subject matter areas that affect their clients. Clearly, too, special interest groups such as Pacific Telephone, Pacific Gas and Electric, Sierra Club, California State Employees' Association, Bank of America, Santa Anita Race Track, California Teacher's Association, the Automobile Dealers Association, and hosts of others have an important impact on policy decisions.

In the next section, we shall consider why lobbies and special interests have had such a strong impact on California state government, and in the following section, we shall discuss how reformers in this state have attempted to cope with special interest power.

REASONS FOR STRONG LOBBIES

By establishing rules, regulations, and taxing policy, state government has always had a strong influence over certain kinds of businesses: banks, insurance companies, mortuaries, dairies, petroleum industries, liquor interests, horsetracks, agribusiness, real estate, construction, and land development. Moreover, many of these groups have actively sought government regulation to protect themselves from competition. These interests, and others, have found it vitally important to be represented in

Sacramento. Historically, five key factors contribute to the strong lobby nature of California politics: (1) Progressive reforms weakening political parties, (2) coterminous development of statehood and lobbies in the western states, (3) the nonprofessional quality of the pre-1966 California Legislature, (4) low public visibility, and (5) campaign contributions.

Progressive reforms

Progressive reforms such as: cross-filing, civil service, prohibitions on political parties making primary endorsements, and the direct democracy devices served to weaken political parties and, concomitantly, encourage special interests. Thus, weak political parties meant that most legislators would look elsewhere for election support and voting cues— the lobbies. Special interests using the initiative process could also hire professional campaign management firms to collect signatures and run their initiative campaigns if the legislature should be unresponsive. Ironically, Progressive reforms designed, in part at least, to curb special interest power often serve to augment their influence.

Coterminous development

The industrial revolution and the development of corporate America occurred during the same period of time that western territories were attaining statehood. As Harmon Zeigler and Michael Baer (1969:37) note:

> In the western states, however, political systems and interest groups developed simultaneously. Interest groups did not have to fight existing political institutions; they shared in the development of the political system; lobbyists and politicians "grew up" together. Furthermore, the political traditions of the western states—nonpartisanship, open primaries, a high rate of participation—invite interest groups (along with everybody else) to compete for the stakes of politics.

Nonprofessional legislature

Another important historical factor helping account for the lobbyists' considerable influence was the amateurish status of the California legislature (see Chapter 9). Through 1966, the California legislature was a nonprofessional, part-time institution. California state legislators were poorly paid, inadequately officed, and understaffed. Indeed, this was the situation in every state legislature in the country at the time. Moreover, some contemporary state legislatures are still strictly nonprofessional. For example, New Hampshire continues to pay its state legislators $100 per year; Massachusetts still does not provide offices for its rank and file members; and a great many contemporary state legislatures have virtually no professional staff. Let us consider some of the major dimensions of nonprofessional legislatures.

LOW PAY

Prior to its modernization, the California legislature met biennially. Once every two years California legislators would journey to Sacramento for a four- to five-month legislative session, and then they would return home after final adjournment to their regular jobs—practicing law, farming, running their businesses, and the like—for the remainder of the year and the following year. During even-numbered years ("off-years"), legislators were sometimes called back to Sacramento for special sessions, or they might be assigned interim committee hearings.[1] When the legislature was out of session, lawmakers performed traditional constituent duties in their spare time back in the district. Excluding their modest basic salary, the only fringe benefit provided California legislators was a single round-trip to Sacramento. The meager legislative salary lawmakers earned could not possibly cover their living expenses while in Sacramento, trips back to the district, house payments or rent, food, clothing, and miscellaneous other expenses. Those who were personally wealthy could afford to serve but, since most legislators were not, they had to seek other sources of income.

Through the 1940s, the California legislature operated under a curious pay system. Legislators were paid $1,200 in the off-year for doing very little legislative work and then paid the same amount during the regular session for doing a great deal of work. The $1,200 annual salary was doled out $12 per day while the legislature was in session, and after 100 days, legislators' salaries were exhausted. Thus, while legislators were receiving their last $12 payment in mid-May, they were not infrequently confronted with a legislative session that might stretch into late June (Buchanan, 1965:20). The motivation behind this pay scheme was that if salaries were cut off, there would be more incentive for legislators to wind up their session and go home.

The meager legislative pay served more as a token of civic gratitude than as a living wage. The view was that the public-spirited citizens who ran for the legislature were, in effect, donating their services in much the same manner that most city council members, school board members, or planning commission members do currently. Some legislators served only a few terms and then "graduated" into the lobbyist ranks and tripled or quadrupled their former legislative salaries. Others returned to their previous occupation to recoup their losses and some ran for higher office.

The imaginative techniques employed by legislators to survive financially in the "good ole' days" became legendary. Some economized by renting rooms at down-trodden Sacramento hotels. One legislator used to save money by hitchhiking back and forth to his Los Angeles con-

---

[1] Between 1948 and 1964, they would meet for at least a one-month budget session in the even-numbered year.

stituency. Others sold their state code volumes to local book stores for extra cash.

But, of course, the normal and accepted means many legislators used to survive financially in this earlier period was to live off the lobbyists. Indeed, a few of the less scrupulous legislators not only survived financially but prospered. Some lobbyists (not all by any means) were more than willing to pay for hotel bills, buy meals and drinks, take legislators on expensive travel junkets, provide tickets to sporting events, or give them gifts of money. Rather than returning to their empty hotel rooms after a long, arduous day at the capitol, many legislators, not surprisingly, found it more appealing to have lobbyists take them out for an evening on the town. Bars and restaurants near the state capitol did a booming lunch and dinner business during those years. The Derby Club, Moosemilk, the Caboose Club, and other regular luncheon meetings of lobbyists and legislators became Sacramento institutions. Additionally, a few lobbyists were known to provide female companionship for some of the temporary-bachelor legislators.

In the 1940s, Artie Samish paid his top staffers $3–4,000 per month as

ILLUSTRATION 7–1
The Cattle Pack, a California cattleman's lobby, hosts lawmakers at an annual breakfast Meeting with legislators at meal time is a traditional lobbying technique.

Photo courtesy Sacramento Bee

contrasted to a legislator's $1,200 *annual* salary! At the height of his powers, Samish did not even bother to go to the state capitol building to testify before committees or buttonhole legislators. Instead, legislators would come to Artie Samish. He would host lavish luncheon buffets daily in his hotel suite and would serve the finest wines, liquor, and gourmet food to legislators. After lunch, there would be card games for interested legislators and lobbyists. While the unofficial rule at lobbyist-legislator social gatherings was that legislative business was not to be discussed, it inevitably did creep into some of the discussions. At the very least, this socializing provided the Third House agents greater access to legislators than that available to lobbyists who could not afford to entertain and helped pave the way to lasting friendships. At its worst, social lobbying may have bought some legislators' votes.

Shrewd lobbyists could direct legal business to a lawyer-legislator's law office, buy insurance from an insurance agent-legislator, invest in real estate from a real estate broker-legislator, or do business with a business-owner–legislator. A favorite device of savings and loans banks was to place local legislators on their board of directors. It provided the bank with increased status and gave the legislator extra income with a minimal amount of work.

In the last analysis, of course, it is impossible to detail comprehensively the endless ways lobbyists influenced poorly paid legislators. Many lobbyists successfully tried to ingratiate themselves with the legislator's staff—particularly the secretaries—by taking them to lunch or giving them gifts. Skillful lobbyists quickly discovered where a particular legislator's interests were—sports, dining, hunting, golfing, cards, drinking, and the like—and would then try to capitalize on them.

INADEQUATE FACILITIES

In the early years, California legislators did not have private offices. Many legislators used their desk on the floor to conduct legislative chores—dictating letters, reading mail, discussing bills with lobbyists, being interviewed by reporters, or chatting with visiting constituents. In all this hubbub, visiting student groups from various junior high and high schools of California would be ushered into the visitors galleries and be duly recognized by the presiding officer. Experienced lobbyists thrived in this bedlam. Bills could be killed or amended or lost in this confusion, and few would know the difference.

LACK OF STAFF

Lobbyists were not only friends and confidants of legislators, they were also prime sources of information. Since legislators could not possibly be expert on all the various subjects with which they had to deal, lobbyists provided legislators with this much needed information. Lobbyists helped draft legislation or provided questions sympathetic legislators might use at committee hearings. Freshmen legislators were particularly grateful to lobbyists who asked them to carry a bill (i.e., to be its author), since this was the way they established a legislative record.

Low public visibility

Up to the last decade or two, the major metropolitan dailies of California tended to give short shrift to Sacramento doings. The major metropolitan papers preferred to concentrate their efforts on national or international news along with a heavy smattering of local news—but paid little attention to state politics. Sacramento tended to be viewed by the major metropolitan newspapers and their readers as a hot, dusty valley town with few cultural refinements, inhabited primarily by political hacks, local satraps, and faceless bureaucrats. And, it was.

Reporters assigned to the Sacramento beat tended to be lethargic—certainly not prone to the sort of Watergate investigative reporting of Woodward and Bernstein. Sacramento reporters usually traveled in the same capitol social circles as legislators and lobbyists, and so were part of the same "good old boy" syndrome. Indeed, until just a few years ago, newspapers were given rent-free office space in the capitol rotunda, and some legislative leaders felt that, given these circumstances, reporters should not be too critical—"Don't bite the hand that feeds you."

The closed, secretive nature of the legislative system of this bygone era further played into the hands of the lobbyists. On the senate side, committee chairs were able to control action of their committees and either pass along or kill bills arbitrarily. Not surprisingly, lobbyists would often concentrate their efforts on the upper house, because it was smaller, its power more diffused, turnover minimal, and partisanship imperceptible. In both houses, committees frequently met in executive session (closed), and, in addition, there was no official record kept of committee votes.

In most cases, lobbyists asked a legislator for just a few votes each year. These were usually technical bills on esoteric subjects where there was little public opinion but which might mean millions to one's clients. This is how one author (Berg et al., 1976:146) described the process:

> If, for example, a lobbyist needs a "no" vote on a bill before a particular legislative committee, he or she drops by the office of those members who are . . . friends and explains the bill in one or two sentences. The lobbyist asks if the legislator is getting any mail on the subject, and wonders in a seemingly questioning way whether a "no" vote would hurt the legislator back home. When it is clear that there has been little or no mail on the

subject (generally only a handful of bills in each session generate the mail), the lobbyist says, "This one means a lot to my principals. If I don't beat it I'll lose the account (or my job). I'd personally appreciate it if you can give me a vote. And I'll let our people in your district know how helpful you've been to us and make sure they give you some help (that's money) in your next campaign.

Campaign contributions

As noted in Chapters 4 and 5, special interests have been and continue to be major contributors to politicians' campaigns. Many lobbyists, or the groups they represented, invariably gave sizable sums to incumbents

ILLUSTRATION 7–2

BEHIND THE GREEN DOOR

Dennis Renault, Sacramento Bee

(who are usually sure winners) as a sort of investment. A regular feature of the Sacramento social scene are legislators who host lavish testimonial dinners at $50 or $100 or $250 a ticket. Lobbyists were expected to buy blocks of tickets and make sure the honored legislator saw them in attendance. The lobbyist role in providing campaign contributions is a subject of some controversy today and is discussed in the following section.

LOBBY REFORM

Given the unbridled power and influence of the Third House in Sacramento, it is not surprising that there have been periodic attempts to reform the special interests and lobbyists. Four reform periods stand out: (1) the Progressive era, (2) the Samish scandal aftermath, (3) the Unruh legislative modernization drive, and (4) the post-Watergate period.

There is little doubt that the style of contemporary lobbying is different from earlier lobbying; however, there is considerable dispute as to whether the stylistic changes that have taken place have *really* made any significant differences. In other words, do wealthy special interests and large mass membership organizations exert the same kind of influence over legislators and administrators currently that they did historically?

Lobby reform—Progressive period

As we noted, the Progressives early in this century made the first concerted attempt to limit special interest influence. For example, the Progressives placed in the constitution a prohibition on any transport company (Southern Pacific was the obvious target) giving any public official a free ride (no pun intended). They also established a state railroad commission to set rates charged by Southern Pacific and other public utilities. The Progressive reform ire, though, was directed more towards political parties, politicians, and special interests rather than toward lobbyists per se. The impetus to control lobbyists came some 40 years later in the wake of the Samish revelations.

Lobby reform—Samish aftermath

In 1949, *Collier's Magazine* published a classic in muckraking journalism, "The Secret Boss of California" (Velie, 1949). The article, based on a freely given interview with the then-notorious California lobbyist, Artie Samish, described how Samish exerted influence over the state legislature and state bureaucracy. Included within the text of the article was a famous color photograph of the gargantuan Artie Samish seated in a chair

ILLUSTRATION 7–3
Artie Samish and "Mr. Legislature"

Photograph by Fred Lyon, *Collier's Magazine,* August 13, 1949. © 1949 by Crowell-Collier Publishing Co.

with "Mr. Legislature," a wooden puppet, being manipulated by Samish. "Said the big man: And how are you today, Mr. Legislature?" Another color photograph showed Artie in his lounging robe smoking a large black cigar, talking on the telephone. His menacing, baleful stare looks today like a studio publicity shot for a 1930s Hollywood gangster movie.

The *Collier's* series for the first time brought to the attention of the California public the behind-the-scenes stranglehold Artie held over state government. After publication of this article, there was a great public outcry and clamor for reform of the lobbying process.

Responding to the Samish scandal Governor Warren commented that, "Disruptable lobbying practices are impairing the efficiency of state government and besmirching the creditable work of the vast majority of our legislators, offices and employees" (Samish, 1959). Governor Warren pushed for lobby reforms including:

1. Lobbyists would report all financial transactions with state elective officeholders.
2. Groups hiring lobbyists would file periodic expense statements.
3. No contingency lobbying (payment only for success) would be allowed.
4. No lawyer-legislators could represent clients before administrative agencies.

Even with the public outcry over Samish, the legislature refused to support Warren's proposals. Legislators and lobbyists have always had a close, symbiotic relationship in California. Many legislators were particularly critical of point 4 above.

In 1949, the legislature passed the Collier Act (named after its author John Collier, not the magazine) which was patterned after the Federal Regulation of Lobbying Act. The Collier Act required lobbyists to register, file monthly financial reports of contributions and expenditures over $10, and list the bills they were supporting or opposing. Because of the confusion in implementing the Collier Act, a year later (1950) the Ervin Act was passed to strengthen and clarify the Collier Act provisions. The Ervin Act required the disclosure of employment of legislators by lobbyists, the prohibition of contingency lobbying, and the establishment of a joint committee to administer the new rules. In 1951, Samish was indicted, convicted of income tax evasion, and sentenced to federal prison.

While the Collier and Ervin Acts may have been of some modest help in opening up the lobby process, in fact, little really changed. The Collier and Ervin Acts were not really regulatory but rather focused on disclosure. "Lobbying" was never defined in the acts. Some lobbyists, in fact, argued that they were not actually lobbyists but were merely governmental representatives for their group, or public relations specialists, or interest group executives. Many who did register provided only the barest of details of their financial dealings, and those who were scrupulous found their reports edited with key sections deleted. Moreover, there was very little interest by those officials in charge of enforcing the law to go after violators vigorously. The annual report of lobbyist spending required by the Collier Act was a compendium of miscellania useless to reporters or scholars trying to understand or discern lobby spending patterns.

Lobby reform—Unruh period

PROPOSITION 1A

In November 1966, California voters approved several major constitutional amendments (Proposition 1A) that significantly changed the legislative process. These amendments gave the legislature authority to set its own session length and salary schedule.

While Proposition 1A did not deal directly with lobby reform, the impact of these changes was keenly felt in the Third House. The then-Speaker of the Assembly, Jess Unruh, argued that passage of 1A would help restore the prestige and dignity of the legislature. Unruh contended that poorly paid legislators were fair game for lobbyists. Lobbyists could influence lawmakers if legislators were dependent upon them for meals, drinks, and other expenses. If legislators were paid reasonable salaries, better educated, more competent citizens would run for the legislature, and they would be better equipped to stand up to the lobbyists. Higher legislative salaries would mean that lawmakers would be freed from depending upon their original occupations to sustain them, and there would be less need for special interests to hire legislator-lawyers or retainers. Full-time legislators would be able to devote their complete attention to complex legislative issues.

Since the approval of Proposition 1A, legislators' salaries have climbed steadily to $25,233. The increased pay, coupled with their other fringe benefits—$46 per diem (tax-free), car-leasing arrangement, and gas and telephone credit cards—make the contemporary legislators' lifestyle quite different from their predecessors.

In addition, the passage of Proposition 1A has affected legislators and lobbyists in several other ways. First, since the legislature began meeting year-round, some legislators, and many lobbyists as well, have found it more convenient to move their families to Sacramento. This has meant fewer lobbyist-legislator dinner outings. Moreover, jet travel allows legislators to commute back and forth to Sacramento and home more easily.

As better educated, more politically astute legislators began to get elected after the passage of Proposition 1A, lobbyists have had to change their *modus operandi* in order to relate to this new breed of legislators. The new breed was far more likely to be influenced by lobbyists with expertise in a subject matter area rather than simply an unlimited checking account. Passage of Proposition 1A meant that legislators no longer *needed* to have lobbyists pay for meals, drinks, and other expenses. While the practice of lobbyists picking up tabs continued, the dependency relationship had been altered. The development of a professionalized legislature meant the concomitant development of a professionalized lobby corps.

Prior to 1966, many legislators had been anxious to "graduate" into the lobby ranks in order to make a more respectable salary. Now, the pendulum seems to be swinging slightly in the other direction. A number of lobbyists have attempted to get elected to the legislature (Wayne Carrouthers, CTA or Bud Porter, San Diego County), and several have succeeded (Frank Vicenzia, Milk and Mass Transit; or Leona Egeland, Zero Population Growth). Indeed, one legislator, Senator Bill Campbell, went from legislator to lobbyist and then back to legislator. While a few recent legislators, such as former Assembly member Frank Murphy or former State Senator Clare Berryhill, have voluntarily retired from the legislature and become lobbyists, not as many seem to choose this path voluntarily today.

Clearly, legislators have become the dominant partner in the legislator/lobbyist relationship. Indeed, symbolic of this shift in power in the late 1960s, a new informal legislative subgroup was formed, a sort of liberal Democratic assembly subcaucus. The name they adopted, "Micemilk," was a direct take-off of the lobbyist-sponsored Moosemilk luncheon buffet. Micemilk members tended to be more independent from the Third House. Lobbyists, who in earlier years had been deferred to by many legislators, came to be treated more casually and with more indifference. While lobbies were still critical in funding campaigns, no one lobby could beat a legislator. Increasing numbers of legislators in the majority and minority parties looked to the legislative leaders of their respective parties for campaign contributions, not just the lobbies. Lobbyists came to need legislators as much as legislators needed lobbyists.

PROFESSIONAL STAFF

Prior to the Unruh years (primarily the 1960s), the California legislature had a small staff. Unruh, in promoting a professional modernized legislature, argued strongly for additional staff. During his tenure as speaker, the assembly added many committee consultants, an Office of Research, personal assistants, and party staff. Instead of relying solely on lobbyists for expertise, legislators now had a new, more neutral source of information.

PARTISANSHIP

Unruh also championed a more partisan legislature. During his speakership years, majority and minority consultants and party leadership staff were added to complement the other assembly professional staff. Majority and minority caucuses became more important, and party voting began to appear. Heightened legislative party discipline meant that legislators would not have to be so dependent on lobbyists for voting cues. Taking its lead from the assembly, the California Senate has also become more professionalized in the intervening years.

REAPPORTIONMENT

One further reform affecting lobby patterns occurred in the California legislature of the 1960s—reapportionment. In 1965, the U.S. Supreme Court ruled in *Reynolds* v. *Simms* that both the lower *and upper* houses of American state legislatures were to be apportioned only on the basis of population (the famous "one man, one vote" decision.)

In 1965, the California State Senate ranked as one of the most malapportioned legislative bodies in the nation. For example, Los Angeles County with nearly 7 million residents had one state senator, while three sparsely populated desert and mountain counties, Alpine, Inyo, and Mono, with a combined population of approximately 14,000 also had one senator.

Prior to 1966, many of Sacramento's more influential lobbyists tended to concentrate their lobbying efforts on the upper house. Since most special interest lobbyists tended to be defensive, i.e., fending off attacks on their groups, it was more convenient to work with a few key senators in killing assembly-sponsored measures. Moreover, some of the key lobbyists were ex-legislators who had been legislative classmates of some of the incumbent senators. Powerful northern rural senators held a stranglehold over committees dealing with urban problems. Since the northern rural senators received little district input on these issues, they could trade favors with lobbyists on bills helping their districts, and, given the small population size of these northern rural districts, a modest campaign contribution in a relatively low cost campaign could be crucial. In fairness, though, many of these northern senators were among the most fiercely independent, incorruptible legislators the capital has ever seen! Today, both houses of the legislature are apportioned on the basis of population.

Lobby reform—Post-Watergate

PROPOSITION 9

The most recent development in legislator-lobbyist relations has come with the adoption of the 1974 Political Reform Act, Proposition 9, by the voters. Proposition 9 is an omnibus reform measure dealing with several different reform areas including lobbying. It affects the lobbying process directly and indirectly.

Overall, Proposition 9 aimed at requiring lobbyists, legislators, and administrators to provide much more extensive information about their dealings (particularly financial) *and* also sought to reduce the influence of wealthy, special interests at the state capitol.

Proposition 9, it should be noted, was an initiative generated, in part, by the Watergate scandal and also by rumors—real or imagined—of corruption at the state level. While a number of bills dealing with governmental reform has been introduced in the California legislature in the early 1970s, such as public financing of campaigns, greater disclosure requirements for campaign income and outgo, or conflict of interest measures, these bills were not greeted with enthusiasm by most legislators. Virtually all were killed or stalled in committee. Finally, in frustration, the reform forces decided the California legislature was either unable or unwilling to act and, hence, an initiative was required.

Proposition 9 was opposed by many of the most powerful political interests in the state including: the AFL-CIO, Teamsters, California Medical Association, Building Trades Council, Taxpayers' Association, Real Estate Association, Growers Association, Chamber of Commerce, Farm Bureau, United Professors, State Employees Association, the Executive Committees of the Democratic and Republican State Central Committees, Young Democrats, Republican Women, and even the central committee of the Los Angeles County Peace and Freedom Party. Many other special interests would have joined the anti-Proposition 9 forces, but they felt it was hopeless to oppose a "motherhood"-type measure in the post-Watergate period and were convinced that any public effort in opposition to Proposition 9 might be interpreted as special interest plotting. In any case, opposition to the reform measure proved futile; voters gave overwhelming approval to Proposition 9 by a nearly 3 to 1 margin (it received a majority vote in all 58 California counties).

Included among the key features of Proposition 9 are: (1) *all* lobbyists are required to register (the Fair Political Practices Commission established a definition of lobbying based on time spent attempting to influence public officials and compensation received); (2) lobbyists can spend no more than $10 per month per public official—legislator, staff member, administrator, or commissioner; (3) detailed reports must be filed periodically with the Secretary of State's Office and the Fair Political Practices Commission dealing with who has been lobbied, subjects discussed, and how much has been spent; (4) Proposition 9 prohibited *lobbyists* from contributing money to state political campaigns[2] and (5) the Fair Political Practices Commission has overall responsibility for enforcing the Reform Act.

Additionally, several other reform features of Proposition 9 impinge indirectly on lobbyists and special interests. There is a tough new *campaign disclosure* law requiring candidates to file regular spending reports on all contributions and expenditures twice during the campaign and once after the election. There is a new set of conflict-of-interest regulations. All state public officials are required to disclose annually all of their income.

Since voter approval of Proposition 9 in June 1974, lobbyists have adopted several different strategies to cope with Proposition 9. The overwhelming majority of lobbyists have grudgingly accepted Proposition 9

---

[2] In the original language of Proposition 9, lobbyists were prohibited from even discussing with their employers which legislators should receive campaign contributions or how much they should receive. This feature has since been struck down by the court.

as a *fait accompli,* and they have been anxious and concerned about not violating any of the new rules or regulations.

A number of key lobbyists have joined together in a new organization of lobbyists, the Institute of Governmental Advocates, to fight Proposition 9 in the courts. One of their first victories came when the courts struck down the prohibition on lobbyists conferring with their clients on campaign contributions. Recently, in an even more important decision, the state supreme court struck the prohibition against lobbyists contributing to campaigns. This decision was appealed to the U.S. Supreme Court, which refused to accept the case. In effect, this upheld the state court decision.

A few lobbyists and special interests have probed for loopholes in the law. Thus, it would be difficult to keep track of the $10 gifting limit of lobbyists if they paid with cash rather than a credit card at a restaurant. Interest group executives can entertain legislators lavishly without the budgetary restrictions of the lobbyists. Finally, whether lobbyists may or may not be able to make campaign contributions, the groups that employ them can, and hence any such prohibition seems a token gesture. Clearly, there probably always will be ways for the opportunistic or devious to get around such laws.

Hence, the debate on Proposition 9 continues. Let's consider some of the major pros and cons of the Reform Act as it relates to lobbying.

CRITICS

Opponents contend that the $10 monthly limitation on lobbyist spending is meaningless or worse—insulting. They argue that only the naive would believe that legislators' votes are exchanged for dinners, drinks, or other gratuities. It is argued, too, that the limitation has impeded the lobbyist-legislator exchange of ideas. Prior to Proposition 9, legislators and lobbyists met at local restaurants and discussed matters in a convivial setting away from ringing phones and endless interruptions; today, critics charge, important and useful lobbyist expertise input has been reduced in the new setting. Some have argued that the law restricts many ethical lobbyists while providing opportunities for the unscrupulous.

In enforcing the $10 limit, the Fair Political Practices Commission has run into a score of practical problems ranging from the sublime to the ridiculous:

1. Must a lobbyist whose young daughter is invited next door to a legislator's daughter's birthday party report the gift on the reporting forms?
2. Does a male lobbyist have to report gifts he gives to his wife if she is a member of the legislative staff?
3. Must lobbyists report that they invited a legislator, perhaps a longtime friend, to their house for dinner?

Not surprisingly, many lobbyists and legislators resented the Proposition 9 intrusions into their private lives.

Proposition 9 critics also argued that to deny lobbyists the opportunity to contribute to political campaigns violated a basic constitutional right of freedom of expression. Furthermore, forbidding lobbyist-client discussions on which candidates should get campaign contributions, though also struck down by the Supreme Court, is nonetheless, outrageous and completely unenforceable. Under Proposition 9, political action committees of various special interests could make campaign contributions, but lobbyists were to be prevented from making them. Critics of the act argue then that nothing really changed. If a lobbyist for a group, such as the CSEA (California State Employees Association), visits a legislator's office seeking support for a particular bill, the legislator is keenly aware whether this particular group has been generous in the past or might be generous in the future. While lobbyists were no longer pressured to buy tickets to legislators' testimonial dinners, lobbyists' clients could buy their lobbyists' tickets to the affair—nothing had changed. Now that the court has struck down the prohibition on lobbyist contributions, lobbyists' mails will be filled with ticket requests to fund raisers once again.

Finally, critics of Proposition 9 focus on the alleged "police state," "big brother is watching you" syndrome created by the act. An annual audit of lobbyists, it is argued, is excessive. The Fair Political Practices Commission, it is charged, is yet another layer of bureaucracy. Worse though, these unelected commissioners tell elected representatives how they should act. As one might expect, there have been repeated run-ins between the commission, on the one hand, and legislators and lobbyists on the other. Drafting rules and regulations implementing Proposition 9 has not been easy. Conflict of interest issues, campaign expenditure reporting, legislative staff involvement in campaigns, campaign procedures, and a myriad of other issues have frequently pitted the FPPC against candidates, officeholders, staffers, administrators, and lobbyists. The claim is made that there is an implicit assumption in Proposition 9 that many legislators, staff members, administrators, and lobbyists are guilty of all sorts of wrongdoings but, in reality, only a very small minority are.

Finally, critics charge that the FPPC requires too much paperwork. Indeed, spokespersons for many of the groups supposedly helped by the reforms of Proposition 9—the League of Women Voters, the PTA and the Sierra Club—have complained that the extensive paperwork entailed in Proposition 9 has worked to their disadvantage. Wealthy groups have the staff or can hire professional accountants to keep track of lobby expenses and fill out the complicated forms; poorer groups do not have this ability.

SUPPORTERS

Proponents would concede there have been some problems in administering the act, but they would argue there are similar problems in implementing any major, complex piece of legislation. Establishing rules and guidelines and dealing with problems of administration never contemplated by the authors of the act are always difficult. For the most part, the FPPC has succeeded, its supporters would argue. Guidelines and rules have been established, compliance achieved, and legislators and lobbyists have learned to live with it. Indeed, Dan Lowenstein, former FPPC Chairperson, is concerned that lobbyists have become so used to the act and its various provisions that it may no longer have the impact and vitality that it once did.

Above all, supporters of Proposition 9 would contend that the act has greatly helped improve the style and tone of lobbying in Sacramento. The extensive entertaining, posh excursions, and lavish gifting have been substantially reduced. Proponents of the act argue that the $10 limitation is strict but reasonable (it still should buy a legislator's lunch or dinner once a month). The $10 limit has helped change access patterns. The big expense-account lobbyists have reduced opportunities to gain influence because of their extensive gifting.

Reform backers argue there is no attempt in Proposition 9 to muzzle lobbyists or reduce legislator-lobbyist interaction as its critics argue. Even if Lobbyist X's $10 minimum has been expended for the month on a legislator, the lobbyist can still have long discussions at lunch or dinner —the only difference is that each would have to pay for his or her own check. Indeed, some legislators seem to prefer it this way, since going "Dutch Treat" saves the lobbyist inordinate time filling out forms and saves the legislator from potential problems with election challengers. In any case, it would seem that whatever initial fears legislators may have had about being listed on these forms has been dispelled. The FPPC reports hundreds of thousands of dollars have been spent by lobbyists over the last several years entertaining legislators, staffers, and administrators.

Proponents of Proposition 9 would probably concede that the prohibition against lobbyists making campaign contributions struck down by the state court had been of limited value in evening the balance between interest groups. However, if nothing else, the Reform Act made the lobbyist's role in campaign funding a little more indirect. Furthermore, it is likely that contract lobbyists (professional advocates representing several clients) were slightly less influential when they could not contribute to campaigns. For example, before Proposition 9's adoption, a lobbyist representing, for example, Santa Anita Race Track and the School Boards

Association could contribute substantial campaign contributions to various candidates from money provided by the horsetracks. This could, in effect, "buy" him access for his other client, the School Boards Association, in a sort of "halo" effect.

Finally, are the various interest groups on a more equal footing now that Proposition 9 is the law? There is no question that "public interest" groups such as Common Cause, the People's Lobby, the Sierra Club, the Planning and Conservation League, the League of Women Voters, and consumer groups have more impact on policy than they had formerly. The various reforms that we have noted, and in particular the Political Reform Act, have helped contribute to this new balance. In addition, some special interests such as utilities, petroleum interests, or the auto industry have had recent image problems because of high prices, shoddy products, and excessive profits. The reputation of these special interests has been tarnished in the public mind and "good-guy" lobbyists such as Ralph Nader or Common Cause have benefited but, clearly, the pendulum never stops. Groups out of favor in one decade may be back in favor the next.

The lobby reforms that have taken place over the last several decades have made contemporary lobbying in Sacramento a much more professional and reputable endeavor. Undoubtedly, the style of lobbying has changed, and the substance of lobbying has also changed to a limited extent. Clearly, interest groups and their lobbyist agents have a right and obligation to promote the governmental goals of their respective groups. Hopefully, new groups representing underrepresented interests will begin lobbying and, of equal importance, hopefully political clout will rest on a variety of factors, not simply monetary resources, in the years ahead. Overall, the various lobby reforms we have described have improved the ethical tone of lobbying.

THE LOBBYISTS

Background

Few contemporary lobbyists knew early in their careers that they would wind up as legislative advocates. There is no prelobby undergraduate major, any graduate school training for aspiring lobbyists, or even an apprenticeship program. Rather, the people who become lobbyists invariably wind up there by chance or accident. Certainly, in the public mind, politicians are viewed suspiciously, but lobbyists have an even more notorious reputation. This is unfortunate, since most contemporary lobbyists are bright, well-educated professionals who are honest and ethical.

Essentially, people gravitate into the lobby ranks from two prime sources: (1) from within the governmental milieu, or (2) from within the particular interest group, business, or trade association. The standard stereotype of a lobbyist in the public mind is the aging ex-legislator who has been hired by a particular interest group because of former friendships and contacts in the legislature. This is seldom correct.

GOVERNMENTAL MILIEU

Currently, several dozen ex-legislators and an assortment of other ex-officeholders serve as lobbyists for various interests in Sacramento. For the most part, ex-officeholders become lobbyists not voluntarily, but because they have lost elections but still have connections. While ex-legislator lobbyists comprise a small portion of the total number in the lobby corps, we should emphasize that these advocates tend to be contract lobbyists associated with lobby firms normally representing a number of clients of key special interests. Obviously, the ex-legislator lobbyist can trade on his or her friendships with former legislative colleagues through intimate knowledge of the legislative process. It should be noted that because of the rapid turnover in legislative membership and the periodic reshuffling of administrative posts, the ex-legislator lobbyist cannot trade very long on old friendships.

Other lobbyists coming from within the governmental milieu include ex-legislative staffers, former bureaucrats from different executive departments, and student interns. Some enterprising individuals have persuaded key legislators to suggest to an interest group looking for a lobbyist that they would be excellent choices. A strong recommendation from Committee Chair X that Group Y should hire Lobbyist Z is not casually overlooked. Lobbyists coming from within the governmental milieu easily comprise several hundred of the more than 600-plus Sacramento lobbyists—but they are still a distinct minority of the total lobbyist membership.

GROUP MILIEU

The great majority of lobbyists attain their positions from within the group they represent. Many corporations have public affairs divisions staffed by attorneys who represent them in Sacramento. Employees with skills in public relations, politics, sales, or advertising are obvious possibilities. Some corporations or businesses assign key executives to their Sacramento beat. Individuals going into lobbying from within a corporation, business, trade association, or public interest usually represent that single client, though a few have branched out into contract lobbying after a successful initial period with a single client. Generally speaking, the major asset lobbyists offer to legislators and administrators in this category is expertise. They are steeped in the knowledge of their business or trade association.

The job—Salaries and workload

It is difficult to generalize about the salaries of lobbyists, since they vary considerably. A few, such as "Judge" James Garibaldi, may make more than $100,000 a year lobbying, while a few others (for example, the lobbyist for the League of Women Voters) receive no salary and virtually no expense money. Generally, most California lobbyists are paid about as well, if not somewhat better, than California state legislators.

To earn their salaries, most lobbyists put in long, tiring days, especially when the legislature is in session. They must keep track of countless details. A typical morning of an average lobbyist might include: an early trip to the Bill Room to pick up the amended versions of several bills he or she is following; a hurried discussion with a legislator in the hallway about a bill coming before that legislator's committee; a walk over to one's office to check the mail, answering some telephone calls, editing the group's newsletter due to be sent; confering with group executives on pending legislation; a short coffee break with a fellow lobbyist to discuss testimony for an afternoon committee hearing; a deadly dull Senate Finance Committee hearing; and lastly, lunch with a committee consultant to discuss a bill that the committee consultant's boss, the committee chair, will soon be introducing.

Then comes the afternoon. . . .

Most lobbyists seem to enjoy their work. It is financially rewarding, meaningful, important, and provides reasonable job security. For the most part, there is an unwritten rule among lobbyists that once a lobbyist has secured a client, other lobbyists are expected not to try to win that client away. The emergence of the new high-powered, professional lobby firms anxious to secure new clients probably means the beginning of a more competitive situation. Thus, there have been a growing number of occasions when an interest group has dropped one lobbyist and hired another to further their legislative goals (Hockenson, 1977).

Types of lobbyists

Presently, there are approximately 600 registered lobbyists in Sacramento who, in turn, represent some 650 different groups. Some groups are represented by many lobbyists. Pacific Gas and Electric has 22 lobbyists; San Diego Gas and Electric, 16; Southern California Edison, 14; Standard Oil, 16; Chamber of Commerce, 12; and County Supervisors, 12. On the other hand, some lobby firms may represent 15 to 20 different interests.[3]

---

[3] For example, the Robert Beckus lobby firm, California Advocates Incorporated, represents: California Judges Association, California Special Districts Association, California Automobile Dealers Association, California Fabricare Institute, Knudsen Corporation,

Clearly, over the last decade there has been a steady increase in the number of people lobbying and the number of groups represented. Any number of factors probably contribute to this phenomenon: first, the increasing complexity and heterogeneity of California society and economy; second, more people have been registered as lobbyists since the adoption of Proposition 9, because of the Fair Political Practice Commission's definition of lobbyist; third, there has been a substantial increase in the number of single-issue lobbies such as death penalty, abortion, or tax reform; and fourth, increased efforts by entrepreneurial lobbyists who actively seek new clients among businesses or corporations either unrepresented at the state capital or represented only in a large trade association.

Lobbies run the gamut in Sacramento—business, labor, farm, occupations, veterans, conservation, religious, social, and trade associations are all there. Any group has the right to be represented by a lobby as long as it pays its $25 registration fee. However, are all groups *truly* represented in Sacramento? And, even if they are represented, is it anything more than token representation? For example, PG&E has 22 lobbyists representing it in their governmental relations division. These 22 lobbyists are expected to explain and defend this multibillion-dollar corporation's views to legislators, administrators, and commissioners. But who represents the views of the consumers of PG&E, gas and electricity? The Tobacco Tax Council pays the Joseph F. Mahoney lobby firm $100,000 a year to represent them, but the American Cancer Association can raise only a nominal amount for lobbying. Students, housewives, consumers, farmworkers, the poor, and the unemployed are some of the groups that traditionally have had little, if any, direct representation in Sacramento. It is true today that these groups are at least better represented than they used to be, but they have a long way to go.

TECHNIQUES OF LOBBYING

Grass-roots function

As everyone knows, particularly college students, keeping abreast of what is going on in the various arenas of American national, state, and local government is not easy. In the California State Legislature alone,

---

Motor Car Dealers Association of California, California Thoroughbred Committee, San Bernardino Valley Municipal Water District, The Sea Ranch Association, Southern California Association of Governments, Standard Oil of Ohio, TRW, Inc., United Hospital Association, Northern California Motor Car Dealers Association, Pomona Valley Municipal Water District Rohr Industries, Concerned Physicians for Malpractice Reform, Costa Mesa Community Water District, Dolphin Investment Co., Inc., Association of Bay Area Governments, Bechtel Corporation, The Adamson Companies, Otay Municipal Water Districts and the Pre-School Association of California.

thousands of measures are introduced each year. If one were to con-
scientiously read a major state newspaper such as the *Sacramento Bee*
or the *Los Angeles Times* daily, plus watch the local TV news shows, this
person might have some small glimmer of what is going on in Sacramento. A *very* interested citizen conceivably could subscribe to the
California Journal, an authoritative journal on state politics, pour over
recorded roll call votes in the *Assembly* and *Senate Journals* (kept in most
major libraries), or study the *Weekly Histories, Recorded Committee
Votes,* and *Daily Files* at a legislator's district office. But obviously, few
citizens have the time or inclination to do this. In order to really keep up
with Sacramento doings as it relates to one's job, business, or political
interests, most citizens inevitably tend to rely on the interest groups to
which they belong for information.

A substantial part of most lobbyist's work day is spent communicating
with the leader and members of the group he or she represents. Most
group publications or newsletters give extensive coverage and credit to

ILLUSTRATION 7–4
"Over the Top" at Rancho Seco nuclear power plant Nuclear power protestors
urge shutdown of plant.

Photo courtesy Sacramento Bee

their legislative friends and describe the status of pending legislation. Many groups extensively coordinate their local membership with their capitol lobbying. Groups such as Common Cause, AFL-CIO, the League of Women Voters, the California Teacher's Association, and the Bankers Association, among others, urge their members to write or call particular legislators or perhaps attend (pack) a committee hearing in Sacramento. Some single-issue groups such as the antigun control lobby have become particularly adept through their use of sophisticated computerized mass mailings to generate impressive letter-writing efforts or raise substantial sums of money.

Information function

Legislators must vote on thousands of measures in a session. To be expert in one or two fields of legislative policy is challenging, but legislators must cast votes in dozens of different policy areas. Hence, lobbyists play another crucial role. They inform legislators of their membership's views and also provide information and expertise to legislators in various policy areas.

While lobbyists make formal presentations before committees in support of or in opposition to legislation, the most critical point is prior to the committee hearings in the legislators' offices, *in the coffee shop,* or over cocktails at a local bar. Most important decisions have been made prior to the committee hearing.

STRATEGY

Some political scientists have argued that the power or influence that any particular lobbyist wields is determined exclusively by the group this person represents. In this vein, one might argue that no matter how slow-witted or ineffective a particular Teamster lobbyist might be, he or she would be an influential lobbyist simply because of the power of the group represented. The Teamsters are a wealthy, large mass-member group with many potential voters. The Teamsters make large campaign contributions to political campaigns, send volunteers to work in campaigns, have a large statewide membership, entertain legislators, and have a nationwide reputation for being tough. To use a familiar cliché, "They don't miss a trick." For example, the Teamsters provide each legislator with a handsome notebook with short biographies of the various legislators. It is this sort of attention to detail that makes the Teamsters a power in the capital. Indeed, given the astute political qualities of the Teamsters, it seems highly unlikely that they would ever hire an inept lobbyist.

ILLUSTRATION 7–5
Howard Jarvis delivering boxes of letters to Sacramento lawmakers urging budget and tax cuts in 1979 This is "grassroots" on a large scale!

Photo courtesy Sacramento Bee

Obviously, a group such as the Teamsters using a variety of techniques of persuasion is going to have power, but we argue that the individual lobbyist adds yet another dimension to this picture. Let's consider what some of the main ingredients of successful effective lobbying are—beyond simply representing a powerful group.

First and foremost, an effective lobbyist has a keen understanding of the complex issues facing his or her client group. A skilled lobbyist is able to explain clearly and concisely the main facets of an issue to a legislator, administrator, staff member, reporter, or another lobbyist. The effective lobbyist knows how to read the legalese of bills, spot flaws, look for key points or problems, and suggest amendments. The effective lobbyist is equally at home at a luncheon meeting at the Sutter Club; in a quiet, informal, frank discussion in a legislator's office; or in a formal representation of testimony at a committee hearing.

Second, an effective lobbyist understands the legislative process and the formal rules governing that process. Effective lobbyists provide input at all the phases of the process: bill origination, bill drafting, assignment to committee, selection of committee members and chairpersons,[4] scheduling of bills, floor action, conference committees, the governor, administrative agencies implementation, court action, and initiatives.

Many of the skills effective lobbyists possess come only with experience. How many votes are necessary to get a bill out of the Assembly Criminal Justice Committee? Are the votes there, or should a bill be held over? How do you avoid a hostile committee? Should one agree to a particular amendment?

For example, John Zierold, Sierra Club lobbyist in 1976, was convinced that former State Senator Tony Bielenson's coastline bill would not clear the Senate Finance Committee. He had carefully counted the votes ahead of time. Zierold persuaded former Assembly Resources Chair Charles Warren and Senator Jerry Smith to hold Smith's scenic highways bill in the assembly committee until the fate of Beilenson's coastline bill had been decided. Once the Beilenson coastline bill was killed in Senate Finance, the coastline bill was amended into the Smith scenic highways bill, passed out of assembly committee, passed on assembly floor, and then went to the senate floor for concurrence in assembly amendments—effectively bypassing *Senate Finance.* The strategy, knowledge, and tactics employed by Zierold in this instance could not be learned from a textbook nor attempted by one inexperienced in the process.

Third, the effective lobbyist knows not only the formal rules but the informal, unwritten rules as well. For example, a cardinal rule in Sacramento is, if a lobbyist determines he or she will have to oppose a bill, the lobbyist is honor-bound to go to the bill's author and discuss the reasons for opposition with that legislator *prior* to committee hearings. The legislative author of the bill might suggest some amendments to the bill in hopes of persuading the lobbyist to not oppose the measure. Indeed, it is entirely possible the legislator may have no strong commitment to the bill but may have introduced it in behalf of an interest in his or her district. The legislator might very well say something like, "Go check with the lobbyist sponsoring the bill and see if you can iron out your differences. Whatever you decide is fine with me."

Among other key unwritten rules—a good lobbyist will never threaten a legislator with defeat. In the first place, he or she probably could not deliver, and in the second place, today's opponent may be tomorrow's ally.

In Sacramento, lobbyists are expected to give those whom they are trying to influence "the straight scoop." Obviously, lobbyists present their

---

[4] For example, the *Sacramento Bee* (November 2, 1979) reported that lobbyists put pressure on the Senate Rules Committee to prevent Senator Alan Robbins from being named chair of Senate Insurance and Finance because they feared he would be overzealous in putting the bite on them for campaign contributions.

group's views in the most favorable light, but they must also be able to explain the pros and cons of a bill to a legislator. A lobbyist that knowingly lies to or misleads a legislator would not only lose that legislator's support henceforth, but would also lose face with (even access to) other legislators. The Sacramento inner circle of legislators-staff-lobbyists and reporters is small and intimate. Word of an important transgression spreads rapidly. If a lobbyist should happen to give a legislator the wrong information, mistakenly, about a bill's effect, the advocate would be expected to get to the legislator and clear up the point as quickly as possible. In short, honesty, discretion, and keeping commitments are essential elements of lobbying in the California State Capitol.

Fourth, the effective lobbyist usually tries to become a friend of the legislator and gets on a first-name basis with that person. An effective lobbyist makes an effort to know about the special interests of the legislator or administrator—whether it's sports, hunting, or antique pipe organs. Many of the more successful lobbyists of the 1970s trade on the sports interests of the new generation of legislators, and invitations to play tennis, racquetball, or golf are as popular lobbyist-legislator activities today as gin rummy or poker was a few years ago.

Fifth, effective lobbyists work cooperatively with their lobbyist colleagues. They often trade information and help one another. Moreover, on any issues of consequence, coalitions of lobbies work jointly to support or oppose measures. Effective lobbyists know how to exploit the power of their group.

Sixth, effective lobbyists help orchestrate the grass-roots organization with the capital operation. Obviously, lobbyists work closely with legislators whose districts encompass significant elements of the lobbyist's group.

FURTHER REFORMS IN THE LOBBYING PROCESS

What additional measures, if any, should be adopted to further reform the lobbyist process? First and foremost, the most essential reform would be some form of public financing of state election races to further reduce the monetary power of special interests with their campaign contributions. Ideally, influence should hinge on information and expertise rather than just "big bucks." The goal should be to help groups compete on more even terms. Second, it would be possible and not unreasonable to whittle down lobbyist gifting further—the amount allowed for honoraria could be further reduced. Third, attempts should be made to plug up some of the loopholes in the Political Reform Act.

Lobbying is an essential and indispensable part of the American governmental process—citizens petitioning their government. The reforms enacted in California have helped improve the lobby process, but there is still much to be done.

SUMMARY

Lobbyists and special interests have been inextricably linked with California government throughout state history. Interest groups are necessary and vital to democratic government, but they also pose a potentially grave threat to democratic institutions through their money influence, entertaining, and "me-first" attitude. The various lobby reforms that have been launched in California have helped reduce the potential for evil, but further reforms are needed.

8

Political parties in California: The perennial power vacuum

In theory, the Supreme Soviet is the highest deliberative lawmaking body in the Soviet Union; in theory, the British monarch presides over the British Commonwealth of nations; and in theory, California's political parties are directed and coordinated by a three-tiered system of state conventions, state central committees, and county central committees. But in reality, none of these happens. For the most part, California's official party organizations play only a minor role in influencing and shaping the state's politics.

The reason that California's political parties have traditionally been so weak and ineffective hinges largely on a key historical feature we have referred to frequently in this text: the Progressive reform movement in the early 1900s. Progressives viewed the rise of corrupt city and state political machines and their boss leaders with alarm. California's major city of that era, San Francisco, was dominated by the Boss Reuf Machine, while the Republican and Democratic parties, as well as all other institutions of government in California at that time, were the captives of the Southern Pacific Railroad. Fremont Older (1926:14), a leading newspaper reporter of the time, noted:

> The Southern Pacific Railroad dominated not only the Republican Party, but also, to a large extent, the Democratic organization. Virtually every one of influence supported the railroad, because it was in control—and thus the sole dispenser of political favors.

160

PROGRESSIVE PARTY REFORM PROPOSALS

When the Progressives eventually came to power in California (and in many of the other western states), much of their reform effort was directed toward reducing the power of the politicians, political parties, and special interests. The reforms enacted by the Progressives made it difficult (some might say impossible) for California political parties to perform their traditional functions: recruiting candidates, endorsing and supporting office seekers in primaries, taking stands on issues, raising campaign funds, organizing campaigns, moderating differences and achieving compromises in the general election. Significantly, with only one or two exceptions, the political reforms instituted by the Progressives remain intact. The changes achieved by the Progressives some 70 years ago still shape contemporary California politics.

Primary election reforms

To remove Southern Pacific tentacles from the state's political parties and to expand the role of voters in the nomination process, Progressives successfully fought for the enactment of the direct primary system. Under this system, voters *elect* party nominees rather than having party leaders at what were often rigged conventions *select* party nominees. Indeed, adoption of the direct primary system allowed for the nomination and election of Hiram Johnson to the governorship in 1910 along with many other Progressive legislators—a Republican convention would not have nominated Hiram Johnson as its gubernatorial candidate.

California was also one of the first states to adopt a presidential preference primary for electing delegations to national nominating conventions. Under the presidential preference primary system adopted by the Progressives, delegates to the national party conventions were popularly elected—not just hand-picked—by party leaders as they had been formerly.

Laws were passed preventing state party leaders or political parties from playing any sort of role in the primary. Parties were expressly forbidden from endorsing candidates or making financial contributions to candidates in the primary. In short, the traditional king-making role of political parties was eliminated.

Antiparty reforms

Among the more important party structural reforms passed by the Progressives, which helped shape future patterns of California politics was the adoption of cross-filing. Under cross-filing, candidates for partisan office were allowed to file not only in their own party's pri-

162

ILLUSTRATION 8–1

ILLUSTRATION 8–1
The Republican presidential convention comes to California U.S. Senators
William Knowland (Calif.) and Bourke Hickenlooper (Iowa) on the floor of San
Francisco's Cow Palace, July 16, 1964.

United Press International

mary but in the opposition party's primary as well. Progressives believed
that party voters should not be limited to their own party's candidates in
the primary, but rather, voters should be able to vote for the best candidate—regardless of party. Unfortunately, however, the opportunity to
vote for other parties' candidates in the primary depended on those candidates' decisions to cross-file. Thus, in fact, cross-filing gave candidates
the option of seeking several parties' nominations, but voters had no
control over those options.

In the 1930s, '40s, and well into the '50s, cross-filers (usually well-
entrenched incumbents) were frequently able to capture both parties'
nominations in the primary. In the November general elections, these
candidates would go on the ballot as hyphenated Republican-Democratic
(or vice versa) candidates. Earl Warren and Pat Brown, former California
governors, were both successful cross-filers during their political careers. Cross-filing, however, on the whole, tended to give Republicans
greater tactical advantages than Democrats. Republicns were usually

better organized, had more newspaper support, and had better financial resources than the Democrats.

Progressives also established nonpartisan local elections in California. Local issues, it was argued, such as road repair, park maintenance, or dog leash laws were not partisan, and parties should not intrude in the local election process. Voters should make voting decisions based on candidate qualifications rather than party designation. On the other hand, as Eugene Lee noted (1978:231), nonpartisan local elections provided activist business community members ("Main-Street" types) distinct advantages they would not have had with partisan voting. Conservative businesspeople knew each other through service club memberships and volunteer community activities and could effectively coordinate political activities. Not surprisingly, nonpartisan local elections further weakened local party grass-roots organization.

Ballot reforms

Progressives championed the adoption of the Australian secret ballot in order to help discourage vote fraud. Additionally, Progressives instituted the office-block system on the election ballot. The office-block system does not allow a voter the option of checking one box at the top of the ballot to cast a straight party ticket. Voters are forced to vote separately for each of the offices. This tends to weaken party ticket voting.

Civil service reforms

In many eastern seaboard states or midwestern industrial states during the nineteenth century and a few today, party organizations tended to be comprised of state and local government employees whose jobs depended upon their party's staying in power. Government jobs in these states were dispensed to party activists and relatives as patronage and not on the basis of merit or qualification. Progressives promoted the concept of civil service reform. Qualifications and test scores were to be used to determine who received government jobs. This meant that the traditional work force of eastern party organizations—government employees—was virtually absent from California political parties. For much of this century, amateurs and volunteers have been the mainstays of California political party organization.

While these volunteers have occasionally played instrumental roles in local campaigns—staffing headquarters, walking precincts, collecting signatures, distributing flyers at supermarkets, stuffing and addressing envelopes, putting up signs, and performing other tasks of the campaign—in statewide races the focus tends to be on money and media (see Chapter 5).

Political party organizational reform

Progressives also promoted laws that extensively reformed how political parties would operate in the state. Rules were established to govern when, where, and for how many days the different party units as specified in the Elections Code would meet—and for that matter, even their dues structure. Under these reform arrangements, there was little coordination linking local party units with the statewide party organization.

STATE CONVENTION

Shorn of any significant functions by the Progressive reform surge, California's official parties have tended to be more form than substance. Theoretically, the most important unit, the *State Convention,* meets once every two years for a two-day session in mid-August. The convention includes the party officeholders and nominees for statewide office (10), Congress (45), and state legislature (120) for a grand total of 175 members. Additionally, Republicans also include a few other party leaders at their conventions.

Prior to the adoption of the direct primary in California, the party convention had the important task of nominating statewide candidates. Today, however, the convention is assigned such "important" duties as: (1) selecting the party's candidates for presidential electors (for the virtually meaningless electoral college), and (2) drafting a party platform (which nobody reads and few care about). For the most part, the state convention seems to serve the primarily symbolic function of getting party officeholders and nominees together. Officeholders, often preoccupied with their elective chores, take little genuine interest in this ceremonial party unit, and party nominees do not really enjoy full status as members of the convention, since many of them are guaranteed defeat by well-entrenched incumbents of the other party.

STATE CENTRAL COMMITTEE

The *State Central Committee* has more than five times as many members as the convention (approximately 1,000). Each party has its own set of rules determining membership on its State Central Committee—officeholders, party nominees, appointees, county chairs, and other party officials are all included. The State Central Committee's prime tasks are to elect a state chair, vice chair, and executive committee, and to assist party candidates in their campaigns for office. Since the State Central Committee is large and unwieldy and has only a very small professional staff and very little money, the amount of support it can provide the many individual party candidates is limited.

For the most part, State Central Committees marshall their modest resources to expend in some of the marginal districts or in helping party candidates in open districts where there is no incumbent. The Republican State Central Committee invariably has more money to spend for Republican candidates than their Democratic counterpart. Money, mailers, and professional assistance are given to a handful of the most promising newcomers in the party, and workshops are organized to help train campaign workers. (It should be emphasized, however, that special interest groups provide the great bulk of campaign funds in California—not party organizations.)

Few would argue that the State Central Committees play a leading role in California politics. It is true, however, that an occasional highly dedicated, energetic state party chair, such as Charles Manatt on the Democratic side or Gaylord Parkinson on the Republican side, has been able to overcome momentarily some of the obstacles to strong party organization in California and has provided effective leadership of the party organization. But these individuals are the exception to the rule. A state chair who tries to intrude into incumbent politics does so at his or her own peril. Democratic chair Dick O'Neil was roundly censured by Republican and Democratic senators alike when he intervened in a leadership squabble in the state senate.

COUNTY CENTRAL COMMITTEE

At the bottom rung of the state political party structure is the *County Central Committee.* However, as with the other party units, County Central Committees have seldom been noted for their political effectiveness. While many voters may not know the names of their assembly representative, state senator, or county councilperson, they are almost sure not to know the names of people comprising their party's County Central Committee. While the County Central Committee is the only party unit that is democratically elected, in only a few of the larger urban counties is there occasionally any spirited competition for committee posts. Since most individuals running for the County Central Committee have little name recognition, there is no real campaign or media coverage of the race— voting frequently hinges more on one's ballot positioning than anything else.

Indeed, in many rural counties, party leaders have considerable difficulty finding enough people to run in order to fill empty slots on the Central Committee, and many committees wind up having to appoint members to fill out terms. It is interesting to note, too, that there is no party unit stipulated by the Election Code below the county level—at the precinct or ward level.

The prime duty of the County Central Committee is to assist local party candidates running for office, and, in effect, maintain the party presence in a particular area. The problems for the County Central Committee are similar, on a smaller scale, to problems of the State Central Committee—little money, absence of professional staff, and apathetic members.

County Central Committees may find themselves sharply divided over how much support or effort should go to assist the campaign of a particular local candidate, since the County Central Committee had no real voice in that individual's nomination. In many states, candidates must, in effect, "pay their party dues" (be active in the local party, contribute money, work in the office) before they can hope to get the nomination of the party. But in California, local party organizations must accept the will of the voters, and at times, they do this with some reluctance.

The problems and difficulties facing local party organizations in California are highlighted by an incident occurring in San Francisco in the 1976 election. San Francisco County is the most liberal Democratic county in the state. Several Republican candidates in this county facing well-entrenched Democratic incumbents attempted legal action against their own Republican County Central Committee of San Francisco because, they claimed, it was not doing what the State Election Code stipulated it was supposed to do, i.e., provide campaign assistance to local Republican candidates.

The dilemma posed to the San Francisco Republican County Central Committee was whether they should concentrate their meager resources backing incumbent Republican State Senator Milton Marks, who was in a tough reelection fight, or squander their money in a series of futile campaigns for various hopeless San Francisco Republican candidates. The Republican County Central Committee of San Francisco decided on the former strategy, and the court did not interfere.

On very rare occasions, County Central Committees can play a decisive role in local politics. If an uncontested party nominee should die before the primary, or if the nominee selected should die before the fall general election, the County Central Committee is given the responsibility of choosing a replacement. Thus, Assemblyman Mike Gage (Democrat-Napa) secured the nomination from the Napa and Solano County Central Committees after his predecessor, former Assemblyman Al Siegler, died of a heart attack a few weeks prior to the June primary. The death of Republican incumbent Congressman William Ketchum just three weeks after the June 1978 primary meant the four Republican Central Committees of the 18th Congressional District had to choose their party nominee for November. In these instances, membership in these local party units becomes very important. Local candidates interested in securing the nomination must woo the County Central Committee members at miniconventions.

Finally, we should not conclude our comments on the weak party organization in California without briefly paying tribute to the small corps of volunteer activists in each party. Unpaid, unrewarded, and overworked, these party activists can be found in virtually every California community. Housewives, teachers, lawyers, students, and local businesspeople are frequently found among these party volunteers. Idealism, excitement, issues, and social contacts are some of the factors motivating these people. They keep the party presence alive at the local level. Clearly, most of their contemporaries spend no time on party activities. California party activists are a unique subset of the state population.

Social setting

Further compounding the weakness of California political parties and discouraging effective state party organization has been the population flux within the state—the migration into and movement within the state (see Chapter 2). In the eastern states, party machines tended to rely on coalitions of ethnic voters. Old-line Irish, Italian, Polish, Jewish, Puerto Rican, Slavic, or black neighborhoods were the important building blocks for the machines. People living in these older ethnic enclave neighborhoods in major eastern industrial cities often knew their precinct captains by name. Precinct captains knew how to cope with the city bureaucracy. If someone had a problem—a pothole in the street in front of their apartment, trash not picked up, a traffic ticket, or children in trouble with the authorities—they knew they could always turn to their precinct captain for assistance in cutting through governmental red tape. In return, the voters were supposed to support the party machine in the polling place. Precinct captains who did not turn out the vote in their districts did not remain precinct captains very long. Today, the government—through food stamp programs, welfare checks, unemployment relief, and social security—has taken over this function.

While there was evidently some potential for boss-machine politics in California (for example, San Francisco's Boss Ruef's Machine in the early part of the 20th century), the pattern never really developed in this state. However, it is true that in a few distinctive areas in California— such as the Irish, Italian, or Chinese neighborhoods of San Francisco, the Jewish population concentration in West Los Angeles and Hollywood (Littwin, 1977), the Mexican-American barrios in East Los Angeles, the black precincts in Oakland-Berkeley (Jacobs, 1976), or the Watts-Compton area—popular local politicians have put together effective political organizations in some ways reminiscent of the old-fashioned political machines. The Waxman-Berman organization in the Jewish neighborhoods of West Los Angeles, the Dymally organization in Watts, or the Dellums organization in Berkeley are examples. But it should be emphasized that these local political machines are headed by local *elected* officeholders. They are also strikingly different from the old-style political machines in that they largely depend upon volunteers, not ward heelers, for the organizational work force. Vote fraud is virtually non-existent, and these local organizations have no patronage and few "goodies" to dispense to the loyal.

Because of the various reforms[1] launched by the Progressives and the mobility of the California population, strong party organization has not been part of the state pattern. Interestingly enough, the antiparty mood of California now appears to be part of the national picture: increasing numbers of voters do not feel committed to any political party and political action committees of special interests—not political parties—are the major funding source for politicians' campaigns.

POLITICAL PARTY SUBSTITUTES

Since political parties were so grievously weakened by the Progressive reforms, other organizations have emerged in California to fulfill traditional party functions.

Extra party groups—Republican

In 1934, a group of moderate Republican leaders (including Earl Warren) decided the State GOP needed to project a more centrist image. California Republicans had just been overwhelmed by the New Deal sweep of President Franklin Delano Roosevelt. These moderates believed the Republicans, to remain competitive, would have to offer voters bright, young, attractive candidates rather than the elderly archconservatives who tended to control Republican nominations. The California Republican Assembly (CRA) was organized to help the more progressive elements in the party survive the primaries and hopefully gain election. CRA was an *unofficial* party group and hence not bound by the legal prohibition on endorsing in the primary.

In a remarkably short period of time, CRA came to play a pivotal role in state Republican nomination politics. It could provide financial assistance, campaign expertise, manpower, and the prestige of its endorsement behind its candidates. Local CRA committees interviewed and questioned prospective Republican legislative candidates prior to their filing for office. After surveying the field, the local committee placed its stamp of approval on a specific candidate. In statewide races, CRA had a special selection panel who interviewed prospective Republican candidates and discussed with them their stand on key issues of the day. This committee, in turn, recommended its choices to the CRA statewide conven-

---

[1] Cross-filing is the only Progressive reform that has been abolished. Modified in 1954, cross-filing was effectively eliminated in 1959.

tion. Richard Nixon got his start in politics by winning the CRA endorsement in a southern California congressional district and went on to beat the Democratic incumbent. Obviously, CRA's endorsing activities tended to narrow the field of Republican candidates and was contrary to the spirit of the Progressives' goal of a free and unfettered primary.

As CRA's prestige grew, many prospective Republican candidates who failed to win endorsement would decide not to file for office. By the mid-1940s, the occasional Republican statewide candidate who ran without a CRA endorsement would invariably lose. Hence, prospective Republican candidates for state office were virtually required to vie for CRA support. The CRA-endorsed candidate would face little or no intraparty opposition and could often poach on the Democratic side under cross-filing and capture each party's nominations.

Though CRA began as a voice of moderate Republicanism, over the years it has become increasingly conservative. The appointment of CRA founder, Earl Warren, to the U.S. Supreme Court, the election of several prominent CRA moderates to office, and the defeat of Richard Nixon for governor in 1962 meant that archconservatives could attain leadership positions in the group. Yet, as conservative as the CRA was becoming, it was not conservative enough for some in the organization. These ultraright-wingers pulled out of CRA to form a new extra party group— United Republicans of California (UROC). In 1964, yet another Republican extra party group, the California Republican League (CRL), was formed to support moderate Republican candidates. This latter group, however, has never really become a major force in Republican nomination politics.

Extra party groups—Democratic

The California Democratic Council (CDC) was organized in 1953, after several earlier attempts to organize a Democratic extra party group had failed. Part of the impetus for CDC's formation came from the enormous popularity of Adlai Stevenson, the Democratic presidential nominee of 1952.

The CDC, while not as important in Democratic nomination politics as CRA was in Republican nomination politics, was, nevertheless, a significant factor in its heyday. Democratic aspirants actively courted the group and CDC's nominating conventions became a critical juncture for Democratic candidates. Unlike the CRA or UROC, which were comprised of relatively small groups of party activists, CDC, for a time, was a large mass-member organization. In 1964, another Democratic extra party group, Democratic Volunteers Committee (DVC), was formed. This group, primarily the inspiration of Speaker Jess Unruh, who was angered by CDC, never really took hold and has long since expired.

Problems of extra party groups

Extra party groups which once played substantial roles in nomination politics a decade or two ago in California have now fallen upon hard times. Each group, of course, has its own individual set of problems, but there are some common difficulties as well. CRA and CDC were able to exert maximum leverage when they had a monopoly on the endorsing function within their respective parties. Competition from UROC, CRL, and DVC lessened the value of CRA and CDC endorsements, since candidates could shop around for support.

Extra party groups tend to attract issue-oriented people to their groups, and, hence, these groups seem to be particularly susceptible to angry wrangling over platforms or bitter strife over the wording of resolutions. Thus, CDC's ranks were decimated by bitter divisions over U.S. involvement in the Vietnam War. While most CDC'ers were opposed to the war, particularly by 1968, many CDC'ers felt the organization should not undercut Democratic President Lyndon Johnson by openly opposing the war—but others did. Individual members and entire clubs pulled out of the organization over this issue.

CRA and UROC have tended to take more conservative positions than Republican rank and file, the CDC has tended to be much more liberal than average Democratic voters. Democratic and Republican officeholders forced to seek compromises in the political arena were frequently criticized by their respective extra party group's zealous adherents who were suspicious of "sell out." As Owens et al. (1970:212) notes, these groups tend to be more issue-oriented than victory-oriented. Clearly, the extra party groups have frequently been out of step with the mainstream of their respective parties.

CDC'ers tended to be white, suburban professionals, while the great majority of Democratic voters were low income, blue collar, and ethnic minorities.[2] CDC members, it was claimed, enjoyed the social features of the organization but were not dependable precinct workers.

Another reason for the demise of the extra party groups is that the campaign workers these groups could offer candidates—door-to-door canvassers, envelope stuffers, placard placers, and so on—have become less consequential in the era of automated statewide campaigns. Firms can be hired today to do the drudgery work of politics, from addressing envelopes to putting up signs, and television is the most significant factor in statewide campaigns.

In any case, one of the extra party groups, DVC, has totally disap-

---

[2] Only in the heavily Jewish neighborhoods of Los Angeles did the CDC have a strong Democratic local base. Most CDC chapters were located in wealthy, white, *Republican* suburbs. CDC could get their local candidate nominated, but the nominee invariably lost to a Republican opponent in the general election.

ILLUSTRATION 8–2
Computerized political mailings Candidates now use high-speed computerized electric typewriters to prepare "personalized" campaign letters.

Courtesy International Business Machines Corporation

peared from the political scene, and the other four (CRA, UROC, CRL, and CDC) have little money, reduced memberships (CDC has gone from 100,000 to 10,000), few professional staffers, and imperceptible impact. In their early years, CRA and CDC leaders and members would often hold leadership positions in the official party structure as well as the extra party group. Today, the extra party leaders and followers increasingly seem to be cut off and isolated from the official parties. CRA's and UROC's shrill opposition to the UN, support for white Rhodesia and South Africa and similar programmatic stances mean that these groups will continue to be on the far-right fringe of American politics. In the same vein, CDC endorsed Fred Harris in 1976 as its candidate for the Democratic presidential nomination. Harris garnered *only 1 percent* of the Democratic primary vote, further attesting to the decline of CDC and the value of its endorsement.

Extra party groups still provide forums for candidates running for office to make speeches and get some publicity. Their endorsements receive some press coverage at least, though since 1966 they must print a disclaimer ("not an official party group") on all flyers. The groups take controversial stands on some of the leading issues of the day and thus encourage public dialogue on these matters, but their impact on the nomination process is virtually gone.

Other party groups

In addition to these extra party groups, other semi-official party groups have from time to time played modestly influential roles in their respective parties—Young Democrats, Young Republicans, women's party groups, college party groups, and the like. However, the most dynamic new political groups on the horizon are not technically party organizations. Tom Hayden's Citizens for Economic Democracy (CED) and Ronald Reagan's Citizens for a Democratic Republic (CDR), at opposite ends of the political spectrum, appear to have greater impact on the state Democratic and Republican Parties than any of the existing extra party groups. Indeed, CDC officials have become increasingly wary of the Hayden organization, feeling that it is competing with them for leadership of the liberal-left community in California politics. While the Hayden organization has been active in only a handful of races up to this time, it promises heightened activity in the years ahead. The youthful exuberance of CED stands in marked contrast to the aging leadership of CDC.

CAMPAIGN MANAGEMENT FIRMS

In the 1930s, another prominent feature of the California political scene emerged: the professional campaign management firm. The now legendary husband and wife public relations firm of Whitaker and Baxter was the first to employ modern advertising techniques in political campaigns—and, on a fee basis, the firm provided expert advice to their clients on the overall management of a campaign, raising money, planning, and wording and placement of ads. For much of their early history, Whitaker and Baxter concentrated primarily on ballot proposition elections.

Between 1933–55 Whitaker and Baxter managed 75 different campaigns and won 70. The Whitaker and Baxter success formula involved several factors. *First,* they did not take on campaigns that looked like "sure losers." *Second,* they had good relations with the state's major newspapers (this was prior to television), because most of the press was Republican and usually endorsed issues that Republicans supported. Whitaker and Baxter was also in charge of several very large commercial accounts and spent substantial amounts of money each year placing that advertising in the state's press. Some of their major commercial accounts were Pacific Gas and Electric, Pacific Telephone and Telegraph, Standard Oil, and the Southern Pacific Railroad. This gave Whitaker and Baxter additional access to many of the state's newspapers. Third, Whitaker and Baxter always paid for their political advertising *in advance* (political campaigns are famous for not paying their bills). In summary, Whitaker and Baxter usually managed attractive ballot measures and relied on a sympathetic press to carry the message to the voters. They almost always won.

After World War II, other firms such as Spencer and Roberts, Baus and Ross, and Murray Chotiner joined the field. The weak party structure, the size of the state, the concomitant need to use mass media to reach voters, and the many ballot proposition campaigns were factors that helped encourage the development of professional public relations firms in California campaigns. Today, (Boyarsky, 1974) there are at least a dozen firms running campaigns either full-time or as part of their varied endeavors. A number of the contemporary firms are spin-offs from some of the original firms.

The professional campaign management firms in contemporary California work for candidates as well as ballot propositions and usually with only one party's candidates—Republican: Spencer and Roberts, Woodward and McDowell, Lyn Nofzeiger, George Young Associates, and Baus and Ross; Democrat: Joe Cerrel, Sandy Weiner and Co. and Winner-Wagner. The Winner-Wagner Company uniquely runs political campaigns and also does contract lobbying. Some public relations firms specialize in gathering signatures to qualify initiatives—Alan Blanchard and Associates (San Francisco). Butcher-Forde of Orange County has specialized in computerized mailings (Jacob, 1979).

In addition to the public relations firms, there are easily several hundred campaign managers and media experts who can offer their expertise to candidates for a fee or salary. For example, San Diego Mayor Pete Wilson spent $1,166 for a one-day communications seminar with Leonard H. Roller, Inc. Roller provided intensive training in press conference psychology and how to respond to "unfriendly" questions. Consultant Don Penny works with candidates on style, content, and delivery of speeches. Media expert Maxwell (Bud) Arnold specializes in television filming of candidates. Given the various professional campaign specialists operating in California, party pros (the few that are around) tend to be relegated to subordinate positions in major state campaigns. Major candidates look to media professionals, not the official party organization, for their campaign advice. Indeed, one 1978 GOP gubernatorial candidate, Ken Maddy, said he felt almost compelled to hire a public relations firm to assist with his campaign in order to give it credibility with major contributors and the media. Before they gave, political action committees and fat cats wanted to know who was managing the campaign for Maddy.

From the early years of professional campaign managers to the present, there has been considerable concern raised over the success rate of these "hired guns" in the election process and, also, of the deterioration in the quality of campaigns because of the Madison Avenue selling techniques used by the firms. Candidates, it has been charged, were being sold to voters much in the same way that mouthwashes, toothpastes, or underarm deodorants were being advertised. Also, the success rate of some of the more prominent public relations firms suggested they could win regardless of the substance of the ballot proposition or the qualities of their candidate.

Whether these public relations firms—through slogans, half-truths, and television spots—have lowered the quality of American campaigns continues to be debated. And, just as major television network spokespersons argue that the trivia, banalities, and sexual sniggering of many typical top-rated television shows are there because this is what the public wants, so too, political public relations specialists say their techniques must be used to reach the typical, apathetic voter. In the old days when there were only one or two firms in professional campaign management, the side that had the public relations firm had a distinct advantage. Today, given the number of firms in the field, any leading candidate for major statewide office who can pay the fee can hire one of these firms. Thus, the public relations firms' effects are neutralized. It should be emphasized, too, that there is no secret formula to a winning campaign. The quality of the candidate, the issues, and the mood of the electorate will all play a part in the outcome. Furthermore, there would seem to be no constitutional way to prevent these firms from taking part in campaigns, but their involvement would likely be reduced if effective limits on campaign spending could ever be achieved.

Last, it should be noted that what started as a uniquely California phenomenon, i.e., professional campaign managers, is now a major feature of national campaigns and elections in many other states.

PARTY IN GOVERNMENT

Legislative leaders

Over the last decade, party leaders in both houses of the state legislature and, in particular, the speaker, have become increasingly involved in raising campaign war chests which, in turn, are dispensed to needy party aspirants. Additionally, some individual members funnel funds to one another. Obviously, IOUs are built up between the recipient of a campaign contribution and a contributing member seeking legislative party office. The aspirant gets campaign help, and the legislative party leader or aspirant solidifies his or her position.

Frequently, consultants from the majority and minority party caucuses, leadership staff, or personal staff take leaves of absence from their offices to work in campaigns of potential newcomers. Staffers have become increasingly careful to separate their official jobs from their campaign work. District offices and legislators' field representatives must avoid getting directly involved in campaigns. If they do, they run the risk of having the Fair Political Practices Commission investigate.

Clearly, the most powerful leader in the assembly in disbursing funds to party hopefuls is the speaker. For example, according to the Fair Political Practices Commission records, Speaker Leo McCarthy raised some $331,167 from special interests between January 1975 and August 1976 in his campaign fund. McCarthy, in turn, parcelled out $168,000 to 21 different Democrats running for office (mainly first-timers). On the senate side, the president pro-tem also provides campaign funds to deserving party candidates.

Legislative voting

Given the antiparty traditions of California politics, it is not surprising that political parties in the Sacramento arena have not displayed the same rigid discipline evidenced in some of the eastern state legislatures. One, of course, must be wary when comparing party voting in the state legislatures. As Keefe and Ogul (1977:300) note:

> . . . there are wide differences in party competition among the states. There are southern states where Republican politicians come in contact with the legislature only by visiting the state capital and northern states where Democratic legislators have a status only a notch above that of the interloper—so dominant are the major parties in their localities. Under conditions of one-party rule, factions lay plans and struggle for ascendancy somewhat in the fashion of political parties, and perform some of their functions as well, but all this bears only a dim resemblance to the idea of responsible party government.
>
> In one state, Nebraska, state legislators are elected on ballots shorn of party designation.

These authors also note the problems of comparing because of the varied environs of each state. Most attempts to compare party voting in state legislatures rely on roll-call data.

In some states, roll calls are rarely taken; in others, roll calls are required on all bills whether they are controversial or not. Notwithstanding these limitations, nearly all of the roll-call studies comparing state legislatures come to several similar conclusions: first, several eastern state legislatures such as New York, Connecticut, Rhode Island, Massachusetts, and Pennsylvania have unified cohesive, legislative parties; and second, the California legislature is invariably grouped at the bottom or near the bottom of these in terms of rankings of the number and percentage of party-division votes. For example, Jewell and Patterson (1966:420–21), while noting some fluctuation over the years, rank the California legislature as one of the least partisan state legislatures. In a similar vein, Professor Hugh Le Blanc (1969:33–57), in a comparative study of 26 different state upper houses, ranked California's senate at the very bottom of the listing—Rhode Island had a 100 percent cohesion score; Pennsylvania, 82 percent; and California, 17 percent.

The authoritative *California Journal,* a leading monthly publication on state politics, has for the last several years traced voting patterns of party mavericks in the California legislature. Beginning in December 1973, on a biennial basis the *Journal* has published a series of articles focusing on the extent to which California legislators have voted against a clear majority of their own party on a list of key votes compiled by the *Journal* for that particular year. Table 8–1 indicates the extent of party-line vote deviating in the two houses of the California legislature.

While there are no strong trends in the maverick vote percentages for the 1970s, nor is there any great difference in independent voting between the two parties in either house, senate Republicans did seem to exhibit a little more independence than the other groups, and assembly Democrats were somewhat less inclined to bolt the party position. How-

TABLE 8–1
Maverick voting patterns in the California legislature, 1973–1978 (percentages)

	1973	1974	1975	1976	1978	Average
Senate Democrats	16%	13%	14%	18%	18%	16%
Senate Republicans	23	21	20	23	18	21
Assembly Democrats	14	9	11	19	19	14
Assembly Republicans	21	18	23	18	19	20

Source: *California Journal* 4, no. 12 (February 1973): 417–18; 6, no. 1 (January 1974): 31–32; no. 1 (January 1976): 34–35; and 10, no. 2 (February 1979): 76–77.

ever, if we consider only 1976 and 1978, differences among the various groups were negligible. Overall, Senator Milton Marks of San Francisco is the leading maverick voting against his party as much as 65 percent of the time. Party mavericks tended to be urban Republicans or rural Democrats. Interestingly, one of the leading Republican mavericks of the mid-70s, Ken Maddy of Fresno, steadily became more of a party regular in his voting patterns in the latter 1970s, at the time he was seeking the Republican gubernatorial nomination.

Exactly why the California legislature has had so relatively few party division votes can be readily explained. As noted previously, for much of this century, the Progressive antiparty legacy has been part of the California pattern. Party voting seems much more likely to take place in the industrialized northeastern states, where party competition is keen, and local party organization is strong.

During most of the 20th century in California, personality, skill, and political savvy were far more important to an ambitious member in getting ahead in the legislative arena than one's party affiliation. After all, many legislators were hyphenated Republicans-Democrats (successful cross-filers) who owed little debt to either party for their election. California legislators quickly discovered it was far more important to have been on the winning side in a fight for speaker or president pro tem than belonging to a particular party, if one hoped to become a committee chair. At least historically, on controversial issues the California legislature, more often than not, tended to be divided along rural-urban, north-south, or special interest factional lines rather than by party.

There is little doubt that the number of party votes has increased over the last decade or so. In each house, majority and minority caucuses attempt with varying degrees of success to unify party members on at least some controversial votes, though there are few binding positions taken. Additionally, the party role of the speaker, president pro tem, other majority and minority leaders, and Democratic and Republican staff have encouraged a more partisan tone in the contemporary legislature. However, while parties are more important in the present-day California legislature, they are still far less unified than the eastern states. Most issues are perceived by California legislators as being nonpartisan. As recently as 1977 (January: 32–33), the *California Journal,* in its rankings of party cohesion of the California state legislature, concluded that there was substantial deviation from the party line for the year and went on to note this had been the pattern for the entire 1970s decade.

Governor as party leader

The California governor, Republican or Democrat, is the leader of his or her respective party. The more popular governors in California history, however, have tended to deemphasize party—governors such as Earl Warren, Goodwin Knight, Pat Brown, and the legendary Hiram Johnson. Those stressing partisanship have not been very effective (see Chapter 9). While recent governors such as Ronald Reagan and Jerry Brown have been important spokespersons for their parties—each has stressed independence from and often disdain for traditional party politics.

Furthermore, the elected plural executive (see Chapter 11) in California has been another factor promoting bipartisan state politics. Normally, at least a few state executives belong to a party different from the governor's. Only the lieutenant governor and governor have traditionally been members of the same party. But even that tradition was broken in 1978, when voters elected Mike Curb, a Republican, as lieutenant governor while reelecting Jerry Brown, a Democrat, as governor.

THIRD PARTIES

Third parties have intermittently played interesting but seldom crucial roles in California politics. In this century alone, there have been a number of significant third-party efforts including: the Hiram Johnson Progressives, Upton Sinclair's Socialist Party of the 1930s, and such contemporary third parties as the Peace and Freedom Party, American Independent Party, and the Libertarian Party.

The problems facing third parties in California are typical of the kinds of problems third parties face nationally: little money, overemphasis on single issues, few "name" candidates, lack of organization, and popular issues borrowed by the major parties.

While some state local legislatures have made it difficult for third parties to qualify for the ballot, this has not been the case in California. Under the generous provisions of the California Elections Code, in order to qualify for a place on the California ballot, a new third party must either: (1) register at least 1 percent of California voters (through 1978: 63,646) into the party, or (2) get 10 percent (636,460) of the voters to sign a petition asking that the party be placed on the ballot. Given the enormous number of signatures entailed, this latter option has never been successfully accomplished. The first option, though, has been used repeatedly.

In 1968, the Peace and Freedom Party and the American Independent Party both easily qualified for the California ballot. Indeed, the Peace and Freedom Party, unlike the more stable American Independent Party, had virtually no party funds, professional staff, or statewide organization, but it was able to register sufficient voters to qualify for the ballot.

In 1976, the California Legislature further modified its election laws to allow third-party *candidates*, another option. Third party candidates could qualify by simply getting 1 percent of the registered voters' names on a petition requesting that the particular candidate be placed on the ballot. Third-party candidates qualifying for the ballot under this option are listed on the ballot as "independents" without any accompanying party affiliation designation. In 1976, presidential candidates of the Communist Party, the Socialist Workers Party, and the Libertarian Party qualified as "independents" under this provision. Though 1976 Communist presidential candidate, Gus Hall, ran seventh in a field of seven on the California ballot, one might well ponder how many of the 12,000 votes that he received were cast by voters believing they were voting for an "independent," and not realizing he was the official Communist Party candidate. In any case, the three separate "independent" third-party presidential candidates, the two bona-fide third parties—Peace and Freedom and American Independent—and the two major parties helped provide a wide spectrum of views and choice for the voters in 1976.

Additionally, in California, staying on the ballot is even easier than qualifying. To remain on the ballot, a party must maintain a registration of at least *one fifteenth* of 1 percent, and second, have at least one of their candidates running for statewide office receive a minimum of 2 percent of the votes cast. The *one fifteenth* of 1 percent means that currently a third party has to only maintain 9,546 registrants to stay eligible. Moreover, there are usually enough disgruntled voters within the two major parties plus third-party voters to secure in one or two of the statewide races the necessary 2 percent to keep the party on the ballot.

Peace and Freedom Party

The Peace and Freedom Party was born out of the frustrations and disenchantment that many American voters felt with the interminable Vietnam War. When the official Democratic Party leadership of Lyndon Johnson and 1968 Democratic presidential candidate Hubert Humphrey sought to continue the American presence in Vietnam until an honorable peace had been achieved, some disgruntled Democrats saw the Peace and Freedom Party as the only viable alternative for opposition to the war. Further inflaming feelings of many Democrats was the fact that the Johnson-Humphrey administration had promised to end U.S. involvement in Vietnam during their 1964 campaign.

As the war stretched on, resistance and opposition to American policy in Vietnam steadily increased. By the late 1960s, substantial numbers of Democrats and many Republicans had become vocal opponents of the war, and Peace and Freedom Party opposition to Vietnam policy was no longer unique. The victory of the Communist insurgency in Vietnam and the hasty withdrawal of American forces meant the Peace and Freedom Party had lost its central issue. Membership in the party has declined steadily ever since. Moreover, prominent radical names of the 1960s (such as Paul Jacobs, Mario Savio, or Eldridge Cleaver) are no longer involved in the party. Illustrative of the depths to which this once proud, socialist third party had fallen came in the 1974 gubernatorial elections. The Peace and Freedom Party's gubernatorial candidate, Elizabeth Keathley, became so upset with the party's lack of visibility or news coverage that she campaigned in the nude on a Venice beach in southern California (to get more exposure?). There seems little doubt that what had once been a serious radical effort had, by the mid-1970s, degenerated into a comical farce.

The American Independent Party

The American Independent Party has also fallen on hard times. For much of its early history, the party leadership had a strange sort of love/hate relationship with George Wallace. In 1968, George Wallace, the presidential candidate of the party (though he was not an official party member), garnered some 13 percent of the national vote. During Wallace's presidential campaign and immediately afterwards, the party was rent with internal strife between Wallace loyalists, who saw the party as a temporary election refuge for the Alabaman's presidential quest, and the elected party leadership, who saw Wallace as the temporary candidate of a new third party. After 1968, Wallace returned to the Democratic fold and sought (and lost) that party's presidential nomination in 1972.

The AIP, in 1972, turned to John Schmitz, a dedicated member of the ultraright John Birch Society and former Republican member of Congress, as their presidential candidate. Once again, though, party officials had to go outside the party to find a "name" presidential candidate. As with the Wallace candidacy, there was considerable dissension within party ranks over whether Schmitz had really left the Republican Party and joined the American Independent Party or whether he was another interloper. Scraping the bottom of the barrel in 1976, the AIP nominated the irascible southern gadfly—Lester Maddox. The steady decline of the national AIP can be noted by the fact that in 1968 Wallace received 13 percent of the national vote; Schmitz received 5 percent in 1972; and Maddox received less than 1 percent in 1976. Further hurting AIP efforts, two other new archconservative parties appeared on the political scene in 1976, causing increased fragmentation of the far-right vote.

Third-party significance

While the AIP and Peace and Freedom Parties have faded into obscurity, as their percentages in statewide races dropped, they have at times played an interesting "spoiler's role" in a few pivotal state legislative races. In close elections, the Peace and Freedom Party candidate can drain a small, but nonetheless significant, percentage of liberal-left votes away from the Democratic candidate. This can throw the election to the Republican candidate. As an example, in 1972 in the 27th Senatorial District, voting results were as follows:

> Robert Stevens (Republican) 136,515
> Catherine O'Neil (Democrat) 132,616
> Ben Perrick (Peace and Freedom) 5,450

Certainly, Peace and Freedom voters could have, and *probably* would have, voted for the Democrat if they had not had the Peace and Freedom option.

The AIP can play a similar spoiler's role by capturing votes that would have gone to the Republican candidate. The voting results in the 1974 election in the 34th Senatorial District were as follows:

> W. Craig Biddle (Republican) 70,597
> Robert Presley (Democrat) 70,849
> Neal Meadows (AIP) 6,394

It is likely that many votes received by Meadows would *probably* have gone to the Republican Biddle if there had been no AIP alternative. Hence, the generous provisions of the State Elections Code allowing nearly moribund third-party corpses to remain in a state of suspended animation on the California ballot can create special problems for Democrats and Republicans in a few marginal districts. However, as the years have gone by, these two third parties have found it hard to field candidates in the state legislative races. In 1978, with 20 state senate and 80 assembly races, the Peace and Freedom Party had a total of 13 state legislative candidates and the American Independent Party, 7.

Perhaps the most interesting new phenomenon in third-party politics has been the rapid growth of the Libertarian Party. Libertarians emphasize free enterprise and laissez-faire economics, which appeal to conservatives. The party also advocates no governmental interference in the private lives of citizens on matters such as gambling, drugs, or prostitution; this has an appeal to many liberals.

Reforming political parties

Should California political parties be further reformed, or perhaps more accurately re-reformed? Clearly, the Progressive reforms have succeeded in relegating the official parties to a relatively modest role in California politics. With the exception of cross-filing, all of the other Progressive reforms remain intact in the state and help shape the style of California politics and the types of candidates that benefit from weak party structure.

The most frequently voiced criticism is that political parties in the California legislature tend to lack the cohesiveness and unity exemplified by parties in the eastern states. While party division votes are becoming more numerous these days, California legislators seem much less party-oriented than many of their colleagues in other states. Hopefully, in the years ahead, a reasonable balance will be found in the California legislature between cohesive, responsible parties on the one hand, and a legislator's personal freedom to vote his or her own personal convictions on important issues.

The most important problem facing California political parties is the lack of participation in party activities at the grass-roots level. This problem, of course, is not unique to California but is part of a national pattern, though the extent of the problem seems particularly apparent in this state. In part, the party substitutes take up some of the slack, but none of them really involves very many citizen participants.

To reinvigorate the local party, California Democrats passed legislation in 1978 to reform the structure of their State Central Committee. Under the new format, the number of appointees on the Democratic State Central Committee will be reduced: for incumbents (7 to 3), and for party candidates (5 to 2). Additionally, some Democratic State Central Committee delegates will be *elected* by county central committees and others will be elected by assembly district caucuses at the rate of one delegate per 20,000 registered Democrats. These changes, it is hoped, will help a little to restore interest in local party activities. Additionally, Democrats have also instituted local caucuses to serve as selection units for Democrats interested in being a delegate for a particular presidential candidate.

Of course, the most obvious reform to add interest and significance to local party groups would be to allow them to make preprimary endorsements for partisan elections—and perhaps nonpartisan elections. Clearly, party involvement becomes more significant if party activists believe they have a substantial voice in influencing the selection process. Admittedly, this reform would negate one of the key Progressive reforms passed 60 years ago, but reforms of one decade can become antireformist in another. Whether allowing local party groups to endorse would truly stipulate greater local involvement is not clear, but considering the dead-end situation facing California parties, it certainly would be worth a try.

SUMMARY

California political parties have been weak throughout this century. Progressive reforms and the mobility of the state population have helped prevent the development of eastern-style politics in the state. Due to the weakness of the official party organizations, extra party groups and campaign management firms have, at times, assumed some of the traditional functions of party organizations in California. Third parties have occasionally played modestly important roles in state politics.

Clearly, the most influential figures in California politics are not the top functionaries of the party but the state elective officeholders. Moreover, party-line voting is infrequent in the California legislature, and overly partisan governors have faced great difficulties leading the state.

9

The California legislature: Cinderella or Frankenstein?

Overall, state legislatures perform four major tasks in the American federal system: (1) lawmaking, (2) oversight, (3) representation, and (4) education. Let's briefly consider each of these functions.

LEGISLATIVE TASKS

Lawmaking

Lawmaking is traditionally considered as *the* critical task of the legislature. Every year thousands of bills, constitutional amendments, and resolutions are introduced in the various state legislatures for consideration. As the policy-making arm of state government, state legislatures are restricted only by the federal and state constitutions and the governor's vetoes in their deliberations. Legislators must spend untold thousands of hours in the tedious, laborious job of working over legislation—bill assignment, subcommittee hearings, full committee hearings, fiscal committee hearings, testimony, amendments, and the like.

In a sense, the rites of legislative bill passage might best be compared to a giant pinball game. Bills (pinballs) bounce madly from one committee to another over to the other house and then, perhaps, back again. Most bills, like pinballs, get sidetracked along the way. And, as in pinball where the same metal balls are used game after game, legislative bills that die in one session are likely to be reintroduced the next session, or the next, or the next. Prime sources of the substantial stream of legislation include:

special interests and lobbies, governors, state bureaucracies, legislative staff, local governments, political parties, constituents, and even legislators at times.

The legislature is the public arena where various competing interests thrash out their policy differences. The prime lawmaking objective is to seek compromise among the bewildering array of conflicting demands.

Oversight

The oversight function is another important legislative task. Being a counterbalance to the governor and keeping track of the state bureaucracy is a formidable undertaking. Most state legislatures have difficulty being a coequal branch with the governor. State legislatures tend to be divided by personal regional and/or party divisions further complicated by two house divisions. The many legislative members have difficulty competing with the single governor for media attention. However, state legislators can make bureaucrats tremble—particularly when the budget of an agency is being reviewed.

Representation

No task is performed so zealously by state legislators as the representative function. Legislators, keenly aware of looming reelection battles, are anxious to serve their constituents. "Bringing home the bacon" and the "pork barrel" are traditional features of American legislatures.

Two classic dilemmas of representative government are: (1) should legislators merely echo the sentiments of their constituents when voting, or should they follow their own judgment or conscience; and (2) should legislators be a typical cross-section of the adult population of a state—racially, socially, occupationally—or should they represent the most able elements of a state's population?

Education

Finally, state legislatures serve an important educational function. The legislature provides a major public forum for discussion of the critical issues of the day. It is the only branch of government where the decision-making process is, to some extent, public, and while the public portion of the legislative process is the tip of the iceberg, citizens can at least see the tip.

Legislative investigations of vexing public issues help focus attention on these problems. For example, in the summer of 1979, the California legislature held special hearings on the gas shortage in an attempt to find out who was to blame for the crisis. Moreover, through newsletters and speeches legislators help keep local citizens informed on developments at the state capitol. Of course, given the public's absorption with daily living problems and other distractions, the educational function does get sidetracked frequently—but there is at least potential.

FORMAL STRUCTURE OF THE CALIFORNIA LEGISLATURE

Patterned after the bicameral Congress and like 48 of the other state legislatures (Nebraska is the sole exception), the California Constitutions of 1849 and 1879, Article IV, vest legislative authority in two houses— the assembly and senate. The California legislature's upper house, the senate, has 40 members elected to four-year staggered terms, i.e., half are elected every two years. In the lower house, the assembly, members serve two-year terms, and all 80 are up for election every two years. From 1923 until 1965, California's legislature operated under the Federal Plan: the assembly's representation was based on population; the senate's on area (counties). Since 1965, the U.S. Supreme Court has required both houses of American state legislatures to be based on population. To be eligible to be elected to the California legislature, one must be at least 18 years of age, a U.S. citizen, an inhabitant of California for three years, and a resident of one's district for at least one year.

Each house is organized differently. In the assembly, the speaker is the key legislative figure, while in the senate, political power is shared by a number of senators including Rules Committee members and key chairpersons.

While the structural framework of the California legislature has remained basically unchanged over the 100-plus years of state history, the legislative style of the chambers has changed considerably over the years. Particularly during the 1960s, the California legislature was transformed from a typical, moribund state legislature into a modern, professional legislature, or, to use the phrase of one expert, the California legislature became the "Cadillac of American state legislatures." (Given the current gas shortage on the one hand, and the limits on governmental spending philosophy of the contemporary period on the other, this accolade may turn out to be a mixed blessing.)

THE PROFESSIONAL LEGISLATURE

For much of the 19th and 20th centuries, American state legislatures tended to be the dustbins of the American federal system. State legislatures tended to be fettered by antiquated state constitutions, outflanked by the national government's new social programs, confused by bureaucrats, dominated by full-time, professional governors, and indebted to lobbyists for meals and sustenance. Further compounding the difficulties facing state legislatures, historically at least, was the problem of representativeness. State legislatures were usually run by rural state legislators. Farm bloc legislators were usually indifferent, if not outright hostile, to urban population needs. As population steadily shifted to urban centers in many American states during the 20th century, these rural solons fought a bitter rearguard action to maintain control. State legislatures came to be labeled in the press as "horse-and-buggy" institutions designed for an earlier, less complicated era. State legislatures through the mid-1960s were a not-very-funny national joke.

Several factors occurred in the 1960s and early 1970s which helped lead a number of state legislatures to modernize and professionalize. One key factor was the series of reapportionment decisions issued by the United States Supreme Court in the early 1960s, culminating in the *Reynolds* v. *Sims* decision in which the Court ruled *both* houses of American state legislatures were to be apportioned on the basis of population. The rural stranglehold on American (and California's) state legislatures was effectively broken.

Background to reform

Through the early 1960s, California's legislature was reasonably typical of other states. Legislators were poorly paid, met only part of every year, had inadequate offices, had haphazard procedures, and had very few professional staff. Through 1965, the California legislature's working conditions were controlled extensively by the state constitution. For example, legislative salaries ($6,000 annually) and the length of session (120 days for general sessions in odd-numbered years and 30 days for budget sessions in even-numbered years) were locked into the constitution. To change either feature required amending the constitution, an always difficult and time-consuming endeavor. First, the amendment would have had to be approved by a two-thirds majority vote in each house (opportunities for grandstanding are legion), then signed by the governor, and, finally, the toughest hurdle of all—submission to an always wary public for final approval. Not too surprisingly, raising legislators' (politicians!) salaries was a difficult notion to sell to the public.

In order to deal with these sorts of constitutional problems as well as to remove obsolete portions from the document, the legislature adopted a concurrent resolution in 1963 establishing a Constitutional Revision Commission. The commission made its initial report to the legislature in February 1966 and recommended revisions of articles dealing with the legislative, executive, and judicial branches of California government. These proposed constitutional revisions were submitted to the voters as Proposition 1A of November 1966 (see Chapter 3).

Under the proposed provisions of Proposition 1A, legislators, henceforth, would set their own salaries and determine for themselves the length of their legislative session. The legislature had previously passed a pay raise bill raising their salary from $6,000 to $16,000. This would become effective if 1A were approved. To assuage the public, safeguards were built into the language of 1A on legislators' pay. Legislators were to be limited to a five percent salary increase per year, and any pay hike approved by the legislature would not become effective until the next legislative session.

1A—The successful campaign

Undoubtedly, the leading proponent of Proposition 1A, and the person most instrumental in getting the constitutional revision approved, was Speaker Jess Unruh. To gain approval of 1A, Unruh sought support from several key sources: (1) he secured the cooperation of the "other party" —many key Republican legislative leaders gave solid support to the effort; (2) he persuaded lobbyists to join the campaign ("take a lobbyist to lunch" became a legislative theme) by warning them that their failure to support 1A with political campaign contributions would be long remembered; (3) he garnered the support of much of the state's press by promising the legislature would pass new, strict conflict of interest rules upon adoption of 1A; and (4) he campaigned tirelessly the length and breadth of the state championing the measure.

Unruh argued that improving legislative salaries would help attract brighter, better educated people to the legislature. Low pay, he believed, tended to discourage able people from running for office and made it nearly impossible for some minority group leaders to run for office. Inadequate pay virtually guaranteed that legislators would be dependent on lobbyists for meals, lodgings, and other sundries. Further, Unruh contended that pay should be based upon the responsibilities of the job, and, hence, legislators deserved more money. Improved legislative salaries would allow legislators a chance to concentrate their full-time attention on their legislative chores. Jess Unruh's protege, Larry Margolis, helped establish the Citizens Conference on State Legislatures, later Legis/50, as a private citizen group urging reform and modernization of American state legislatures.

In November 1966, California voters, by a spectacular 3-to-1 margin, voted approval of Proposition 1A. The campaign had succeeded. After the overwhelming vote of approval for Proposition 1A, Speaker Unruh was invited to address university groups, public forums, and other state legislatures on the topic of legislative reform and the California success story. In addition, delegations of legislators from other states came to visit the California capital almost like pilgrims visiting Mecca to discuss

ILLUSTRATION 9–1
Jess Unruh   He led the legislative reform movement in California.

Photo courtesy California State Library

with their California colleagues how this "miracle" might be achieved in their states.

Since the passage of 1A, base pay for California legislators has been raised several times to the present yearly salary of $25,555. In addition to salary, California legislators enjoy other perks (perquisites) of office that provide additional resources to legislators.

Perks

Currently, California legislators receive $46 daily (per diem) for living expenses while the legislature is in session. This generally adds another $9–$10,000 tax-free income to a legislator's income. (A sum greater than basic salaries for legislators in about half the states.) Among the other major perks (most were adopted when the constitution limited pay increases) are (1) $225 monthly for car leasing; (2) a gasoline credit card providing free gas and car maintenance service on their leased car; (3)

money provided to pay for district office rent; (4) a telephone credit card; (5) office supplies and office furniture; (6) money for five constituent newsletters and/or questionnaires per session; (7) options for life, medical, and dental insurance programs; (8) a generous retirement system, and (9) salaries for personal staff to assist legislators.

STAFF AUGMENTATION

As noted previously, even prior to the 1960s the California legislature had a small but competent professional staff. In addition to a small clerical—secretarial—housekeeping staff, there were three key staff offices operating prior to the decade of the 1960s which provide important staff assistance to the legislature. These offices are:

1. *Legislative Counsel* (1913) provides technical bill drafting and bill amending services to legislators. Presently, there are nearly 60 attorneys in this office.
2. *Auditor General* (1955) provides independent postaudits of state agencies to insure that funds appropriated are spent according to law. Currently, there are nearly 50 auditors plus support staff comprising this office.
3. *Legislative Analyst* (1957) provides fiscal expertise to legislators and prepares the *Analysis of the Budget Bill*. This latter document, in effect, sets the agenda and establishes the parameters for budget deliberations by the Senate Finance and Assembly Ways and Means Committees. At present, there are 56 program and administrative analysts and support staff in this office. Because of the skill, personal style, and strict nonpartisan stance of its former long-time director, Alan Post, this office developed a national reputation.

During the Unruh speakership years in the 1960s, there was a rapid expansion of assembly legislative staff. Since legislators inevitably have to be generalists, professional staff could provide legislators badly needed policy expertise. A skilled professional staff, it was argued, would allow legislators to concentrate on their more important legislative chores (staff could handle the more routine duties) and, equally significant, would provide legislators a neutral informational source freeing them from the lobbyists. This neutral information is particularly important when legislators must evaluate legislation drafted by lobbyists and state bureaucrats. A few years after the assembly had augmented its staff, the senate began its own staff development program.

Committee consultants

Prior to the 1960s, only a few major assembly and senate committees had consultants. By 1963, under Unruh's prodding, every assembly committee had at least one consultant, and several of the more important committees had more than one. For example, currently, the Assembly Ways and Means Committee has 12 consultants to assist members. (Ways and Means is the only assembly or senate committee with a formalized majority (8) and minority (4) consultant arrangement.) Committee consultants have prime responsibility for doing bill analyses, coordinating testimony at committee hearings, and finally, carrying out other tasks assigned by the chair.

Research staff

In 1962, Speaker Unruh helped create the Assembly Legislative Reference Bureau, which two years later was transformed into the Office of Research. The office has three prime responsibilities in the assembly: it provides long-range and short-range research; it provides expertise on a variety of technical subjects; and it also provides a third reading analysis of pending bills. While complaints were raised in the early years of the AOR's history that it was primarily a staff vehicle for the speaker and the majority party, under its last two directors, Jim Hurst and Richard Brandsma, the AOR has become more nonpartisan. Currently, the director of the office is responsible to a bipartisan Committee on Policy Research Management for its overall direction.

Additionally, on some research projects, the legislature has found it useful to contract with private consulting firms to carry out specialized research on various topics. For example, the Rand Corporation, a private research consulting firm, has done several research projects for the legislature on energy-related matters.

Personal staff

By 1963, each assembly member was provided with at least one administrative assistant, two capitol secretaries, and a secretary/field representative in the district office. The legislator's personal staff perform a variety of functions—answering constituent mail, handling constituent problems, working on legislation, attending district functions, and sending out news releases and newsletters.

Leadership staff

Each of the assembly party leadership positions—speaker, speaker pro tem (the presiding officer) minority leader, majority and minority floor leaders, Rules Committee members, and caucus leaders—is provided additional staff to augment their regular personal staff. For example, the current assembly speaker has seven legislative aides in his Sacramento office to assist him in the management of the lower house.

Party staff

Another significant expansion of staff during the Unruh years came with the development of the majority and minority consultant offices. Currently, there are 19 majority and 18 minority party consultants. Since 1969, majority and minority consultants and caucus staff personnel have provided assistance to members of their party (especially newcomers) on matters such as preparing newsletters and news releases, drafting speeches, analyzing voting patterns, and providing assistance on issues.

Before the adoption of Proposition 9, the Political Reform Act of June 1974, many party consultants, and sometimes leadership staff, would work for their party's candidates during election campaigns while still on state payroll. Under the new reform format, this practice is forbidden.

Today, during the campaign season, majority and minority consultants working on campaigns go on leaves of absence from their offices and off the state payroll. During this period, their salaries must be paid by the candidate for whom they are working. Legislative staffers who violate this rule run the risk of having the FPPC (the enforcement commission established by Proposition 9) investigate their activities and possibly fine them. One assemblyman was recently fined by the FPPC for having a legislative consultant working in his campaign—on state time. The bad publicity engendered by such a violation could be disastrous to a campaign. Undoubtedly, party staff and leadership staff have helped contribute to a more partisan tone in the contemporary state legislature.

Housekeeping staff

Overall administration of assembly staff is handled by Assembly Rules and its consultant, the chief administrative officer of the assembly. Other housekeeping staff include: the chief clerk, who keeps track of floor session details and bill assignments; the sergeants-at-arms staff; the mail room assistants; the secretarial pool; Bill Room employees and messengers.

Senate staff

Clearly, the senate has moved more slowly in modernizing and professionalizing itself than has the assembly. The assembly has led the way in staffing, and the senate has followed—with some reluctance. While there is parallel staff in each house, the senate has fewer committee consultants, party staff, and research staff. Individual senators, however, have larger personal staffs than their assembly counterparts (partially due to the larger districts they represent).

The senate has placed more emphasis on recruiting experts already established in their specialties to join their staff, while the assembly has tended to recruit young men and women, many straight from law or graduate schools, who have proven themselves in legislative internship and/or campaign positions.

One receives the impression that assembly members view expert staff more as equals; senators, on the whole, seem more conscious of the fact that they are the members, not the staff. One cynical senate aide was heard to remark that senate staff are used primarily for retinue services and other ritualistic purposes—not advice. Undoubtedly, the senate has moved in the staff direction with less enthusiasm than the assembly.

Interns

In addition to its regular legislative staff, there is one other source of work assistance to California legislators—interns. The California Assembly was one of the first state legislative bodies in the nation to offer college graduates an opportunity to work for the legislature for a year and, in return, receive a modest stipend. Since 1957, the California Assembly Internship Program (now called the Fellowship Program) has provided additional legislative staff assistance to the assembly. Fellows assist members and staff in their legislative chores, and, in return, are provided a unique educational and job training experience. Many of the ex-fellows hold paid legislative staff positions today. Some have been elected to the legislature. The state senate also has established its own fellowship program.

In addition to assembly and senate fellows, an increasing number of California colleges and universities allow students an opportunity to receive academic credit for work experiences with the legislature. With few exceptions, interning is probably one of the very best ways young people have to learn about the legislature and possibly work into legislative staff positions.

PROCEDURES

As the California legislature has become more professionalized over the last several decades, there has been impressive progress in streamlining and routinizing the legislative process to make it more orderly and less vulnerable to behind-the-scenes maneuvering. In the "good ole' days," floor sessions were chaotic. Members used to have to use their floor desks to do their legislative office work, and anyone who wanted could get a floor pass. Today, access to the floor is strictly limited to members and their secretaries. Each legislator has his or her own microphone, and floor debates usually proceed smoothly. In the assembly, an electrical roll call system is used to record votes, though the senate still uses the more time-consuming oral roll call.

Committees used to frequently meet in closed-door, executive session. A few committees used to meet ahead of time to decide their course of action, and some committee chairs used to control the actions of their committees. Activities such as these are increasingly uncommon in contemporary Sacramento capitol politics. The two-year session, public announcement of hearings, orderly procedures, and the right of anyone so desiring to testify, all help contribute to a relatively open process.

To keep track of the legislative flow, the senate and assembly publish several important documents: the *Daily Journal* (contains the official proceedings of each house and the roll calls on all votes taken); the *Files* (announcements of committee hearings and listing of bills scheduled for action); and the *Weekly History* (an index of legislative subjects and a record of actions taken on a bill). Bills, constitutional amendments, and resolutions are printed and made available to the legislature and the public as soon after introduction as possible. As Chief Clerk of the Assembly, James Driscoll (1972:121) commented, "The California legislature maintains the most complete and sensitive information system of any legislative body in the world."

EFFECTS OF PROFESSIONALIZATION: CINDERELLA OR FRANKENSTEIN?

What effect has this professionalizing trend had on the California legislature? Overall, it is difficult to prove that these legislative reforms have or have not made a great difference. Let's examine the arguments of each side on the issue.

Cinderella case

Proponents of legislative professionalization would argue the California legislature has changed markedly, and for the better, over the last decade or so. The legislative reforms enacted have meant substantial improvements in a number of key areas.

MEMBER QUALITIES

Clearly, contemporary California legislators are better informed and better educated than their preprofessional colleagues. Nearly every member of the present-day legislature has completed at least some college work, and most have advanced graduate degrees. These members have the ability to deal with the complex problems confronting California. Contemporary California legislators tend to come from four major professional occupational backgrounds: attorneys (35–40 percent of each chamber), former local politicians, exlegislative staff, and people from the business community.

Since 1966, when the pay and overall prestige of the California legislature was improved, many more minority politicians have run and have been elected to the legislature. Obviously, a host of reasons account for the growing numbers of minority members getting elected to the California legislature, including reapportionment and a growing political awareness in the minority communities, but the increased pay and status of the legislature has helped. Clearly, the white "Gentlemen's Club" atmosphere of the legislature of earlier years is absent from the present scene.

It is true that historically, at least, the less professionalized the legislature, the higher the percentage of women members in that chamber. Perhaps more women were able to get elected in less professional legislatures, because there was less (male) competition for elective office. However, if California is at all typical, this seems to be changing. Increasing numbers of women are running and getting elected to the contemporary and highly professional California legislature. Table 9–1 shows the increases in minority and female representation in the California legislature over the last decade.

TURNOVER

One of the frequently cited criticisms of nonprofessional state legislatures is the problem of constant turnover in membership and the instability this creates. While there are reasons for extensive turnover (usually about one fourth of the state legislators are freshmen in an average session), the most frequently noted is low pay. As Keefe and Ogul comment (1977:131), "Burdened by low pay, high costs, and the frustrations of the job, members serve a brief tour of office and drop out."

However, it is true that even in the professionalized California legislature, there is usually substantial turnover in membership, although not as great as in a nonprofessional legislature. For example, the recent record for longevity is held by Assemblyman John Knox, who was first

TABLE 9–1
Minority and female members in the California legislature, 1965–1978

	1965	1978	Percent of state population
Blacks	2	8	7.0%
Chicanos	0	6	18.0
Women	1	11	51.0

elected in 1960. And he has announced that he will not be running for reelection in 1980—there does seem to be a considerable amount of "burn-out" in the legislature. The job is *very* demanding. Only a handful of assembly representatives have served more than ten years in the lower house, and the senate is not too different.

While a very few assembly members die or voluntarily retire from the legislature, most will eventually run for higher office—state senate, Congress, or statewide office. Some get appointed to important judicial or administrative positions. In most other states, legislators simply return to their former occupations.

HIGH RANKING OF THE CALIFORNIA LEGISLATURE

Not surprisingly, a variety of recent studies rating state legislatures have come to the same conclusion: The California legislature is one of the best in the nation. The Citizens Conference on State Legislatures (now called Legis/50), in their pioneering survey of American state legislatures (Burns: 1971), ranked California's legislature first in the functional criterion, third in accountability, second in the informed category, third in independence, second in representativeness, and most important, first in overall performance.

Professor John Grumm (1971:291–322), in another study, concluded that professional legislatures seem to respond to the demands of urban populations better than nonprofessional legislatures. A study by Fisher et al. (1973:40) suggests that professional legislatures seem more supportive of public education than nonprofessional legislatures. It would also seem that the most innovative state governments have, for the most part, the most professional state legislatures (Walker, 1969; and Gray, 1973).

SUBSTANTIVE DIFFERENCES

Perhaps the two most significant differences between the California legislature before and after 1966 are first, the reduction in special interest power, and second, the growing ability of the legislature to play a co-equal role with the governor.

Clearly, the Artie Samish style of corrupt and flamboyant lobbying of the 1930s–40s era is largely behind us. Reasonably compensated, well-staffed California legislators are no longer as dependent on lobbyists for handouts or for information as they once were. While lobbyists still exert leverage through campaign contributions and social entertaining, they no longer dominate the legislature.

On the second point, admittedly, there is little "hard" evidence to support the view that present-day governors have found the professional legislature a more formidable adversary. Veto overrides or gubernatorial appointment rejections may not be as rare as they once were, but so many other political variables are involved on these votes that they are not very satisfactory indicators of legislative independence. Impressionistically, we can note, since 1966, the angry confrontations between Speaker Unruh and Governor Pat Brown; the delicate compromises finally worked out between Governor Reagan and Speaker Moretti; the open conflict between Governor Brown and Speaker McCarthy related to the former's championing of a constitutional convention to limit federal spending. Legislative leadership seems increasingly assertive. Governor Jerry Brown's eight item veto overrides in July 1979 were probably due more to his lack of good working relations with the legislature than to any institutional conflict.

Certainly, governors would no longer dare get involved in legislative leadership contests as they once did, and they seem more concerned about checking with the legislature on local appointments. Our view is that present-day California governors must work harder than their historical predecessors to achieve results in the legislature.

Frankenstein case

Clearly, not all scholars, journalists, or politicians are convinced that professionalized legislatures should be emulated. It is contended that the expensive, full-time features of professionalized legislatures are ill-suited for many rural, small state legislatures. These legislatures can manage quite nicely meeting for a few months every other year without having all the trappings of a modern legislature.

Patterson (1978:216) argues that much of the discussion of legislative reform seems to miss the point. He suggests that legislative experts tend to lump minor, remedial changes in a legislator's work schedule— getting an extra secretary, being provided rent money for a district office, or getting per diem living expenses—as critical "reforms." Reform, Patterson argues, should connote substantive changes affecting the significant operations of a legislature.

Perhaps the most frequently heard criticisms raised against professional legislatures is that: (1) they are costly; (2) there is no "hard" evidence to prove conclusively that professional legislatures produce qualitatively better legislation than their nonprofessional counterparts; and (3) professional legislatures are less responsive to the public than nonprofessional ones.

Other frequently heard criticisms leveled against professional legislatures are that:

1. Substantial legislative salaries attract greedy, overly ambitious types to the legislature, not public-spirited citizens.
2. Part-time legislators are more representative—they come from a wider variety of occupations, from a wider span of age groups, and have a higher percentage of women members.
3. Professional legislators tend to be comprised of a successful elite.
4. Per-diem expense allowances serve to lengthen legislative sessions so that legislators can continue to pocket their expense money.
5. Professional, full-time legislators spend too much time in the state capitol—they should be back in the district listening to constituents.
6. Professional legislators tend to become prima donnas expecting preferential treatment.
7. Legislative staff become a sort of "shadow government" in professional legislatures, making many behind-the-scenes decisions for their bosses and insulating them from the public.
8. Ex-legislative staffers frequently run for open seats in professional legislatures, and this creates an unhealthy inbreeding in these institutions.

Last, one could note that even though the professional California legislature has reams of information (perhaps almost too much) and the structural capacity to make enlightened decisions, their record in resolving several key current state issues—property tax relief, malpractice disputes, no-fault auto insurance, preserving agricultural land, statewide land use planning, implementing Proposition 13, the Serano decision, or promoting political reform—is hardly exemplary. If it were not for the initiative *or the threat* of the initiative, many of these issues would still be unresolved. Indeed, it can be argued that professional legislatures may have more difficulty resolving conflict than nonprofessional ones. The many bright, assertive, independent legislators in the new reformed legislature are all anxious to make their contribution, and this makes compromise more difficult. The old legislature's members could be (and were) led more easily by leadership.

POLITICS OF THE LEGISLATIVE PROCESS: THE ASSEMBLY

The speaker of the California Assembly is unquestionably the most powerful single member of the lower house and, indeed, of the legislature. There are five important questions to consider in examining the role of the assembly speaker. (1) What are the speaker's powers? (2) How does a member get to be speaker? (3) What criteria does the speaker use in making committee assignments? (4) What are the limits to the speaker's powers? and (5) What is the relationship between the speaker and the minority party?

The speaker's powers

The speaker of the California Assembly is unquestionably the most powerful single member of the assembly and, indeed, the California legislature. The speaker is second only to the governor in terms of influence within the California governmental milieu. In the assembly, the speaker has total control over: (1) selection of standing committee chairs; (2) selection of select committee chairs, vice chairs, and subcommittee chairs; (3) assignment of members to committees (Rules Committee is the single exception); (4) assignment to subcommittees, joint committees (i.e., the assembly members), and select committees; (5) assignment of bills to committees; (6) selection of the other majority party leadership positions—majority floor leader, caucus chair, speaker pro tem (presiding officer), and party whips; (7) control of assembly floor action; (8) chief rule enforcer; and (9) through the Rules Committee chair, determination of matters such as the location of the member's capitol office, whether the member might get an extra secretary, or even whether a member will be allowed a second district office.

Electing the speaker

Before Jess Unruh's tenure as speaker, speakers were elected by a vote of the entire membership every two years after the general election. This became the most important single vote of the session for members. Candidates for speaker would promise choice committee assignments to members in return for their support. Not infrequently, the governor might throw his support to a particular legislator. Party affiliation was a relatively minor factor in the speakership elections. Usually, Democratic and Republican assembly members would vote for one of their own party's colleagues—but not always. However, Republicans were the majority party for most of the first half of the century, and hence, most speakers tended to be Republicans. If a member were on the winning side in a speakership contest, that legislator could expect to be rewarded, but if a member were on the losing side. . . .

Unruh changed, in effect, the way speakers were to be elected. Previously, the crucial decision-making arena was the assembly floor; under Unruh's prodding, it was shifted to the majority party caucus. In 1964, Unruh successfully secured an agreement within the Democratic Party caucus that all members of the majority party be *pledged* to vote on the floor for the candidate receiving the most votes in the majority caucus (i.e., Unruh). This meant the minority party, in effect, had no real voice in the speakership vote. The formal vote of the entire assembly was meaningless. This has been the pattern ever since. However, in an intra-party speakership battle in November 1974 between incumbent Speaker Leo

McCarthy and challenger Willy Brown, the latter sought the support of Republican assembly members along with other disgruntled Democrats in an attempt to oust the speaker. All Republicans voted for Brown plus a few Democrats, and they nearly toppled McCarthy from office. Since this was the second time of a McCarthy-Brown fight, McCarthy punished assembly dissidents severely.

In addition to the traditional bartering of committee assignments and chairs to get pledges of speakership support, Unruh added a new dimension—campaign contributions. As a powerful legislator and former chair of several "juice" committees (committees where powerful financial interests had policy interests) and a good arm-twister, Unruh was able to raise a substantial Democratic assembly campaign kitty. This money, in turn, was dispensed to "deserving" Democratic incumbents or grateful Democratic candidates in open districts. Interestingly, 1970's Speaker Leo McCarthy faced his most serious leadership challenge in December 1979 because of the speaker's campaign war chest. Howard Berman, once the speaker's top lieutenant and majority floor leader, sought to topple McCarthy from the speakership because, it was claimed, McCarthy was amassing campaign funds for his own future state race in 1982—not to assist Assembly Democrats in marginal districts. Northern Assembly Democrats tended to stick with San Franciscan, Leo McCarthy, while many southern Democrats supported West Los Angeles Assemblyman, Howard Berman. Though McCarthy lost a 26–24 vote in the Democratic caucus in January 1979, he was able for the time being to retain his position since Berman could not muster sufficient strength in the caucus necessary to bind it to him, and he needed to put together 41 votes on the floor to replace McCarthy. Clearly, both McCarthy and Berman were political "losers" in this bitter struggle for power.

Selection to committees

Since the speaker appoints all committee chairs and selects nearly all committee members, his or her appointment powers are virtually total. The assembly committee selection process is therefore quite different than the system used in its federal counterpart, the House of Representatives. In the U.S. House, members normally acquire chair positions through a seniority system process. Generally, the most senior member of the majority party with the longest continuous service on a committee becomes its chair (assuming this person gets the approval of the majority party caucus). The congressional chair selection process is marked by relatively little politicking, (except perhaps in the caucus vote), little backstabbing, and an almost ironclad guarantee that the chair will be a congressional veteran in his or her 50s or 60s (and sometimes 70s or 80s) with years of acquired expertise in the particular subject matter area of the committee.

In the assembly, seniority counts for little. Party affiliation is of some consequence, though traditionally the minority party gets at least some of the committee chairs, depending on the numerical size of the minority party, their cooperativeness, and other variables. But seldom would minority members chair the most important assembly committees. In the assembly, chair determination is left entirely to the speaker. The speaker's selection criteria generally include: (1) loyalty, (2) competence and ability, (3) political philosophy, (4) party affiliation, (5) friendships, and (6) occasionally, seniority. Obviously, the more secure the speaker, the less the emphasis on loyalty for committee selections. Assembly committee chairs are frequently legislators in their 30s or 40s, and often only in their second or third term. The assembly system is more political than the House of Representatives, but new ideas and young, dynamic individuals can also quickly assume leadership positions.

The speaker will generally use the same criteria listed for chair selection for committee selections. Obviously, the speaker wants to retain solid, safe majority party dominance of the major policy committees. Also, unlike chair selections, members are sent forms by the speaker, and they are asked to rank their choices for committees. Selections to committees depend heavily on the interests, background, and district of the legislator. A legislator representing a rural district would probably want to get on the Agriculture or Water Committees; a former school teacher would probably want to get on the Education Committee; an ex-insurance agent on the Finance and Insurance Committee, and so on.

The speaker also designates his or her choices for other assembly majority party leader positions. The majority floor leader is second-in-command and is responsible for shepherding key bills of the majority party through the legislature. The caucus chair and whip work to forge unified party stances on major issues. The speaker pro tem is the presiding officer, and usually a highly respected senior member of the majority party. Finally, Rules Committee and the Ways and Means Committee chairs are other key figures in the assembly leadership group. Given the reasonably small size of the assembly, the many standing committees, the select and joint committees, and the diversity of interests of the membership, it is normally not too difficult for a speaker to give at least one or two committee assignment requests to a member.

Because of the California speaker's extensive appointment powers, the congressional apprenticeship pattern (i.e., the newcomer "should be seen but not heard" and should defer to party elders) is totally absent. In the assembly, new members are expected to take part right away. If the freshman legislator has expertise in a subject matter area, he or she may exert influence in policy development immediately. Of course, a freshman will *probably* not be selected as a committee chair, be placed on Ways and Means, get elected to Rules, carry major bills, or have a large office. Traditionally, one freshman from a "class" is selected for hazing on the floor by senior colleagues when the new member presents his or her first bill. But, other than these minor difficulties, within a few months new members are treated as veterans.

The speaker—Rule enforcer and limits

The style and tone of the assembly is set by the speaker. From items as mundane as dress standards to serious breeches of legislative ethics, the speaker plays the central role. The speaker alone has the power to punish members. As with any social organization, in addition to formal rule structures, there are many unwritten rules and customs that develop over the years to facilitate group processes. Among the unwritten rules in the California legislature are items such as: honoring commitments, keeping one's word, never attacking a colleague personally, supporting committee integrity, granting a colleague's request for reconsideration of a bill, never testifying in opposition to another member's bill, or never calling public attention to necessary, but embarrassing, features of the legislature such as absentee voting. Clearly, some rules do change over time. Dress code standards have changed to a more informal attire. It used to be that members would not campaign against one another, but some do today in the more partisan legislative setting. Indeed, some lobbyists complain that contemporary members no longer can be counted on to honor a commitment.

While a rule violator or maverick can be cold-shouldered by colleagues or not included socially, it is the speaker who is the ultimate disciplinarian. Depending upon the severity and frequency of the offense, a speaker could remove a member from a good committee, sack the member from a chair position, move the member to a smaller office, not allow a legislator extra staff, not honor a member's request for money to attend an out-of-state meeting and other such penalties, or ultimately, attempt to reapportion the legislator out of his or her district. (Reapportionment takes place every ten years with the Federal Census.)

Technically speaking, of course, the state constitution stipulates that each house judges the qualifications and elections of its members and on a two-thirds vote can expel a member. But expelling a member seems a remote possibility. In fact, there is no blackballing of members in the legislative club—voters, not legislators, determine membership. Legislative leaders must put up with the "accidents of democracy" washed upon the legislative shore. On the few occasions when state legislatures have attempted to exclude a legally elected member, the courts have generally sided with the aggrieved legislator.

Obviously, a legislature comprised of many mavericks would clearly be unmanageable and not very productive. On the other hand, maverick legislators, by refusing to pay homage to the leadership, by challenging stuffy traditions, and by adhering to their principles, add a breath of fresh air to the sometimes stale legislative atmosphere. Having a few mavericks in the legislature adds an important dimension to the legislative process.

Clearly, there are risks and liabilities for speakers if they find they must discipline a member. Heavy-handed disciplining would be resented by many members and probably not viewed favorably by the public. It is interesting to note that Leo McCarthy's chair of Ways and Means, Don Boatwright, was the legislative proponent favoring a constitutional convention to balance the federal budget, while Leo McCarthy was the legislature's leading opponent of this strategy. Yet, there was never any question that Boatwright would remain as McCarthy's choice for chair of Ways and Means. In the long run, persuasion and consultation seem to be more effective for speakers than force.

Finally, while the speaker is a powerful political figure within the assembly, the office has not been a good launching pad to other state elective positions. Some former speakers, such as Jess Unruh and Bob Moretti, developed reputations for being overly partisan or ruthless and hurt their gubernatorial quest. Clearly, skills in running the assembly do not automatically transfer to a statewide campaign. Obviously, too, when a speaker announces for another office, he or she becomes a lame duck unable to reward or punish effectively. Since present speaker Leo McCarthy has indicated he will be stepping down soon, there is considerable speculation as to whom his successor will be.

The speaker and the minority party

The minority party has a similar leadership hierarchy: floor leader, caucus chair, and whip, with roughly corresponding duties to the majority party. Perhaps what is most unique in the minority party leadership structure is the paucity of power of the minority leader. None of the powers accorded minority party leaders in most other state legislatures reside in this office. Minority members are selected as chairs, placed on committees, or assigned offices by the speaker—not the minority leader —though Speaker McCarthy's intraparty challenge has forced him to seek accommodation with Republican assembly leaders.

The size of the minority membership, the political climate, personality, the skills of the minority leader, and other factors, help determine the extent to which the speaker consults a minority leader counterpart. To get press coverage, former minority leader Paul Priolo got into the habit of scheduling his press meetings in the same room immediately following Speaker McCarthy. His efforts to capture the media's attention finally evolved into joint press conferences. Of course, if the minority leader is too cooperative, this may alienate minority colleagues. When Priolo, assembly minority leader, announced his candidacy for the 1980 U.S. Senate race, he found himself a lame duck. In the battle that ensued to oust Priolo, some Republican members voted for his eventual replacement, Carol Hallett, because Priolo, it was claimed, worked too well with Speaker McCarthy.

Finally, minority leaders are expected to raise campaign contributions for their party colleagues and are also expected to increase their party numbers in the assembly.

POLITICS OF THE LEGISLATIVE PROCESS: SENATE

Prior to the U.S. Supreme Court-ordered reapportionment of 1966, the California Senate was a much different legislative body than the assembly. The motto in Sacramento used to be, "the assembly proposes —the senate disposes." The senate, on the whole, tended to be less innovative, more conservative, more northern and rural-oriented, less partisan, and less professionalized. Typically, conservative measures would be voted out of the senate and killed in assembly policy committees. And, vice versa—liberal measures would be torpedoed in senate committees. Since 1966, however, differences between the two chambers have narrowed perceptibly, though some still persist.

Clearly, the senate is the more prestigious body. It has the sole responsibility for approving the governor's appointees. Senators serve four-year terms rather than the two-year terms of assembly members. Hence, senators get a "free-ride" political advantage in the middle of their term. They can run for higher office and still hold their senate seat. Assembly members who want to move up to other offices must gamble with their political careers, since they cannot file for another state office and the assembly simultaneously. There are half as many senators (40) as assembly representatives and, therefore, they are better known. Senators occupy approximately half the space in the state capitol building, and consequently tend to have larger offices than their assembly counterparts. Prior to the capitol restoration, senate chambers tended to be more elegant and sumptuous than the assembly—an ambience befitting upper house members. Finally, assembly members run for the senate when there is an opportunity; senators would never voluntarily run for the assembly.

"Old guard"

As members of the pre-1966 senate retire from office, one crucial difference between the two houses remains: the leadership structure. The assembly is led by one person, the speaker, while the senate is governed by a five-member Senate Rules Committee. The president pro tem of the senate is the chair of the Rules Committee, but, in truth, this officer is merely one of five votes on the committee. The pro tem's influence rests less on formal authority and more through informal persuasion. An occasional pro tem, for example, Hugh Burns, has been nearly as powerful as most assembly speakers. Most pro tems, however, are not. The senate pro tem cannot make the same sorts of committee assignment/chair promises to colleagues that a speaker can. The senate pro tem must work with other Rules members to be effective, and all decisions are part of a collective process.

Election of the pro tem comes on a vote of all members of the senate. Party affiliation, while of considerable consequence, is not crucial, though the likelihood of the senate electing a minority party pro tem seems extremely remote. Once in office, a speaker is rarely challenged; his or her position usually becomes more secure over time. The pro tem is in a much more precarious position, since senate leadership is a collective enterprise. Hence, the senate tends to be a more volatile and unstable chamber than the assembly, somewhat like an Arab sheikdom or Latin American banana republic with plots, coups, and rumors of coups.

The other four members of the Senate Rules Committee are nominated by the two-party caucuses and tend to be veteran members. Again though, there is no ironclad tradition that overlooked members of a party caucus will not look for support from the opposition party.

In the "good old days," powerful senior senators tended to chair, dominate, and overlap on a few key committees. Seniority was an important criterion for promotion to chairs. Many "old guard" senators believed that new senators ("young Turks") had to be properly trained into senate traditions and customs before they could be given important assignments. Party leadership positions in the senate: floor leader, caucus leader, and so on, tend to be of lesser importance than their assembly counterparts, while committees tend to be more powerful and independent.

In 1966, Pro Tem Hugh Burns faced an unprecedented situation: 22 of the 40 senators (a clear majority) were new to the chamber. These 22 (14 were former assembly members) had been elected in the aftermath of the 1966 reapportionment. Burns treated all 22 as "freshmen," giving no preferential treatment to the former assembly members in the group. The disgruntled freshmen and other Burns opponents coalesced to eventually oust Hugh Burns. Today, power is more diffused in the senate, but, nevertheless, old senate hands tend to cluster on key senate committees, such as Rules, Finance, Revenue and Taxation, and Government Efficiency.

One last feature of senate leadership should be noted. Technically, the presiding officer of the senate and theoretically one of its leaders is the lieutenant governor. Since presiding over the senate is a minor and routine duty, most lieutenant governors have spent little time with the gavel. Indeed, after one year in office, Lieutenant Governor Curb had never presided over the senate. This is primarily because Curb is concerned with potential problems of conflict of interest if he makes a floor ruling, and then later has to sign or veto the same bill. Additionally, in cases of ties, the lieutenant governor can cast the deciding vote—but this seldom happens. Clearly, the lieutenant governor is not one of the powerful leaders in the upper house. (The lieutenant governor's powers as acting governor when the governor is absent from the state are discussed in Chapter 11.)

POLITICS OF THE LEGISLATIVE PROCESS: MECHANICS

In Illustration 9–2, the reader can view the flowchart of the bill process in the California legislature. While the various "nuts-and-bolts" facts are included in the diagram, the essence of the process, frankly, cannot be depicted neatly on a flowchart.

In any given session, literally thousands of bills, resolutions, and constitutional amendments are introduced in the California legislature. While many bills are killed or held for further study, about 2,000 will pass both houses and be signed by the governor. A few bills are the inspiration of individual legislators, who have researched a particular issue, but most bill ideas are generated by interest groups, local governments, legislative staff, executive agencies, party organizations, and occasionally constituents. Most legislators want to author legislation. They are usually receptive to carrying bill proposals from different groups. Indeed, freshmen legislators consider it a favor if a group provides a bill for the new member to sponsor. Some legislators refuse to "author" a bill with which they are not in accord, other legislators introduce nearly everything offered them, though they may make only half-hearted efforts for bills on which they are ambivalent.

Status among one's legislative colleagues hinges, in part, on the ability of members to steer important legislation through the houses—being able to explain your measure, knowing when to accept amendments, knowing how to provide leverage, and knowing how to persuade your colleagues. In capitol parlance, the legislative lightweight "couldn't even get a Mother's Day Resolution through." (In the 1977 session, the legisture passed a resolution honoring grandparents!) Of course, a legislator's reputation is enhanced by being able to help kill a bill skillfully, too.

Each proposed bill is first sent to the legislative counsel's office, which drafts it into proper legal form and indicates the proposed changes in the existing law. The bill is then "placed across the desk" and given a number and dated. After this first "reading," the bill is assigned to committee (in the assembly, the speaker does this; in the senate, the Rules Committee). Most of the time, assignment of bills to committees is routine: bills are sent to *the appropriate* policy committee. However, there are

ILLUSTRATION 9–2
Legislative process

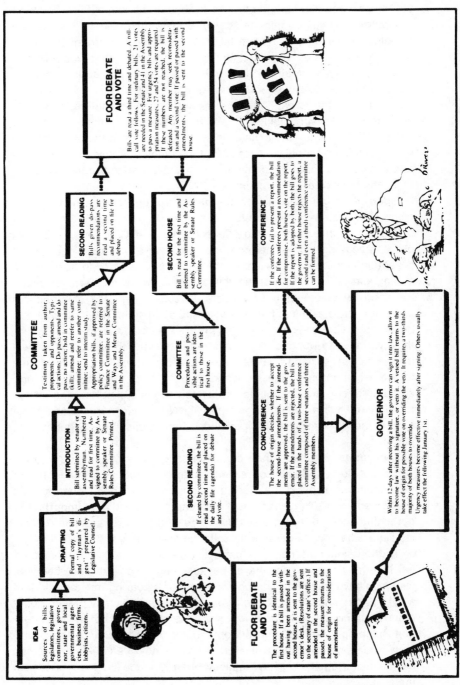

IDEA

Sources of bills: legislators, legislative committees, governor, state and local governmental agencies, business firms, lobbyists, citizens.

DRAFTING

Formal copy of bill and "layman's digest" prepared by Legislative Counsel.

INTRODUCTION

Bill submitted by senator or assemblyman. Numbered and read for first time. Assigned to committee by Assembly, speaker or Senate Rules Committee. Printed.

COMMITTEE

Testimony taken from author, proponents and opponents. Typical actions: Do pass, amend and do pass, no action, hold in committee (kill), amend and rerefer to same committee; refer to another committee; send to interim study.

Appropriation bills, if approved by policy committee, are referred to Finance Committee in the Senate and Ways and Means Committee in the Assembly.

SECOND READING

Bills given do-pass recommendations are read a second time and placed on file for debate.

FLOOR DEBATE AND VOTE

Bills are read a third time and debated. A roll-call vote follows. For ordinary bills, 21 votes are needed in the Senate and 41 in the Assembly to pass a measure. For urgency bills and appropriation measures, 27 and 54 votes are required. If these numbers are not reached, the bill is defeated. Any member may seek reconsideration and a second vote. If passed or passed with amendments, the bill is sent to the second house.

SECOND HOUSE

Bill is read for the first time and referred to committee by the Assembly, speaker or Senate Rules Committee.

COMMITTEE

Procedures and possible actions are identical to those in the first house.

SECOND READING

If cleared by committee, the bill is read a second time and placed on the daily file (agenda) for debate and vote.

FLOOR DEBATE AND VOTE

The procedure is identical to the first house. If a bill is passed without having been amended in the second house, it is sent to the governor's desk. (Resolutions are sent to the secretary of state's office.) If amended in the second house and passed, the measure returns to the house of origin for consideration of amendments.

CONCURRENCE

The house of origin decides whether to accept the second-house amendments. If the amendments are approved, the bill is sent to the governor. If the amendments are rejected, the bill is placed in the hands of a two-house conference committee composed of three senators and three Assembly members.

CONFERENCE

If the conferees fail to present a report, the bill dies. If the conferees present a recommendation for compromise, both houses vote on the report. If the report is adopted by both, the bill goes to the governor. If either house rejects the report, a second conference committee can be formed.

GOVERNOR

Within 12 days after receiving a bill, the governor can sign it into law, allow it to become law without his signature, or veto it. A vetoed bill returns to the house of origin for possible vote on overriding the veto. It requires a two-thirds majority of both houses to override.

Urgency measures become effective immediately after signing. Others usually take effect the following January 1st.

208

occasions when a bill might go to several different committees. Power to assign to a *particular* committee could be instrumental in a bill's passage or defeat. For example, a farm labor bill favoring the organizing rights of farm workers could be sent to the agriculture committee (comprised of rural legislators sympathetic to farmer's needs) or the labor committee comprised of large city liberals sympathetic to the union movement.

Essentially, the key policy decisions are made in committee. What the committee does with a bill is crucial. If a committee rejects a bill, it is "dead" for the rest of the legislative session. If a committee unanimously recommends that a bill be passed by the complete house, it almost certainly will be. In short, the committee process is vital to proposed legislation—the floor vote is a formality.

Upon receiving the bill with the author's request for a hearing, the committee chair sets the date for hearing as soon as possible and has it published in the *Assembly* or *Senate File*. The California legislative process does not allow chairs to refuse to hear a bill or seriously delay scheduling hearings on measures that they oppose. Prior to hearing, the author and lobbyist supporting the proposal will work hard to secure the approval of committee members, in some cases, by securing co-sponsors. Once a commitment is given by a legislator, it is supposed to be honored. Lobbyists opposing the bill are expected to inform the author they will have to oppose the measure. Frequently, the bill's author will invite lobbyists for and against a measure to get together ahead of time to see if compromises can be worked out. Ideally, for the bill's author, agreeing to certain reasonable amendments may suffice to head off opposition and guarantee passage of the bill. Nothing is more welcome to a bill's author than to have no opposition offered; this virtually guarantees passage.

Legislators who know their constituents are solidly opposed to a bill would be highly unlikely to be persuaded by a lobbyist, colleague, or party leader to support the measure. However, most bills generate little public sentiment. These technical bills can be exceedingly important to particular interests but are seldom discussed in the press and, hence, legislators have considerable flexibility in their voting.

To the uninitiated, hearings can often be anticlimatic and disappointing. Meeting times can be delayed because there is no quorum; observers who may have traveled hundreds of miles for a hearing may be told that a bill has been held over (put off); or expert witnesses may present testimony to committee members who are either not there, not paying attention, sleeping, or conferring with one another. The reason for this seemingly bizarre behavior by legislators is usually not due to lack of interest, but because legislators have usually already made up their minds on the issue.

Committee members may have already discussed the bill with experts, lobbyists, and staff; read the reports; sat through endless hearings on the bill in previous years; know the governor's and legislative party leader's stands; and checked for district impact. Thus, hearings usually do not provide legislators with new information. They tend to be more for the public record and for publicity from the press—though there are occasionally a few legislators on the fence who can be swayed one way or the other by expert testimony. Some groups, in an all-out effort to get committee approval, will pack the committee hearing room with their supporters in hopes of intimidating committee members to support a bill. This may or may not help their cause.

After arguments are presented for and against the bill, committee members can propose amendments that probably, but not necessarily, will be accepted by the bill's author. If the bill's author is unwilling to accept the amendment, the legislator runs the risk of having the bill defeated in committee. Thus, the member usually accepts the proposed amendment. Sometimes authors must offer clarifying amendments to soften opposition.

After action on the bill is completed in the committee, a member of the committee will move to report the bill out "do pass" or "do pass as amended." A majority of "Aye" votes is necessary to report a bill out; abstentions or "taking a walk" (to avoid voting) count, in effect, as "No" votes. The chair may hold the roll open if members have been called away or have not arrived at the hearing. If sufficient "Aye" votes are not there, a member may move to hold the bill over so that the bill's author can have more time to persuade some of his or her colleagues to support the bill.

If the committee wants to kill a bill nicely, or if it's on a new subject, the committee may recommend the bill for interim study. Occasionally, bills are reported out of committee without recommendation. Sometimes these are measures that must be forwarded to Ways and Means in the assembly or Finance in the senate to consider their fiscal impact. Any bill

ILLUSTRATION 9–3
Governor Jerry Brown appears before an assembly committee hearing He knows where the important decisions are made in the legislative process.

Photo courtesy Sacramento Bee

having *any* fiscal impact (nearly every important bill) must go to Assembly Ways and Means and Senate Finance.

A few measures are reported out to the floor without recommendation (committee members may have problems with the bill but feel the matter is important enough to give all members a chance to be recorded on it). Such a move is a sure-fire guarantee that the bill will be defeated on the floor.

After clearing committee, the chair presents a report to the house indicating what the committee recommends, and it is read a second time. The committee's proposed amendments are always accepted, and then the bill is engrossed (a check for accuracy). The next step is the final (third) reading of a bill where the bill's author makes a presentation on the floor, as do its opponents (if there are any). (Noncontroversial measures can be placed on the consent calendar for pro forma approval.) Most "do pass" or "do pass as amended" legislation will be approved on the floor and sent to the other house, though a few will die on the floor. On some occasions, a bill's author, seeing formidable opposition to the bill, may ask to have it re-referred to committee for further study.

Certainly, one of the best ways to assess the status of a committee chair is to see what happens to measures clearing his or her committee. Skillful chairs normally have little difficulty getting bills with a "do pass" recommendation approved on the floor. Weaker or less astute chairs sometimes have measures rejected on the floor.

A clear majority, 41 votes, is needed in the assembly and 21 votes in the senate to pass a bill. Two thirds, 54 votes, are needed in the assembly and 27 votes in the senate for the budget, constitutional amendments, and urgency measures. The bill then goes to the other house for another round of hearings and committee action. Measures passed by both houses but in substantially different form will be threshed out in conference committees. Finally, the last hurdles in the process are the governor's signature and the bill's administrative implementation.

REFORMING THE LEGISLATURE

What are the important steps lying ahead for legislative reform in California? Two significant reform proposals have been discussed extensively: public financing of legislative elections and the unicameral legislature. However, now that the Watergate reform surge has abated, the chances of either one of these measures winning acceptance in the near future seems remote (except, perhaps, by the initiative process).

Public financing

The ever-mounting costs of state legislative campaigns and the continued impact of special interest contributions attest to the need for spending limits and public financing. In two special election assembly races in southern California, the winners, Democrat Mel Levine and Democrat Michael Roos, each spent in excess of $200,000 in their campaigns. In a 1979 special state senate race, Ken Maddy spent over $400,000 in defeating John Thurman, who spent more than $300,000. But the record in costly campaigns was won by State Senator John Schmitz, who spent more than $500,000 in 1978. For the average citizen, the thought of having to raise $200,000 to $500,000 to have a realistic chance of getting elected to the legislature is mind boggling. And, of course, with inflation, these figures will continue to increase. (See Chapter 5 for more discussion.)

Unicameral legislature

Currently, Nebraska is the only unicameral state legislature in the nation. Momentum to achieve a single-house legislature has increased slightly over the last decade, because of the court reapportionment decision basing representation in state legislatures on population.

Unicameralists argue that a single-house legislature would mean:

1. Fewer legislators and more salary savings for taxpayers.
2. Fewer staff members (no more duplicate committee consultants for Ways and Means and Finance, each repeating what the other has done).
3. Less delay and foot-dragging.
4. Smaller, more compact legislative districts and less confusion for voters as to who is their representative.
5. Less time wasted by the haggling between the committee chairs of the same policy committee in the two houses as to which should get credit for a particular bill.
6. Accountability would be heightened—the other house could not be conveniently blamed for action not taken.

Only a few contemporary legislators seem interested in the unicameral approach. Former legislators such as Jess Unruh and Hugh Burns and present Governor Jerry Brown support the single-house concept, but gaining legislative approval is another matter. Again, the initiative process is probably the only hope for achieving this reform.

Other reforms

Other reforms that have been proposed include: (1) limiting the number of terms a legislator might serve (to encourage more turnover), (2) limiting the number of bills a legislator might introduce during a particular session, (3) reducing the number of legislative committees, (4) establishing an independent commission to set legislative salaries and do reapportionment (turned down by the voters in June 1976), (5) allowing committee members to elect their own chairs, (6) dispensing with the various legislators' perks but increasing their salaries substantially, (7) extending assembly terms to four years, (8) ending the legislative log jam at the close of the session, (9) paying the leaders of each chamber greater salaries than the rank-and-file members, (10) limiting the amount of moonlighting in which a legislator can engage, (11) forbidding legislative aides from working in political campaigns—even on their own time, (12) reducing the power of the speaker, (13) opening caucuses to the public (Republican legislators in the assembly have already established this policy), and (14) shortening sessions to allow legislators more time in the district.

SUMMARY

California has the most modern, professional legislature in the nation. It has served as a model for other state legislatures in their modernization efforts. However, there is considerable dispute in academia and media circles whether professional legislatures do anything very differently from nonprofessional legislatures.

The speaker and Senate Rules hold the key to legislative power in the California legislature through their ability to select members to committees, pick committee chairs, and assign bills.

While there are admittedly problems, delays, confusion, and skullduggery at times in the California legislature, on the whole, California's top-rated legislature has a well-deserved reputation.

10

California's governors

Unquestionably, executives have become *the central political figures* in contemporary governments. Even in democratic governments, the executive proposes, implements, coordinates, and other interprets policy. At all three levels of government in the United States—national, state, and local—the day-to-day activities of government most often seem to focus on the executive. Indeed, the very word—executive (to execute)—suggests action and authority.

Executive preeminence, however, has not always been the case in the United States. The balance of power between legislative and executive changes. In the 13 original colonies, governors acting as the king's agent held most of the power during the early years of settlement and growth. Following the American Revolution, partly in reaction to the king/governor's authoritarian position, governors were stripped of many of their powers. In a number of states, governors became, essentially, figure heads with little or no power. The same pattern existed at the national level. Indeed, under our first constitution, the Articles of Confederation, there was no chief executive for the national government. *At the end of the 18th century, legislatures were the dominant political institutions.*

But the chaotic, aimless drift of the new government under the Articles soon convinced the Founding Fathers that there was a need for some kind of executive authority. And when the second constitution was drafted, the office of president was created.

Over time, need for continuous program direction and policy coordination and the need for someone to "manage the store" while the legislature was not in session (which was most of the time) forced the states and the nation to establish minimal executive authority. And, given the part-time, amateur-politician composition of state legislatures in our early history, the gradual emergence of full-time professional executives was inevitable. By the latter half of the *19th century, governors had become the dominant figures in state politics.* Those from large electoral vote states were frequently considered prime presidential timber.

From the Civil War to the Great Depression of the 1930s, governors were major national political powers. They headed one of their state's major political parties and frequently went on to be elected to the U.S. Senate—and even the presidency. Between 1876 and 1932, 8 of the 15 presidents elected had previously served as governors. However, the Great Depression of the 1930s—which gave rise to the New Deal—and the emergence of the United States as a world power following World War II substantially enlarged the national government's powers. In turn, states and their *governors declined in national politics.* (It is significant that Jimmy Carter was the first governor to be elected president since 1932—a lapse of 44 years.)

Governors though, may be coming back in vogue as presidential possibilities. In 1976, on the Democratic side, Milton Shapp (Pennsylvania), Terry Sanford (North Carolina), Jerry Brown (California), George Wallace (Alabama) and the eventual nominee Jimmy Carter (Georgia) were all governors or former governors. And on the Republican side, Ronald Reagan (California) was also a former governor. Nineteen-eighty presidential hopefuls included Reagan and Brown (again), and John Connally (Texas).

Though most governors are not as prominent in national politics as they once were, *they remain key political figures within their own states.* And, governors of large electoral vote states—New York, Texas, Illinois, and California—are inevitably prominent in national politics. Indeed, in 1976 and 1980, California Governors Jerry Brown and his predecessor, Ronald Reagan, were contenders for their respective party's presidential nominations. Interestingly, the national stature of California governors increases their political powers within the state. Political and community leaders are often reluctant to oppose a potential president.

The sheer size and complexity of California further enhance the governor's powers within the state. California is too large and diverse to be dominated by any single regional group or leader. Thus, there is no single urban or regional power base from which someone can challenge the governor. The last governor to be defeated after one term was Culbert Olson in 1942. Earlier in California's political history, most governors served only one term. Recently, governors have been reelected to a second term. Earl Warren won a third term, and Ronald Reagan might have won a third term had he wanted it.

And, in recent years, most successful candidates for governor have held statewide office at the time of their campaign. Since 1934 (11 elections), only two governors have been elected who did not hold some statewide office at the time—Culbert Olson and Ronald Reagan. The other five became governor while holding another statewide office: two were lieutenant governors, two were attorney generals, and one was secretary of state. And Ronald Reagan was a well-known TV personality.

Through circumstance, custom, constitution, and law, the governor of California is a powerful political figure. As we shall see, these powers make the governor chief executive, chief legislator, voice of the people, and head of party. Combined, these make the California governor the single most powerful executive within the state and a powerful national political figure as well.

FORMAL POWERS AND AUTHORITY

Constitutional

There is no single source of executive authority in California's Constitution. As discussed in Chapter 3, Article V is devoted to the Executive and sets forth the basic powers of the governor, lieutenant governor and attorney general. In addition, this article establishes the qualifications, terms of office, and salary provisions for most executives. But other articles of the California Constitution also contain significant executive provisions. In fact, one must look at 8 different constitutional articles to find the basic authority and powers of the state's 11 elected executives.

California is similar to most states with its system of plural executives. Historically, statewide elections of several administrative officials were another part of the antigovernor feelings rooted in early colonial experience. The constitutional division of executive power into several positions means that no one person can exercise all executive authority. It is, in a sense, a kind of checks and balances system within one branch of government. Thus, it is important to note that the governor is only *1 of 11* elected state executives, and this does restrict the powers of the office. (The other executives are discussed in Chapter 11.)

Qualifications for and terms of office

The constitution stipulates that to become governor one must be a registered voter, a citizen of the United States, and a resident of California for at least five years prior to election. Elected to a four-year term, the governor currently receives a salary of slightly less than $50,000 a year and an expense allowance of about $45,000 a year. While there is no formal constitutional limit on the number of terms, most early governors served only one term. More recently, California governors have usually run for a second term and been reelected. And, one, Earl Warren, was elected to a third term.

Major powers

Among the 50 states, California's governor clearly ranks as one of the most powerful. One recent study of state governors ranked California 6th out of 50. Historically, California entered the Union after the era of weak governors (late 1700s and early 1800s), and the first California Constitution (1849) gave the governor substantial powers. While the second California Constitution (1879) added little to the governor's formal powers, voters in 1922 approved a ballot measure that gave the governor substantial new budget authority. At present, the four most significant legal powers are: budget, veto, special sessions, and appointments.

BUDGET

In theory, the legislature has the "power of the purse," but in fact, since 1922, the governor has had the authority and the responsibility to prepare the annual state budget and to *present it to the legislature* every January.

The budget contains a statement of both anticipated state revenues and expenditures. In contrast to the federal government, the state budget must be balanced. If anticipated revenue does not cover anticipated expenditures, the governor is required by the state constitution to suggest sources for additional money (new taxes). The constitution also prohibits the state legislature from passing any bill which would spend money (an appropriations bill) before the budget has been passed. (The only exception is an *emergency* bill recommended by the governor and passed by two thirds in both houses.)

The annual state budget is, in effect, a dollars and cents statement of governmental priorities and programs. Of course, there are also moral/ethical policies which are not included in the budget. For example, state policy establishing the death penalty, decriminalizing marijuana, and lowering the voting age to 18 years have essentially no budget implications. Other important policies may involve very little expense—utility regulation, coastline development, or fair employment practices. But since most major policies require the spending of some money, and since all state expenditures are in the budget—it is the budget that engenders the most dispute in the state capitol.

Placing the budget at the top of the legislative agenda and giving the governor authority to prepare it, puts the governor in the legislative driver's seat. Executive policies and programs come first, while the individual legislator's ideas are considered later and must conform to the limits of the budget. If the legislature should try to ignore the budget's priority or spending limits, the governor has the power of the veto.

VETO

One of the governor's most important legislative powers is the veto—or, the implicit threat of its use. The California governor has two kinds of veto—the *general veto* and the *item veto*. (The governor no longer has the "pocket" veto; it was abolished in 1967.) To override a veto requires an absolute two thirds vote in both houses of the legislature. This happened to a California governor only three times between 1946 and 1977. (This compares strikingly to the 27 presidential veto overrides between 1945 and 1975.) Neither the President of the United States nor half the other states' governors has such powerful veto weapons.

The veto has been an enormously important power of California governors. Recent governors have vetoed approximately seven percent (about 1 out of 14) of the bills passed by the legislature. Governor Reagan, facing a hostile legislature in his second term, vetoed more than 12 percent of the bills sent to his desk. In one particularly difficult year (1972), he vetoed over 16 percent. Governor Jerry Brown in his efforts to slow budget growth vetoed over 10 percent of the bills sent him in his first three years as governor.

The general veto   This applies to any bill passed by the legislature. The governor can reject any legislation within 12 days after passage by sending it back to the legislature. Normally, the governor makes a short statement of reasons for vetoing the bill.

The item veto   This applies only to an appropriation bill—typically the annual budget. By using the item veto, the governor does not have to choose between accepting or rejecting all of the budget bill. The item veto allows the governor the opportunity to remove the parts not liked and approve the rest. Moreover, the item veto allows the governor not only to *eliminate* a particular part of the appropriation but also to *reduce* it as well. Thus, if the legislature puts an appropriation into the budget which the governor does not like, it can be eliminated. If the legislature increases an appropriation which the governor had in the budget, it can be reduced to the original figure. (The governor may not, however, increase any appropriation after the legislature has passed an appropriations bill.)

In 1979, Governor Jerry Brown suffered eight veto overrides in July. All but one involved a major conflict between Brown and the legislature over state employee salaries. Adding to the conflict was a long-simmering personality clash between Brown and lawmakers. Such a rash of veto overrides is not likely to happen again.

SPECIAL SESSIONS

The governor may call the legislature into a special session at any time. During special sessions, legislators may consider only those issues presented by the governor. This enables the governor to control the agenda. Before 1967, governors would call special sessions for one of two basic reasons: (1) the legislature was not in session, and there was an important issue which the governor thought required immediate action; or, (2) the governor wanted the legislature to consider an issue which it was ignoring while in regular session.

Between 1863 and 1966, the legislature met only for limited periods of time, sometimes every other year and sometimes with sessions limited to 30 or 120 days per year. Hence, over a two-year span, the legislature was seldom in session, and thus in emergencies or for political reasons, the governor could call a special session. Between 1849 and 1970, the legislature was called into special session 53 times. (The record was set in 1940 when Governor Culbert Olson called five sessions.)

Since 1967, the legislature has met every year with essentially no limits on the length of sessions. Now like Congress, the legislature meets for a two-year period and is usually in session. Today, the only real reason for a governor to call a special session is to force legislators to consider an issue in which the governor is interested. For example, Governor Reagan called a special session of the legislature in 1973 to force consideration of his tax reform proposal. The legislature was opposed to it and though called into special session for this express purpose, ignored (in effect, rejected) the governor's proposal. Governor Jerry Brown used special session calls in 1975 to get passage of housing and malpractice legislation. And, in January 1978, the governor called a special session of the legislature to consider property tax relief. That special session ran concurrently with the regular session and was clearly designed to focus legislators' attention on what had become a very hot political issue.

More important, legislation passed by a special session becomes law in 90 days. Legislation normally does not become law until the following January 1st, unless passed by a two-thirds vote in both houses. Since it is difficult to get a two-thirds vote (called an "urgency measure") the governor can use the special session where only a simple majority is needed.

APPOINTMENTS

The governor's appointive powers add substantially to the influence of the office. Generally, we might categorize appointments as follows: (1) key administrative (full-time), (2) part-time commissions and councils, (3) judicial, and (4) executive-political.

Key administrative The governor appoints about 170 key administrators, including agency heads, department heads (except Justice and Education who are elected), the Director of Finance, and members of several important boards and commissions. Salaries for these positions are usually substantial; about 40 pay between $35,000 and $45,000 a year. Another 100 pay between $25,000 and $35,000 a year. Most of these positions are subject to confirmation by the state senate. However, almost without exception, the senate approves the governor's choices. Traditionally, senators tend to go along with the governor's appointments to key administrative positions, since these appointees are supposed to reflect the governor's policy. And, the governor tries to avoid making appointments which will engender senate opposition.

These 170 appointees have the important task of implementing the governor's policies. For example, Governor Jerry Brown's agriculture policy is shaped by seven individuals he appoints: the Director of the Department of Agriculture and Food, the five members of the Agricultural Labor Relations Board, and the Board's General Counsel. Another example, Governor Brown's energy, resources, and utility policy is largely implemented by his five appointees to the Energy Resources Conservation and Development Commission and the five he appoints to the Public Utilities Commission. These are just two examples of important state policy areas that are subject to the governor's influence through appointive powers.

Since many commissioners are appointed to terms of office which overlap that of the governor or may have terms of office longer than four years, it may take a governor several years to gain a majority on a particular board or commission. A one-term governor (four years) may never gain control of several commissions and boards—for example, the University of California Board of Regents. (Regents are appointed to the board for 12-year terms. This unusually long term was specifically designed to remove the board from political pressure.)

Commissions and councils   There are about 2,200 people who serve part-time on over 300 commissions and boards. They are usually paid a flat daily fee for each meeting ($25–50) or are reimbursed for actual costs. These commissions and councils review state policy in specific policy areas and make recommendations for change to the appropriate department or directly to the governor or legislature. A few have direct authority to license practitioners and change policy. Licensing is critical to practitioners, such as barbers, auto repair mechanics, car dealers, and others.

A typical cross-section of these commissions and councils would include: the California Commission on Aging, the Cancer Advisory Council, Commission on Fair Employment Practices, the Medical Quality Review Committees, the Student Aid Commission, the Commission on the Status of Women, and the many county fair boards.

Judicial   Whenever vacancies occur, the governor appoints judges to the California State Supreme Court, appellate courts, superior courts, and municipal courts. In total, there are slightly more than 1,000 judicial positions, but the average governor usually appoints only about 200 judges during a four-year term.

After the initial appointment—to fill a vacancy—a judge serves out the term and then must run for reelection (see Chapter 12). Judges usually serve until death or retirement; few are ever defeated in an election. Thus, judges serve on the bench long after the governor who appointed them has left office. Obviously, the governor's initial judicial appointment is much more important than the subsequent elections. Judges appointed by Governor Culbert Olson (1932–42) continued to serve until well into the 1960s. While the voters rejected Olson in 1942, the judges he appointed continued in office for another 20 years!

Governor Jerry Brown has made a successful effort to appoint many women and minorities to judicial positions. Table 10–1 compares his appointments to those of two previous governors, Ronald Reagan and Pat Brown. Almost 40 percent of Jerry Brown's judicial appointments have been women or minorities compared to about 10 percent for Reagan and Brown, Sr.

Executive/political The governor also has the authority to fill vacancies for a number of important executive/political positions including: the state's two U.S. Senators, elected state executives, and county supervisors. Governors do not often make these appointments, but when they do, they can be very significant.

For example, seven of the 38 U.S. Senators from California were initially appointed by a governor—about 20 percent. Governor Reagan appointed Ed Reinecke to the position of lieutenant governor, when the elected incumbent resigned in 1969. And, each year the governor makes several appointments of county supervisors.

Summary Clearly, there are substantial political considerations involved in the governor's appointments. Some positions, such as agency secretary or department head are politically sensitive—these are the people who are in charge of the governor's program. Many of the boards and commissions are also politically sensitive, since they both formulate and administer policy—the Farm Labor Relations Board, Public Utility Commissions, or the Coastal Conservation Commission for example.

TABLE 10–1
Judicial appointments, 1959–1977*

	Percent minorities†	Percent women	Total number
Edmund (Pat) Brown, Sr.	7%	2%	400
Ronald Reagan	7	3	491
Edmund (Jerry) Brown, Jr.	24	14	160

* Excluding state supreme court.
† Black, Chicano, and Asians.
Source: California Common Cause, *Los Angeles Times,* July 12, 1979.

Given the politics of appointments, governors may use them to secure support from legislators or key interest groups. For example, the 477 appointments to the District Agricultural Associations are typical patronage. Appointments to many minor commissions, councils, and boards are also often used to reward the party faithful, the governor's supporters, or to gain support from various organizations or groups. Governor Jerry Brown's appointment of ex-Speaker Bob Moretti to the Energy Resources Commission was criticized by many as a political pay-off. Moretti, who had run against Brown in the Democratic primary, subsequently supported Brown in a very close election against the Republican candidate, Houston Flournoy.

Even judicial appointments are frequently partisan—governors usually appoint judges who are members of their own political party. But more important to the governor is the appointee's social philosophy, judicial/legal reputation, specific views on issues relative to the position and the demands or needs of interest groups, legislators, and community leaders.

When Ronald Reagan appointed Judge William Clark to the California State Supreme Court in 1973, he stressed Clark's conservative political and judicial philosophy. Clark, the Governor's cabinet secretary, had had little experience as a judge or in practicing law, but Reagan liked his conservative views. Four years later, when Governor Jerry Brown appointed Rose Bird Chief Justice of the California Supreme Court, he too stressed her political philosophy (as well as administrative experience). Bird had had no prior judicial experience but had been a member of Brown's cabinet. Moreover, Governor Brown was anxious to appoint the court's first female justice.

Governors often try to balance appointments to commissions and boards. Thus, in late 1976, Brown appointed two very different people to the University of California Board of Regents. One, Verne Orr, a conservative Republican and Director of Finance for Governor Reagan, had long been a vocal critic of the University system's financial policies. The other appointee, Vilma S. Martinez, General Council for the Mexican-American Legal Defense and Education Fund, had been a strong critic of the University's programs for Chicano students. Clearly, the Governor was sending the Regents a pointed message: be conservative in money

TABLE 10–2
Governor Jerry Brown's appointments, 1975–1979

Women	1,030	29%
Hispanics	345	10
Blacks	260	7
Asians	129	4
Other minorities	54	2
Total	3,548	

Source: *Sacramento Bee*, October 7, 1979.

matters, but be sensitive to social needs. Governor Brown has also made more appointments of blacks, Chicanos, and women to important administrative positions than has any previous governor.

Over the years, California governors appear to have been very successful in appointing qualified people. The state court system and the administrative bureaucracy have had national reputations for ability and integrity. However, the prolonged investigation of the state's supreme court in 1979 badly hurt its reputation (see Chapter 12). Of course, regardless of who is appointed, governors find appointments a two-edged sword. The governor pleases the person appointed but often angers the many people who were not.

Just as the governor may appoint someone to a position, the governor may also remove someone whose actions or judgments run counter to the administration's policy or needs. The removal power is weaker, however, than the appointive power. Persons appointed to positions for fixed terms cannot be removed before the end of the term without good reason. About 2 out of 3 governor appointments are for fixed terms. Such reasons can be illegal actions or gross incompetence. But a single error, personality clash, or difference in philosophy are not good reasons for removal. Furthermore, the governor's removal powers in many instances are limited by due process. That is, the governor may not remove someone from a middle administrative level without following prescribed procedures. Governor Brown discovered this after he removed a controversial and acknowledged lesbian, Dr. Josette Mondanaro, from her administrative post in the Department of Health. Dr. Mondanaro's specific offense was writing an alleged obscene letter on state stationery during working hours. After a five-day hearing, she was reinstated by the State Personnel Board.

Minor powers

In addition to the governor's major powers and functions discussed above, there are several others which are relatively minor in nature. This is not to suggest that they are unimportant or meaningless, but only that they do not add much to the governor's overall position of power. The minor powers we will consider briefly are clemency, military, and ceremonial.

CLEMENCY/EXTRADITION

The governor has the power to pardon criminals, commute sentences, and issue stays of execution. In doing this, the governor has the advice of the California Adult Authority and his clemency secretary— but the final decision is the governor's. This *minor power* can sometimes produce *major problems* for governors. The most publicized problem in this regard is that of the death penalty. Both Governors Pat Brown and Jerry Brown opposed the death penalty on moral grounds. But both, as governors, were required to uphold the laws and constitution of the State of California.

Extradition, a corollary power, applies to persons who (1) live in California and are charged with a crime by another state, or (2) who live in another state and are accused of a crime by the State of California. Persons who are charged with a crime by another state can only be forceably transported to that state with the approval of the governor. Normally, California's governors approve extradition automatically. However, once in a while, a governor will not. Recently, Governor Jerry Brown refused to extradite Indian activist Dennis Banks to South Dakota because he believed that Banks would not get a fair trial in that state.

MILITARY

The governor is commander-in-chief of the State National Guard. In times of emergency—earthquakes, floods, or riots—the governor may call out the guard to help survivors, provide transport, deliver food or medical aid, or keep order. When riots occur, the governor may use the guard to help local police. In addition, the governor is responsible for the state's civil defense program.

CEREMONIAL

As head of state, the governor is, in effect the personal representative of California. For example, it was Governor Brown who welcomed and entertained Britain's visiting Prince Charles in November 1977 and who met the President of the United States at Los Angeles International Airport in the spring of 1978.

The governor's mansion is symbolic of this function. During Governor Reagan's administration, planning and construction began on a new mansion at a total cost of about $1.3 million. Much more than a residence, the mansion has substantial facilities for entertaining state guests and holding conferences and other meetings of government officials.

Though the mansion was completed in time for the new governor in 1974, Jerry Brown refused to move in, saying it looked like a Safeway Supermarket. Brown's austere lifestyle did not fit the opulence of the mansion, and he moved into an inexpensive downtown Sacramento apartment.

PERSONALITY AND CIRCUMSTANCES

In the long run, the governor's effective leadership is based only in part on constitutional authority. Personality, style, energy, and circumstances are exceedingly important. What a governor wants to do—or not do, which party controls the legislature, the nature of emerging issues, and the political ambitions of others—all may have a substantial impact on the state's chief executive powers.

PARTY LEADER

Governors of California automatically become leaders of their party. Of course, not all governors have enjoyed playing the role of party leader, and some have not been successful in playing it. The most successful governors appear to be those who have been able to be a party leader and yet rise above partisanship.

Compare, for example, Culbert Olson and Earl Warren. Olson assumed that the new (depression) majority of Democratic voters would automatically support Democratic Party candidates. He ran as a straight Democratic Party partisan and lost his reelection bid to Earl Warren who better discerned the California voters' attitudes. Warren could have played the role of party leader but chose not to do so. Basically, he seldom took partisan stands on issues, nor did he try to lead the Republican majority in the state legislature.

Today, 30 years after Earl Warren, California governors are faced with an even more complex social and economic system. They are required to work with a much more partisan state legislature, are now viewed as potential presidential candidates, and, as a result, are hard-pressed to avoid being party leaders. It is expected of them. Whether this position of party leader adds or detracts from a governor's overall power is difficult to determine. Governors normally receive support from voters and lawmakers of their own party and expect opposition from lawmakers and voters of the other party.

Voters

Republican governors tend to have a somewhat more philosophically unified party than do Democratic governors. Democratic governors must lead a party which spans a wide ideological range. Thus, 40 percent of California Democrats consider themselves conservatives, while another 40 percent consider themselves liberals. The remaining 20 percent tend to be swing voters. No Democratic governor can afford to ignore either wing of the party, much less alienate them.

Depression Democrat Governor Culbert Olson antagonized large numbers of conservative Democrats by his liberal policies, and he lost his reelection bid to Earl Warren. The next Democratic governor, Pat Brown, tended to be more middle of the road or moderate but would sometimes respond to one group of voters or another on a specific controversial issue, such as opposition to the death penalty or support for fair housing laws. The present governor, Jerry Brown, does not appear to have a clear or consistent political philosophy. In his 1974 campaign and during most of his first term, he appeared to be a conservative Democrat—his tight budgets, for example. His repeated comments about "lowering expectations," his successful pledge of "no new taxes," and opposition to new programs which would cost money all helped develop a conservative image. Brown has denied he is a conservative—describing himself as "just cheap" (*Playboy*, 1976).

But, Brown's opposition to the 1978 property tax initiative (Proposition 13) badly hurt his conservative image. Overwhelmingly approved by the voters in June, the taxpayers' revolt forced Brown to jump on the bandwagon. Going on statewide TV, he announced his own proposal for limiting government spending.

Nor is Brown's liberal image any more clear. His opposition to LNG landing sites, indifference to Dow Chemical's problems in constructing a petrochemical facility, and opposition to nuclear energy are attractive to many liberals and conservationists. But his efforts to get Japanese auto makers to build in California, his switch on farm land limits, and statements to organized labor that jobs are more important than the environment distress these same voters. Thus, one spokesperson of the liberal wing of the Democratic Party, Tom Hayden, recently described Jerry Brown as merely "recycled Reagan."

Part of Brown's conservative-liberal mix comes from his view that California is entering an era of limits—that government cannot tax any more or regulate any more than it now does. Part of his political philosophy clearly comes from his own nonmaterial lifestyle. But even more important, his ambivalent political stance is rooted in an uncertain and narrow political base. His first election as governor was by a razor-thin 50.2 percent of the vote. Four years later, in 1978, he overwhelmed his Republican opponent by 1.3 million votes. But his opponent, Evelle Younger, was a weak candidate, and the vote meant little. Equally important, Democratic party leaders and voters are badly split on a number of key issues. Governor Brown must try to keep the major factions happy. As Brown recently observed, he has to "paddle his (political) canoe first a little on the right and then a little on the left."

In contrast, Governor Reagan (1967–74) was clearly *the spokesperson* for most of his state party. Unlike Democrats, California Republicans tend to have a more unified political philosophy—about two thirds view themselves as conservatives. Thus, Governor Reagan's leadership of his party could be more strongly ideological. In fact, his election in 1966 was part of the successful campaign by conservative Republican Party workers to wrest control of their party from moderates. (Reagan won his party's gubernatorial nomination by a 2-to-1 vote over a moderate oppo-

ILLUSTRATION 10–1

Caucus

by HüGo

nent.) In tune with most party leaders, workers, and members, Reagan has clearly been the dominant Republican leader in California since 1966.

Reagan's party leadership was also based on his personal popularity with California citizens, Democrats as well as Republicans. Many liked him because he was not a professional politician. When he defeated the incumbent Democratic governor, Pat Brown, in 1966 by a margin of 1 million votes, he received about 750,000 Democratic votes in the process. Four years later (1970), he won again by a half-million votes. In Ronald Reagan, California Republicans had a proven winner in a state which has many more registered Democratic voters than Republicans. Thus, Reagan's party leadership stood on two legs—he was "correct" on the issues with most of the Republican rank-and-file, and he was a winner with the voters.

Republican candidates for governor must get a substantial vote from Democrats if they hope to win. Thus, they must pursue policies that will attract conservative or moderate Democrats and, at the same time, not alienate Republican voters. Democratic candidates for governor do not need Republican votes to win, but they must satisfy the demands of both wings of the Democratic party. Thus, Republicans tend to avoid a strong partisan stance and concentrate on issues, while Democrats avoid issues and stress party loyalty.

Party organizations

Generally, California governors have not paid much attention to their party's statutory organizations—county and state central committees— since these organizations tend to have little political consequence (see Chapter 8). For example, in the Warren era, Governor Warren would often go to a football game instead of attending State Central Committee meetings. And, today, even though partisanship has become more important in California politics, governors continue to pay little attention to the statutory organizations.

Moreover, governors have not been very closely identified with their party's volunteer groups either. As candidates, they normally seek support from the party volunteer workers, but as incumbents they tend to stay away from the ideological bickering and factional in-fighting that seem to typify party clubs. Earl Warren was a prime mover in the formation of the California Republican Assembly, but after attaining the governorship, he had little time for CRA activities. Pat Brown, indifferent to the California Democratic Council at the time of its birth, never felt comfortable with the organization—their relationship was arms' length at best. Ronald Reagan, elected through his own efforts, owed little to Republican club members, but they admired his conservative views so much that their support was always assured. Jerry Brown received considerable support from CDC activists in 1974 but has not involved himself with the organization since. Political club members can be important to gubernatorial *candidates* in a party primary election. *But incumbent* governors, on the other hand, must respond to a much wider constituency than that represented by doctrinaire club activists (see Chapter 8).

Legislative party leader

Four factors strongly shape governors in their role as a party leader in the legislature. First, overall popularity with the voters, particularly the governor's own party's voters. Second, the partisan make-up of the legislature. Which party has a majority in either, or both, houses of the legislature? And, how large a majority—more than two thirds? Third, whether the major issues before the legislature tend to be partisan in character. And fourth, the level of support a governor provides his or her party's legislators when they seek reelection.

POPULARITY

Governor Reagan's convincing win in the Republican primary and general elections of 1966 put him in a position of strong party leadership with Republican legislators. On the other hand, Governor Brown's narrow win, both in the Democratic primary and in the general election of 1974, put him initially in a weak position of party leadership with Democratic legislators. Between elections, the governor's popularity as measured by public opinion polls affects leadership capacity.

PARTISAN BALANCE

Reagan, as Republican party leader, could not afford to be highly partisan in his dealings with the legislature, because Republicans never controlled the legislature during his administration. To pass legislation, he needed Democratic votes. Additionally, since it takes a two-thirds vote to pass the budget, Democrats were in a strong bargaining position. However, Governor Brown's partisan position has been fundamentally stronger, because there has been a strong Democratic majority in both houses which often agrees with him.

PARTISAN ISSUES

A number of issues have pitted Democrats against Republicans in the legislature in recent years. For example, farm labor relations, tax policy, marijuana possession, welfare support, and some environmental bills have become partisan issues, with Democrats taking one side and Republicans the other. Outnumbered Republicans often turned to Governor Reagan for a veto in order to defeat the Democratic majority. And, Democratic legislators had to work with Governor Reagan in order to get some of their legislative packages signed into law.

CAMPAIGN SUPPORT

Governors are expected to hit the "rubber chicken" circuit—appearing at fund-raising dinners for their party's legislative candidates and praising the candidates' fine qualities. Legislative candidates—incumbents or aspirants—like to be seen rubbing elbows with the governor. It makes them look important to the home folks. Helping the incumbent legislator raise money (typically $10,000 to $40,000) at a dinner which features the governor as guest speaker puts the legislator in political debt to the governor. Both understand that the governor may collect that IOU during the next legislative session.

ILLUSTRATION 10–2
Governor Jerry Brown with Assembly Speaker Leo McCarthy and State Senate President Pro Tem Jim Mills The Governor's relationships with legislative leaders is crucial to his program.

Photo Courtesy Sacramento Bee

LEGISLATIVE LEADER

In general, a governor's dealings with the legislature are only partially influenced by partisan considerations. How governors use their constitutional powers (discussed previously), their public popularity, and the goals of their administration may have a much more profound effect on events. Consider, for example, governors Ronald Reagan and Jerry Brown as legislative leaders.

Popular base

Governor Reagan used his broad popularity to influence and sometimes intimidate legislators. Because of his sustained popular appeal, he was frequently able to overcome Democratic majorities in both houses. In part, Reagan's popularity was ideological—a clear majority of Californians (Democrats and Republicans) liked what he stood for. And, in part, his popularity was based on image, style, and quick wit. Once, when confronted with student demonstrators, he observed, "Their signs said, make love not war, but they didn't look as if they could do either." His basically antigovernment stand had wide popularity. Though criticized by some for his anti-intellectual and probusiness stance, Reagan's public popularity remained consistently high during his eight years as governor. Not only did he win both of his elections by large majorities, but when he left office, according to the California Poll (August 1974), 2 out of 3 people in California thought he had done a good job.

In contrast, Governor Jerry Brown's initial popularity was not as great as Governor Reagan's. Brown barely won election, and his failure to secure passage of a farm labor initiative in 1976 weakened his early relations with the legislature. On the other hand, his solid victories over Jimmy Carter in several 1976 presidential primaries demonstrated a growing national support base among the general public. After three years in office, 80 percent of those interviewed by the California Poll (October 1977) thought he was doing a "good" or "fair" job as governor. And by 1978, Brown was so popular that no Democrat made a serious attempt to challenge him in the gubernatorial primary. His increased popularity gave Brown new strength in the legislature.

On the other hand, Brown's diminishing presidential chances in mid-1979 and his announcement that he would not seek a third term weakened his position with the legislature. Symbolic of that weakness were the eight veto overrides in July 1979.

Personal relations with legislators

Aside from voter appeal and general popularity, a governor's personal relations with legislators are important. Most legislation, whether coming from the governor's office, lobbies, local governments, or elsewhere tends to be nonpartisan. If the governor supports a bill, it is easier to get a legislator's vote if the legislator and governor are "friends."

Neither Ronald Reagan nor Jerry Brown have had the same warm personal friendships with lawmakers that Earl Warren, Pat Brown, or Goodwin Knight enjoyed. Both Reagan and Jerry Brown became governors on "antipolitician," "anti-Sacramento," and "antigovernment" positions. Legislators were also offended by both Reagan's and Brown's "holier-than-thou" attitudes toward lawmakers and civil servants.

For most of his eight years as governor, Ronald Reagan did not get along well with Sacramento lawmakers. Robert Monagan, speaker for the two years that Republicans had a majority in the assembly (1969–70), observed:

> [Reagan] didn't operate on a personal basis, I can remember when Pat Brown was governor—even when we were fighting with him as Republicans —we could always go down and Pat would put his feet up on the desk and we'd tell a lot of stories and argue about the issues. It was always a kind of relaxed personal relationship and I never felt I had that with Reagan. (*Los Angeles Times,* September 29, 1974)

Moreover, Reagan got little that he wanted in his first term. What he achieved was essentially negative. He could and did veto legislation and cut the budget. But to get new laws required support from the legislature.

Reagan's second term as governor was marked by better relations with the legislature. Reagan wanted to reform the state's massive welfare system and implement property tax relief. Democrats wanted more school funds and improved medical aid. Each of these programs required both legislative action and approval by the governor. Democratic Speaker, Bob Moretti, looking toward his 1974 campaign for governor, wanted to establish a positive record. Reagan and Moretti worked together, compromised their differences, and the governor got more of the legislation he wanted than he had in his first term.

Governor Jerry Brown has also had personal problems with lawmakers. As secretary of state, he irritated many legislators with his political reform activities—in particular his support for Proposition 9 (the Political Reform Act). Many legislators also felt that Jerry Brown's election was based more on his father's record and name than on any demonstrated ability. Some felt the governor was "flakey," because of his interest in Zen, his antimaterialist attitude, and his nonpolitical friends. Perhaps more important in the long run, as one knowledgeable observer commented:

> Brown . . . is not especially known for massaging the egos of his staff, political allies and legislators. He has not worked at developing good will among lawmakers . . . Few legislators know Brown well or express any personal warmth for him. (Ed Salzman, *California Journal,* October 1975)

Brown's failure to provide legislative leadership further damaged his relations with lawmakers. The Democratic majority, after fighting with Reagan for eight years, looked forward to close working relations with the new governor. But Brown's run for the Democratic presidential nomination in 1976 further harmed his relations with legislative leaders. Many felt the governor was spending too much time on the campaign trail and not enough at his desk in the state capitol.

At one point in the 1976 legislative session, legislative leaders refused to act on the governor's program, until he filled some long-standing vacancies on several key commissions. Fortunately for Brown, he was able to establish a good working relationship with Assembly Speaker Leo McCarthy in his first year as governor. But by 1978, their relationship had obviously cooled. By 1979, Brown's relationships with lawmakers were so bad that he suffered a record number of veto overrides. Much of this was due to his failure to work with legislators on a personal basis.

In any overall evaluation, however, it should be emphasized that while neither Reagan nor Brown had any "buddy-buddy" relationships with legislators, and while both governors were sometimes the butt of legislator's wisecracks, they were able to exert substantial leadership with the legislature because they were very popular with the voters.

Administration goals

The success or failure of governors as legislators is substantially influenced by the goals of their administration. Reagan's basic policy—to cut back on government activity—did not need much legislative action. Thus, Reagan had a tactical advantage in dealing with the Democratic-controlled legislature—he often did not need them. He could and did cut the budget without legislative approval. And in administering state government, he could and did reduce the scope of government action without approval of the legislature.

Governor Brown, on the other hand, had goals which often required legislative action. For example, the governor needed legislation to establish farm labor collective bargaining rights, to close tax loopholes, and to revise criminal sentencing policy. (It is significant that these policies did not cost the taxpayers much money). But even for laws that cost very little money, the governor must get support from the legislature.

In addition, the governor's own goals may be in conflict. Brown's no-new-taxes policy directly conflicted with other goals of increased medical aid, property tax relief, and implementation of the *Serrano* decision. In such cases, the governor has to sort out goals and prioritize them. These kinds of decisions are often made within the office of the governor by the staff and cabinet.

OFFICE OF THE GOVERNOR

The governor is more than an individual; *the person* elected in November *soon becomes an institution*. No one individual can hope to manage the State of California. In playing their many roles and in meeting their many responsibilities, governors must delegate authority to others. And, obviously, they need some oversight of that delegation of power. To do this, governors have a staff of nearly 100 aides. Clearly, the styles of governors are reflected in the ways in which their offices are organized. Basically, that organization falls into two parts—staff and cabinet.

Staff

Because the basic tasks of the governor remain largely the same over time, regardless of the office's occupant, the major staff positions are part of every administration. These major staff positions reflect the ongoing concerns which every governor has:

Executive Secretary acts as chief of staff, coordinating the governor's staff.

Legal Affairs Secretary is concerned with the problems of clemency, pardons, and extradition. He or she tends to be involved in other areas as needed.

Press Secretary is the link between the governor and the press and, hence, the public.

Legislative Secretary is in charge of liaison with the legislature.

Appointments Secretary is in charge of screening applicants for the many appointments which the governor makes.

In addition, governors create other special staff positions as they need them.

In some cases, staffing changes with circumstances. Reagan's concern with higher education led him to appoint an education secretary— Alex Sherriffs. Sherriffs had been a professor of psychology at U.C. Berkeley but became disenchanted with higher education in California. Partly because of his background, Sherriffs was appointed to advise the governor on education policy and maintain liaison with the independently elected superintendent of public instruction. Governor Jerry Brown appointed a space advisor, former astronaut Rusty Schweikert, and an arts advisor, Jacques Barzaghi.

Reagan depended on his staff of specialists and department heads for policy recommendations. He relied heavily on assistants and seldom bothered with detail. Brown, just the opposite, has been a detail man who looks to his assistants for information and expects debate—he may spend 15 hours a day immersed in a particular problem.

Cabinet

The governor's cabinet, unlike the staff, is focused on one area of concern—program administration. Like the staff, it is composed of appointees: the secretaries of the four major agencies, the director of finance, and the governor's executive secretary. Conspicuously absent are the heads of two major departments—Justice and Education. Since they are independently elected, the governor has no direct control over them (see Chapter 11).

At times, an unofficial group of close friends and political advisors may also be important in policy formulation. This sometimes invisible group—often known as the "Kitchen Cabinet"— may be a significant part of the governor's administration.

SUMMARY

The governor *dominates the executive branch* of government. The legal-formal powers of budget control, veto, appointment, authority to call special sessions of the legislature, and a host of minor powers provide the state's chief executive with a formidable political arsenal. The less tangible but no less real authority of public popularity and party leadership further enhances gubernatorial powers. This is particularly true in California, because of the national stature of the state's governor. Finally, the governor's appointment powers exert an influence on state government and politics long after that governor is gone. Undoubtedly, the governor is the *central political figure* in California.

Yet, the governor is also a person—a personality—about whom each of us can have some personal feelings and attitudes. This *personality dimension* is seldom found in other state political figures such as legislators, administrators, or judges, because they are identified with a larger group. Other officeholders are, in a sense, lost within their office. A legislator is one of 120 lawmakers; a judge is one of 1,000 judges. But the governor *is the governor*—there is only one. So the office takes on a personality—the personality of the incumbent. This is usually to the advantage of the governor, because people feel that they "know" this person. They feel comfortable in referring to the governor as "Jerry" or "Ronnie" or "Pat." Not many other officeholders in state government are on a first-name basis with their constituents.

11

Administration: Executives, civil servants, and money

While the political spotlight most often shines on the governor as the state's chief executive, hundreds of other executives are busy in the day-to-day administrative processes of government. The voters elect a lieutenant governor, five department heads, and four members of a state tax agency. The governor appoints about 200 other important administrators. There are also a few hybrid agencies made up of a mixture of elected officials and appointed administrators. Finally, there are some "predetermined" boards of major importance.

In addition, there are some 200,000 state employees who do the work —from digging ditches to filling medical prescriptions. The vast majority of these state employees are hired under civil service, a merit plan.

How these executives and civil servants do their jobs is important to all Californians. Few of us have direct contact with elected public officials; few of us even know their names. But, nearly all of us, citizen or alien, have frequent direct contact with state employees.

PLURAL EXECUTIVE

California is similar to other states in that it elects many statewide executives. Most states elect at least six executives in addition to the governor (see Table 11–1).

California (like most other states) also elects local executives called county supervisors. These supervisors are popularly thought of as local government officials. However, in fact, county supervisors spend most of their time administering programs mandated by the state. (We will examine the county as an administrative agent of the state in Chapter 13).

TABLE 11–1
Comparing California's plural executive with other states

Office	California elects	A majority of other states elect
Lieutenant Governor	Yes	Yes
Attorney general	Yes	Yes
State treasurer	Yes	Yes
Secretary of state	Yes	Yes
Superintendent of public instruction	Yes	Yes
State auditor	No	Yes
Controller	Yes	No
State Board of Equalization	Yes	No

Source: *The Book of the States, 1976–77.*

Constitutional provisions

No single article of the California Constitution completely encompasses California's plural executive. Article V, while devoted to the state's executive powers and functions, is only one of eight different constitutional articles which contain significant executive provisions. Article XIII delineates the powers and responsibilities of the treasurer and controller. Three different articles contain important powers of the secretary of state (IV, XVI, and XXIII). The superintendent of public instruction's powers are mainly established in Article IX, but important authority is also found in Article XXIV. Finally, the Board of Equalization's authority comes largely from Article XIII.

LIEUTENANT GOVERNOR

The lieutenant governor's role in state government resembles the vice president's role at the national level. As one California governor observed, the duties of the lieutenant governor are "to preside over the senate and each morning to inquire solicitously after the governor's health." These are hardly monumental tasks. Yet, there are some duties of significance. And, in some ways, the lieutenant governor has more power within the state setting than the vice president has at the national level.

Unlike the vice president who becomes president only on the death or disability of the president, the lieutenant governor becomes *acting governor* whenever the governor leaves the state. (Also, the lieutenant governor becomes governor on the death or resignation of the governor.) Since California governors travel out of state frequently, the lieutenant governor can sometimes have an opportunity to exercise important powers.

As acting governor, the lieutenant governor usually performs only routine functions. Typically, the governor and lieutenant governor have an agreement about the lieutenant governor's actions while the governor is out-of-state. But emergencies can happen. Lieutenant Governor Glenn Anderson, acting governor while Pat Brown was on vacation in Greece, had to make socially crucial and politically sensitive decisions at the start of the 1965 Watts Riots.

And, for the first time in the 20th century, voters in 1978 elected a governor and lieutenant governor of different parties. As a result, substantial conflict developed between the two. In the spring of 1979, when Governor Jerry Brown was out of state, Lieutenant Governor Mike Curb appointed a judge to the appelate court. When Brown returned, he withdrew the appointment and substituted his own. (Under pressure from Curb, Brown hastily made over 30 additional judicial appointments in less than a week and then left the state again!)

Both the Governor and Lieutenant Governor appealed to the California State Supreme Court to resolve their dispute. After evaluating the arguments on both sides, in December of 1979 the court upheld the Lieutenant Governor. Thus, it is clear that when the governor is out of the state, the lieutenant governor *is governor in fact*.

Perhaps, more significantly, unlike the vice president, the lieutenant governor is not chosen by the head of the ticket to be a running mate in the election. The lieutenant governor is elected independently from the governor in the party primaries. And each runs independently from the other in the general election. Yet, the lieutenant governor has often become governor. Of this century's 14 governors, 4 were originally lieutenant governors. Of all the statewide executives, the lieutenant governor has the best chance of becoming governor. And, the odds may be getting better as California's governors are now "natural" candidates for the presidency or vice presidency.

On those rare occasions when the state senate is locked in a 20–20 tie vote, the lieutenant governor is authorized to cast the tie-breaking vote. For example, Lieutenant Governor Mervyn Dymally flew from Denver to Sacramento to cast a tie-breaking vote on the "consenting adults" bill in 1976.

The lieutenant governor also automatically serves on three important governmental bodies: (1) the State Lands Commission, (2) the University of California Regents, and (3) the California State University and College Board of Trustees. Finally, like the vice president, the lieutenant governor can be given important assignments by the chief executive. Hence, the lieutenant governor's role in the state's political milieu depends heavily on the willingness of the governor to make meaningful assignments.

ILLUSTRATION 11–1
California's plural executive

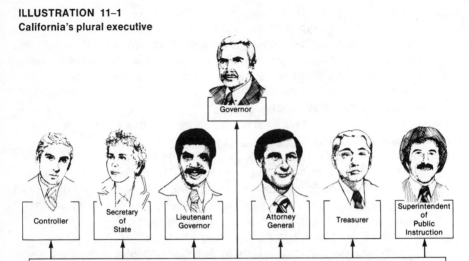

CALIFORNIA VOTERS

ATTORNEY GENERAL

Second only to the governor, the attorney general is the next most important elected executive in California. As head of the Department of Justice, the attorney general is, theoretically, responsible for enforcing all state laws. In fact, because of the strong tradition of "home rule" in the counties and cities, the attorney general seldom enters into local law enforcement matters.

Thus, the attorney general operates typically at the state level. This is a particularly important task, since in the American federal system, "law and order" remain primarily a state function. Law and order cover a wide range of activities including both civil and criminal law, investigation, legal advice, and, in emergencies, authority over local law enforcement. The attorney general is much more than just a supercop or investigating attorney.

In recent years, the office of attorney general has been a major stepping stone to the office of governor. Both Earl Warren in 1942 and Pat Brown in 1958 went from attorney general to governor. In 1978, the incumbent attorney general, Evelle Younger, captured the Republican gubernatorial nomination (see Chapter 4). After a lackluster general election campaign, Younger lost badly to incumbent governor Jerry Brown. But, Younger's defeat does not make the office of attorney general any less politically powerful. As can be seen in Illustration 11–2, the party out of power has frequently held the attorney general's office in recent years. Clearly, it has become an important base for political advancement.

CONTROLLER

The controller is chief fiscal officer of the state. The main duties of the controller are to pay state bills and keep track of state accounts. This officer is responsible for four major programs: fiscal control, tax administration, local government fiscal affairs, and administration.

The controller's authority in administering the inheritance tax has given this office a decidedly political flavor. Inheritance tax appraisers are not covered by civil service, and appointments have long been considered a political plum. Yet, interestingly, controllers tend to have low political mobility. Only two controllers have been able to move up politically—both to the U.S. Senate. Controller Houston Flournoy captured the Republican gubernatorial nomination in 1974 but was narrowly defeated by Jerry Brown in the general elections. Moreover, controllers have been unable to isolate themselves from strong political tides affecting their political party—winning and losing seems to be tied to their party's fortunes (see Illustration 11–2).

ILLUSTRATION 11–2
Partisan control of executive offices 1923–1982

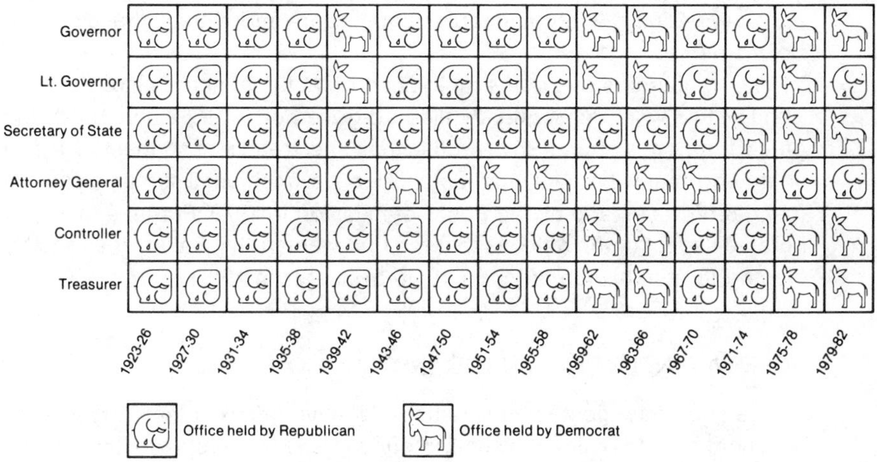

SECRETARY OF STATE

The secretary of state is guardian of documents and records for California. In addition, the secretary serves as the state's chief elections officer. Until recently, the office aroused little interest among the electorate. Two people, Frank C. and Frank M. Jordan (father and son), held the office from 1911 to 1970 except for three and one-half years. Others have held it for an average of one term.

When Jerry Brown was elected secretary of state in 1970, he used the office to promote campaign reform and generate personal publicity. In an era of Watergate, his activity made the office more visible. He capitalized on the situation and won the election for governor in 1974 as a reform candidate. Brown was the first secretary to go on to higher office. His successor, March Fong Eu, was the second woman and first Oriental elected to statewide office.

TREASURER

The treasurer is state banker and investment counselor. There are four major duties—two are important but not very exciting to the average voter, and two are relatively unimportant.

The most important duty is to prepare, sell, and redeem state bonds. With an annual sale of over $500 million in general obligation bonds, it is important that the treasurer secure the lowest possible interest payments. A difference of 1 percentage point is equal to $5 million per year. In addition, by carefully managing the state debt, the treasurer plays an important part in maintaining state credit.

The treasurer's second important job is to invest state surplus funds. These temporarily idle funds average about $2.5 billion dollars which earn over $200 million in interest each year—more than the cigarette tax yields.

The treasurer is one of the most obscure political figures in California. Though two were subsequently elected governor (in 1862 and 1922), the office today has such a low profile that one treasurer suggested a few years ago that it be abolished as an elective position. The same recommendation was made by the Post Commission in 1979. Perhaps the most notable aspect of the office is that the first woman (Ivy Baker Priest) to be elected to a statewide office became treasurer in 1967.

SUPERINTENDENT OF PUBLIC INSTRUCTION

The superintendent is an unusual executive officer. Elected statewide on a nonpartisan ballot, the superintendent is responsible to a ten-person board of education appointed by the governor. As the administrative head of the State Department of Education, the superintendent is expected to implement board policy. Yet, this officer is elected and, hence, ultimately responsible to the voters rather than to the board. Further compounding the complexity is the fact that most of California's education is delivered at the local level. Most Department of Education policies directly impact the state's local school districts. But, the vast bulk of K–12 educational funds (approximately 98 percent) are spent by local districts.

State and local education programs cover a wide range of activities in addition to the three Rs: child-care centers, migrant child care, preschool and early childhood education programs, programs for the disadvantaged, and programs for the physically handicapped, to list a few (see Chapter 13).

An important and often controversial area for the Department of Education is its text adoption authority for school grades kindergarten through eight. Local districts may only use texts on the approved list. Controversies over "God and science," sex education, and "fundamentals or frills" often end up on the superintendent's desk.

With over one third of the state budget flowing through the Department of Education, the superintendent is clearly a major figure in California government. Since the state supreme court (*Serrano* v. *Priest*) ruled that local property taxes do not provide equal funding opportunities for every child, California state government has been forced to substantially increase its support to local school districts. Most recently, voter approval of Proposition 13 in June 1978 cut local school district revenues by about one third. The state replaced most of the lost funds out of its budget surplus. Increased pressure for more state money as a result of Proposition 13 promises to make the superintendent's position both more powerful and more politically sensitive than in the past.

Since the superintendent is elected on a nonpartisan basis, the office has not normally served as a springboard to higher elective office. For example, Max Rafferty, superintendent from 1963–71, failed in his bid for the United States Senate in 1968. Wilson Riles, elected in 1970, became the first black to hold a statewide elective office in California.

The only nonpartisan statewide office, superintendent candidates appear on all ballots in the June primary. If, as happened in June 1978, a candidate receives a majority of the votes cast, he or she is elected in the primary. That cannot happen in any other statewide election.

STATE BOARD OF EQUALIZATION

This board has five members. Four are elected from approximately equal population districts, and the fifth member is the state controller. The board has two major functions: collecting sales taxes and supervising property tax assessments by the counties.

The Board of Equalization's most important function is to administer and collect state and local sales and use taxes. It also has the responsibility for several state excise taxes, including those on alcoholic beverages, cigarettes, and gasoline. In all, it collects about half of state tax revenues each year.

The board's other major function is to review each county's tax assessments and procedures. It is responsible for maintaining equal assessment-to-market-value ratios among the counties. The board also trains property appraisers. And, where needed, the board may issue rules governing assessment procedures.

Board members, though elected on a partisan basis, have an exceedingly low political profile. Once elected, they are usually reelected. Since 1942, board members have averaged better than three terms (over 12 years) apiece. One member, George R. Reilly, first elected in 1938, served on the board for more than 40 years! In recent years, no board member has gone on to higher office.

POSSIBLE REFORM

California's plural executive has been the subject of considerable debate. Several reforms have been suggested ranging from abolishing all of the minor offices to elimination of one or two.

As discussed above, the duties of the secretary of state, controller, treasurer, and Board of Equalization are largely routine and administrative. They involve little policy making or policy discretion. It has been suggested that they should be appointed by an elected official who is clearly a policymaker—the governor. Further, the argument goes, by electing executives who have little or no policymaking functions, the office *becomes* unnecessarily political. Politics, according to this point of view, should play no part in the activities of these executives.

Another argument for reducing the number of elected statewide officials is that it would shorten the ballot. Many think that the California ballot is too long now and that it is confusing to most voters to make decisions on eight statewide elections plus assembly, state senate, congressional, and U.S. Senate races, as well as the dozen or more ballot propositions. One way to help the voter focus on the most significant elections would be to remove the relatively minor offices from the ballot.

A third argument for eliminating some of the elected executives is that they are elected on essentially a *coattail* basis or *party-line* vote. Illustration 11–2 shows this. It presents the party affiliation of the statewide elected executive between 1923 and 1982. Clearly, the vote for the minor offices usually conforms to that cast for the governor. (Of the past 75 elections for minor executive office, only 14 [19 percent] produced winners from the party which lost the governorship. Of these unusual

14 elections, 7 were for attorney general. Excluding that one office, California's voters have voted a party ticket for the other minor executive offices over 90 percent of the time.)

Finally, the unusual situation of placing the elected nonpartisan superintendent of public instruction under the authority of a board appointed by a partisan governor has evoked repeated criticism. A more rational arrangement would be to elect the board which would then appoint the superintendent.

Another suggested reform would be to have the lieutenant governor run on the same ticket as the governor—as in half the states and in presidential/vice-presidential elections. This is because voters under the present ground rules could elect a lieutenant governor from one party and a governor from the other (as they did in 1978). Since the lieutenant governor is often the state's acting governor, the argument is that the occupant of that office should be someone who is in general agreement with the governor on the major issues.

Those who argue against change point out that historically, the lieutenant governor has almost always come from the same party as the governor. Further, they suggest the lieutenant governor has more authority acting as an independently elected official.

There are, also, several good reasons why no change should be made. First, making some of these positions appointive would increase the governor's powers. Many feel that the governor is strong enough (or too strong) now. Second, electing these minor executive officers gives minorities and the politically disadvantaged an opportunity to get into politics at a statewide level. For example, two women, two blacks, and an Oriental have recently been elected to some of these offices. Third, and perhaps most telling, is that the *rational-logical arguments* for change miss the *political argument*. California's voters are not likely to give up their power to elect minor executives.

Predetermined executives

Membership on several executive boards and commissions is in some cases predetermined. For example, most of the State Lands Commission and Franchise Tax Board members are automatically "appointed," because they hold some other elective office. To a large extent, then, these government bodies are independent both of direct control by either the voters or some appointive authority.

STATE LANDS COMMISSION

The State Lands Commission is a little known but very important government body comprised of the lieutenant governor, controller, and director of finance. It has control over the management of all state lands. Increasingly important is its authority to administer state land leases, permits, and sales of state oil, gas, and minerals. The commission closed the Santa Barbara Channel to new oil drilling in 1969 after the famous oil spill, and in 1974 it ordered the channel reopened for further development.

The commission generates revenues for the state in excess of $100 million per year, largely from the sale of oil. About two thirds of these funds go to building new facilities for higher education in California.

FRANCHISE TAX BOARD

The Franchise Tax Board is comprised of the controller, chair of the State Board of Equalization, and the Director of Finance. It has responsibility for administering three major tax programs: (1) personal income tax, (2) bank and corporate tax, and (3) senior citizens property tax. It is also charged with auditing campaign and lobbyist financial reports.

California's personal income tax provides the state with its second largest source of revenue—about one third of the total collected. The board supervises income tax withholding, collection and refunds, processing about 8 million individual returns each year.

The bank and corporation tax is the third largest source of state revenues—over one tenth of the total collected. In this program, the board's activities are similar to those under the personal income tax. The board also supervises payment of property tax relief to about 350,000 of the state's senior citizens each year.

Finally, the board is required by the Political Reform Act of 1974 (Proposition 9) to audit all statements and reports of lobbyists, candidates (or their committees), and elected officials who fall under the provisions of the act. (The details of this activity are discussed in Chapters 5 and 7.)

SEMIPREDETERMINED EXECUTIVE BODIES

A number of governmental bodies are comprised of some predetermined and some appointed members. Among these are the State Board of Control, the California Educational Facilities Authority, and the Wildlife Conservation Board.

Appointed executives

Appointed executives are also important in the operation of California state government. The following offices and departments are examples of the some 170 important appointed executives.

DEPARTMENT OF FINANCE

The Department of Finance is the governor's budgeting and fiscal control agency. Its director is appointed by the governor and is normally the second ranking member of the administration. The department is responsible for (1) preparation of the annual fiscal plan (usually called the budget), (2) administration of the plan, (3) analysis of program effectiveness and efficiency, and (4) economic and demographic research. The department's own annual budget is over $6 million, and it employs slightly more than 260 people. This is small compared to most other state departments, but nevertheless, it is the single most important and powerful department in California government, because it controls the state budget.

In overseeing the state's annual financial plan, the Department of Finance both prepares the budget and assists the legislature in its budget evaluation (see Legislative Analyst in Chapter 9). After the budget bill becomes law, the department then exercises administrative control by making sure that all expenditures are as authorized.

The department's second most important policy activity is its analysis of state programs. This means more than simply an audit of some agency's accounts; it includes an evaluation of program management and effectiveness in achieving program goals. From this information, the governor will decide on the worth of the program and the priority to be given to it in future budget allocations.

The director, in addition to overall management of the department, has other important responsibilities. This officer is a member of the State Lands Commission, State Public Works Board, and the Franchise Tax Board. It is worth noting that the director has a vote on these boards and commissions just as do the elected members—the controller, treasurer, legislators, and lieutenant governor. In fact, the director may have more power as the governor's representative than do the elected statewide officeholders.

It is obvious that the director and the governor have a close political relationship. And, since most state policy involves the expenditure of state funds, the Director of Finance is a very powerful person.

THE SUPER AGENCIES

Much of California's administrative system is organized into four super agencies—each of which houses several departments, boards, and commissions (see Illustration 11–3). The governor appoints each agency head, called a "secretary," and in addition, the governor appoints the department heads and most members of the many boards and commissions. The basic function of the agency secretaries is to provide com-

ILLUSTRATION 11–3
California's administrative structure

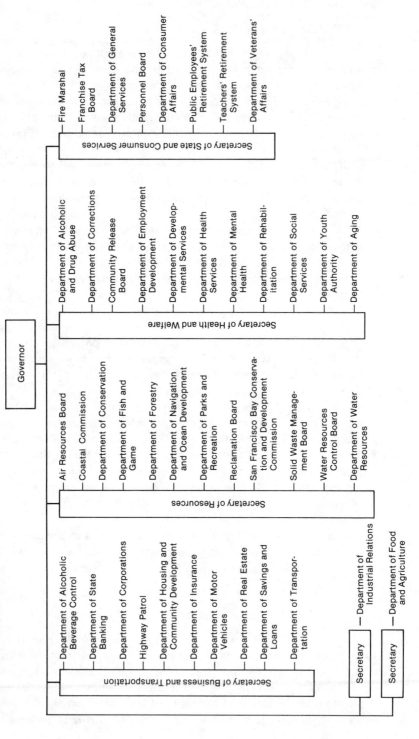

Governor

Secretary of Business and Transportation
- Department of Alcoholic Beverage Control
- Department of State Banking
- Department of Corporations
- Highway Patrol
- Department of Housing and Community Development
- Department of Insurance
- Department of Motor Vehicles
- Department of Real Estate
- Department of Savings and Loans
- Department of Transportation

Secretary — Department of Industrial Relations

Secretary — Department of Food and Agriculture

Secretary of Resources
- Air Resources Board
- Coastal Commission
- Department of Conservation
- Department of Fish and Game
- Department of Forestry
- Department of Navigation and Ocean Development
- Department of Parks and Recreation
- Reclamation Board
- San Francisco Bay Conservation and Development Commission
- Solid Waste Management Board
- Water Resources Control Board
- Department of Water Resources

Secretary of Health and Welfare
- Department of Alcoholic and Drug Abuse
- Department of Corrections
- Community Release Board
- Department of Employment Development
- Department of Developmental Services
- Department of Health Services
- Department of Mental Health
- Department of Rehabilitation
- Department of Social Services
- Department of Youth Authority
- Department of Aging

Secretary of State and Consumer Services
- Fire Marshal
- Franchise Tax Board
- Department of General Services
- Personnel Board
- Department of Consumer Affairs
- Public Employees' Retirement System
- Teachers' Retirement System
- Department of Veterans' Affairs

munication, coordination, and information. They are not program managers per se but are responsible for program implementation through the civil service staff.

State and Consumer Services Agency Until Governor Jerry Brown reorganized this agency, it was a catch all. But in 1977, the Departments of Food and Agriculture and Industrial Relations were removed and each given their own secretaries (cabinet status). Now the agency is clearly devoted to serving the state's public employees and consumers.

Business and Transportation Agency As one might expect from the title, this agency contains two distinct kinds of departments. One kind is concerned with transportation activities—the California Highway Patrol and Department of Motor Vehicles, for example. The other kind is made up of departments oriented toward business activities—the Department of Banking and the Housing Finance Agency, for example.

Resources Agency This agency is responsible for the state programs related to management and preservation of water, air, land, natural life, and recreational resources. Typical departments include the Department of Conservation, Air Resources Board, and State Lands Division. The Coastal Zone Conservation Commission also functions through this agency.

Health and Welfare Agency This agency covers health, welfare, and corrections programs. Typical departments are: (1) Department of Health, (2) Department of Corrections (see Chapter 12), (3) Department of Benefit Payments, and (4) the Office on Aging. Given the rapid increase in costs of health and welfare, the controversial nature of abortions and drug treatment programs, the middle-class reaction to welfare programs, and the budget squeeze imposed by Proposition 13, these programs and agencies are under intense political pressures.

INDEPENDENT DEPARTMENTS

Department of Food and Agriculture Part of a super agency until 1977, when the governor gave it independent status with its own secretary, this department serves the state's agricultural interests. Its cabinet status reflects the political and economic significance of California's agricultural enterprise.

Department of Industrial Relations Also part of a super agency until 1977, this department is concerned with labor and conditions of employment in California. Its cabinet status also reflects the political importance of organized labor in California.

COMMISSIONS AND BOARDS

Commissions and boards differ from agencies and departments in several important ways. First, a commission or board is comprised of several people (typically five or seven) each of whom has an equal vote in the making of policy. While a commission or board will elect a chair, responsibility for program control and policy decisions is shared equally by all members. Second, commissions and boards have broader policy-making authority than do department heads. Third, members serve part-time. And, fourth, they are frequently provided with a small staff.

Public Utility Commission The Public Utility Commission is one of the state's most important regulatory agencies. It has five members, who are appointed by the governor with state senate approval. The commission, established by constitutional amendment in 1911, is theoretically politically independent. The staggered six-year terms of members were designed to make it difficult for a governor to "pack" the commission. In fact, however, the commission often reflects the governor's position on utility issues (by 1979, all five members of the commission had been appointed by Jerry Brown).

The commission is charged with regulating utility rates (natural gas, water, and electricity) and transportation rates within the state. These rates are supposed to provide utilities and common carriers a fair return on their investment. To do this, the commission uses a cost-plus formula.

At the same time, the commission is also supposed to protect the consumer against unreasonable rates and see that the utilities and common carriers provide adequate facilities and services. In essence, the commission has to balance demands from consumers with demands from utilities and common carriers. It is both an administrative and quasi-judicial body. Appeals from its decisions may be made only to the state supreme court. Consumers, the regulated utilities, and common carriers are substantially effected by commission rulings.

Governor Pat Brown's appointments were usually considered "pro-public"—favoring low rates. Governor Ronald Reagan's appointments were usually considered "pro-utility." But, in his pro-utility and economizing drive, Reagan cut back on the commission staff and as a result, utility requests for rate increases were long delayed. Moreover, during the Reagan years, rate increase requests went from 48 per year to 70, and public complaints went from 12,000 to 30,000 per year. This increased work load overwhelmed the reduced staff, and both the utilities and the consumers were hurt.

Energy Resources Commission Legislative concern over the inability of the Public Utilities Commission to fulfill its responsibilities, its apparent bias in favor of utilities, and the energy crisis led to establishment in 1975 of a new commission—the Energy Resources Conservation and Development Commission. This new commission was given power over utility rate structure. In addition, it was given the authority to approve all new power plant facilities in the state. It shares this authority with the Coastal Commissions for coastal power plant sites. As a result, the power of the Public Utilities Commission was substantially reduced.

The Energy Resources Commission also has substantial powers in the areas of energy conservation and land use regulation. Thus, the commission recently changed utility rates to discourage the excessive use of natural gas and electricity. Under earlier rate schedules, the more energy a consumer used, the lower the unit costs. Under the new rate schedule, as a consumer increases energy use, the unit costs go up. Other energy conservation regulations adopted include changes in design rules, particularly in lighting, insulation, and climate control (heating and air-conditioning) systems.

Finally, the commission has been authorized to make long-range studies of energy use and resources. It has already adopted the development of alternative energy resources including solar and geothermal as a top priority.

Agricultural Labor Relations Board After years of turmoil, including strikes, violence, and consumer boycotts, the state finally established an agricultural relations board in 1975. Creation of this board was, itself, a controversial act. The legislature had considered such an act in every session since 1959. But Governor Reagan vetoed such legislation when it finally passed the legislature. And voters rejected a ballot measure in 1972 which would have regulated relations between growers and farm workers.

When Governor Brown signed the 1975 Act, there was hope that the long-simmering conflicts over working conditions, pay, fringe benefits, and collective bargaining could be resolved. However, bitterness between growers and farm workers (UFW) and attempts by the Teamsters Union to organize farm workers led to continued conflict. The board was so overloaded with charges of unfair labor practices, bargaining elections, and challenges to its rules that it exhausted its first year's budget in 30 weeks.

When the board requested additional funds from the legislature, growers' representatives were able to delay them. In retaliation, the UFW resorted to a ballot initiative (Proposition 14) in November 1976. The initiative would have protected the board's authority and funding from the legislature. Following a bitter contest, Proposition 14 was rejected by the voters, and farm-labor disputes remained unresolved. It is worth noting that while directly affecting only those few who work on farms or own them (about 4 percent of the state's population), the board's policies affect each of us as consumers of food.

State Board of Education This board consists of ten people appointed by the governor to staggered four-year terms subject to state senate confirmation. The board sets policy and exercises oversight of the Department of Education (see discussion above of Superintendent of Public Education).

CIVIL SERVICE

State employees are responsible for delivering the goods and services which California provides. Patrolling the state freeways, distributing tax forms, checking the accuracy of gas station pumps, helping campers at state beaches, and collecting and distributing money require people. The standards by which state employees are hired, promoted, or fired are important in determining the quality of service provided to California citizens.

About 2 percent of California's work force is employed by the state. Though a small part of the work force, state government employment has grown twice as rapidly as the rest of the state in the last 20 years. Essentially, all (99 percent) of the state's employees are hired under civil service or some form of merit plan. There is very little patronage.

Historically, like most states, California's public employees were at one time hired on a political-patronage basis with little or no concern about their ability to do the job. One of the major reforms of the Hiram Johnson Progressive administration was to partially establish a civil service system. And in 1934, civil service was extended to virtually all state employees by an initiative constitutional amendment (Proposition 7).

At present, civil service is under attack from two directions. Affirmative action programs which require the hiring of the disadvantaged have challenged the validity of traditional civil service exams. These tests, according to critics, have a built-in bias that favors white males. One knowledgeable critic, San Francisco Police Chief Charles R. Gain, challenged police promotion tests saying that ". . . [you could] draw straws and accomplish the same thing."

State Personnel Board data show that about half of state jobs are held by women, but most of those are in the lower ranks. Blacks and Chicanos are not employed in numbers proportionate to their percentage of the state population, and again, those that are hired tend to be in the bottom ranks.

Collective bargaining for public employees is another challenge to civil service. Under collective bargaining, pay scales, promotion criteria, and working conditions are subject to negotiation. This will clearly alter the traditional role of the State Personnel Board. While the state has not established collective bargaining for all state employees, it has enacted laws that provide for it at the local level (see Chapter 13). Both the AFL-CIO and Teamsters are trying to win members away from the

ILLUSTRATION 11-4
Two state employees looking over some files   The bureaucracy feeds on paper!

Photo *courtesy* Sacramento Bee

State Employees Association in anticipation of collective bargaining elections.

And, though the San Francisco police strike and New York City's record of public employee strikes cause concern, there appears to be more support for collective bargaining than in the past. For example, an attempt to ban public employee strikes failed in late 1977. Supporters of an initiative measure, which would have outlawed such strikes, failed to secure enough signatures to get it on the ballot. Collective bargaining for public employees appears to be emerging as a major issue which will have a profound effect on state personnel practices.

PROBLEMS AND REFORM

How responsive to the needs of the public is California's bureaucracy? Being immune from political pressure, is the bureaucracy so independent that it pursues its own goals and ignores the public's?

In theory, the constitution and state statutes establish two kinds of executives—those who make policy and those who administer it. Those who make policy are either elected by the public or appointed by elected officials to positions *exempt* from civil service.

On the other hand, those who administer policy—deliver services— are required to secure their positions by passing tests. Elected officials and exempt appointed officials are subject to election results; civil service personnel are not. In theory and in law, it appears that policy-makers are subject to public will. But reality and theory are not always the same.

The plural executive clearly obscures public responsibility. The average voter does not often know which elected executive is responsible for which policy area—nor do the state's political parties provide much policy control.

The some 2,000 part-time executives who serve on the various boards and commissions broaden the base of citizen participation in the administration of government, but, at the same time, these citizen executives are sometimes in conflict-of-interest positions. This is particularly true for the professional and sales bodies.

Until recently, these boards and commissions were dominated by the very people they were supposed to regulate. Attorneys were appointed to the California Bar, dentists to the Board of Dental Examiners, doctors to the Board of Medical Quality Assurance, real estate brokers to the Real Estate Commission, and termite exterminators to the Structural Pest Control Board. The few "public" members on these bodies were heavily outnumbered. Under Governor Jerry Brown, many of these boards and commissions now have a majority of public members.

And, there are substantial pressures for more change. Betwen 1970 and 1978, there were 16 ballot measures submitted to the voters which would have further modified the executive branch.

SUMMARY

Clearly, in a democracy there can be conflict between a professional civil service and the public. The pressures for affirmative action and for patronage appointments are good examples of that conflict. The plural executive obscures policy responsibility. And, citizen executives are sometimes in conflict-of-interest positions. Yet, in comparison to other states, California has a very efficient and responsible executive-administrative-bureaucratic system.

Whether the administrative system needs a major overhaul or just a tune-up is debatable. Nevertheless, the pressures for change will continue.

MONEY: TAXES AND THE BUDGET

Regardless of position, each government official is concerned with delivering a service, enforcing regulations, or distributing monies according to law. The entire bureaucracy, from governor, treasurer, and controller down to the lowest paid clerk is involved in some way in these activities. In this section, we will take a close look at taxes, budgets, and some of the pressures for change in the ways California collects and spends public money.

No other current domestic issue has been as controversial, so widely discussed, and so directly related to most other policy decisions as taxation. In California, Proposition 13 (1978), reduced property taxes by 55 percent, generated massive support and drew 6.5 million voters to the polls. Approximately 750,000 citizens voted on Proposition 13 only—ignoring all other candidates and measures.

The success of Proposition 13 followed repeated earlier attempts to reform California's tax system. In 1968, two measures appeared on the ballot. Proposition 1A, exempting $750 in assessed home value from taxation, was passed by the state's voters. At the same time, they rejected a much more sweeping property tax limit measure—the Watson Amendment (Proposition 9). In 1972, Governor Ronald Reagan and Assembly Speaker Bob Moretti agreed on a tax reform measure that raised the sales tax to 6 cents but also increased the property tax exemption to $1,750 and gave renters a $50 tax credit. But another major attempt by Reagan to reform taxes was rejected by the voters in a special election in 1973 (Proposition 1). Reagan's proposal would have limited taxes and government spending. At the time it was considered too extreme.

In the next five years, inflation and a shortage of housing caused a rapid increase in home prices. Property taxes, based on market value, also increased rapidly. By 1978, California's homeowners were ready to vote for the extreme measures contained in Proposition 13.

Like most tax reform, the effects of Proposition 13 have been slow to materialize. But regardless of the results of Proposition 13 or other subsequent tax/budget reforms, the problems of taxation and government expenditure—the budget—will remain central to politics and public policy.

Budget Growth

California has a tradition of growth, including its budget. In 1950 the state budget was $1.1 billion; in 1980 it reached $21.2 billion.[1] But, at the same time, California's population grew from 10 million to 23 million, and inflation cut the value of the dollar by two thirds.

Having more people to serve with dollars that buy much less, the state's budget has had to grow just to provide the same services each year. Illustration 11–5 shows the impact of population growth and inflation on the state's budget.

California's population growth contributed about 9 percent to its budget increase between 1950 and 1980. During the same period of time, inflation added another 28 percent to budget growth. Obviously, as long as population grows and inflation continues, the state's budget will continue to grow even with no new programs. But new programs have been the major cause of budget growth in the past. Real budget growth in terms of new and/or expanded programs accounted for well over half (63 percent) of budget increases.

Taxes

Whatever government spends under California's constitution, it must have adequate tax revenues. Unlike the federal government, there are

ILLUSTRATION 11–5
Budget growth 1950–1980

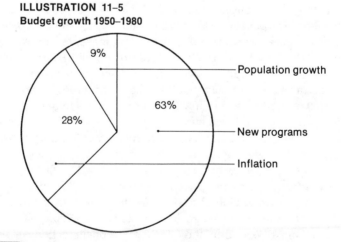

9%
28%
63%
Population growth
New programs
Inflation

---

[1] The general budget of $16.4 billion plus $4.8 billion in additional funds to local government combined produced a total of $21.2 billion.

no deficit budgets in California. Thus, in preparing each year's budget, the governor and legislature must estimate how much tax monies they will collect.

California collects many different taxes and fees, but most of the money comes from two sources: (1) the sales tax, which provides 38 percent of state government revenues, and (2) the personal income tax, which provides another 32 percent. The other 30 percent comes from a variety of taxes and fees (see Illustration 11–6).

SALES TAX

California's largest single source of governmental revenue is its sales tax of 6 cents on each dollar of taxable purchase. Some basic necessities such as food, prescription drugs, and utilities are not taxed. The major attractiveness of this tax is that it is easy and inexpensive to collect and generates large revenues ($5.6 billion in 1978–79).

But the sales tax is considered *regressive* by many critics, because it imposes a heavier burden on the poor who spend more of their income on sales tax items than do the rich.

PERSONAL INCOME TAX

California's second largest revenue source is its personal income tax. The tax rate is *progressive*—the rate increases as the income taxed increases. But, like other states, the tax rates are low—1 percent to 11 percent. This is because the income tax rates levied by the federal government are considerably higher (14 percent to 70 percent).

ILLUSTRATION 11–6
The California budget dollar by revenue source 1978–1979

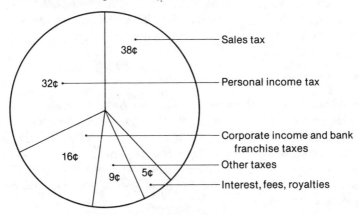

Source: *Controller's Annual Report, 1978–79.*

Since 1971, California has utilized payroll withholding to collect income tax. This has increased compliance and produced a steady flow of revenue into the treasury. This tax generated $4.8 billion in 1978–79. In 1979, the legislature reformed the tax rate schedule, indexing it to the cost of living. Before 1979, when an individual received a cost-of-living pay increase, her or she would move up into a higher income tax bracket. As a result, the income tax went up, even though real income remained the same. The net result was a cut in take-home pay. Now the tax brackets move up with inflation.

BANK AND CORPORATE FRANCHISE AND INCOME TAXES

The state also levies taxes on business income and collects a fee for the right to do business in California. Corporations pay an income tax of 9 percent on earnings, while banks pay 13 percent. Until 1976, corporation taxes could not be raised without a two-thirds vote in both houses of the legislature. This made it harder to raise their taxes compared to others. However, voter approval of Proposition 5 in June 1976 amended the constitution and now permits an increase in taxes on banks, corporations, and insurance companies by a simple majority vote in both houses of the legislature (the same as for all other taxes).

Business taxes generated $2.4 billion in revenue in 1978–79. They are the third ranking source of governmental funds in California.

OTHER TAXES

Several other taxes generate about 9 percent of the state's revenues. These include the motor vehicle fuels tax (7 cents a gallon), vehicle fees, gift and inheritance taxes, alcoholic beverage taxes, a tax on cigarettes (10 cents a pack), and a tax on bets placed at horse race tracks. No one of them produces more than 2 percent of total state revenues, but combined they constitute an important source of funds.

NONTAX REVENUES

In addition to monies collected by various taxes, the state also derives some income, about 5 percent, of its annual revenue from nontax sources. Royalties and bonuses for oil, gas, and other minerals extracted from state-owned lands; personalized license plates; fish and game licenses; and interest on temporarily idle state funds generated over $700 million dollars in fiscal year 1978–79. The recent rise in oil prices may mean more money for the state.

Budget

All of California's various tax dollars and other revenues support a wide range of programs. As we saw in Chapter 10, each year the governor prepares and presents to the legislature the state's annual budget. In California, most governmental services are provided by or through local governments—cities, counties, school districts, etc. Thus, a very large part, about 80 percent, of the state's annual budget is devoted to local assistance. This means that out of a state budget of $17.0 billion, almost $13.7 billion was given to local governments to spend (fiscal year 1978–79). Of course, these expenditures were under the direction and control of the state's government—legislature, governor, and bureaucracy. As we will see in Chapter 13, counties and school districts perform many of their activities as agents of the state. And it is as agents of the state that they receive billions every year.

For example, in 1978–79 the state provided local school districts with over $5.0 billion for educational activities. Counties received over $2.3 billion to provide local health and medical services. This contrasts markedly to the much smaller amounts of money spent directly by the state—$1.4 billion on higher education and about $.5 billion on health.

Looking at the state's budget by activity (see Illustration 11–7), it is obvious that education, health, and welfare make up most of the budget. Seventy-six cents out of every state dollar is spent on them. The other large expenditure—property tax relief—went directly to various local governments to spend as they needed. It is also in these major expenditure areas that any substantial changes in the budget must be made.

ILLUSTRATION 11–7
The California budget dollar by policy/program 1978–1979*

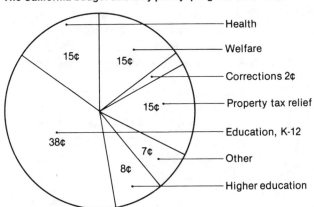

* Including both local assistance and direct state expenditures.
Source: *Controller's Annual Report, 1978–79.*

Tax/budget change

Taxes and budgets, like other governmental activities, are constantly changing. In California, the property tax has been traditionally a local government revenue source (see Chapter 13). However, in 1978, the state's voters implemented a major change in the property tax limiting it to 1 percent of market value. But even before Proposition 13, the state recognized the substantial tax burden placed on many property owners and provided local governments with funds to relieve that load. In fiscal year 1977–78, before Proposition 13, local governments received $1.4 billion in property tax relief from the state.

Following implementation of Proposition 13, local governments lost $7 billion in tax revenues, and the State of California had to replace much of the loss. Fortunately, the state had a surplus from which to provide some $4.2 billion to local government in 1978 and $4.8 billion in 1979.

The impact on California's state budget was staggering. Local assistance increased from $8.5 billion to $13.7 in one year. The $7 billion cut in property tax revenues plus another $1 billion reduction in income tax enacted by the legislature in the summer of 1978 dropped California from 3rd to 21st among the states in per capita tax burden. Governor Brown immediately froze all state employee salaries and cut almost $1.5 billion from his initial 1978 budget in order to help supply the increase in local assistance funds. Again, in 1979 the state's budget was kept under tight control.

But it was California's large budget surpluses which enabled it to provide massive support for local government. These surplus billions represent tax dollars collected but not spent (see Table 11–2). And, these annual surpluses have engendered several more tax cut proposals.

On the other hand, Governor Brown repeatedly stated in 1978 and 1979 that there would be a decline in state revenues in the early 1980s, and no massive tax cuts should be made. He urged instead tight budgets and program reductions. However, by mid-1979, the Governor's predictions had failed to materialize. Moreover, a prestigious group of UCLA

TABLE 11–2
California's state budget
surpluses 1975–1979 ($ billions)

Fiscal year	Surplus
1975–76	$0.9
1976–77	1.9
1977–78	3.8
1978–79	2.8

Source: *Controller's Annual Reports, 1975–76; 1978–79.*

economists estimated that California's governmental revenues would continue to be greater than expenditures until well into the mid-1980s.

As a result, repeated demands have been made for more tax cuts and/or budget reductions. In early 1979, Paul Gann's "Spirit of 13" initiative measure to limit government spending qualified and was placed on the November 1979 special election ballot. A group known as CAST (Coalition to Abolish the Sales Tax) was established in mid-1979. Its goal was to place an antisales tax measure on the June 1980 ballot. And Howard Jarvis declared in April 1979 that he would lead a fight to cut the state's personal income tax in half. His measure qualified for the June 1980 ballot.

The Gann spending limit allows government budgets to grow only at the same rate as population growth and inflation. If such a measure had been law in 1950, the state's 1980 budget would have been only $8.4 billion instead of $16.4 billion. Gann's measure, Proposition 4, approved by voters in November 1979 ballot appears to make it impossible to add new programs or expand existing ones without eliminating or reducing other existing programs.

The CAST proposal to abolish the sales tax in three equal yearly steps would eliminate the state's largest single revenue source. It would also make the state's tax structure more *progressive* in that it would place a larger burden on the personal income tax. The income tax would provide half of the state's revenues by 1983, if the CAST initiative were approved in 1980.

Howard Jarvis' proposal to cut the income tax in half would, on the other hand, shift a slightly greater burden onto the sales tax. By 1983, the sales tax would produce $8.1 billion and provide over 40 percent of the state's revenues. The Jarvis measure would make California's tax structure slightly more *regressive*.

If all three proposals were passed, local government revenues would be cut by about 36 percent and state revenues by about 70 percent (post-1979). Obviously, California state and local government budgets are under heavy attack. Even if some of these recent proposals pass, the "go-go" growth attitude of past decades is at an end for some time.

In addition to legislation or direct initiative by the voters, California's tax and budget structure is subject to control by the courts. In 1971, California's supreme court upheld a lower court decision in *Serrano* v. *Priest,* declaring the property tax an unconstitutional source of funding for local public education (see Chapter 13). The immediate result of that decision was the addition of $1.0 billion in state expenses to support local education.

In 1976, the court reviewed state progress in equalizing pupil expenditures and found significant differences. And, in 1979 after a protracted struggle among school districts, the legislature, and the governor, significant differences continued to exist. Assembly Bill 8 (1979), as finally approved, brought only about half of the state's student enrollment into compliance with the court's requirements. According to state estimates, it would take until 1983 or '84 before the court's goal of equal education funding would be substantially achieved.

Finally, as we have seen, both inflation and population growth exert a significant influence on the state's budget. Neither factor can be controlled by the state. In recent years, the decline in population growth has slightly reduced pressures on the budget, but the massive inflation of the '70s was the major contributor to budget growth during the Ronald Reagan and Jerry Brown administrations.

12

California's justice system

For most of us, the state's justice system is the traffic officer, "bail by mail," and lurid headlines in the newspaper about the latest sensational trial. Yet, the system is much more than that. And, for students of state government, the justice system is highly significant, because it is one of the few governmental activities which is still largely a state function. While many state and local functions have been taken over by the federal government in the last 200 years (health, welfare, transportation, etc.), the justice system is still, essentially, a state system.

Nine out of ten court cases are heard before state courts; attorneys are licensed to practice by the states; and corrections—jail, prison, parole, and probation—are largely state activities. For most citizens, it is state laws which have the most frequent and immediate impact. It is the state courts, as Justice William Brennan once observed, that deal with the day-to-day issues of life, liberty, and property. It is the state justice system that deals with life and death matters—marriage, divorce, annulment, juveniles, will probate, contracts, consumer protection, and a variety of other subjects. And, for most of us, the courts and other parts of the state's justice system are our most frequent contact with government.

It must be emphasized, however, that the justice system is not just the courts. Courts are only part of it. Equally vital are the police, district attorneys, public defenders, private attorneys, witnesses, trial and grand juries, jail guards and prison officials, probation and parole officers. Each plays an important part in adjudicating conflict, allocating rewards, imposing punishment, and attempting to rehabilitate—all functions of the state justice system.

Typically, these functions are divided into two categories—criminal and civil. A criminal case involves the state as plaintiff against an individual. The individual is charged with violation of some state law and the state is a party to the case. A civil suit, on the other hand, is between two private parties; the state is not a party to the dispute.

FUNCTIONS OF JUDICIAL SYSTEM

Criminal

Criminal cases fall ino three categories: felonies, which are the most serious; misdemeanors, which are less serious; and infractions, which are minor violations. Felonies involve criminal acts such as murder, rape, and armed robbery. Conviction of a felony may carry a penalty of one year or more in state prison, a heavy fine, or both. Misdemeanors involve less serious crimes such as assault, drunk driving, or speeding. If found guilty, the defendant may be imprisoned in county jail, fined, or both. In felony and serious misdemeanor cases, the defendant must appear before the court and enter a plea ("guilty" or "not guilty"). In light of the penalties involved, defendants have the right to legal counsel. They may request the court to appoint counsel if they cannot afford an attorney.

For less serious misdemeanors—an illegal U-turn, for example—the accused may post bail (often by mail) and, failing to appear, automatically plead guilty and forfeit bail as a fine. The less serious crimes, called infractions, are acts such as jaywalking, driving a motor vehicle with a faulty headlight, illegal parking, and some minor animal control laws. In an effort to relieve the courts of an ever-increasing crush of cases, the legislature has eliminated the right to a jury trial in these cases, and the accused is not guaranteed legal counsel. Punishment is limited to fines, and there are no jail sentences. It is worth noting that the bulk of criminal cases involve illegal parking—over 8 million a year.

Civil

The state courts hear over 1 million civil cases each year. Essentially, there are two kinds of civil cases. A civil case *in law* is when one person sues another for "damages." Such suits arise from property damage, personal injury, medical malpractice, or failure to live up to a contractual obligation. A civil case *in equity* is brought to prevent harm or irreparable damage (for example, an injunction). Equity also involves such things as probate of wills, administration of trusts, or divorce.

In civil cases in law, *the plaintiff* sues *the defendant* for damages— usually a certain amount of money. If damages are $750 or less, the case is heard in small claims court. Municipal and justice courts hear suits for more than $750 and less than $15,000. If damages are more than $15,000, the case is heard in superior court.

In following sections of this chapter, we will look at each component of California's justice system. While California enjoys one of the best systems in the United States, we will see that there is considerable room for improvement.

ESTABLISHING THE SYSTEM

Much of California's justice system is established in Article VI of the state constitution. Included are features such as: the court structure, the Judicial Council, Commission of Judicial Performance, and the state bar. Article I provides for basic citizen rights including grand juries and trial juries. Article I also allows the state to imprison a person for a crime. Article V establishes the state's attorney general (see Chapter 11), and the police operate under the home rule provisions of Article XI (see Chapter 13).

The state legislature is another major source of laws affecting the justice system. The Department of Corrections was established by an act of the legislature. And, more recently, lawmakers set up three night trial courts on an experimental basis to determine the need for them. Another example would be the "instant trial" procedures for minor traffic infractions. Under this system, if defendants waive trial, they are, in effect, automatically pleading guilty. Since bail is posted by mail, it then becomes the amount of the fine. More substantial examples are the recent reforms in the laws changing civil divorce proceedings and abolishing the state's indeterminate sentencing laws replacing them with a form of fixed-term penalties.

The California Supreme Court also plays a key role in the justice system through its interpretation of the state constitution and laws. Recently, for example, the supreme court ruled that justice court judges had to be attorneys (*Gordon* v. *Justice Court,* 1974). This has led to a substantial change in justice court organization and procedures.

Another important source of legal rules is the California Judicial Council which, under the authority and limits of the state constitution and codes, has the power to establish court rules of procedure. A good example of this would be the 1977 change in juvenile court rules. The bulk of juvenile court law is found in the Welfare and Institutions Code. But the council, after a two-year study, set forth new rules detailing practices and procedures designed to provide greater uniformity and application of the code in the counties.

Counties and cities play an important role, too. The availability and quality of prosecuting attorneys and public defenders is largely under control of the County Board of Supervisors. And sheriffs are elected in each county. Finally, each city determines the quality of its own police department (see Chapter 13).

Clearly, the justice system is neither neat nor symmetrical. In fact, as one police chief recently observed, there really isn't any system. It's more a jumble of pieces and parts which have an effect on each other but which operate more or less independently.

COURTS

There are four levels to the California court system (Illustration 12–1): (1) municipal and justice courts—sometimes known as "inferior courts," (2) superior courts, (3) district courts of appeal, and (4) the state supreme court. Generally speaking, the municipal, justice, and superior courts are trial courts where cases are first heard. District courts and the supreme court are appeals courts; they hear cases brought to them on appeal from the trial courts. Overseeing the entire operation of California's court system is the Judicial Council.

Inferior courts

Municipal and justice courts handle the vast majority of court cases in California—about 96 percent of over 17 million filings per year. These are the courts which most of us have come into contact with. In 1977–78, they processed 9.5 million parking citations and over 5 million traffic violations. (Nine out of ten parking and traffic cases never go to trial but are settled at the bail clerk's window.) Additionally, these courts handle over 450,000 small claims cases.

JURISDICTION

The jurisdictions of municipal and justice courts are the same. They hear civil suits of less than $5,000, small claims ($750 or less), minor traffic violations, and some lesser crimes which do not have penalties of more than one year in jail or a fine of more than $1,000. These courts also hold preliminary hearings for more serious cases that may be tried in superior court. In the preliminary hearing, the judge decides if there is sufficient evidence to justify holding the accused and conducting a trial.

Justice courts serve rural areas of the state with populations of less than 40,000. As California has become more urban, the number of justice courts has declined from 349 in 1953 to 107 in 1978. Municipal courts serve urban areas. In 1978, there were 455 judges serving in 90 municipal court districts with populations of over 40,000.

ILLUSTRATION 12–1
California court system

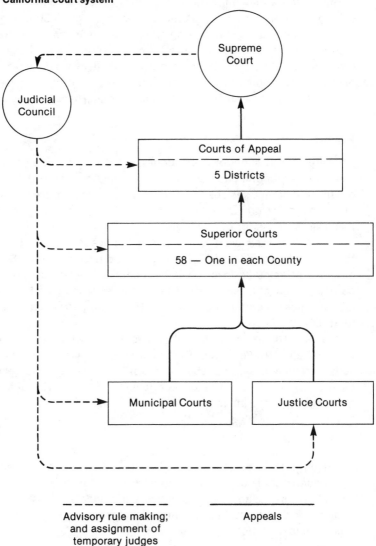

- - - - - - - - - -   ─────────────
Advisory rule making;   Appeals
and assignment of
temporary judges

SMALL CLAIMS

Both justice and municipal courts serve as small claims courts. These courts hear cases involving amounts of $750 or less. Unlike other courts, no attorneys are allowed. The parties to disputes such as a dog bite, defective refrigerator, or smashed fender, argue their own case before the judge (there is no jury). And, unlike cases before other courts, most small claims go to trial (about two thirds). Appeal from the decision of the court may be made by the defendant but not by the plaintiff.

Small claims may not, however, be the "people's court" as it is often said to be. A 1979 study by the state's Department of Consumer Affairs and the state Judicial Council revealed that almost six out of ten cases filed in small claims courts were by corporations, other businesses or governmental agencies. These cases most often involved suits over credit or loan transactions. Equally significant, in six out of ten cases heard in small claims, the defendant fails to appear and, hence, loses by default.

Superior court

There are 551 superior court judges in California. Each county has at least one superior court, and large counties are divided into several divisions—with judges specializing in various kinds of law (family, juvenile, probate, or criminal). Los Angeles, the largest county in the state, has over 170 superior court judges.

Superior courts have original jurisdiction over (1) all civil cases where the suit is for at least $5,000, (2) divorce and dissolution of marriage regardless of amounts involved, (3) probate, (4) all major crimes which carry a penalty of a year or more in state prison, and (5) all cases involving juveniles. Superior courts also act as courts of appeal from the inferior courts.

A small proportion of all court cases are heard in superior courts— approximately 700,000 a year (out of 17.3 million). Of these, less than 1 in 10 is a criminal case. And, about 1 out of 7 involves juvenile delinquents. Most superior court cases involve family law and civil suits, and the great majority are settled prior to trial.

PROBATION

Attached to each county superior court is a probation department. This department is concerned with criminal cases as well as custody of juvenile wards of the court. Probation departments provide background information to the court about criminal defendants which is important in determining sentence.

Courts of appeal

DISTRICT COURTS

California is divided into five districts, each with a court of appeals. In 1978, 56 appelate judges received more than 13,000 cases. About two thirds were appeals from decisions by lower courts. These cases were brought to the courts of appeal on *points of law*. A case on appeal is heard by three judges (compared to one in a trial court). Arguments are presented in written form, and there is seldom any oral argument, nor is there a jury.

Relatively few cases are appealed—about 1 out of 60 from the superior courts. Since the appeal is made on a point of law, when the courts of appeal make a decision, they are usually *making policy* by interpreting law.

SUPREME COURT

This is the top state court. Its decisions are final except for appeal to the United States Supreme Court (which rarely happens). The California State Supreme Court has six justices and one chief justice. Most cases reach the supreme court after having been tried in superior court and appealed to one of the district courts of appeal. In addition, the supreme court automatically reviews all death penalty cases. Only a very few cases reach the court—less than 4,000 a year.

The California Supreme Court usually has discretionary jurisdiction— it decides if it wants to hear a case. As a result, the supreme court hears only about 3 percent of the cases submitted to it. Essentially, the court considers only cases involving a substantial question of public policy. The seven members of the court receive both written and oral arguments. Their written opinions—about 200 per year—are the authoritative interpretation of California laws and Constitution.

Judicial council

California, like most other states, has a judicial council which oversees the state court system. The Chief Justice of the California Supreme Court chairs the council and appoints 14 judges to it. The state bar appoints four members, and each house of the legislature appoints one.

The major responsibility of the council is to study the state's court system continually and make recommendations to the legislature for needed constitutional or statutory changes. In addition, the council may make administrative rules so long as they conform to state law.

SELECTION AND RECRUITMENT OF JUDGES

All California judges must be members of the state bar when appointed. In addition, they must meet different standards for the different levels of the court system. The governor appoints all judges except justice court judges who are appointed by the County Board of Supervisors. In every case, judges must stand for nonpartisan election at the end of their terms (until recently, this was only a minor formality).

ILLUSTRATION 12–2
Qualifications and terms for California courts

Court	Term	Qualifications*
Justice court	6 years	Member of state bar
Municipal court	6 years	Member of state bar for five years or judge of a court of record
Superior court	6 years	Member of state bar for ten years; citizen of United States for five years; resident of county for two years
District court of appeals	12 years	Member of state bar for ten years or judge of a court of record; citizen of United States
State supreme court	12 years	Same as district court

* Judges must also be registered voters in order to run for reelection.

Few judges are originally elected to office; most are first appointed to fill a vacancy. Appelate court judges have usually served on lower courts, typically a county superior court. Sometimes, however, the governor will appoint someone to a district court of appeals or the state supreme court who has had little or no prior judicial experience. Governors usually justify such "inexperienced" appointments on the basis that the supreme court is a policymaking body and that the appointees' social philosophy and personal values are of greater importance than judicial experience. The record of these inexperienced court justices does not appear to be markedly different from that of "experienced" justices.

In any case, the governor's power to appoint judges is very important. Superior Court Judge Robert Kenny once observed: "A judge, you know, is just a fellow who knew a governor." The governor's appointments to the supreme court and the appelate courts are subject to confirmation by the State Commission on Judicial Appointments. Appointments to the superior and municipal courts are not subject to confirmation.

Governors usually appoint judges who share their own values and frequently belong to the same political party. This does not mean that the appointees are not qualified, but rather that politics is an inseparable part of the judicial process.

In theory, judges are subject to election at the end of their term. In fact, most judges seldom have had trouble getting reelected. It is rare for a judge to be defeated in an election. Defeat requires an unusual set of circumstances. Thus, in 1970, a judge of the Los Angeles Superior Court, Alfred Gitelson, lost reelection after he issued a highly unpopular decision in a school desegregation case. And, in 1974, a San Francisco Superior Court Judge lost an election because voters thought he had been too lenient in sentencing a rapist.

In 1978, an unusually large number of superior court judges were challenged for reelection. Out of the 158 judges who sought reelection, 28 (18 percent) were challenged. In 1974, of the 78 judges seeking reelection, only 3 (4 percent) were challenged. However, as a general rule, most judges have not been challenged and under California law are thereby deemed to be reelected. Their names are not even put on the ballot.

Appelate court elections take another form (see Illustration 12–3). The ballot simply asks, "Shall _____ be elected to the office for the term prescribed by law?" The voter has a choice of "Yes" or "No." There is no opponent. Under law, if the judge is rejected, the office is declared vacant, and the governor appoints someone else to fill it. This has never happened, though now and then an unpopular judge will be the object of a vigorous "No" campaign. In 1978, Chief Justice Rose Bird of the supreme court was vigorously attacked by two groups in an attempt to defeat her. One group, located in southern California and headed by ultraconservative State Senator H. L. Richardson, attacked her for being too "liberal" and "soft" on crime. The other group, centered in California's rich farming areas, attacked her because of her previous role in assisting the United Farm Workers. Underlying the efforts of both groups was a steadily increasing criticism of courts in general. Highly controversial decisions involving school busing, abortions, public financing, death penalty, and rape cases have made the courts more subject to public attack.

ILLUSTRATION 12–3
Ballot for the supreme court elections

JUDICIAL		
For Chief Justice of California **Para Presidente de la Corte Suprema de California**		
Shall **ROSE ELIZABETH BIRD** be elected to the office for the term prescribed by law?	**YES SI**	
Debera **ROSE ELIZABETH BIRD** ser elejido para el oficio por el termino prescrito por ley?	**NO**	

Source: Official sample ballot.

Chief Justice Bird narrowly escaped defeat, with a 48 percent "No" vote against her. Three other associate justices also on the ballot received an average 34 percent "No" vote. These were all-time records for "No" votes against members of the state's supreme court.

In 1979, the Law and Order Committee, headed by State Senator H. L. Richardson, examined the records of over 200 superior court judges who would be up for reelection in 1980. After analysis, it was announced that the Committee would try to defeat about 20 (10 percent) of the judges because they were incompetent or too lenient in sentencing criminals.

Commission on Judicial Appointments

The Commission on Judicial Appointments has the authority to approve or reject the governor's appointments to California's appelate and supreme courts. The commission has three members—the Chief Justice of the California Supreme Court, the attorney general, and an appelate court judge. Aside from this commission and the constitutional requirements, there is no other formal check on the governor's judicial appointing power.

In 1940, the commission rejected a supreme court nominee. This is the only rejection of a governor's nominee since the commission was first established in 1934. In 1973, Governor Ronald Reagan's nomination of William Clark to the supreme court drew considerable criticism. It was argued that Clark had very little judicial experience and an undistinguished legal career. He was nominated, it was claimed, because he shared Reagan's political philosophy. But, by a 2-to-1 vote, the commission approved the appointment. In 1974, another Reagan appointment (to the court of appeals) was so sharply criticized that the nomination was withdrawn—the first to be withdrawn since 1942. And, in 1977, the commission approved by a 2 to 1 vote the appointment of Rose Bird as Chief Justice of the California Supreme Court. This appointment, too, caused an unusual amount of controversy, since she had never served as a judge prior to her taking the supreme court position. However, most appointments cause little controversy, but also, most governors try to make appointments which will meet with the commission's approval. Thus, though seldom fully exercised, the commission's power is important.

Commission on Judicial Performance

The Commission on Judicial Performance reviews the quality and performance of judges after they have been appointed. The commission receives, investigates, and evaluates all complaints against California judges. The Commission has nine members: five judges appointed by the supreme court, two lawyers appointed by the state bar, and two lay-persons appointed by the governor (subject to senate approval). If the commission finds that a judge has performed in an unprofessional manner, it makes a report to the state supreme court, and the court has the authority to remove the judge.

The supreme court has censured several judges and removed a few for felony convictions or gross misbehavior. In 1973, the commission recommended for the first time that a judge be removed for willful misconduct in office. He was removed. And, in 1977, the commission heard evidence charging a member of the state supreme court, Marshall McComb, was no longer able to function due to advanced senility. After considerable negotiation, the justice was removed from the court.

Each year, the commission will hear about 260–80 complaints. Of these, about 200 will be about a judge's judicial ruling or some other legal problem. These are not considered. But about 70 complaints will deal with unprofessional or improper conduct and will be investigated. In about 20 cases, there will typically be enough evidence of misconduct to require some action by the commission. In two or three cases, there may be public action taken by the supreme court upon recommendation by the commission. In 1979, one judge voluntarily resigned and another was censured. Clearly, the commission plays an important role in maintaining high judicial standards in California.

In December 1978, the commission was requested to investigate the state supreme court following charges that the court (or some of its members) deliberately delayed highly controversial decisions until after the November 1978 elections. Central to the charges were long delays in handing down case decisions involving rape, separation of church and state, and the power of grand juries. Most crucial of all was the highly publicized Tanner case ("use a gun—go to prison").

The commission's hearings—held in public—revealed a court badly split by both ideological and personality conflicts. Eventually, on appeal of Associate Justice Stanly Mosk, the commissions's public hearings were completed in private. On November 5th 1979, the commission issued its final report, simply stating it would not bring charges of misconduct against any of the seven supreme court justices. But the year-long investigation, costing over $500,000, did not clear the court of suspicion. One commission member observed later that the court was not exonerated.

Generally, the California judicial system is considered to be one of the best in the nation. Moreover, the supreme court has usually been considered one of the finest in the nation. Its decisions frequently carry great weight in other states and with the United States Supreme Court. *The Wall Street Journal* said in 1975 that "The California Supreme Court is to courts what UCLA is to basketball." However, the 1979 hearings of the

Commission on Judicial Performance into supreme court case delays and several controversial decisions have badly damaged California's courts.

ATTORNEYS

No one may practice law in California *or act as an attorney* for a client, without being admitted to the state bar. The bar's authority is provided by the state constitution, which gives it the power to set ethical standards, admit to practice, discipline, and expel attorneys. "Admit to practice" is the key power. It means, essentially, passing an examination administered by the bar.

Attorneys occupy a central position in California's justice system. Judges (except for a few in the justice courts) must be members of the state bar. The attorney general, prosecuting attorneys for cities and counties, and public defenders must also be members of the bar. And, with few exceptions, in major cases heard before a court, both parties to a conflict depend on attorneys to represent them.

Prosecuting attorneys

The district attorney is the government's prosecuting attorney at the county level. After an arrest is made by the police, this official decides whether to prosecute, change the charge, or drop the case. Given the statutory time limits, limited staff, and backlog of pending cases before the courts, the prosecuting attorney has to limit the number of cases pursued. In some counties, the prosecuting attorney may drop as many as half of the felony cases and prosecute the rest. But very few will actually go to trial.

Usually, the district attorney will reduce the charge in exchange for a guilty plea. This is commonly called "plea bargaining" or "copping a plea"—about 90 percent of prosecuted felony cases are decided this way. In effect, most criminal trials are negotiations between the district attorney and the defendant's attorney. The negotiated plea of "guilty" to a reduced charge is then formally presented to the judge in court.

Defense attorneys

The California Constitution provides that the accused (in a criminal case) has the right ". . . to appear and defend in person and with counsel." In other words, everyone has the right to have an attorney represent them in a criminal case. In fact, prosecution may not begin until the defendant has had an opportunity to secure legal counsel. In a few instances, the court may allow individuals to defend themselves without legal counsel, but there is no absolute right to do so. Those who can afford to will hire a private attorney, but the great majority of criminal defendants have limited financial resources and must depend on the public defender or assigned counsel. Inability to make bail is generally considered adequate proof of poverty.

PUBLIC DEFENDER

The public defender, like the district attorney, is a county employee, but the job of the defender is to defend the accused. Since the district attorney usually prosecutes cases only where there is a good chance of conviction, the public defender, given staff limits, usually tries for reduced charges through plea bargaining. In 1975, the Office of State Public Defender was established to represent the poor on appeal and assist county public defenders during pretrial and trial proceedings.

ASSIGNED COUNSEL

In small counties where there is no public defender, the court uses *assigned counsel,* i.e., appoints an attorney in private practice to defend the accused. These attorneys tend to be young and inexperienced.

CLINICS/GROUPS

In the last few years, new types of legal assistance have emerged to assist defendants who cannot afford private counsel. These new forms include legal insurance ("liticare") and legal service clinics such as the California Rural Legal Assistance or the Western Center for Law and Poverty. Additionally, the American Civil Liberties Union has a long history of defending accused in cases involving constitutionally protected liberties. Here and there, private law firms have also donated their services. And, in some counties, the local bar organization will station attorneys at court houses, available to defendants.

CIVIL SUITS

For those involved in a major civil proceeding—divorce, probate of a will, or suit for damages—a private attorney must be hired. Even in cases which do not go to trial, legal counsel is needed.

POLICE

The police officer is a key individual in the criminal justice system. Police are usually the first public officials to arrive at the scene of the crime. In earlier times, police were concerned primarily with protecting government officials and providing a crude level of law and order. Today's police are civil servants involved in a broad range of social and personal problems—family fights, runaway children, neighborhood disputes, enforcement of racial integration, crowd control at demonstrations and marches, or keeping the peace at an athletic event. But more time is consumed by *automobile-related* activities than any other—traffic control, parking, and accident investigation. (Sometimes it is hard to see how the police have any time and effort left for crime prevention and the apprehension of criminals.)

Under the California Constitution, law enforcement is a local function—an important part of home rule—vested in the counties and cities (see Chapter 13). Each of California's 58 counties has a sheriff who is responsible for law enforcement within the unincorporated areas. Elected on a nonpartisan basis, the sheriff is one of several elected county officials. In addition to law enforcement, the sheriff also provides crime lab and other technical services to city police within the county and jail facilities for cities without them. The sheriff also has custody of those accused awaiting trial who cannot make bail and those who have been sentenced to short terms in jail.

ILLUSTRATION 12–4

"WOULD YOU LIKE TO WRITE OUT THE TICKET?"

Cartoon by Robert Minter

The bulk of police work is done by city departments, where most Californians live. City departments are headed by police chiefs who are usually appointed either by the city manager or by the city's police commission. Problems facing city police departments are varied. Large city police departments such as Los Angeles, San Diego, Oakland, San Francisco, or San Jose frequently deal with serious crimes such as murder, arson, or armed robbery. Smaller cities are more frequently concerned with traffic and burglary.

In addition to city and county police, there is also the California Highway Patrol, which is largely responsible for traffic on state freeways, and state police, who have responsibility for guarding major government buildings.

Police training

There are no required standards for police recruitment and training in the state. California has established some voluntary police standards known as POST. Police completing the course of study receive a certificate. But, essentially, each city and county establishes its own recruitment and training standards. Los Angeles and Oakland have, for example, their own police academies which give new officers basic instruction in police practices and the law.

In larger counties, the sheriff's department will have some training facilities, too. Smaller police departments will often send their new officers to such facilities. Some cities send selected officers to the FBI Academy for advanced training. But in many small cities, on the other hand, police training is only "inservice"—the new officer rides along with a senior officer for a month or so.

Promotion in most departments requires some education beyond high school—usually beyond the first two years of community college. Larger cities and counties often require an MA in police science or public administration for promotion.

CITIZEN PARTICIPATION

The citizen also plays a direct role in the state's justice system as a witness and as a member of trial or grand juries. About 1 out of 6 Californians has been in a court as a witness, while about 1 out of 12 has served on a trial jury. Very few ever serve on a grand jury (Field, 1974).

The right of a defendant in a court trial to have witnesses testify is provided by both the California and United States Constitutions. It is an important right that cannot be denied. Right to trial by jury is also guaranteed by both constitutions but is not an absolute right and is, in fact, not often used.

Trial juries

This jury form is used only in trial courts—justice, municipal, and superior courts. Most cases, of course, do not go to trial but are settled by plea bargaining, so there is no jury involved. Of those cases which do go to trial, only about 1 in 20 is argued before a jury.

Under California law, every adult citizen is required to serve on a trial jury when called. Until recently, many people were excused from jury duty because they were employed in "crucial" occupations—doctors, hospital employees, teachers, and utility workers, for example. They no longer are excused. Police officers, lawyers (and their wives), and some government employees are still automatically excused from jury duty. In 1979, the state's supreme court upheld a state law which excludes ex-felons and aliens. Most counties use lists of registered voters from which to draw names of potential jurors. But, increasingly, counties are also using lists of drivers' licenses. These newer practices are designed to produce juries which are representative of all the people living in a community.

Grand juries

Grand juries are quite different from trial juries. Grand juries indict suspects (charge them with crimes). They also investigate the operation of governmental agencies within the county. Every county has a grand jury, usually 19 citizens, selected by the county's superior court judges. Serving one year, the grand jury is the county "watchdog." While grand juries get most of their publicity when they return an indictment, this represents little of their total time and activity. District attorneys take very few criminal cases to the grand jury—less than 1 out of 50 felonies prosecuted in the state. (The district attorney almost always goes to the court with a direct accusation—called "information.")

Grand juries spend most of their time and effort investigating the conduct and operation of local governmental agencies and the needs of the county. Typically, in a year, they will make several investigative reports on various agencies and departments, calling attention to deficiencies, citing needed improvement, and perhaps making recommendations for reform.

Witnesses

All parties to a trial—the accused, the plaintiffs, and the defendant—have a constitutional right to present witnesses in their behalf. It is therefore logical that everyone has an obligation to appear as a witness when asked to do so. And, in fact, the court has the authority to compel people to testify (except against themselves).

RIGHTS OF THE PEOPLE

Every person, regardless of citizenship or residence, has a right to justice. As each of us within the jurisdiction of the state is subject to its laws, so each of us is also entitled to the protection of its laws and use of the system to protect our rights.

Rights of the accused

The accused has many rights, some of which are directly provided by the federal and/or state constitution. Other rights are provided by legislation or by court-adopted rules. Among these rights are: proper notification of a suit (subpoena), correct arrest and interrogation in a criminal case, knowledge of the charges, bail (in most cases), the advice of legal counsel, a fair trial, trial by jury (in most cases), and the right to appeal an adverse decision (in most cases). While some of these rights are not absolute (as noted), the limits exist only for minor infractions. Most restrictions on these rights are time and costs—not law or practice.

For an individual charged with a crime, first contact with the justice system is usually arrest by a police officer or sheriff's deputy. After booking, the suspect may make at least one phone call to an attorney, friend, relative or bail bondsman. At the time of arrest, police are required to inform the suspect that *under the constitution* he or she has the right to (*a*) remain silent and (*b*) have an attorney. Suspects also have the right to know the charges under which they were arrested. Both the California and U.S. constitution protect the individual against self-incrimination.

Before trial, the suspect is brought before the court—usually a municipal judge—and *arraigned.* At arraignment, the judge formally notifies the suspect of the charge, his or her legal rights, sets a date for a preliminary hearing, and establishes bail.

The right to reasonable bail is guaranteed by Article I of the California Constitution and may not be denied except in a capital case (death penalty). Persons of good character charged with minor crimes may be released without bail or on their own recognizance (OR). If the accused cannot make bail, they are held in jail pending trial.

In a civil case, the plaintiff brings the defendant to trial by filing a complaint with the clerk of the court and having a subpoena issued. Being served with the subpoena notifies the defendant of the suit and requires the defendant to appear in court.

In both criminal and civil cases, the defendant has the right to legal counsel (except in small claims). This right is essential in our complex and technical justice system. But attorneys are expensive, costing *at least* $50 per hour. The expense of legal counsel is one major reason why so few civil suits actually go to trial (less than 10 percent). Most are settled out of court.

Juveniles

Juveniles (anyone under the age of 18) are treated differently than adults in our legal system. This difference in treatment comes from the basic idea that juveniles are *not responsible for themselves.* A felonious act (arson, manslaughter, robbery) committed by a juvenile is usually not treated as a crime but rather as an act of someone who should not be held responsible for it. Thus, juveniles are also not liable to a civil suit—contracts with juveniles are not enforceable. Juveniles are not allowed to engage in substantial business activities (as individuals responsible for their own actions). For example, a successful child movie star's contract, salary, expenses, and other business activities are controlled by the court through a court-approved agent—usually the parents. Typically, the juvenile's case is heard in juvenile court. The juvenile criminal becomes a ward of the court which attempts to isolate him or her from the conditions which contributed to the juvenile's problem. Juveniles are not punished by terms in jail or prison. They may be housed in a detention facility, placed under probation, or put into some form of counseling program. The essential difference is that in criminal cases involving an adult, the court acts to protect society. In cases involving a juvenile, the court acts to protect the juvenile as well as society.

PENALTIES, CORRECTIONS, REHABILITATION, AND DAMAGES

Courts are involved in both the determination of guilt (in criminal cases) and liability (in civil cases). Following a criminal trial, the court begins what is known as the *penalty phase* of the proceedings. In a civil suit, the court determines the dollar amount of the settlement—*damages.* In suits in equity, the court may order performance or issue an injunction.

Corrections, penalties, and damages are vitally important to the justice system. In criminal cases, penalties and corrections are supposed to provide *punishment, deterrence,* and *rehabilitation.* In civil suits, the damages awarded or orders are supposed to *right the wrong.* If these aspects of the justice system fail, the rest is meaningless.

Determining penalty

CRIMINAL

Following conviction, the court requests that the county probation department recommend a suitable sentence. In addition, the district attorney and defense attorney also make recommendations. In imposing sentence, the judge weighs several factors. First, what are the statutory penalties? How severe was the crime? What are the circumstances surrounding the crime? Does the defendant have a prior record? The defendant's age, mental competency, and community status will also be considered.

Between 1917 and 1977, California law provided for an "indeterminate sentence." The judge would remand the convicted defendant to the California Adult Authority for an indeterminate period of time (for example, 1 to 10 years). The goal of the indeterminate sentence was rehabilitation. Felons were to be incarcerated until, in the judgment of the parole board, they were rehabilitated and ready to rejoin society. However, in the past few years, most legal experts have concluded that criminals are not rehabilitated in prison (see discussion of reform at end of chapter).

California courts now impose sentence under a new law (The Uniform Determinate Sentencing Act of 1976). This act provides three specific periods of time which may be imposed by the judge in sentencing for a specific crime. For example, a person convicted of robbery may receive a minimum sentence (three years), a medium sentence (four years), or the maximum sentence (five years). The circumstances of the crime must be considered in adding to the basic sentence imposed. If the robber had a prior conviction, the judge may add three more years to the sentence. If a firearm was used, two more years may be added. If someone were injured during the crime, another three years may be added. Thus, a first-time offender under mitigating circumstances might be sentenced to three years. But the same crime committed by someone with a prior record during which a person was injured could lead to a sentence of 11 years.

CIVIL

Following determination of liability in a civil suit, the court (or jury) may award the damages asked by plaintiff. Or, the award may be less. The award may simply be the amount needed to pay for repairing an automobile or the doctor's fees. Such an amount is easy to calculate. But if the award is for loss of a leg or an eye or a life, what is the correct amount? How much should be awarded for pain and suffering?

Most civil suits are settled out of court. The attorneys for the plaintiff and for the defendant agree on a settlement and the judge then records that agreement and orders the liable person to pay.

Imposing penalty

PROBATION

Rather than fill the jails and prisons, judges often place the convicted person on probation. This is particularly true for first-time offenders who are unlikely to commit another crime. Often, an individual will be given a sentence of time to be served in jail, with two thirds of it on probation. Technically, the convicted person is sentenced to a specific time in jail but is then *placed on probation* and allowed to remain free. A county probation officer is assigned the case, and the convict is required to report at specified intervals. A person on probation may be restricted in travel, required to perform some appropriate community service, or restricted in associations. Failure to meet the requirements of probation can lead to a return to jail.

INCARCERATION

As an agent of the state, each county has a jail which is administered by the county sheriff. The State Department of Corrections also administers 12 institutions. County jails have two types of prisoners. First, persons held for trial who have been denied bail, those who cannot make bail, or those who do not qualify for release on their own recognizance. Second, jails hold persons convicted of lesser crimes. Many of these convicts might have been sent to a state facility 10 or 15 years ago.

State institutions house persons convicted of violent crimes and/or serious drug offenses. In the past, prisons contained people convicted of some lesser crimes—burglary or forgery, for example. But today, the number of convicts sentenced for serious crimes equals or exceeds the state's prison capacity, so those convicted of lesser crimes are sent to jail instead.

Today, the California prison population is comprised largely of "repeaters." About 4 out of 10 have been in prison before, and another group, about half, have been in a county jail or a juvenile facility before.

PAROLE

California's lockup facilities have not kept pace with state population growth. Judges are able to sentence only the most serious cases to the state prison system which has a capacity of about 21,000 inmates.

Under law, after serving two thirds of a sentence, a prisoner is eligible for parole. Parole for each eligible inmate is considered once a year by the California Adult Authority and is granted on the basis of the inmate's behavior and prior record. A prisoner with a record of "good time" will probably be granted parole, unless there is a prior record to suggest that parole will be violated. Anyone on parole is still under the jurisdiction of the California Adult Authority and may be returned to prison for violation of the terms of parole. Arrest on another charge or carrying a firearm would be an automatic violation of parole.

Under Governors Reagan and Jerry Brown, the California Adult Authority was pressured to release unusually large numbers of prisoners on parole. Both governors wanted to avoid having to build new prison facilities. Both governors found, however, that a large percentage of "early" parolees were soon back in prison, frequently convicted of another criminal act. Both governors eventually returned to the more traditional stringent parole policy.

JUVENILES

Juveniles detained for a criminal act may not be kept in custody with adults. After a hearing, juveniles may be placed on probation, placed in custody of the county, or sent to the California Youth Authority (CYA). Only the most hardened juveniles, who are found guilty of a very serious offense or repeated acts ("incorrigible"), are sent to the CYA. County facilities typically include a secure facility called a *Juvenile Hall* and some "camplike" facility. Most large counties have foster home programs as well. But, as a general policy, judges of juvenile courts prefer to have juveniles remain at home and place them on probation.

REHABILITATION

Sentencing and rehabilitation give rise to a whole range of strong emotions and philosophies. California's 60-year "experiment" with the indeterminate sentencing law was based on the hope that criminals could be rehabilitated while in prison. Today, it would be accurate to say that California has abandoned attempts to rehabilitate criminals in prison. Prisons and jails, it is generally believed, do not rehabilitate. In fact, prison and jail are fine places for the young criminal to learn more about crime.

The motives and reasons for criminal activity do not appear to be modified or eliminated by incarceration. Rehabilitation efforts are essentially focused on the individual *under probation* or *on parole*. Foster homes and intensive counseling are considered to be more effective than Juvenile Hall or the CYA for juveniles.

COURTS AND POLICY MAKING

A simplistic view of the judicial system is that courts are *not supposed to make policy*. Thus, the argument goes, given the American governmental framework, legislatures make policy, executives administer policy, and courts make sure that everything is done according to the laws and constitution. It's this last expectation which leads to the court's policy making.

Judicial policy making occurs when judges are *asked to resolve a conflict* between two laws or between a law and a constitutional provision. Policy is also made when courts *interpret* a law or constitutional provision. Frequently, legislators will enact a law in general terms, doing little more than stating their purpose or *legislative intent.* The legislature will not spell out the details, definitions, or specific applications of the law. This they leave to administrators and the courts. Thus, the courts find themselves inevitably making policy.

In fact, appellate courts and the state supreme court were established to resolve conflicts between and uncertainties within laws and the constitution. It is also important to realize that a state supreme court has the constitutional authority to significantly interpret or modify United States Supreme Court decisions involving their state's activities.

Thus, for example, the California Supreme Court in 1975 significantly restricted police searches of suspects. The U.S. Supreme Court had earlier ruled that full-body searches by police of persons arrested for minor offenses did not violate the U.S. Constitution. But, the California State Supreme Court, citing the California State Constitution substantially restricted police searches *in California.*

Courts may also review the substance of referendums and initiatives.

ILLUSTRATION 12–5

"If you think the political reapportionment map is a hassle, wait until we have to get into this one!"

Dennis Renault, Sacramento Bee

Those who lose in such an election may feel that some constitutional rights have been denied or infringed upon and go to the court for an opinion. For example, the California Supreme Court modified or completely nullified 5 of the 7 constitutional initiatives passed by California's voters between 1962 and 1976. In one instance, California voters approved a constitutional initiative measure in 1972 that outlawed school busing to achieve racial balance within school districts (Proposition 21). That constitutional amendment was challenged in the courts, and the state supreme court ruled the initiative unconstitutional. The court held, in that case, that not even a majority of voters could deprive anyone of their basic constitutional rights. And, immediately following passage of the property tax initiative (Proposition 13) in June 1978, several adversely affected groups asked the state supreme court to declare it unconstitutional. The court, however, upheld its constitutionality.

The courts are also frequently asked to interpret laws. The state's 1973 death penalty law was challenged, and the state supreme court held the law unconstitutional because it was inflexible. The state court relied on an earlier U.S. Supreme Court decision in this case (as contrasted to the police search case).

Finally, it should be noted that the court makes law in some instances. It ordered the state legislature to equalize public school financing in *Serrano* v. *Priest*. That decision required the addition of $1 billion to the state's budget in 1972 and another $4.3 billion in 1977. And, reaching into the heart of the political process, in 1973 the court reapportioned the state legislature, after the governor and legislators became deadlocked on the issue.

The policy-making role of the courts is essentially inevitable. The controversial issues of our society get to the court, because those who lose the struggle in other political arenas hope for success in the courts. Those who opposed the 1972 school busing initiative (Proposition 21) lost the election fight but won the court battle. Those who opposed the death penalty won a modified victory in the courts after losing in the legislature. Those who were adversely affected by the traditional method of financing local public education went to the courts and won a victory that could not have been achieved in any other political arena. The authority of courts to resolve conflicts in law is a vital part of our governmental process.

As long as the courts are empowered to resolve conflicts, they will be involved in controversy and the making of public policy.

REFORMING THE SYSTEM

Each part of the California justice system has come under criticism. Some see the system as arbitrary; others see it as too soft on criminals; still others see it as too hard on minorities. Almost everyone is concerned about the deterrence of crime, but there is little agreement on how to do it. Almost everyone wants to make the courts more available to people and to speed up the civil calendar, but not everyone wants to spend more money to do it.

Police

Two major police reforms are most frequently suggested: (1) increased training and standards, and (2) civilian review boards.

The quality of police training, recruitment, and training standards varies considerably among the cities and counties in California. At present, less training is required to be a police officer than to be an electrician or barber. Opposition to uniform and statewide standards comes from many cities and counties who want to maintain their own requirements and hold down police salaries.

Civilian review boards have become a controversial issue. Most police are bitterly opposed to having any outside control in reviewing police actions. On the other hand, many citizens feel that the city council, police commission, mayor, and/or city manager do not adequately control the police. Charges of police brutality or unnecessary use of force revive the demand for greater civilian control of the police. This attitude is particularly strong among racial minorities, homosexuals, and members of civil rights organizations.

Courts

More demands for reform center on the courts than on any other component of the justice system. These reform issues include: (1) the role of the press, (2) jury size and selection, (3) civil case backlog, and (4) night courts.

The press wants greater access to court trials. Reporters argue that the right to a public trial is meaningless if they cannot provide complete coverage of a trial.

However, the press sometimes reveals facts which a judge might feel damages the judicial process. Judges have sometimes demanded that reporters reveal their sources. Newspapers traditionally refuse to reveal sources, and in Los Angeles and Fresno, reporters have recently been jailed for their refusal to do so. Most newspaper reporters believe their sources should not be revealed. They argue the public is best served by providing more, not less, information. Judges, on the other hand, are concerned about what they view as unfair publicity and violations of a defendant's rights to a fair trial.

One of the major problems plaguing courts is the civil case backlog. Delay in hearing civil cases has been steadily increasing in California. More civil cases are now waiting trial than ever before. The average wait to have a civil case tried is two years. If "justice delayed is justice denied," the civil case backlog is a major problem.

Delay in appeal cases has also become an issue. In the fall of 1979, suit was brought against the state's supreme court justices charging them with violating a constitutional provision requiring disposition of a case 90 days from final hearing. Over 20 cases were cited which substantially violated that requirement. The trial court found for plaintiffs and the justices paychecks were withheld. On appeal, the lower court's decision was reversed. But the problem of slow appeal still remains.

Prosecution/Defense

Plea bargaining or "copping a plea" is viewed by many to be one of the most pressing reforms in the area of criminal prosecution and defense. Given the present number of courtrooms, judges, and clerks, plea bargaining is an absolute necessity. If every criminal case went to trial, there would have to be about 770 new judges, courtrooms, and so on, in addition to the 551 superior court judges as of 1978. Few people have been willing to support such a costly expansion of the court system. On the other hand, many feel that the accused should be tried for the crime committed—not allowed to plead guilty to a lesser charge.

Bail reform is another important item on the list of needed reforms. A bail bond is an amount of money deposited with the court to guarantee that the defendant will appear for trial. The right to post such a bond (except for homicide) is guaranteed in the California Constitution. The court sets bail at a dollar amount designed to insure that the individual will appear for trial. The more severe the crime (and penalty), the higher the bail bond. Failure to appear means forfeiture of bail.

If the accused cannot raise the amount of bail, he or she stays in jail until trial. However, this means that a poor person stays in jail, though not yet convicted of any crime.[1] One fruitful reform program has been OR (own recognizance). Under OR a person with no prior arrest and good reputation need not post any bail except in serious cases.

A major reform in bail bond procedures was enacted in 1979 permitting those accused of a misdemeanor to deposit 10 percent of the required bail directly with the court. Following disposition of the case, the court will return the 10 percent (less a nominal processing fee) to the defendant. No such return is made by the bail bondsman.

The bail bondsman lobby strongly opposed the reform, asserting that it would cost local government $2.4 million a year in bail forfeitures. Those supporting the reform asserted that it would permit return of most

---

[1] Testifying before a legislative committee hearing on bail reform in April 1979, Los Angeles District Attorney John Van de Kamp asserted that more than half the people in jail are there because they cannot afford to post bail before trial.

of the 10 percent to the defendants, who lost their deposits under the previous system whether or not they were found guilty.

Juvenile justice

The juvenile justice system has been under reform pressure from two directions: (1) those who see it as too harsh on juveniles and (2) those who see it as too lenient.

The first group has won a partial victory in eliminating the status offense detention because of an act which is illegal only for a juvenile (e.g. curfew). Another reform which appears to be close to adoption is use of an adversary hearing process in juvenile court. In California, juvenile courts have been closed to the public to protect the juvenile's identity. Recent court decisions have held, however, that juveniles are entitled to a public hearing and an attorney.

Treating some juveniles as "responsible adults" is the goal of some reformers who view the juvenile justice system as "soft on juvenile felons." Should a youth of 17 charged with premeditated homicide be tried as an adult? It would be hard to say without knowing other facts. Should a youth of eight charged with premeditated homicide be tried as an adult? Most people would say "no." At what age is an individual "responsible?" Most of the debate over juvenile justice hinges on the answer to that question.

Grand jury

Grand juries are sometimes criticized because they may indict a person on evidence which would not be admissible in court. Thus, grand jury indictments, while relatively few, may violate the commonly agreed-upon rules of a fair hearing. The suspect may not have an attorney present while being questioned. Indeed, the accused has no right to be present unless subpoenaed by the grand jury.

Those who argue in favor of the present system point out that the grand jury is often concerned with political corruption and organized crime. Such cases might not get a balanced hearing in court.

In general, it is argued, grand jury indictments are usually based on solid evidence. Judges deny their indictments about 13 percent of the time compared to denial of 9 percent after usual preliminary information hearings.

Trial procedure

Several major reforms offer a potential for improvement of the justice system. The use of video-taped testimony by witnesses unable to appear in court physically has been suggested and sometimes used. A much larger issue is the admissibility of illegally obtained evidence—the "exclusionary rule." Under Article I of the California Constitution (and Fourth Amendment to the U.S. Constitution), there is a guarantee of "the right of the people to be secure in their persons, houses, . . . against unreasonable seizures and searches." California courts tend toward strict interpretation of this prohibition.

Corrections

A much broader issue of reform is the goal of the state's prison system. Under the indeterminate sentencing law, there was a strong rehabilitation theme—or at least hope. The new determinate system is clearly designed to punish. The theory is that punishment will act as a deterrent to crime, if the potential criminal knows he or she will go to prison if caught and convicted.

The legislature's enactment of a mandatory prison sentence for anyone using a gun to commit a crime is a good example of the punishment-deterrence theory. As yet, no one knows for sure if the theory will work.

SUMMARY

In this chapter we have looked at the various parts of the California justice system. Two major features stand out. First, it is not so much a system as a number of governmental agencies functioning in the same area. And, second, the system is under heavy pressures due to increased use and for reform.

Each year, there are more court cases—more civil suits and more criminal trials. And the largest number of cases comes from our use of the automobile. (What would a highly efficient, inexpensive public transportation system do to the court load?)

Pressures for reform fall into three categories. First, there are the demands for change that will make the justice system more fair. Rules of evidence, bail bond practices, and the method for selecting trial juries are examples of this concern. Second, there are demands for greater accessibility. Night traffic courts, night small claims courts, reduced delay in getting a civil suit to trial, and bail-by-mail are examples.

Third, there is the larger debate over the function of the criminal justice system itself. What should be its goal? Can the wayward juvenile be saved from a life of crime? Should jails and prisons serve as agents of rehabilitation? Or should the criminal system be concerned only with making the streets safe for law-abiding citizens? Much of this debate is rooted in our view of crime and of human nature. The wide-ranging debate over the death penalty is a good example.

Californians place a heavy burden on the state's justice system and have made many demands for reform. Change and reform are difficult to achieve, but it is encouraging to see that some advances have been made.

13

Local government in California

Local government in California (and in other states) is different from state and national government in two significant ways. *First,* local governments have no inherent constitutional existence but are, rather, agents of the state. *Second,* local governments share jurisdictions with other local governments; their territorial areas often overlap those of other local governments.

There are four basic kinds of local government in California: county, city, school, and special district. California has 58 counties, 417 cities, almost 1,300 school districts, and some 5,000 special districts. These local units provide most of the day-to-day services we associate with government—police, fire, education, parks and recreation, streets, sewage disposal, libraries, land use regulation (including zoning), water, public transportation, and flood control. In addition, many local governments also provide services such as electricity and gas, harbors and airports, hospitals, cemeteries, and housing.

In California, 8 out of 10 state government dollars are spent by one of the several thousand local governments. Moreover, most government employees, 7 out of 10, work at the local level. Local government is obviously important.

California has a tradition of "home rule." Elements of this tradition may be found in both the state's constitution and in the political values of citizens and politicians. In theory, much of our local government could be abolished, consolidated, or sharply reduced by legislative action. In fact, political pressures from citizens, locally elected public officials, and many interest groups would make it difficult for legislators to change dramatically the powers and scope of local government.

But in spite of the importance of local government, few citizens are involved in it. Local government tends to be government by local elites and activists.

CONSTITUTIONAL PROVISIONS

The authority of the state to create city and county governments, organize their structures, and define their powers is found in Article XI of the California Constitution. Section 1 provides for county governments: "The State is divided into counties which are legal subdivisions of the State . . . The Legislature shall provide for county powers and an elected governing body in each county."

Section 2 of the same article provides for city government: "The Legislature shall prescribe uniform procedure for city formation and provide for city powers." Finally, Section 3 sets up the process by which local voters may establish a *chartered* city or county. Other sections provide for local lawmaking power (called ordinances) and the powers to tax and regulate.

Two other articles in the constitution deal with local government. Article IX provides for local school districts, county schools, basic financial aid to local schools, and the authority to borrow money. It also provides for school boards to govern local schools. Article XIII is concerned with the taxing authority exercised by local governments.

Special districts (sometimes called public districts) are not directly established by the California Constitution. Most of them are created by counties, some by cities, and a very few by the legislature.

COUNTY GOVERNMENT

When California entered the Union, it was divided into 27 counties. As population grew, more counties were created until there were 58 by 1907. Counties serve as local administrative agencies for state programs as well as providing other services. Each of the state's counties is organized in one of two ways—by charter or general law.

County forms

GENERAL LAW COUNTIES

General laws, enacted by the state legislature over the years, provide for a consistent statewide pattern of structures and powers for counties. Each general law county has the same basic form. Elected officials include five members of the Board of Supervisors, a sheriff, district attorney, coroner, assessor, tax collector, superintendent of schools, and

290

ILLUSTRATION 13–1
Counties, 1974

five other minor officials. Many general law counties (particularly the smaller ones) combine some of these positions. For example, Alpine County (population 700) elects a combined county clerk-auditor-recorder, and several other counties combine the position of sheriff and coroner.

Each county is divided into five geographic districts which elect a

representative to the County Board of Supervisors. The board is authorized by the state legislature to enact county ordinances (laws) governing
the county. The board is also authorized to prepare an annual budget,
to collect the county's property tax, and to receive state and federal funds
designated for locally administered programs (welfare and roads, for
example).

The board is also empowered to appoint a number of minor administrators as well as several important officials. The most important person
appointed is the county's chief administrative officer. Other important
appointed officials include the director of social services, head of public
health, head of the planning department, chief probation officer, and
head of public works (roads, bridges, sewers, etc.).

CHARTER COUNTIES

Eleven counties have adopted their own charters (constitutions). With
approval of the local voters, charter counties are able to set up different
political structures and to exercise additional powers. This is supposed
to give them greater ability to meet local needs. Los Angeles was the first
county to adopt a charter (1912). Since then, ten others have joined the
list: Alameda, Butte, Fresno, Sacramento, San Bernardino, San Diego,
San Francisco, San Mateo, Santa Clara, and Tehama.

Charter counties tend to be urban (excepting Butte and Tehama) with
large populations. San Francisco, "The City," as it is known in northern
California, has a unique charter. It is a mix of both city and county forms.
It combines the office of mayor and an enlarged (11 members) board of
supervisors. San Francisco exercises both the powers of a city and a
county. With over 600,000 people living on only 46 square miles, such
a hybrid form appears to be reasonable.

The main advantages of a charter form are: (1) it can make the lesser
administrative officers appointive rather than elective; (2) it can determine the county's own salary schedule; and (3) it can reorganize administrative structure more easily.

Actually, the number of elected administrative officials in charter
counties is not much different from the number in general law counties.
Nor does the power to reorganize and set salaries appear to have made
much difference in the day-to-day operations of county government.
Regardless of the supposed advantages, California's charter counties
are not very different from general law counties.

County administrator

The top appointed official in county government is the chief administrative officer. In some counties, this official is known as the County
Executive and in others as the Chief Administrative Officer. Whatever the

title, over 40 counties have someone who manages the day-to-day administration of county services, oversees county operations, and controls expenditures. In many counties, the administrator will also make policy and budget recommendations to the Board of Supervisors.

Those few counties which do not have such an official are generally small, with populations of less than 33,000. Government in these rural "cow counties" tends to be part-time and small-scale. But in most California counties, the populations are large, and government is full-time.

Major county programs/services

WELFARE

Regardless of county size, welfare programs have historically been the largest part of the budget. In San Francisco, 1 out of 4 residents receives some form of public welfare. In Los Angeles, the ratio is 1 out of 7. Aid to Families with Dependent Children (AFDC) is the largest part of the welfare budget (about 75 percent). But other forms of welfare are important too—aid to the blind and infirm, hospital care for the poor, and general relief for those who are needy but do not meet the requirements of other welfare programs.

In recent years, the federal government has provided a major part of the funding for welfare. And since passage of Proposition 13, which put limits on property tax collections, the state has picked up more of the costs. In 1979, the local costs of welfare were largely eliminated, but counties continue to administer the programs.

PUBLIC SAFETY

The sheriff, courts, jails, flood control, and fire protection combine to make the second largest part of the typical county's budget. The sheriff heads the county's police department. This officer is an independently elected public official, frequently well-known and powerful. It is important to remember, however, that the Board of Supervisors controls the sheriff department's annual budget.

The county jail and juvenile hall are other major areas of public protection expenditures. Many criminal suspects are kept in the county jail or juvenile hall prior to pretrial hearings. If not released on bail or on their own recognizance, the suspect will remain in county custody. Finally, after conviction, most felons who are given sentences will serve time in the county jail rather than in one of the state's prisons.

The district attorney, public defender, trial courts, and probation department are also important parts of the public safety program (see Chapter 12).

ENVIRONMENTAL PROTECTION

Environmental management, including pollution control, land use planning, and zoning in unincorporated areas, has recently become a significant county activity. Much of California's population growth has taken place in the suburbs—often in unincorporated areas. The county's zoning and land use plans are crucial in preventing destruction of natural resources, open spaces, and agricultural lands. Recently, however, their authority has been diminished in some counties by the creation of Local Agency Formation Commissions (see LAFCO section later in this chapter).

PUBLIC HEALTH

Health and sanitation are central activities to the ongoing life of a county's residents. Such activities as water quality control and sewage disposal are obviously necessary, as is inspecting restaurants for cleanliness. In addition, many counties maintain a public hospital for care of the indigent. And, often unnoticed but crucial, is "vector control"—keeping the community safe from rats and rabid or other disease-carrying animals.

RECREATION

Parks and recreation are another traditional county activity. This is particularly important in the urban counties (and cities) where crowded living conditions place a premium on open space. As gasoline prices go up and supplies become short, many people may find that parks and public recreation centers are very important.

ROADS

Road construction and maintenance are other important county activities. Citizens tend to take "surface transportation" for granted until roadbeds crumble or are flooded out. Perhaps if mass rapid transit becomes a reality, less stress will be placed on roads and streets.

Selected problems

In recent years, California's counties have had increasing difficulty in meeting their citizens' needs. First, because there are so many elected public officials (on the average seven or eight per county) responsibility and authority are scattered. Voters seldom know who is in charge.

Second, in the larger counties, supervisorial districts have too many citizens to permit meaningful representation. In Los Angeles County, the average district has 1.4 million residents. In Orange County, the average is 340,000, and in San Diego the average is about 320,000. Statewide, the average supervisorial district has about 77,000 residents.

Third, there is no county executive comparable to a governor or mayor. Thus, there are no checks and balances in county government excepting San Francisco. In 1978, Los Angeles voters considered setting up a county mayor but rejected the idea.

Fourth, many problems which counties face originate outside their boundaries and are not capable of being solved by the individual counties. For example, pollution, poverty, and unemployment are subject to little or no county influence.

And fifth, the passage of Proposition 13 reduced the average county's annual revenues by almost 20 percent and required significant cuts in programs even with state aid. Along with state aid has come increased state control over local government—for example, the denial of pay increases to local government employees in 1978.

CITY GOVERNMENT

Cities, unlike counties, are not created by the state. Any group of residents who decides that county services do not meet their needs can (with a few restrictions) form a *municipal corporation*—a city. And, as California has grown, so have the number of cities. Today, almost 420 cities from Amador (population 160) to Los Angeles (population 2.7 million) provide a wide range of services to their residents.

ILLUSTRATION 13–2
Los Angeles in 1853—a small pueblo on the fringe of civilization

Photo courtesy California State Library

California's first cities were established during the Spanish era long before the state was formed. San Diego, the state's first city, was founded in 1769, followed by Monterey (1770), San Francisco (1776), and Los Angeles (1781). After California became a state, these early cities were incorporated under provisions of the new state's constitution.

Sometimes cities are formed for unusual or unique reasons. The cities of Vernon, Commerce, and Industry in southern California, and Emeryville in northern California, were formed to provide tax benefits to the businesses located there and to protect them from the regulations and property taxes which would have been imposed if neighboring cities had annexed them.

Sometimes cities are formed to provide greater local political control —to protect their residents from being "swallowed up" by larger neighboring cities. And sometimes cities are formed as a matter of local pride and identity. Thus, Chicano activists have twice tried to form a city in the

ILLUSTRATION 13–3
Modern Los Angeles, the state's largest city, stretches beyond the horizon

Photo courtesy California State Library

east Los Angeles area which would be, they believe, more responsive than the county to their social and cultural needs.

Usually, however, municipal incorporation occurs when an area's residents need additional governmental services. Cities are often formed to provide:

1. More control over land use and zoning.
2. Traffic control.
3. Control over expenditures for services.
4. Better sanitation and/or sewage disposal.
5. Better police and/or fire protection.

Many cities have been formed as a result of suburban migration—people moving from major cities to the suburbs surrounding them. Those who leave the central cities often complain about dirt, noise, and crime rates, and many are looking for more room and privacy. In recent years, many Californians have left the central cities because of racial tensions or fears. Often called "white flight," middle-class residents have moved to the suburbs and formed new cities over which they hope to have more control.

As we saw in Chapter 2, most of California's population growth has been in the suburbs. Each of the 21 cities incorporated in the 1970s was on the outskirts of a major metropolitan area. But as California's population growth has slowed, so too has the formation of new cities. Not since the Depression decade of the 1930s have there been so few new municipal incorporations as in the 1970s. And this low rate of municipal growth is likely to continue into the 1980s, due to continued slow population growth and, in addition, the lack of adequate tax funds since adoption of Proposition 13.

City forms

California's cities are organized in one of two basic ways—under the state's general laws or by charter. Unlike counties, which are established by the constitution, a city does not exist until a group of people decide to incorporate. Once incorporated under the state's general laws, each city has a city council, mayor, and administrative structure. It also has authority to provide a wide range of services. Charter cities usually modify the basic mayor-council structure and provide additional services not available under the general law form.

GENERAL LAW CITIES

Most California cities (almost 350) are incorporated under the state's general law provisions. At one time, incorporation was relatively easy.

But, in response to the haphazard city formation of the late 1940s and 1950s, state law was altered to make municipal incorporation more difficult.

If the residents of a specific area decide to incorporate, they must follow a specified procedure:

1. Apply to the County Local Agency Formation Commission (LAFCO).
2. Must have at least 500 inhabitants in the proposed city.
3. Show that the proposed new city boundaries do not overlap those of an existing city.
4. Show that the proposed new city boundaries do not intrude into another city's sphere of influence (see the LAFCO section).
5. Show that there is a need for the proposed city.

If the LAFCO approves, sponsors must then obtain signatures of support from at least 25 percent of the proposed city's property owners who must also own 25 percent of the proposed new city's real estate by value. These petitions are then submitted to the County Board of Supervisors. If the board, after public hearings, approves the formation of the new city, there will then be a special election. Voters in that election will be asked:

1. "Should there be a new city of _____?"
2. Vote for five city council members.

If a majority of voters approves formation of a new city, the five candidates receiving the most votes become the new city's first city council.

The new city's council selects one of its members to be mayor, an honorary position, to preside at council meetings. Mayors in general law cities have no more power than any other member of the city council. All formal political authority resides in the council which makes policy for the city. Most general law city councils appoint a city manager to administer city policy and take charge of the day-to-day city activities and services.

City managers have responsibility for hiring and firing city employees, preparing and submitting the city's annual budget, and proposing new city laws. While not elected, the typical city manager exercises functions and powers similar to those of the governor or other elected executives.

CHARTER CITIES

California has almost 80 charter cities. The residents of these cities have decided that the general law city form is not adequate for their needs. Typically, charter cities are large. All of the state's major cities and most of those over 100,000 population have charters.

Charter cities are formed in much the same way as general law cities

—by petition and election. Charters, like constitutions, can be amended by the city's voters. One of the strongest arguments for a charter is that a local community's voters can make changes in city form and powers.

Charter cities can adopt forms which are different than those available under the general law. For example, Los Angeles has a city council of 15 members elected by district and a mayor elected at large. Santa Ana, a medium-sized city in Orange County, has a city council of seven members, nominated by districts but elected at large. San Francisco has a board of supervisors, with 11 members elected by district and a mayor elected at large.

While most charter cities retain the council-manager form, some have established a strong mayor form. As a rule, larger cities will elect council members by district and their mayor at large. The mayor is not a member of the council. This pattern more closely resembles the pattern of executive-legislative separation of powers found in the national and state governments. These independently elected mayors often have substantial administrative and budget authority similar to that exercised by governors.

City activities

POLICE

One out of 5 city dollars is spent on the police. This is the largest single budget item in a typical city. Since most Californians live in a city, it is the city in California which provides most of us with our police services.

Police tasks vary somewhat depending on the kind of city. In general, police tasks or activities can be listed as: regulation of traffic, investigation of traffic accidents, patrol, crime prevention, investigation of reported crimes, apprehension of suspects, gathering and presenting evidence, detention of suspects, and custody of property.

Traffic control, which includes parking regulation, is the single largest police activity in the typical California city. About 75 percent of a city's police budget and personnel are used for traffic regulation and control.

Rapidly rising crime rates, particularly in central urban areas, are also a major police concern. In one recent survey of California residents, 45 percent reported that they or some member of their family had been the victim of a crime in the previous year (Field, 1974). In addition, over half of those interviewed expressed fear of leaving their home. This is particularly true in urban centers.

Until recently, most Californians give police good marks. In 1972, 8 out of 10 citizens rated police "somewhat good" to "extremely good"

(Field, 1974). However much could be done to improve city police both in recruiting and training (see Chapter 12). In most of the larger urban areas, there have been frequent demands for some form of civilian police review process. Police departments often appear reluctant to investigate or punish an officer charged with illegal or unprofessional acts committed in line of duty, though one study of complaints filed against police in Los Angeles found that over half were valid (*Los Angeles Times,* 1974).

It may be that the public has become less supportive of the police in the late 1970s. A 1979 survey taken in Los Angeles revealed that approval of the city's police department had dropped from 69 percent to 51 percent in 18 months. And while minority respondents (black and Hispanics) were particularly critical, whites increasingly expressed disapproval (*Los Angeles Times,* 1979).

FIRE

Fire fighting and prevention is the third largest budget item in the typical California city—about $1 out of $10 spent. In addition to the usual fire problems associated with residential, commercial, and industrial structures, many California cities also have severe problems with brush fires. This is particularly true in southern California where many homes are built in the hills.

STREETS

Slightly more than 1 of 10 city dollars is spent on street construction, maintenance and repair, parking, lighting, and storm drains. This is the second largest city budget item. In California, where the automobile is a way of life, an adequate street system has high priority.

PARKS AND RECREATION

Slightly less than 1 out of each 10 city dollars is spent on parks and recreation. Due to California's rapid population growth, large communities of tract homes frequently have few parks or community recreation facilities. Center-city and ghetto parks are often small and poorly maintained. The accessibility of beaches and mountains has until recently reduced the desire for parks among many of the middle class. But as travel costs increase, more demands will be made for them. Many cities now cooperate with local school districts for after-school use of playgrounds for recreation. And a few cities now require developers to set aside specific areas for parks. But tight budgets will mean cities will have little or no capacity to provide more parks.

UTILITIES AND TRANSPORTATION

Many of the state's cities provide water and electricity to their residents. San Francisco brings water 150 miles from the High Sierras via the Hetch Hetchy Aqueduct. Similarly, Los Angeles gets much of its water from the Owens Valley (170 miles northeast of the city) and from the Colorado River (240 miles) on the Arizona border. San Diego and many other southern California cities also get their water supply in part or entirely from the Colorado River Aqueduct.

Most major cities also provide airport facilities (Los Angeles, San Francisco, San Diego, Sacramento, and San Jose, for example). Bus and street cars are often provided either by a city (Santa Monica and San Francisco) or jointly with other cities in regional transportation districts. The seaport cities of San Diego, Long Beach, Los Angeles (San Pedro), San Francisco, and Oakland have substantial harbor facilities. Stockton and Sacramento, both about 65 miles inland, also have major harbor facilities on their rivers.

LAND USE AND PLANNING

One of the major functions of most cities is the control of land use and planning. While not a significant budget item, it is important to the quality of life and economic health of every city. In fact, several cities have been incorporated because their residents wanted to control local development and growth and feared county control of the process.

One major feature of land use and planning in growing cities—usually in the suburbs—is development policy. How large shall residential lots be? What is the best mix of single unit dwellings and apartment houses? How wide should streets be, and how shall the city control traffic flow? Where should shopping centers and commercial and industrial facilities be located? All of these questions are central to land use planning and are frequently the most controversial in new or growing cities.

There is another whole set of land use and planning problems which emerge as a city ages and begins to decline. How can a city, with limited financial resources, attract investment capital into the inner core? How can the city facilitate construction of low-cost housing for the poor? Often, these questions are closely related to the problems of job opportunity, new industry, and public transportation. Restoring blighted areas is one of the major challenges facing our older California cities.

Cities have considerable power over land use. They zone land areas for type of use—single-unit or multiple-unit housing, commercial, industrial, light, or heavy manufacturing, and so on. Under California law, each city (and county) is required to have a long-range land use plan. Zoning and zoning changes are supposed to conform to the plan. But as population patterns change and as the needs of people change, zoning patterns may also have to change.

Selected problems

Like counties, California's cities seem to be increasingly burdened with problems they cannot solve. Typically, many of these problems originate beyond the city's authority. Smog, transportation, much of land use, and crime problems are not localized within the cities' boundaries. The whole range of economic problems—inflation, unemployment, housing, and tax resources—are national problems.

But it is important to note again that most of us live in a city. Perhaps the city is an outmoded governmental form. If it cannot solve our problems, why keep it? Perhaps all local government should be concentrated in county agencies. But as we have discussed, county government has its own problems, too. Perhaps regional governments would help.

Proposition 13 has compounded the city's problems. Left largely on their own in the search for revenues (compared to counties and school districts which receive substantial state assistance), cities may simply cease to deliver their traditional services in the future.

SCHOOL DISTRICTS

Public education in California has historically been a local activity. In 1977, there were 818 elementary school districts, 151 high school districts, 255 unified school districts, and 70 community college districts. Student enrollment in all of these was 5.4 million, costing taxpayers $9.4 billion dollars.[1] Public education is clearly a major part of local governmental activity in the Golden State.

Each public school district is governed by a five-member board of trustees often called the "school board." Trustees are usually elected at large on a nonpartisan basis. Los Angeles Unified School District is an exception—since 1978, it has been governed by a seven-member board elected by district.

School boards, like most city councils, are part-time. They usually meet once or twice a month on a week night. Board members are, typically, homemakers, businesspeople, occasionally an attorney or an accountant, sometimes a downtown merchant.

Board members are not professional educators. School boards set policy but do not attempt to be directly involved in the day-to-day management of the district's business. School boards hire a district superin-

---

[1] There were in addition, about 2,800 private schools (K–12) with 434,000 pupils. About 8 out of 10 of these students attend a church-affiliated school.

tendent who is a professional educator to manage the district. Authority and responsibility for management of the school district lies with the superintendent. He or she prepares the annual budget, hires and fires school personnel, and prepares policy proposals.

Almost 200,000 teachers are employed in California's public schools. In addition, there are thousands of administrators, teacher aides, pupil service employees, clerks, secretaries, gardeners, janitors, maintenance personnel, and others. All together, California's public schools have over 350,000 employees.

The course of instruction offered in the state's schools is varied. Each school is required to offer 175 days of instruction (35 weeks) each year. Every child over 6 and under 18 years of age is required to attend. However, a certificate of proficiency is available to those who pass an exam. Students who pass that test need not continue school. The certificate is not the same as a high school diploma, however.

California is the only state that prints its own textbooks and provides them free of charge to elementary school districts. High schools purchase their own texts directly from the publishers. Some of the curriculum is determined by the local district board of trustees. But the State Board of Education (appointed by the governor) establishes instructional guidelines and requirements for graduation.

Bilingual education is an example of a state special education program. A 1975 survey conducted by the State Department of Education found over 233,000 school children who spoke little or no English. At that time, slightly more than 14,000 teachers were proficient in Spanish. Under state law, school districts must provide bilingual instruction if they have Spanish-speaking students, and the state has a loan program to help new teachers learn Spanish.

California also provides funds for education of the physically handicapped and the mentally gifted. Additionally, the state provides financial assistance for programs on conservation and requires driver education in the high schools. These are only a few of the many state-mandated and/or funded programs required of local schools.

Even more significant than the state-mandated programs in affecting local control of education has been the tendency for major social and political issues to become centered in the schools. Because of segregated housing, community schools have also become segregated. Under several court orders, schools have been forced to integrate—often busing children long distances within districts to achieve racial balance. And in 1978 in response to "white flight," courts began looking at *metropolitan busing.* By transporting white children from surrounding suburban school districts, proponents of integrated schools hope to achieve a "desirable" racial mix. Opponents view such plans as a death blow to their community schools.

School hiring practices have been modified by affirmative action which requires them to make an extra effort to hire blacks and Hispanics. This is one area of employment, however, where women tend to be overrepresented. As school enrollments decline, the disadvantaged will have greater problems in gaining employment as teachers. Ironically, males might use affirmative action suits to displace women applicants!

Collective bargaining for public employees is now available to teachers in California's public schools. School boards increasingly find themselves under pressure from the local teacher's union for higher pay and better working conditions. But at the same time, school funds have been reduced by declining enrollments and Proposition 13 limits on the property tax.

In addition, California's Supreme Court in *Serrano* v. *Priest* (1971) held the property tax to be an unconstitutional base for funding public schools. The court observed that (Post and Brandsma, 1973):

> . . . the California public school financing system, with its substantial dependence on local property taxes and resultant wide disparities in school revenue, violates the equal protection clause of the Fourteenth Amendment.

The court reasoned that the wide differences in financial support for children in different school districts produced an unacceptable difference in the quality of education they received.

Holding that education may not be a function of any particular school district's wealth, the court required the legislature to provide equalization funding. Yet, in spite of repeated attempts by the legislature, differences in funding of education remained as great in 1979 as in 1971 (Post, 1979a). As of 1979, the only effect of *Serrano* has been to give greater control of local school district funding to the state government.

Selected problems

Proposition 13 and the *Serrano* decision have effectively removed local control from the school districts. With 80 percent of local school revenues provided by the state, effective control and direction of education are now in the hands of the state. California's tradition of local control of education appears at an end.

At the same time, the highly controversial issues of racial integration and busing have torn apart many of the state's school districts. Public education is under attack by a proposed voucher plan which would enable parents to send their children to private schools at state expense. And, as budgets are cut, teachers have become increasingly militant in their efforts to unionize and engage in collective bargaining. The 1980s will be a decade of change in California's public education system.

SPECIAL DISTRICTS

Probably less is known about special district government and functions than any other form of local government, yet these 5,000 governmental units provide a wide array of vital services to their residents. While they provide many different kinds of services, they are relatively simple in organization. As the state controller recently defined them, a special district is a ". . . legally constituted governmental entity, which is neither a city nor county, established for the purpose of carrying on specific activities within . . . defined boundaries."

Most special districts provide one service, are governed by a board of directors, and are located within a single county. A few special districts may encompass territory in two counties, and a handful are regional in scope (see the section on regional government).

Some 60 different kinds of services are provided by special districts. The greatest number of districts are: (1) county service areas, (2) county maintenance, (3) fire protection, (4) highway lighting, and (5) cemetery. These five types constitute almost half of all the state's special districts. Other special district activities include: parking, library, garbage disposal, citrus pest control, hospitals, irrigation, and mosquito abatement.

Reasons for forming a special district

While an area's residents may want additional governmental services, they may not want to form a municipal corporation—a city. Among the state's first special districts were those designed to provide for and regulate the use of water in the gold fields. Irrigation districts and reclamation districts were also among the early needs served by special districts. Miners and farmers did not need a city to provide them with water. They did need some governmental agency, however.

Special districts have been so successful in meeting the specific needs of their residents that they are the fastest growing governmental form in the United States. In California their number has grown from 891 in 1950 to 4,915 in 1977. Because of their rapid growth and due to lobbying pressures from cities and counties, Governor Ronald Reagan appointed a Local Government Reform Task Force in 1974 to examine special districts. After extensive study, the task force reported that special districts are effective, efficient, and politically responsible forms of local government (Salzman, 1974).

District types

DEPENDENT DISTRICTS

About 40 percent of the state's special districts are, essentially, administrative agencies of county government. (A few have also been established by a city.) They are known as dependent districts because they are governed by their parent agency and have no independent revenue or taxing authority. The 700-plus county service areas are the best example of this. Another 1,200 are also governed by a County Board of Supervisors —typically maintenance and highway lighting districts.

Such districts are typically established by a County Board of Supervisors in response to requests from an area's residents for either increased services or new services. Usually the area is not part of a city, and its residents want a specific service—water, road maintenance, or street lighting. City-dependent special districts are typically established to provide housing or some form of community redevelopment.

MUNICIPAL ADVISORY COUNCILS

An interesting new variation of the special district form is the Municipal Advisory Council (MAC). Typically, they are found in some of the more rapidly growing unincorporated suburbs or in isolated unincorporated communities. MACs are formally established by a County Board of Supervisors in response to a petition by area residents. Examples may be found in the suburbs of Los Angeles, Orange and San Mateo Counties, and in Big Bear, a remote mountain community of San Bernardino County.

MACs have no independent authority or tax base. They are essentially advisory groups that express their area's needs to the board of supervisors. Members of a MAC are selected in regular elections.

A notable exception to the so-called advisory function is the East Palo Alto MAC which was established by the San Mateo Board of Supervisors in 1967. This MAC has become a meaningful political force in its community, because its advice is almost always taken by the county's supervisors.

The history of MACs is too short to know how they will develop. Some communities which have MACs hope that they will lead to municipal incorporation. Other MACs are simply advisory, and there is no intention that they be anything else.

INDEPENDENT DISTRICTS

About 60 percent of the state's special districts are independent. Their governing boards are wholly (or at least partially) elected by district residents, and they have an independent taxing power. Typically, independent districts provide fire protection, water, and cemetery services. These districts are established much like cities. A group of residents get together and decide to form a special district, define its service activity, and define its geographic boundaries. The plan is then submitted to the county's LAFCO and if approved is then submitted to the area's residents for a vote (see section on LAFCO in this chapter).

District governance

Dependent districts are governed by their parent agency, usually the County Board of Supervisors, or in a few instances a city council. Election to the County Board of Supervisors or city council is the same as election to the board of directors of such special districts.

Independent districts hold separate elections to fill some or all seats on the board of directors. These boards usually have five or seven members who are seldom opposed for reelection. In fact, there will often be no candidate for one of the open seats on the board of directors. In such cases, other directors try to recruit someone. Mid-term vacancies often occur, and the County Board of Supervisors fllls the position by appointment.

Programs and budgets

Special districts, unlike other forms of government, usually offer only one service—water, fire protection, parks, or for whatever purpose they were organized. Their annual budgets are based on four sources of revenue: (1) fees for service and material, (2) the property tax, (3) state funding since Proposition 13, and (4) federal funds. Some districts derive most of their funds from service fees or material charges. Harbor, airport, transportation, water, utility, and hospital districts all collect substantial revenues for services rendered. These districts are called *enterprise districts*. On the other hand, such activities as pollution control, fire protection, flood control, and parks and recreation do not generate much revenue from users. These districts depend largely on taxes and are called *nonenterprise districts*.

Local agency formation commissions

Local Agency Formation Commissions (LAFCOs) are a unique kind of special district. LAFCOs were established by the California legislature in 1963 in response to the explosive growth of cities and special districts following World War II. Their primary purpose is to (1) discourage urban sprawl and (2) encourage the orderly formation and development of local government agencies. Each of California's counties has a LAFCO except San Francisco. Each LAFCO has jurisdiction within its county.

Each LAFCO has five members—two from the County Board of Supervisors, two selected by the county's cities, and one public member chosen by the first four. LAFCOs hear proposals for (1) new cities, (2) new independent special districts, and (3) all annexations.

LAFCOs have authority under state law to accept, modify, or reject these proposals. As a result, they can exercise great power within a county in the development of local government agencies and in the implementation of a county's master plan.

Recently, the legislature gave LAFCOs authority to establish city "spheres of influence." By definition, each city's sphere of influence is that city's probable ultimate boundary. By making such definitions LAFCOs, in fact, control each county's long-range growth plan.

Those LAFCOs which have fully exercised their powers appear to have been successful in creating order and structure in the growth of established local government. But the development of new cities and special districts does not appear to have been affected by the commissions.

Regional districts

Most of California's population is located in its urban counties. But it is a highly mobile population with many people living in one city and working in another. In the same way, many of our social and governmental problems cross city and county lines. Smog ignores governmental boundaries; the need for urban area transportation transcends city and county lines; and the metropolitan area's need for water cannot be met by local supplies. In these and similar situations, the ability of a single city or county to meet or solve its problems is sharply limited.

For example, when the city-county of San Francisco was first formed in 1853, it was the dominant economic and political center of the bay area. Today, however, it is only a small fraction of the area's population and government. In 1979 the San Francisco Bay area included 9 counties, 93 cities, 184 school districts, and 706 special districts—in sum, 992 governmental units.

Similarly, the number of governmental units in the Los Angeles-Orange-San Bernardino-Riverside area is staggering. Four counties, 137 cities, 212 school districts, and 943 special districts comprise the 1,296 governmental units struggling with the regions' problems in 1979.

In an effort to work through some of their common problems, the governmental units of an urban area will sometimes form regional districts. But any attempt to form a regional government inevitably means reducing or eliminating the power or authority of already established local governments. Such proposals thus trigger automatic opposition. As a result, regional government has been typically limited to two functions.

REGIONAL ACTIVITY

First, regional governments often serve an advisory or communicative capacity—these are Councils of Governments (COGs). Two prime examples of COGs are the Association of Bay Area Governments (ABAG) and the Southern California Association of Governments (SCAG).

The second function of regional government is to deliver a specific service or material which the individual governments within the region cannot provide. Smog control, water, mass rapid transportation, and coastal conservation are prime examples of such single-service regional governments.

Air quality control is clearly a problem that crosses county and city boundaries. For example, Los Angeles, which has long had a smog problem, could not control the air emissions of industrial plants outside the county limits. Thus, four counties—Los Angeles, Orange, Riverside, and San Bernardino have formed the South Coast Air Quality Management District. Similarly, the San Francisco Bay counties have established the Bay Area Air Pollution Control District.

Los Angeles and much of southern California has to import its water a long distance. Local supplies are simply not adequate. The Metropolitan Water District of Southern California (SCMWD), which includes Los Angeles, Orange, and San Diego counties and most of their cities and water districts, is a prime example of regional government meeting a regional need. The district constructed a water delivery system from the Colorado River including dams, tunnels, pump stations, artificial lakes, and all the other components of a complex water system in order to deliver water over 200 miles to the region. Another example is the East Bay Municipal Utility District which delivers water from the High Sierras.

Perhaps the most famous of California's regional governments is BART—Bay Area Rapid Transit district. This subway system has helped reduce traffic problems in the three bay area counties which it serves.

REGIONAL GOVERNMENT

Regional government, as it has developed in California, is usually managed by an appointed board of directors rather than by an elected body. Appointment is usually by constituent units—the cities, counties, or special districts—which are a part of the region served. For example, the SCMWD Board of Directors is appointed by member cities and water districts. Each member gets at least one representative on the board plus additional representatives based on its total assessed property value. Each member casts votes based on its total assessed property values. Until recently, the giant city of Los Angeles had half the votes on the board, because of its total assessed property values.

The BART district was originally governed by an appointed board, but since 1974 it has been governed by an elected nine-member board of directors. The BART district is divided into nine equal population areas, each of which elects one representative to the board.

One of the more interesting developments in regional governments in the state is the California Coastal Commission and its regional commissions. These regional commissions were initially established by the state's voters when they approved Proposition 20 in 1972. Proposition 20 established one state and six coastal regions. Half the regional commissioners are appointed by the local governments within each region. The other half are appointed by the governor, Senate Rules Committee, and speaker of the assembly. Half the state commissioners are similarly appointed, and the other half are made up of representatives from each of the regional commissions. In 1976, the legislature established the commissions on a permanent basis as provided by the 1972 initiative.

Regional government will probably continue to grow. Continued urbanization of the state, large numbers of local governments, overlapping jurisdictions, diminished capacity to effectively govern as a result of Proposition 13, and the increased interdependence of the state's economic and social system all will contribute to this regional trend.

LOCAL POLITICS

Local politics are substantially different from state politics in California. The comparison in Illustration 13-4 lists some of these major differences. From these differences flow a wide range of situations which are important to understand.

Citizen participation

City elections typically attract few voters; normally about 1 out of 3 registered voters goes to the polls. Voter participation in school district and special district elections is even lower. Only county elections, which are held at the same time as state and national elections, have substantial turnouts.

One obvious reason for the lack of voter participation in local elections is their timing. City, school board, and special district elections are usually held in odd-numbered years and sometimes in the spring before

ILLUSTRATION 13-4
Comparison of local and state politics

Structure and function	Local	State
Citizen participation	Low	Moderate
Elections	Nonpartisan	Partisan
Legislative elections	Usually at large	By district
Legislative bodies	Unicameral	Two houses
Executive	Usually a figurehead and appointed	Powerful and elected

national and state elections. This effectively separates them from the supposed partisan effects of state and national elections. It also substantially reduces visibility and citizen interest. Thus, only citizens with strong political motives and interests in local government go to the polls.

Elections

PARTISANSHIP

All local elections are nonpartisan. There is no indication on the ballot of the candidate's party affiliation (see Illustration 13–5). Traditionally, partisan political organizations do not become involved in local elections. But recently, there has been a growing partisan interest in some local

ILLUSTRATION 13–5
Typical local nonpartisan ballot

For MEMBER of the CITY COUNCIL Para MIEMBRO del CONCILIO de la CIUDAD	Vote for No More Than Two Vote por No Mas De Dos
ROBERT (ROB) D. CROMWELL Community Relations Director (Director de Relaciones de la Comunidad)	
CHARLES ROSEN U.S. Treasury Officer (Oficial de la Tesorería de Los Estados Unidos)	
JACK H. REID Self-Employed (Empleado de Su Parte)	
BARBARA C. ADY Air Traffic Controller (Controlador de Tráfico Aereo)	
JACQUELINE (JACKIE) HARRISON Homemaker (Ama de Casa)	
ERNEST W. (BILL) HARVEY Manufacturing—Wood Products (Manufactura—Productos de Madera)	
HENRY W. WEDAA Incumbent (Incumbento)	

Source: Official sample ballot, City of Yorba Linda.

elections. Political clubs in San Francisco, Berkeley, San Diego, and parts of Orange and Los Angeles County have supported candidates for city council, school board, and board of supervisors. In addition, Tom Hayden and Jane Fonda's Campaign for Economic Democracy (CED) has been active in some local elections since 1977.

Of course, candidates for local office are usually registered Republicans or Democrats. In California, city council members tend to be more Republican than the community they represent. One recent study of the many San Francisco Bay area city and county elections reveals that Republicans enjoy about a 15 percent bias. That is, the percentage of Republican-elected officials is about 15 percent greater than the percentage of Republican voters (Scott, 1968).

Another recent study of city council members suggests that Democrats are more concerned with social problems than are Republicans (Hawley, 1973). But Democratic city council members were not much more inclined than Republicans to use government power to solve the problems. Some of this reluctance may be a result of the way in which most city council members are selected.

DISTRICT OR "AT LARGE"

Most cities, school districts, and special districts hold their elections "at large." Only County Board of Supervisor elections are by district. In an "at-large election," candidates seek votes within the entire city or district. There are no election districts as in state or national legislative elections. This tends to favor candidates from the local elite—those whose friends and business associates are active in local government and who have access to the local press and civic groups. At-large elections tend to discriminate against those who are poorer and who come from communities where few people are politically active.

A few cities elect by district. Los Angeles, San Francisco, and San Jose are good examples. Their legislative bodies tend to be more representative of all people in their city. In a recent attempt to provide more equal representation, the Los Angeles School District voters adopted a district election system for the school board in 1978.

Santa Ana, an Orange County city of 175,000, has a combination of at-large and district elections. Candidates must live in the district they want to represent, but they are elected by a citywide (at large) vote. In 1977, a black woman candidate for city council won the election in her district but lost to a white male who got more votes from the total city than she did.

While at-large elections are typically biased in favor of the white middle class, they are also biased for any group of people who are organized and politically motivated. Thus, public employees tend to have a strong voice in local government. Gays have considerable influence in San Francisco, and students wield power in university towns.

Women also do better as candidates in school board and city council races than in supervisorial or state legislative races. Over half of California's cities have at least one woman council member and about 10 percent have women mayors.

Legislative bodies

Local government is unicameral in California. There is only one legislative body as compared to two in the state's legislature. Local legislative bodies are also small, typically having five members. And, unlike the state legislators, most local government legislators are part-time. They have no staff and no offices. Local legislators tend to rely upon their bureaucracy for information and expertise. Local government is amateur government.

Executive

Most city mayors are members of the city council. They serve for one year as presiding officers and are primarily figureheads. A few of the larger California cities have independently elected mayors. They run for the office of mayor and are not part of the city council. They usually have considerable political power.

Big city mayors are sometimes candidates for statewide or national office. Several mayors of Los Angeles, San Francisco, and San Diego have run for governor or U.S. Senator, but none have won. In fact, being mayor of a big city may hurt one's political aspirations more than it helps. City problems often defy solution, and mayors can seldom build a support base outside their own city.

There is no independently elected executive in county, school, or special district government. The legislative bodies for these agencies will select a chair to preside over meetings. But the executive function is typically shared by all legislative members and substantially delegated to a full-time professional employee—the superintendent of schools, district manager, or county administrative officer, for example.

Lobbying

Interest groups operate at the local levels just as they do at the state and national levels. There are some significant differences, however. First, there are fewer interest groups, because there are fewer issues on any particular local government's agenda. Second, more of the lobbying is amateur and casual—a few homeowners meeting with a member of the city council to discuss a traffic problem, or a delegation from the PTA conferring with the school superintendent about an after-school sports program.

But some interest groups tend to become formal and permanent— public employee and property-owner groups, for example. Civic, community, and business groups such as the Chamber of Commerce, PTA, Rotary, Kiwanis, or Lions are often involved in local issues. Less formal, but very powerful groups, such as realtors, land developers, bankers, and construction unions will be found in growing suburban cities and counties. Finally, local newspapers are often politically influential—particularly in larger cities and counties.

Candidates for county supervisor and city council are particularly susceptible to pressure from interest groups. Lacking support from their political party, these candidates must turn elsewhere for campaign workers and campaign money. Groups which have a supply of potential campaign workers—public employees, labor unions, and the PTA—can exercise considerable influence if they are organized. Groups or individuals which can supply funds are also powerful, because campaigns for city council and County Board of Supervisors in the larger cities and counties are becoming expensive.

LOCAL GOVERNMENT REVENUE

There are four broad generalizations that describe local government revenues. First, there are many revenue sources. Second, local governments have been historically dependent upon other governments (state and federal) for a substantial part of their total revenues. Third, the property tax which at one time was the major source of local government revenues has been reduced by Proposition 13. Fourth, the long-run impact of Propositions 13 (1978) and 4 (1979) is unclear and other pending tax reforms (see Chapter 11) further cloud the future.

Table 13–1 summarizes local government revenue sources and types before passage of Proposition 13 in 1978. Many different kinds and sources of revenue combined to make up the complex funding patterns for California's local governments. Taxes, fees, licenses, permits, and penalties combined accounted for about half of local government funds. Cities had the widest range of such resources, while schools were limited, essentially, to the property tax and state funds.

Other governments (federal, state, and local) accounted for the second largest source of funds. Counties and school districts, typically, were most dependent on other governments. Special districts and cities were less dependent.

Finally, it is important to note that cities had (and have) a substantial revenue source in their service fees. Charging for governmental services has been possible for cities, because the recipients can frequently afford to pay for them.

TABLE 13-1
Local government revenue sources, before Proposition 13 (fiscal year 1976–1977)

	School districts	Cities	Counties	Nonenterprise special districts
Sources of revenue:				
Property tax	53%	24%	35%	46%
Sales tax	—	15	2	—
Other taxes, licenses, permits, fines and penalties	—	14	3	1
Federal funds	6	16	24	23
State funds	40	14	25	13
Service charges	—	9	9	6
Miscellaneous	1	8	2	11
	100%	100%	100%	100%
Total funds ($ billions) . . .	$7.2	$5.0	$7.4	$0.8
Dependent percentage (federal and state funds) . . .	46%	30%	49%	26%

Source: *State Controller's Annual Report of Fiscal Transactions (1976–77)* for school districts, counties, cities, and special districts.

Property tax

Approximately 40 cents out of each revenue dollar received by local government before Proposition 13 came from the property tax. In California, this had been the single largest source of local government revenues. In theory, many local government services were associated with property—fire, police, flood control, zoning and land use, streets, sewers and parks. All these services protected or enhanced the value of land and property. Thus, it seemed reasonable that property owners should pay for these services. But in recent years, local governments have assumed or have been assigned other tasks unrelated to property. Welfare, health, and education had little to do with property ownership.

Ironically, over time, the state's school districts came to be the most heavily dependent on property tax revenues. Since their services were provided to children, there was no rational relationship to the tax source (see *Serrano* v. *Priest*).

State funds

Even before Proposition 13, California's state government was the second largest source of funds for local government. Some of these funds come from the state's general fund and are subject to the budget process each year. Other funds are distributed on a formula basis. Some of these are known as shared funds—local governments get some of the revenue and the state gets some. Other funds are totally distributed to local government—the state simply acts as a collecting agent.

SHARED REVENUES

Sales tax   Out of each 6 cents collected by the state, 1.25 cents is returned to the cities and counties. Cities get most of these tax dollars—about two thirds.

Cigarette tax   The state collects 10 cents on each pack of cigarettes purchased. Of this, 3 cents is returned to the cities and counties. Cities get most of these funds, about 80 percent each year.

Fuel tax   The state collects 7 cents per gallon on motor fuel. Of this, 3 cents is returned to local government. County governments get a little more than half these funds—about 57 percent, while cities get the rest.

COLLECTION AGENCY

Motor vehicle license fees   The cities and counties each get half of the funds collected.

Trailer coach fees   These fees are collected by the state in lieu of a property tax on mobile homes. The funds collected are returned to the county, city, and school district based upon location of the trailers taxed.

Federal funds

The federal government provides local government with funding for specific programs—usually called grants. In addition, under the shared revenue program, it provides funds which cities and counties may use as they wish. Federal funding has been a significant source for counties, cities, and some special districts. Flood control, highway construction, municipal airports, and harbors are examples of such funding.

Much of welfare is also funded by the federal government. In 1977–78, the federal government provided 46 cents out of every welfare dollar distributed by county government in California. Overall, about 16 cents out of every dollar received by California's local government is from the federal government.

Other sources

A large number of other revenue sources provide substantial funds for cities, counties, and nonenterprise special districts. Cities have the richest source of such funds, with about 31 cents out of every revenue dollar coming from permits, fines, licenses, service charges, and miscellaneous taxes. Nonenterprise special districts receive about 18 cents out of every revenue dollar from service charges, fees, stand-by charges, return from investments, and a few minor taxes. Counties get slightly less —about 14 cents—of every revenue dollar from similar sources.

PROPOSITION 13

Basic provisions

Proposition 13 limited property taxes to 1 percent of assessed market value. It also restricted assessment increases to no more than 2 percent per year, except when property is sold or exchanged. The sale or exchange value then becomes the new assessed value. A third important feature of Proposition 13 is its restriction on new taxes. At the local level, a two-thirds vote of the electorate is required to establish a new tax or to increase one already in existence. At the state level, a two-thirds vote of the legislature is required to increase tax rates or change the method of computation in order to increase tax yields.

Impact on local government

Proposition 13 reduced property tax revenues by 57 percent. Local governments had expected to collect about $12.45 billion in property tax revenues in fiscal year 1978–79. Due to Proposition 13, they collected only $5.40 billion—a loss of $7.04 billion. Table 13–2 summarizes the immediate impact of Proposition 13.

The biggest losses were suffered by the state's school districts and counties which had been heavily dependent on the property tax (see

TABLE 13–2
Impact of Proposition 13, fiscal year 1978–1979

	Property tax revenues (billions)		Change	
	Anticipated (before Proposition 13)	Actual (after 13)	Dollars	Percentage
Property tax	$12.45	$ 5.41	−$7.04	−57%
State "bail-out"	—	4.40	4.40	—
All other sources	11.85	11.85	–0–	—
Total	$24.30	$21.66	−$2.64	−11%

Source: Post, *Commission on Government Reform*, 1979a.

Table 13–1). School districts lost almost $3 billion, while counties suffered a loss of $2.2 billion.

Cities and counties were best able to adjust to their losses. With a wide range of revenues sources before Proposition 13, they were able to increase service and other fees. In many cases, cities and counties began charging for services which had been free to users before Proposition 13. They also reduced park and recreation, library, and cultural events budgets.

School and special districts had little choice but to cut their budgets. Both looked to the state for relief. Ironically, school enrollments declined by over 300,000 in school year 1978–79 so the budget cuts did not hurt as much as they otherwise would have.

State response

Following voter approval of Proposition 13 in June 1978, the governor and legislature moved quickly to replace most of the lost funds. Appropriating $4.4 billion out of the state's surplus, they also cut the state budget by $1.4 billion. The heaviest cuts were in state employee salaries, mental health services, medical, and welfare.

The state also required local governments who received any "bailout" funds to deny pay raises to their employees and prohibited cuts in police or fire budgets.

In 1979 the governor and legislature developed a long-range program for funding local government. The state committed itself to replacing most of the property tax losses—providing $4.85 billion in fiscal 1979–80. The state has now become the major revenue source for much of local government. Thanks to the state, Proposition 13 did not cut very deeply into local government budgets.

SCHOOLS

California state government has now assumed a major long-term obligation to fund local school districts. Shifting $757 million in property tax revenues from schools to the other local governments, the governor and legislature agreed to replace these funds with additional state funds. State government now provides about 80 cents of every school budget dollar.

COUNTIES

As state agents, counties have been recipients of massive support by the state. The state has assumed responsibility for welfare and medical costs. The state now provides about 45 cents out of every dollar received by the counties.

318

United Press International

SPECIAL DISTRICTS

In 1979, the state increased its aid to special districts from $190 million to $200 million. California now provides about 25 cents out of each revenue dollar received by special districts.

CITIES

The state eliminated all Proposition 13 financial aid to cities in 1979. (It had provided about $250 million in 1978.) But the cities' share of the property tax was increased by $207 million. Essentially, cities with their

ILLUSTRATION 13–7

"*THAT WAS JUST TO GET THE RANGE!*"

Dennis Renault, Sacramento Bee

many sources of revenues have been left on their own in the post-Proposition 13 financial adjustments.

Side effects

Proposition 13 cut local government budgets by about 11 percent. The state's budget was cut by 10 percent in 1978. Thus, overall state and local government expenditures were reduced by slightly more than 10 percent in 1978 as a direct result of Proposition 13.

About 17,000 government employees were laid off because of budget cuts following approval of Proposition 13. Another 85,000 positions were eliminated through attrition—as government employees resigned or retired, their positions were not filled. Many of these employees had been recently hired under affirmative action programs. Proposition 13 hit hardest at the young, black, Hispanic, and women government employees.

Proposition 13 obviously reduced the direct burden on property taxes by about $7 billion. But it shifted much of that burden to those paying sales taxes and income taxes. It also increased by over $600 million the amount of federal income tax paid by California residents in 1978 (Post, 1979a:13).

SUMMARY

California government is largely urban government. Over 90 percent of the state's population lives in an urban area. The many governments in California's urban area—almost 6,000 of them—provide most of the services we associate with government. Moreover, the money which California's local and state governments spend is largely generated from urban areas. The major problems of our society—education, welfare, housing, crime, pollution, transportation, racial and ethnic equality—are largely urban problems.

However, there is no rational urban governmental structure to attack these complex and difficult social and economic problems. There is, instead, a jungle of jurisdictions with overlapping authority, complex boundary lines, divided responsibilities, and conflicting powers. The average urban resident, for example, probably pays taxes to as many as eight different local governments:

1. County.
2. City.
3. Elementary school district.
4. High school district.
5. Water district.
6. Flood control district.
7. Sanitation district.
8. Community college district.

Those who are responsible for the management of these governments are elected by the voters residing within the district, city, or county, but most voters are not able to follow the workings of all of them.

It is not surprising that the average citizen is confused. Faced with a problem, where does the citizen go? The problem may overlap from one jurisdiction (i.e., city) to others (i.e., county, planning commission). Because there is no single urban government, local governments can only work with the citizens' problems on a piecemeal basis.

Growth

Much of the complexity exists as a result of California's rapid population growth which has spread out from the major central cities. As suburban tracts are completed, new residents think of incorporation and of establishing their own school districts. One of the basic motives in California's suburban growth has been the drive for identity. Politically, this has been expressed in the formation of new cities and school districts.

The recent decline in the state's growth rate has helped slow the growth of new local governments. Between the late 1960s and mid 1970s, many California cities lost population. A number of school districts closed schools. But since 1975, the state's growth has begun to increase.

Despite the fluctuating population growth and the crippling effects of Proposition 13, the drive for local autonomy remains strong. Recent attempts have been made to create new counties in Los Angeles, Orange, and San Diego. And one new city was formed in the November 1978 election.

Change

The decade of the 1980s will be crucial for California's local government. The restrictions on local government revenues and budgets combined with a recent upturn in population growth present substantial problems for local government. Schools and county governments (following Proposition 13) have become dependent upon the state for financial support. Only cities have remained independent to any appreciable degree.

With local government revenues declining and with population increasing, local governmental services may be sharply restricted in coming years. It has become a common observation that Los Angeles, as a place, doesn't exist. But the problems of urban blight in Los Angeles, San Francisco, and Oakland do exist. These are the realities from which thousands flee to the suburbs each year. And in the past, the suburbs welcomed them with open arms.

But some cities and counties no longer view growth as desirable. San Diego, Petaluma, Golita, Davis and others have attempted with some success to stem the tides of growth.

In addition, the costs of housing and transportation appear to have immobilized many who would otherwise follow the freeway to their suburban dream. Denied escape and engulfed by the problems of our urban centers, what will the average citizen do? Can local governments solve the problems? The past record suggests that they cannot. At best, the future of local government is uncertain.

References

Chapter 1

"Battle over Gay Rights." 1977 *Newsweek* 89 (June): 16–26.

Berg, Larry L., H. Hahn, and J. Schmidhauser 1976 *Corruption in the American Political System.* Morristown, N.J.: General Learning Press.

Bradshaw, Ted K. 1976 "New Issues for California, The World's Most Advanced Industrial Society." *Public Affairs Report* 17 (August): 1–6.

Burdick, Eugene 1965 "The Three Californias." *Holiday* 37 (October): 60–74.

————— 1963 "From Gold Rush to Sun Rush." *New York Times Magazine* (April): 37–39.

Crotty, William J. 1977 *Political Reform and the American Experiment.* New York: Crowell.

Dasmann, Raymond 1965 *The Destruction of California.* New York: Macmillan.

Davie, Michael 1973 *California: The Vanishing Dream.* New York: Dodd.

Field, Marvin 1977 "California Still Ranks High as One of the Best Places to Live." Field Institute Release 941 (May).

Gentry, Curt 1969 *The Last Days of the Great State of California.* New York: Ballantine.

Gray, Virginia 1973 "Innovations in the States: A Diffusion Study." *American Political Science Review* 67 (December): 1174–85.

Lamott, Kenneth 1971 *Anti-California: Report from Our First Parafascist State.* Boston: Little, Brown.

La Porte, Todd, and C. J. Abrams 1976 "Alternative Patterns of Post Industria: The California Experience," in *Politics and the Future of Industrial Society,* Leon Lindberg, ed. New York: McKay.

McWilliams, Carey 1949 *California: The Great Exception.* New York: A. A. Wyn.

Peirce, Neil 1972 *The Megastates of America.* New York: Norton.

Peirce, Neil R., and J. Hagstrom 1978 "California's Urban Policy—A Searchlight on the City." *National Journal* 10 (April): 432.

Salzman, Ed 1977 "Does the Golden State Deserve Its Tarnished Reputation?" *California Journal* 8 (May): 148–51.

Seidenbaum, Art 1975 *This Is California: Please Keep Out.* New York: Wyden.

Starr, Kevin 1973 *Americans and the California Dream.* New York: Oxford.

"An Urban Strategy for California." 1978 State of California: Office of Planning and Research.

Walker, Jack L. 1969 "The Diffusion of Innovations among the American States." *American Political Science Review* 63 (September): 880–89.

Wilson, James Q. 1967 "Californians Lead the 'Best Life'." *Los Angeles Times* (October 22).

Chapter 2

Beck, Warren A., and **Ynez D. Haase** 1974 *Historical Atlas of California.* Norman: University of Oklahoma Press.

Caughey, John W. 1953 *California.* New York: Prentice-Hall.

Durrenberger, Robert W. 1971 *California: Its People, Its Problems, Its Prospects.* Palo Alto: National Press.

MacGregor, Bruce 1979 "The Ties that Bind: Southern Pacific's Hidden Empire." *New West* (March 12).

Trzyna, Thaddeus, et al. 1975 *The California Handbook.* Claremont, Calif.: Center for Public Affairs.

Warren, Charles, Carey McWilliams, Stanley Mosk, and **Alan Cranston** 1977 *California Perspective.* Berkeley: Institute of Governmental Studies.

Chapter 3

Friedrich, Carl J. 1950 *Constitutional Government and Democracy.* New York: Gian.

Hyink, Bernard L. 1962 "The California Legislature Looks at the State Constitution." *Western Political Quarterly* (March).

————— 1969 "California Revises Its Constitution." *Western Political Quarterly* (September).

Mason, Paul 1973 "Constitutional History of California." *Constitution.* Sacramento, Calif.: State Printer.

Strum, Albert L. 1976 "State Constitutions and Constitutional Revision." *Book of States.* Lexington, Ky.: Council of State Governments.

Sumner, Bruce 1979 "Happy Birthday Constitution." *California Journal* 10 (June): 213–15.

Chapter 4

Boyarsky, Bill 1968 *The Rise of Ronald Reagan.* Chicago: Random House.

Burke, Robert E. 1953 *Olson's New Deal for California.* Los Angeles: University of California Press.

Cannon, Lou 1974 "The Reagan Years." *California Journal* 5 (November).

Delmatier, Royce D., et al. 1970 *The Rumble of California Politics.* New York: Wiley.

Lee, Eugene C. 1963 *California Votes, 1928–1960, with 1962 Supplement: A Review.* Berkeley: University of California, Institute of Governmental Studies.

—————, and **Bruce E. Keith** 1974 *California Votes, 1960–1972: A Review and Analysis of Registration and Voting.* Berkeley: University of California, Institute of Governmental Studies.

Mowry, George E. 1951 *The California Progressives.* Los Angeles: University of California Press.

Older, Fremont 1926 *My Own Story.* New York: Macmillan.

Rogin, Michael P., and **John L. Shover** 1969 *Political Change in California.* Westport, Conn.: Greenwood.

Chapter 5

Anderson, Totton J. 1962 "California Enigma of National Politics," in *Western Politics,* Frank Jonas, ed. Salt Lake City: University of Utah.

Boyarsky, Bill 1970 "Fat Cats: Men behind Political Campaign Funds." *Los Angeles Times* (April 7).

Constantini, Ed 1967 *The Democratic Leadership Corps in California.* Davis, Calif.: Institute of Governmental Affairs.

Fay, James 1974 "Changing Regulations: Campaign Finance in the

324

Golden State." *Public Affairs Report* (April).

Gottlieb, Robert, and Irene Wolf 1977 *Thinking Big: The Story of the Los Angeles Times*. New York: Putnam's Sons.

Greenwood, John C. 1974 "Legislative Candidates and Campaign Spending in California." Institute of Governmental Affairs, University of California, Davis.

Gregg, James 1966 "Newspaper Endorsement and Local Elections in California." Institute of Governmental Affairs, University of California, Davis.

———— 1970 "California Newspaper Editorial Endorsements: Influence on Ballot Measures." Institute of Governmental Affairs, University of California, Davis.

Olson, Lance H. 1978 "Practical Guide to State and National Campaign Reform Laws." *California Journal* (March supplement).

Putt, Allen D., and J. Fred Springer 1977 "Impacts of Campaign Disclosure and Lobbying Provisions of the Political Reform Act of 1974." Sacramento: Evaluation Research Consultants.

Quinn, Tom 1978 "Why the State Hasn't Bought Public Financing of Elections." *California Journal* 9 (February).

Rogin, Michael P., et al. (See Chapter 4 reference.)

Salzman, Ed 1977 "The New Political Map of California." *California Journal* 8 (January).

Wolfinger, R. E., and F. I. Greenstein 1969 "Comparing Political Regions: The Case of California." *American Political Science Review* 63 (March).

Chapter 6

Berg, Larry 1978 "The Initiative Process and Public Policy-Making in the States: 1904–1976." Paper prepared for the annual meeting of the American Political Science Association.

Brestoff, Nick 1975 "California Initiative Process Needs Reform." *Los Angeles Times* (February 5).

Burns, John 1971 *The Sometimes Governments*. New York: Bantam.

Duscha, Clara L. 1975 "The Koupal's Petition Factory." *California Journal* 6 (March): 82–86.

Georges, Joseph 1976 "Undertaking the Tough Task of Bouncing a Local Official." *California Journal* 7 (March): 105–106.

Gregg, James (See Chapter 5 reference.)

"Initiative Makes a Big Comeback as Groups Seek to Bypass the Legislature." 1972 *California Journal* 3 (August): 229–30.

Lee, Eugene 1978 "California." In Butler, David, and A. Ranney, eds. *Referendums: A Comparative Study of Practice and Theory*. Washington, D.C.: American Enterprise Institute for Public Policy Research.

Lutrin, Carl E., and A. K. Little 1975 "The Public and Ecology: The Role of the Initiative in California Environmental Politics." *Western Political Quarterly* 28 (June): 352–71.

Mueller, John E. 1969 "Voting on the Propositions: Ballot Patterns and Historical Trends in California." *American Political Science Review* 63 (December): 1197–1212.

Older, Fremont (See Chapter 4 reference.)

Price, Charles M. 1975 "The Initiative: A Comparative State Analysis of a Western Phenomenon." *Western Political Quarterly* 28 (June): 243–62.

Quinn, Tony 1978 "How the Establishment Destroys Initiatives Like Jarvis." *California Journal* 9 (March).

———— 1979 "Recall Fever." *California Journal* 10 (November).

Samish, Arthur H., and B. Thomas 1971 *The Secret Boss of California*. New York: Crown.

Wolfinger, Raymond E., and F. I. Greenstein 1968 "The Repeal of Fair Housing in California: An Analysis of

Referendum Voting." *American Political Science Review* 62 (September): 753–69.

Zeigler, L. Harmon, and H. J. Tucker 1978 *The Quest for Responsive Government: An Introduction to State and Local Politics.* North Scituate, Mass.: Duxbury.

Chapter 7

Buchanan, William 1965 *Legislative Partisanship: The Deviant Case of California.* Berkeley: University of California Press.

Fisher, Joel, C. M. Price, and C. G. Bell 1973 "Legislative Role of Interest Groups." *The Legislative Process in California.* Washington, D.C.: American Political Science Association.

Fredericks, Laura 1979 "Sacramento's Top 15 Lobbyists." *California Journal* 10 (August): 31–37.

Grumm, John 1971 "The Effects of Legislative Structure on Legislative Performance," in *State and Urban Politics,* Richard I. Hofferbert and Ira Sharkansky, eds. Boston: Little, Brown.

Hockenson, Jill 1977 "Politicizing the Doctors' Lobby." *California Journal* 8 (June): 207–9.

Keppel, Bruce 1972 "The State's Biggest Lobbyist: Executive Agencies before the Legislature." *California Journal* 3 (December): 356–59.

"Lobbying the Legislature: Facts, Friendship, Favors, and Flim Flam." 1972 *California Journal* 3 (August): 31–37.

"The Lobbyists the Public Pays: One Out of Every Ten Advocates in Sacramento Represents Local Government." 1972 *California Journal* 3 (October): 292–96.

Lowenstein, Daniel H. 1979 "Forecast More Campaign Scandal." *California Journal* 10 (March): 103–5.

Purnell, Don 1978 "Cal-Tax: Big-biz." *California Journal* 9 (October): 332–33.

Quinn, Tony 1968 "Goodbye, Small-Time Spenders." *California Journal* 9 (March): 96–98.

Samish, Arthur H., and B. Thomas (See Chapter 6 reference.)

Simmons, Bob 1970 "Lobbying: The Case of the Freeway Establishment," in *The Challenge of California,* Eugene Lee and W. Hawley, eds. Boston: Little, Brown.

Velie, Lester 1949 "The Secret Boss of California," *Collier's* 124 (August 13 and 20).

Wahle, Chris 1974 "Sacramento's Most Influential Lobbyists." *California Journal* 5 (September) 293–96.

Ziegler, Harmon, and Michael Baer 1969 *Lobbying: Interaction and Influence in American State Legislatures.* Belmont, Calif.: Wadsworth.

Chapter 8

Boyarsky, Nancy 1974 "The Image Makers." *California Journal* 5 (May): 149–55.

Buhler, Lois 1976 "County Central Committees: The Elected Officials Nobody Knows (or Needs to)." *California Journal* 7 (July): 237–38.

Carney, Francis M. 1958 *The Rise of the Democratic Clubs in California.* New York: Holt, Rinehart, and Winston.

"The Growing Independence of Assembly Democrats." 1977 *California Journal* 8 (January): 32–33.

Jacob, Nora B. 1979 "Butcher-Forde and the Jarvis Touch." *California Journal* 10 (May): 162–64.

Jacobs, John 1976 "The Coalition Politics of Dellums' East Bay Machine." *California Journal* 7 (August): 258–60.

Jewell, Malcolm E., and D. M. Olson 1978 *American State Political Parties and Elections.* Homewood, Ill.: Dorsey.

Jewell, Malcolm E., and S. C. Patterson 1966 *The Legislative Process in the United States.* New York: Random House.

Keefe, William J., and M. S. Ogul 1977 *The American Legislative Process.* Englewood Cliffs, N.J.: Prentice-Hall.

Le Blanc, Hugh L. 1969 "Voting in State Senates: Party and Constituency Influences." *Midwest Journal of Political Science* 13 (February): 33–57.

Lee, Eugene, and W. D. Hawley, eds. 1970 *The Challenge of California.* Boston: Little, Brown.

"Legislative Maverick Ratings." 1979 *California Journal* 10 (February): 76–77.

Littwin, Susan 1977 "Power Brokers in L.A." *California Journal* 7 (December): 405–7.

"1974 Independence Ratings for California Lawmakers." 1975 *California Journal* 6 (January): 31–32.

Older, Fremont (See Chapter 4 references).

Owens, John K., E. Constantini, and L. F. Weschler 1970 *California Politics and Parties.* New York: Macmillan.

Peterson, Larry 1979 "Richard O'Neil's Political Resurrection." *California Journal* 10 (May): 177–79.

"Who Are the Party Mavericks?" 1976 *California Journal* 7 (January): 34–35.

"Who's Who in Party Loyalty Rankings." 1973 *California Journal* 4 (December): 417–18.

Chapter 9

Bardach, Eugene 1972 *The Skill Factor in Politics.* Berkeley: University of California Press.

Bell, Charles G., and C. M. Price 1969 "Pre-Legislative Sources of Representational Roles." *Midwest Journal of Political Science* 13 (May): 254–70.

——— 1975 *The First Term: A Study of Legislative Socialization.* Beverly Hills: Sage.

Blair, George S. 1962 *American Legislatures.* New York: Harper and Row.

Brodie, Fawn 1968 "Big Daddy v. Mr. Clean." *New York Times Magazine* 21 (April).

Burns, John 1971 *The Sometimes Governments.* New York: Bantam.

Driscoll, James 1978 *California's Legislature.* Sacramento: State of California.

Fisher, Joel, et al. (See Chapter 7 references).

Gray, Virginia (See Chapter 1 reference.)

Grumm, John G. 1971 "The Effects of Legislative Structure on Legislative Performance," in *State and Urban Politics,* Richard I. Hofferbert and I. Sharkansky, eds. Boston: Little, Brown.

Herzberg, Donald G., and J. Unruh 1970 *Essays on the State Legislative Process.* New York: Holt, Rinehart and Winston.

Jewell, Malcolm E., et al. (See Chapter 8 references).

Keefe, William J., et al. (See Chapter 8 references).

Kreisher, Otto 1979 "The New Ball Game." *California Journal* 10 (April): 133–34.

Price, Charles M., and C. G. Bell 1970 "Socializing California Freshmen Assemblymen: The Role of Individuals and Legislative Sub-Groups." *Western Political Quarterly* 23 (March): 166–79.

——— 1970 "The Rules of the Game: Political Fact or Academic Fancy?" *Journal of Politics* 32 (November): 839–55.

Rodda, Richard 1977 "How Our Lawmakers Rate: Still Number One." *California Journal* 8 (August): 264–66.

Patterson, Samuel 1978 In *Legislative Reform and Public Policy,* Susan Welch and J. G. Peters, eds. New York: Praeger.

Walker, Jack (See Chapter 1 reference.)

Chapter 10

Boyarsky, Bill (See Chapter 4 reference.)

——— "Brown Appoints More Minorities." 1979 *Los Angeles Times* (July 12).

Cannon, Lou (See Chapter 4 reference.)

DeVries, Tom 1979 "See Jerry Run." *New West* (June 18): 47–59.

Harvey, Richard 1969 *Earl Warren: Governor of California.* New York: Exposition Press.

Los Angeles Times 1974 Interview with Robert Monagan (September 29).

Melendy, H. Brett, and **Benjamin F. Gilbert** 1965 *The Governors of California.* Georgetown, Calif.: Talisman Press.

Pack, Robert 1978 *Jerry Brown: The Philosopher Prince.* Briarcliff Manor, N.Y.: Stein & Day.

Playboy 1976 Interview with Governor Jerry Brown (April)

Roberts, Cynthia 1978 "A Conducted Tour of the Governor's Office." *California Journal* 9 (May): 155–58.

Salzman, Ed 1975 "Brown's First Legislative Record." *California Journal* 6 (October): 359–61.

Schlessinger, Joseph A. 1971 "The Politics of the Executive," in *Politics in the American States,* H. Jacobs and K. Vines, eds. Boston: Little, Brown.

Chapter 11

Bell, James R., and **Thomas J. Ashley** 1967 *Executives in California Government.* Belmont: Dickenson.

California Journal. A series of articles: Lieutenant Governor (January 1971); Controller (March 1972); Attorney General (April 1971); Secretary of State (February 1971); Treasurer (July/August 1971); and Department of Finance (December 1970).

Governor's Office Annual *Economic Report of the Governor.* Sacramento.

Hackett, Bruce M. 1967 *Higher Civil Servants in California.* Davis: Institute of Governmental Affairs.

Legislative Analyst Annual *Analysis of the Budget Bill.* Sacramento.

Post, A. Alan 1979 "California's Fiscal Future." *Tax Revolt Digest* (July).

Quinn, T. Anthony, and **Ed Salzman** 1978 *California Public Administration.* Sacramento: *California Journal* Press.

Rubin, Hal 1978 "New Fiscal Watchdog, Same Old Tricks." *California Journal* (October): 329–31.

State Controller Annual *Annual Report.* Sacramento.

Street, Carolyn 1977 "The Public-Member Siege of the State Licensing Boards." *California Journal* 8 (September): 309–11.

"Study Contradicts State Forecasts on Fiscal Surplus." 1978 *Los Angeles Times* (December 8): 1.

Willett, Cynthia 1979 "The Confrontation Politics of Rival State-Employee Unions." *California Journal* 10 (September): 325–27.

Chapter 12

Blume, William W. 1970 "California Courts in Historical Perspective." *Hastings Law Journal* (November): 121–95.

Cleaver, Eldridge 1967 *Soul On Ice.* New York: McGraw-Hill.

Cook, Beverly B. 1967 *The Judicial Process in California.* Belmont, Calif.: Dickenson.

Field, Merve, and **Stanley Scott** 1974 *Public Opinion of Criminal Justices in California.* Berkeley: Institute of Governmental Studies.

Judicial Council of California Annual *Annual Report.* Sacramento.

Kang, K. Connie 1979 "Why the Bird Court Is in Constant Turmoil." *California Journal* 10 (April): 128–30.

Rubin, Hal 1979 "The Drive to Kill the Bail-Bond Business." *California Journal* 10 (March): 109–11.

Salzman, Ed 1974 "The Great Prison Debate." *California Journal* (July): 216–21.

———— 1977 "Chief Justice Bird— Elevating the Law of the Masses." *California Journal* (May): 157–58.

———— 1979 "Richardson's Attack on Judges—Most Significant June Ballot Issue?" *California Journal* 10 (December): 424–26.

State Attorney General 1973 "The Police in the California Community." Sacramento.

Stolz, Kit and **Preble Stolz** 1978 "Are the Voters Forcing Judges to Act Like Politicians?" *California Journal* 9 (September): 296–99.

Chapter 13

Burns, Jerry 1979 "The Centerist Politics of San Francisco's New Mayor." *California Journal* 10 (February): 40–43.

Field, Merv, and **Stanley Scott** (See Chapter 12 reference.)

"54 Percent of Complaints on Police Held Valid." 1974 *Los Angeles Times* (March 3).

Hawley, Willis D. 1973 *Nonpartisan Elections*. New York: Wiley.

LeGates, Richard 1970 *California Local Agency Formation Commission*. Berkeley: Institute of Governmental Studies.

Nakao, Annie 1978 "What's Wrong with Our Public Schools?" *California Journal* 9 (November): 348–50.

Post, A. Alan 1979a *Commission on Government Reform*. Sacramento (January).

Post, A. Alan 1979b "California's Fiscal Future." *Tax Revolt Digest* (July).

Post, A. Alan, and **Richard W. Brandsma** 1973 "The Legislature's Response" to *Serrano* v. *Priest*." *Pacific Law Journal:* Vol 4: 28–46.

"Public Taking Dimmer View of L.A. Police." 1979 *Los Angeles Times* (May 15): 1, 18.

Salzman, Ed 1974 "Reagan Task-Force Surprise: Special District Is the Most Efficient Form of Local Government." *California Journal* 5 (January): 28–31.

Scott, Stanley 1968 *Governing a Metropolitan Region*. Berkeley: Institute of Governmental Studies.

——— 1975 *Governing California's Coast*. Berkeley: Institute of Governmental Studies.

Shores, Randall 1973 "Regional Government: . . . ." *California Journal* 4 (January): 15–22.

State Controller Annual *Annual Transactions of California's Cities*. Sacramento.

——— Annual *Annual Transactions of California's Counties*. Sacramento.

——— Annual *Annual Transactions of California's School Districts*. Sacramento.

——— Annual *Annual Transactions of California's Special Districts*. Sacramento.

Index

Thurman, John, 211
Torres, Art, 129
Townsend Plan, 60
Transcontinental railroad, 23
Treasurer, 240
Treaty of Guadalupe Hidalgo, 26
Trial jurors, 276
Tunney, John, 74, 88, 98
Tuttle, Holmes, 65

U

Unemployment, 14
Unicameral, 19, 211, 312
Union Pacific Railroad, 30
United for California, 94
United Farm Workers, 11, 249, 269
United Republicans of California (UROC), 64, 169, 170–72
U.S. Supreme Court, 8–9, 124
University of California Regents, 237
Unruh, Jess, 19, 68–70, 92, 104, 143–44, 169, 188, 197, 199, 211

V

Van de Kamp, John, 285
Velie, Lester, 133, 140
Veto, 217
Vicenzia, Frank, 143
Vietnamese refugees, 38
Voters
  behavior, 88
  ideology, 89
  participation, 90–92
  partisanship, 87–88
  regionalism, 100

W

Walker, Jack, 20, 196
Wallace, George, 180, 214
Ward, Baxter, 100
Warren, Earl, 5, 8, 55, 60–62, 133, 141, 162, 168, 178, 218, 224, 227, 230, 238
Watergate, 71
"Watergate" Democrats, 7
Watson, Phillip, 51, 253
Watts race riots, 16, 237
Waxman-Berman organization, 167
Weiner, Sandy, 173
Whitaker and Baxter, 172–73
Wilson, Pete, 98, 101, 173
Winner-Wagner, 173
"Winner take all," 5
Women
  in executive, 221, 243
  in judiciary, 220
  in legislature, 195
Woodward and McDowell, 173
Workingman's Party, 18, 47, 54–57, 80

Y–Z

"Yellow Peril," 35, 54
Yorty, Sam, 66, 69, 94
Young, George, 173
Young Democrats, 172
Young Republicans, 172
"Young Turks," 205
Younger, Evelle, 72, 75–76, 94, 97, 225, 238–39
Zeigler, Harmon, 131, 134
Zero Population Growth, 143
Zierold, John, 157

This book has been set Linotype in 9 and 8 point Helvetica, leaded 3 and 2 points respectively. Chapter numbers and titles are 36 and 20 point Avant Book respectively. The size of the type page is 26 by 45½ picas.